# Dealings With The Inquisition
## Or, Papal Rome, Her Priests, And Her Jesuits

*By*

Giacinto Achilli

# Dealings With The Inquisition
## Or, Papal Rome, Her Priests, And Her Jesuits
### by Giacinto Achilli

Copyright © 2024

All Rights reserved.

No part of this publication may be reproduced, stored in a retrieval system, or transmitted in any form or by any means, electronic, mechanical, photocopying or Otherwise, without the written permission of the publisher.
The author/editor asserts the moral right to be identified as the author/editor of this work.

ISBN: 978-93-61150-12-8

Published by
## DOUBLE 9 BOOKS
2/13-B, Ansari Road
Daryaganj, New Delhi – 110002
info@double9books.com
www.double9books.com
Tel. 011-40042856

This book is under public domain

# ABOUT THE AUTHOR

Italian Dominican friar "Giacinto Achilli" gained notoriety in the 19th century for his critiques and disapproval of the Catholic Church. He was educated in theology and at first joined the Dominican order after being born in Italy. But his views changed, and he broke with the Church as a result. Achilli clashed with church authorities over his divergent opinions and criticisms of Catholic principles, especially those about the Inquisition and the Jesuits. He thus faced imprisonment by the Catholic Church and excommunication from the Dominican order. During an era of significant religious and social upheaval, Giacinto Achilli's life and writings contributed to the larger discourse on the issues faced by people who questioned or broke away from the authority of the Catholic Church. Achilli's activities contributed to bringing attention to institutional problems in the Church, notwithstanding the controversy that surrounded him.

# CONTENTS

PREFACE ............................................................................. 7

**CHAPTER I**
MY REASONS FOR GIVING THE HISTORY
OF MY IMPRISONMENT TO THE WORLD ................... 8

**CHAPTER II**
OF THE SUBJECTS TREATED
UPON IN THIS NARRATIVE .......................................... 19

**CHAPTER III**
MY CREED ...................................................................... 26

**CHAPTER IV**
THE INQUISITION IN
THE NINETEENTH CENTURY ....................................... 39

**CHAPTER V**
THE SUBTLETY OF THE INQUISITION ........................ 53

**CHAPTER VI**
THE PROTEUS-LIKE CHARACTER
OF THE INQUISITION, BOTH IN
ANCIENT AND MODERN TIMES ................................. 67

**CHAPTER VII**
THE JESUITS .................................................................. 80

**CHAPTER VIII**
THE DOMINICANS, AND
MY LIFE AMONG THEM .............................................. 98

**CHAPTER IX**
MY CONVERSION ....................................................... 122

**CHAPTER X**
MY FAREWELL TO ROME .......................................... 144

**CHAPTER XI**
NAPLES AND THE NEAPOLITANS .......... 169

**CHAPTER XII**
THE MONKS OF NAPLES .......... 192

**CHAPTER XIII**
MY EXILE .......... 203

**CHAPTER XIV**
THE ITALIAN CHURCH .......... 211

**CHAPTER XV**
MY MISSION .......... 225

**CHAPTER XVI**
THE CASTLE OF ST. ANGELO .......... 257

**APPENDIX** .......... 277

# PREFACE

The first edition of the ensuing pages having been disposed of very shortly after the publication of it, the Author has availed himself of the opportunity afforded him by a second being called for, to make several important additions, which will be found in the Appendix; and to subject the whole to a minute and careful revision: nor can he send forth his work again before the Public, without expressing the heartfelt gratification it has given him to find the simple narrative, which has been written "for conscience sake," so generally appreciated in the very light in which he was most anxious for it to be viewed; viz. as the humble instrument of use in the cause of religious freedom and gospel truth; a cause sacred in itself, and indissolubly connected with the moral and political prosperity and happiness of the whole family of the human race.

# CHAPTER I
# MY REASONS FOR GIVING THE HISTORY OF MY IMPRISONMENT TO THE WORLD

It was in the month of July, 1842, that I was released, by order of Pope Gregory, from my first imprisonment in the dungeons of the Inquisition. On this occasion, one of the Dominican monks who serve the office of Inquisitor, inquired of me, with a malicious look, whether I, also, intended, one day, to write an account of the Inquisition, as a well-known author had done before me, with respect to Spielberg, in his celebrated work, "*Le mie prigioni.*" Perceiving at once the object of this deceitful interrogation, which was only to afford a pretext for renewing my incarceration, at the very moment when liberty was before me, I smiled at my interlocutor, and exclaimed, "How is it possible, *Padre Inquisitore*, you can imagine I can have any idea of vindicating myself, on account of the imprisonment I have undergone? No, be assured, whatever injustice you may have committed towards me, I shall attempt no vindication. You know full well that in this country there exists no tribunal higher than your own: even that of conscience is silent here, and prostrate before you. Should I make my complaint elsewhere, and appeal to the justice of another land, how could I hope, unknown and unfriended as I am, that my story would be listened to? Distrust is natural to man. One only Tribunal remains; from that neither you nor I can escape; and it is to that same Tribunal that I shall be able to summon the Pope and his Cardinals. Nay, setting aside the idea of my own appeal, they will be summoned there by the great Judge himself. I believe in the declaration of Scripture, 'We shall all appear at the judgment-seat of Christ.' And it is there, *Padre Inquisitore*, that our cause will be tried, and the justice of your decrees adjudicated. Moreover, I shall not, at the present time, describe my imprisonment; not because I have not sufficient materials, but because it shall not be said that I seek to avenge myself, in publishing to the world what you study to hide. This time I shall make it my business to write concerning my liberty, rather than my confinement. The latter, indeed, might gratify the merely inquisitive; but the former will be a source of satisfaction to many kind hearts. If I speak of my imprisonment alone, I merely enjoy the advantage— perhaps a useless one—of engaging for awhile the ear of the public; but if I treat of the liberty I have gained, *O Padre Inquisitore*, the holy and the real liberty I have achieved, then indeed I may hope to see around me those generous spirits who, also escaped from their imprisonment, flock to the true standard of liberty—to the word of God."

At these words the Inquisitor appeared perplexed, and, abruptly remarked: "You say you shall not write an account of your imprisonment this time; have you then any idea of returning here?"

"At any rate, you may rest assured, that should I ever again be shut up in the Inquisition, no consideration will then prevent me from giving a full account of all I may have seen or heard, as soon as I am released."

"Oh! another time you would not get away so easily."

"I can readily imagine it. Indeed, I do not know how it has happened that I have got off so cheaply in the present instance, with only three months' confinement. But in case you should lay hands on me again, would you then, *Padre Inquisitore*, permit me to give a short account of my treatment?"

"Only let us see you back, and then it will be time enough to talk about it," replied the Inquisitor, with an air of spiteful derision, that sufficiently indicated what kind of treatment I might expect.

Now, as it has happened that my return did take place, I feel myself authorized, and indeed called upon, to keep my word. The Inquisitor no doubt resolved that if I ever again fell into his power, I should not a second time escape; and his purpose was very near being realized. Every precaution was taken to render my confinement more severe, and every means of escape provided against. And as it was imagined that the prisons of the Inquisition were less secure than those of the Castle of St. Angelo, I was speedily removed to that fortress. In fact, everything indicated a determination, on the part of the Church of Rome, to keep me in perpetual incarceration; so that I should altogether have despaired of ever knowing the blessing of liberty again, had my chance of obtaining it rested on the will of my enemies. Often, no doubt, the Inquisitors have said among themselves, "Ah! this time our prisoner will have no opportunity to write his narrative." And I, on the other hand, kept repeating to myself, "This time I shall effect my escape, even better than the last: they trust in their gaolers, and in their doors of iron; and I in that invisible hand which throws open the doors, and lays the gaolers asleep."

They had apparently as much reason and probability on their side as I had on mine. Their prognostications, however, completely failed, while mine were realized; a proof, at any rate, of the superior value of my principle, compared with their own. How often may they not have been tormented with the thought that I might possibly effect my escape! And all the while I had no intention of the kind. I shall show, hereafter, how many offers of assistance were made, both to myself and to my friends, in case of my attempting flight, which they, as well as myself, had the resolution to refuse. In short, the Inquisitors were miserable, lest they should fail in their promise to retain me in their custody whenever they caught me again. Why should not I observe mine towards them? Since our first contest is decided, the performance of it naturally follows.

But ought this to be my sole motive why I should give an account of my imprisonment? No, indeed, there are others of a better and a higher nature; and the principal one of all arises from the reverence I feel for the truth, to my devotion for which my imprisonment bears testimony.

The Church of Rome, which has become the church of Satan,[1] incessantly boasts itself as the sole Church of Christ, under the title of Catholic and Apostolic; and, according to its old practice of lying, it has endeavoured to persuade the world that we, the people of Rome, are so penetrated with its doctrines, and so attached to its rites, that the denomination "Roman" may be considered synonymous with that of "Papist." And in order that it may not belie itself, it has established a sacrilegious tribunal, wherein the Romans are taught that neither human reason nor divine authority ought to stand in their way of promoting its views; and that, if they are but faithful to the system it has framed, all imaginable sins will be pardoned them; nor will the means of leading a life of pleasure be withheld;—but, on the contrary, if they express an opinion adverse to this priestly sect, every species of malediction will be showered upon their heads; they will be imprisoned, persecuted, and even put to death; their families consigned to want or exile, and their very names loaded with infamy and held in execration.

An actual hell seems indeed to be at the command of this Church, and it may be known by the name of the Inquisition.

What direful evils have not been reported respecting this institution! and few indeed of them have been overcharged. I do not intend here to repeat concerning it what may be found in various historical relations. The "History of the Spanish Inquisition," by Llorente, and the "Mysteries of the Inquisition," by Fareal, afford abundant information on the subject. But, without consulting history, so universal is the present detestation of the Inquisition, that its name alone is sufficient to excite in the minds of all rational beings a sentiment of horror and repugnance, little inferior to what Christians experience with respect to hell itself; with this difference—that with the idea of hell, however terrible, is associated that of eternal justice, which punishes only sin; while the Inquisition, based on extreme wickedness, strives to persecute virtue and to punish good actions. No one complains of the existence of hell; not even the unhappy wretches who are confined there can impugn the justice of the eternal Legislator; but every voice is lifted up against the Inquisition, and every unfortunate being who may be thrown into its dungeons will raise his cry against so detestable a tribunal. Let us suppose a soul released from the horrors of hell; such a one would doubtless abundantly praise the Divine mercy; but should any one be freed from the Inquisition, even on the score of mercy, still he would complain of the injustice that had confined him there, though it were for a short time only, and would detest it ever after accordingly.

The Inquisition is truly a hell invented by priests. To unmask and to destroy their infernal work is, therefore, the main object I have before me, in writing this account of my imprisonment.

It has of late years been pretty generally believed that the Inquisition at Rome—thanks to the civilization of the age—had been altogether abolished, or at any rate so greatly deprived of power as to be merely employed in settling points of controversy, censuring books, or granting dispensations: very few had any idea that it still exercised in the present day the power of imprisoning those among the Italians who, although they believed in the Bible, had no faith in the Council of Trent. Who would then ever have credited that under the pontificate of Pope Pius IX. and the constitution he had granted, there would have been found any vestige of it remaining? For my own part, I can truly aver, that having been absent seven years from Rome, I could not have believed it possible. How could the Chamber of Deputies and the Inquisition be compatible with each other? A Chamber of Priests alone could be expected to support so execrable a tribunal.

Impressed with this idea, it was about the beginning of last year that I left London for Rome. I well knew that the Inquisition had existed in full vigour during the whole period of the pontificate of Pope Gregory; but I naturally thought it was extinct under Pius IX. Indeed I felt quite persuaded that the Inquisitors, not only in Rome, but throughout the whole of the Papal States, had no longer any opportunity for the exercise of their abilities; that the localities of the Holy Office, throughout all the States of Rome, were converted to other uses; that all its prisons were thrown open; that the immense host of secretaries, officers, clerks, familiars, of every description, who were its spies and agents, were altogether dismissed, and that its very name would no longer be known in Rome.

On the 5th of February, 1849, the Constituent Assembly met at Rome; on the evening of the 8th, it was solemnly decreed that the temporal power of the Pope should cease, in consequence of his flight from the city, and his desertion of his subjects; and the new Government assumed the title of the Roman Republic. The day following, this decree was proclaimed from the Campidoglio, and in a moment the aspect of all things was changed. The Rome of the popes became the Rome of the people. The papal arms were torn down, ecclesiastical rights and privileges abolished, onerous taxes done away with—everything was altered. To the priests, no other possession remained than the Church; and even of this the property was vested in the popular authorities.

A fortnight after the new Government had been in power, it was arranged that the deputies, the triumvirate, the military, and the people, should assemble together, on the Sunday, in the Church of St. Peter, to offer up their solemn thanksgiving in a *"Te Deum."* I was myself present on the occasion, accompanied by some friends; and we all of us, from our hearts, offered up our thanks to the Lord, for having delivered our country from the heavy yoke of the pontifical government; and to my thanksgiving I added a prayer for the overthrow of the popish religion—the most pernicious and corrupt system of moral slavery that has ever been invented by the ingenuity of man.

"Oh!" I exclaimed, "let us pray that the infamous government, which, for worldly ends, has violated everything that is most sacred—our religion—may never more be re-established. Let us supplicate that the idolatry of popery may be abolished, and that, from the present period, the worship of statues and pictures, expressly forbidden by God in the second commandment of the Decalogue, may be discontinued, throughout the whole world. Let us pray that the 'mystery of abomination' may at length be taken away, and that to all the people may be discovered and made known 'the man of sin,' the son of perdition, the adversary; he who exalts himself above every one, and is called a divinity or god, who sits in the temple of God, as God, showing himself to all, and asserting that he is God. Let us pray that the holy name of Jesus Christ may be no longer profaned and blasphemed by a class of people who have unworthily usurped it, and, as it were, solely to abuse it. And let us pray that the holy Word, the Gospel of the Redeemer, be no longer persecuted in Rome, and incarcerated in the Inquisition."

At these words my companions started. "Is it true then," said one of them, "that the Bible itself is persecuted by the Church of Rome, and that the followers of the sacred Evangelists are incarcerated in the Inquisition?"—"By the way," exclaimed another, "can you tell me what has become of the Inquisition? Is it shut up?" "I imagine so," observed a third. "I should like to ascertain the fact," was the remark of the fourth. "Let us go to it," was the general cry; "let us go and see whether it be shut or open, and let us endeavour to penetrate into its recesses."

The service being concluded, every one hastened to leave the church. We directed our steps towards the far-famed Holy Office, which is to the left of St. Peter's, behind the colonnade. It was built by Pius V. about the middle of the sixteenth century, on account of the old building in the Via di Ripetta having been destroyed by fire, by the Romans, after the death of Paul IV. We had no difficulty in entering; there were no guards to prevent us; and we saw no one in our way. All was silent, but nothing was in disorder. "Oh! there is nobody here," said one. "And yet," observed another, "the place does not appear to be abandoned. Let us knock at the door." "But, unquestionably," was the remark of all of us, "there can be no one there. Not the Inquisitors themselves would have the hardihood to attempt to carry on their proceedings under the present Government. A Republic and an Inquisition would indeed form a curious anomaly!"

We had not yet finished our disquisition on the absurdity and even the impossibility of such a coalition, when, aroused it should seem by the noise made by our party, a Dominican friar made his appearance at one of the doors. His countenance expressed doubt and apprehension, and his step was uncertain. He cast his eyes around, and as he saw that we were, for the most part, young men, he appeared greatly to doubt our prudence and moderation. Who knows what his sensations were at first seeing us! With a faint voice he asked what we wanted; and understanding that we were desirous to inspect the place, and more especially to visit the prisons of the Inquisition, he hesitated, drew back a few paces, and excused himself, saying that he had not the power to conduct us about, as he was only there with his superior. In fact, he was a lay-brother, and servant to the most reverend father, the Commissioner General of the Inquisition.

I knew this friar very well, but he was not aware of my presence, as I did not at first address myself to him.

"*Frate mio*," said I to him, "I do not wonder that you are afraid of us, since every thing must be an occasion of dread to those whose lives have been an incessant source of reproach to them. Nevertheless, I own I am surprised that up to the present hour, when the Government and the people have sung the *Te Deum* for the Roman Republic, you and your superior, with as many as surround him, should have the assurance to show yourselves in this place, if not to continue your former evil practices, at least to testify your readiness to do so. And tell me, my dear Dominican, for by this time you have sufficiently recognised me, do you not think I deserve to be called your friend, if I save you from the outrage to which you have rendered yourself liable this day? Neither I nor anybody else could answer for your life, if it were known that, through your means, the Inquisition still existed in Rome. Tell me without hesitation, who and how many are here."

"All," replied he, "are here at present who were here originally. There are the same number of officials, and they occupy their usual quarters. The head commissioner is in yonder apartment, with his whole suite, and at this very moment they are at table."

"Pray," demanded I, "are his companions with him?"

"One is there; the other is away."

"Are the keepers of the prison here?"

"Yes, all three."

"Then there are still prisoners?"

At this interrogation the poor Dominican, who, among many bad, might be termed a good man, made no other reply than shrugging his shoulders, leaving me to guess his meaning. It was too evident that there were still prisoners remaining, and that the hateful tribunal still existed in full power!

My friends insisted on visiting the building: I dissuaded them, however, from attempting it, assuring them that no one of its inmates would open the doors to us, without our using a degree of violence which would be highly unbecoming. The monk had already left us, and we descended the stairs we had previously mounted. The great gateway of entrance was no longer unoccupied: the porter was there with some other persons; among them I recognised one of the gaolers, whom I well remembered, as he was the same that kept me in custody, in the year 1842. Two others also I knew, who were spies of the Inquisition. The gaoler was courteous enough in his way.

"Good day, Signor, how fares it with you?"

"And how fares it with you?" I returned. "Are you still gaolers of the Inquisition? Have they not yet dismissed you?"

"No, we have not been dismissed, we are still in the exercise of our functions; we are all paid as usual, and as long as that is the case, you know, we are bound to continue our service."

"It is an evil employment: how is it that you are not ashamed to be found in it? Besides, it is a dangerous one now. The very name of the Inquisition is sufficient to compromise any one, at the present juncture. Take my advice, my friend, and before you are turned out by force, depart of your own accord. Should the people be given to understand that the Inquisition still continues, that all its officials are still in this place, judges, commissioners, clerks, keepers, spies, and consequently dungeons and prisoners, I assure you, the building would soon be set fire to, and those consumed who belong to it."

I have entered into this minute detail, to show that the Inquisition, as it existed in former times, still continued under Pius IX.; and that when he took flight with his cardinals, he left it on the same footing as usual. Indeed, I am not wrong in asserting that Pius IX. and the cardinals gave strict orders that no one belonging to the Inquisition should quit his post on pain of certain expulsion. A further proof of this is, that after our visit to the Inquisition all the inmates remained at their post, until the Triumvirate sent to turn them out by force, and took possession of the place with all that it contained.

It is a fact, then, that Popery is always the same; barbarous, as in the middle ages, in which it took its rise; ferocious, as in the time of Gregory VII.; increasing in cruelty more and more, as under Innocent III., Boniface VIII., Paul IV., Pius V.; and stolid, as since the restoration in 1815: always seeking to connect itself with kings, and to model its cabinet on the plan of that of Austria and of Russia. Popery always has the same spirit, and the same laws; though, with respect to its habits and temper, it not unfrequently wears a mask. Thus, Pius IX. put on the show of liberality; but this pope, believed so liberal by many, was always secretly combined with the Jesuits and the Inquisition.

It is, therefore, to unmask and to expose Popery, as it is at the present day, that I undertake the writing of this work; that the world may know that in Rome, and in the Roman States, excepting during the five months of the Republic, the infamous and hateful Inquisition has always been in existence. The fact is, that Christianity suffers more now than in former times, under this harsh slavery. Religion, being an affair between God and man, cannot be bound, limited, or prescribed, by human laws; she must be free as thought itself. To this conclusion the civilization of the present day has arrived; and all sound philosophy teaches, that what we wish for ourselves, we ought to allow to others. In matters of religion, every one desires the enjoyment of the most complete liberty. None are more tenacious on this point than the priests of Rome themselves: they complained bitterly when the Turkish Government, and that of the Czar, forbade them the performance of their rites, or the attempt to gain a proselyte. Do not they desire their liberty most ardently, in all those countries where the Greek Church is predominant? What would they not say to the Genevese if they attempted, in their own city of Geneva, to subject the papist to any privation or restraint? All the world knows how they swarmed to the British parliament, to obtain the famous emancipation. And even that was not enough for them: how incessantly have they not since presented themselves before it, with fresh demands and renewed audacity? The papists, throughout the whole of England and Scotland, desire to possess the liberty to talk, to write, to preach, and to assemble themselves together. In every quarter they desire to build churches; and found colleges, schools, and houses, for the seclusion of men and of women. In this country are to be found priests of various orders; and numerous companies of Jesuits have established themselves in different parts of the British dominions, whence they send forth their missionaries to every part of the habitable globe. All these desire to possess the most unrestrained liberty. And I by no means blame either those who seek or those who grant it.

I maintain, however, that these very priests, who, in other countries, seek not only to be in entire freedom themselves, but even to rule arbitrarily over others, refuse, in their own, to grant the least liberty of thought to any one whosoever. The Roman clergy insist on their right to speak and to act in England, in Scotland, and in Ireland, in the same manner as they do in Rome; but they do not allow either the English, the Scotch, or the Irish, to act as they please in the Papal States. It is known to every one how many new churches the Roman Catholic priests have built in various places in this island, in addition to those they already possessed; but to the English, on the other hand, in Rome, not even a single church is allowed; and it was made a great favour that they were permitted to assemble for Divine worship in a humble building beyond the gate of the Piazza del Popolo, outside of the walls of the city.

So habituated are the Roman Catholic clergy to act in this manner, that the complaints and remonstrances of the whole world have no influence whatever upon them, either in changing their conduct, or in rendering them ashamed of it. So many years have they practised their iniquity, that they have lost the power of blushing; and such is the evil consequence of their habits, that they no longer feel the least pang of conscience, either at the continual neglect of their own duties, or their perpetual invasion of the rights of others.

Viewing things in this light, no one, I may venture to hope, will blame me, if I speak out boldly of many things which have lately taken place. Doubtless I shall incur the severe censure of the Papal Court, which will rise up against me, and loudly pour forth its heaviest maledictions. Truly, instead of the furious outcries in which the partisans of the Pope have hitherto indulged, I would counsel them to endeavour to answer me in a more worthy manner, and with the same pacific spirit by which I shall be guided in my writing. As to their clamour and their upbraidings, nay, even their slanders, they will excite in me no more fear than my imprisonment occasioned me; neither will any extent of abuse they may try to cast upon me, remove from their own heads the disgrace of the accusations I shall bring against them, and the truth of which I challenge them to disprove. I shall call things by their proper names, and shall distinguish persons according to their actual merits, or otherwise; but, that no one may conclude that I am instigated by a spirit of vindictiveness, or a desire to injure the reputation of those at present belonging to the Court of Rome, I shall be careful to speak of individuals as little as possible; for as no base motive inspires my pen, so I do abhor, above all things, to defile my paper with unworthy matter.

In treating of any subject of a dishonourable nature, I shall spare the names of some who may be connected with it, and endeavour to act with charity towards those who are yet living. Nevertheless, I propose in these pages to give a warning for the time to come; I shall unfold in them the iniquity of the present day, in order that they may serve as a lesson for the future. It will however be necessary, occasionally, to state openly through whose fault such things as I may relate were effected. I should be sorry for it to be thought that I undertook this work to gratify any bad feeling; my sole motive has been to make the truth evident, that all may apprehend it. It was for hearing and speaking the truth, that I incurred the hatred of the papal Court. It was for the truth's sake, that I hesitated at no sacrifice it required from me; and it is for the truth, and for that alone, that I lay the present narrative before the public.

It is of little importance what outcry may be raised against me. Abuse is the only reply that has hitherto been offered me; but I disregard it and return it not. If any one writes in opposition to me, all that I ask is a fair opportunity of replying to him; I know my own fallibility to be great, and I have always hitherto been disposed to acknowledge an error, when it has been pointed out to me by candour and common sense. I refer principally to matters of religion. If any one opines that my language is not consonant with Scripture, I should desire that I might be called upon to explain it; because as I write to elicit the truth, whoever corrects in me an error, also promotes the same object. And this is my rule of conduct with respect to others. The time is now arrived for the full development of the truth; mankind, wearied of being so long enchained, by the opinions of others, in the darkness of error, now make the most strenuous efforts to free themselves from their mental bonds. It is a struggle between the oppressors and the oppressed. Those who continue to advocate the right of oppressing, will be hated by society, as well as those who desire to preserve the privilege of lying. Falsehood is no longer a venial offence; it is a serious crime, and when resorted to by persons in authority, it is always for the purpose of oppression. The motto of the present age is Liberty and Truth.

### FOOTNOTES:

[1] I speak of the Church of the Pope and of the Cardinals, of the Priests, and of the Jesuits; not of the few true believers to be found here and there, even in Rome, hidden from the eyes of the world, and who may truly be called "first-begotten children, whose names are written in heaven."

# CHAPTER II
# OF THE SUBJECTS TREATED UPON IN THIS NARRATIVE

The title of this work has reference chiefly to my six months' imprisonment in the Inquisition, at Rome; consequently, it will principally treat of the Roman Inquisition, both as it exists at present, and as it existed in the more flourishing times of the Roman Court.

Is the Inquisition of the nineteenth century, as it existed under Gregory XVI., and as it now exists under Pius IX., the same as the Inquisition of the sixteenth century, under Paul IV. and Pius V.? This is the important question which every one asks, and to which it is fitting that I should reply.

How, it will be next demanded, is it that the Inquisition, which for three centuries has waged war against civilization in all countries where popery has flourished,—how is it that it has existed so long, loaded as it has always been by the protests, the complaints, the threats, and the execrations of all people? To this question, also, I shall reply.

What advantage, it may then be asked, has popery actually derived from the Inquisition, on account of which it has incurred so much odium on all sides? This is a fair subject of inquiry, and I shall lend my hand thereto, and state my views thereupon. But at the very outset we shall have to pause in amazement at the incongruous spectacle presented to our contemplation in French and Austrian soldiers marching side by side with the Jesuits, and becoming the tools of this same institution.

Let all those who have not hitherto sufficiently observed these things, during the progress of the late events, observe them now; note them well, and learn to draw a right inference from them. It is for us to transmit to posterity the record of what has passed in our own times. Why should we refrain from speaking of it? Through fear of offending the two powers who have, in the affairs of Rome, so basely granted their aid to support the despotism of the pope? I am not accustomed to disguise my sentiments. I call him base, who commits a base action, were he my own brother.

That Austria and France have dishonoured themselves, in lending their services to the pope, in the bombardment of the three principal cities in his dominions, in order to bring them back to the rule of the Jesuits and the Inquisition, is a fact that admits of no question. The people of these two countries may seek to excuse themselves, by throwing the blame on their respective governments; but I am of opinion that the army, however employed by the government, represents the nation, more especially in the case of a Republic. I shall offer, therefore, a few observations on this subject, which may serve to elucidate more problems than one. Such as, Whether the papacy be a religious or a political system? Whether the papacy can reform itself, now that it is reduced to extremities? Whether the overthrow of papacy would injure the cause of real religion in Italy? And here we shall have to define what papacy really is, and in what respect it differs from pure and primitive Christianity. We shall also give a brief statement of the doctrines of the Church of Rome, its conduct as respects the Holy Bible, and the reasons that have influenced the popes to prohibit the reading of that inestimable treasure. This will bring us to consider, whether it be possible for a system of nominal Christianity to exist, in an enlightened age like the present, contrary to the institution of Christ himself, and to the doctrines of His Apostles? Whether the Italians, especially those of Rome and the Roman States, can be compelled to maintain such a system, in opposition to the convictions of their own judgment; and whether the civilized nations of Europe could, in the present day, calmly look on upon a religious persecution? Whether liberty in matters of religion ought to be confined to mere liberty of thought, or whether it should not extend to liberty of speech, and forms of worship? Whether, while all other nations seek this liberty for themselves, to the Romans alone every reasonable demand for it should be invariably refused?

All these points will be fully treated of in the present work; and no degree of discussion or opposition that it may draw forth will be unacceptable or displeasing to its author; for in disquisitions like those which I propose, it is desirable that every voice should be heard. Should my arguments or my representations be contradicted? So much the better: the public will decide which is in the right. I have no objection to be attacked, or even to be overcome, should it be fairly shown that I am in the wrong. When I throw down the gauntlet I desire it should be taken up, and I am pleased when I meet with a resolute antagonist. Should I declare, for example, that the popes and their adherents have been guilty of uttering falsehood, I must prove it, or I am myself the culprit. But should I establish the truth of my assertion, I have then a right to demand that the popes and their adherents should be stigmatized as false, accordingly.

Am I to be told that a pope is not to be censured because he is infallible, or in other words, because he is pope? If the fact of his falsity be established, is he to be held guiltless through reverence to the imaginary keys of St. Peter? And with respect to these keys, what is to be understood by them? Are they really given to the popes? and how, and for what purpose? Well may it be said that one question leads to another. Suppose I happen to have no more respect for the popes than they have shown, and still show, towards those whom they call heretics; I shall feel myself at liberty to tell the whole world what my opinion of them is, and why I am led to entertain it. On all other matters I make it a sacred rule to explain my views with all possible clearness, and on every occasion to tell the entire truth. Why then am I to conceal or palliate it in this? How many have failed in their object in consequence of concealing a part of the truth; how many others, through declaring it little by little, have had their lives sacrificed before they had concluded! No such temporising will be mine; I am resolved to declare it entirely, at once, and without reserve or disguise, whatever may be the result. It is a great and holy cause which I have undertaken to advocate, and one in which I have already learned to suffer without a murmur. And what could my enemies inflict upon me worse than they have done already? I verily believe they indulge the hope of getting me a third time into the Inquisition. Should it be realized, my life would unquestionably be forfeited to their revenge. But shall I be terrified at the thought? Assuredly not; fear has never yet been allowed to take root in my breast. Should I again fall into their hands, let them do with me as they think fit. In the mean while they cannot, at any rate at present, prevent me from doing what best pleases myself; that is to say, what my duty calls upon me to do; what my most sacred obligation as a minister of the religion of Christ demands of me. I shall declare the truth to the world; before God, and in the face of man I shall make it known: and at the present juncture are there not thousands, nay millions, disposed to listen to it?

Now since it is an incontrovertible fact that I was imprisoned in the Inquisition from July 29, 1849, to January 19, 1850, on this topic I shall also write and disclose every particular connected with it. Six months of close imprisonment, under the most barbarous of tribunals, without any sufficient cause, is not a circumstance to be lightly passed over; neither ought I to be silent with respect to the cruelties and injustice to which any one, however innocent, may be subjected under its tyranny.

The story of my imprisonment presents a new feature in the annals of the Inquisition. Secure of their privilege, satisfied with the possession of their prey, which they were persuaded no earthly power could force them to surrender, they delayed my condemnation, partly because the tribunal was not yet entirely re-organized, owing to the absence of the Pope and the Cardinals, and partly because—in consequence of the fact of my imprisonment being well known, and many persons of high consideration having declared themselves interested in my favour—they feared their designs might be frustrated, were it made public that I had received my final sentence. Their only course, therefore, was to condemn me to suffer in secret. But hundreds were continually inquiring as to my fate, and it would therefore have been highly impolitic, in the priestly party, to afford any opportunity for commenting upon it.

In cases of this kind the principal object of the subtle Inquisitors is to gain time; and in the mean while to spread abroad vague and uncertain reports, relating to further accusations than those originally alleged, in order to distract the attention and confuse the minds of the friends of the party accused. And this measure was speedily adopted with regard to myself. A report was circulated that I had been guilty of other crimes than those for which I was placed in the Inquisition. We shall soon see what these crimes were, and how quickly they vanished away. The fact was, that I was detained captive in order to grace the triumphal car of Pio Nono, on his return to Rome. I was expected to acknowledge, once more, the sovereign and the pontiff, in him whose temporal supremacy and spiritual infallibility I had alike denied. I was to humble myself before him, confess my guilt, abjure my present creed, implore forgiveness; and then, after many supplications for mercy, I might, if really repentant, hope to be permitted to vegetate, during the remainder of my days, in nominal freedom and positive bondage.

Such probably were the intentions of my persecutors, which were in a single moment rendered vain and hopeless by my quietly withdrawing myself from their *protection*, when they least expected it. It will be well that I should explain the system usually observed by the Inquisitors, and show their manner of calculating, which, except in the present instance, has perhaps been hitherto infallible. A prisoner to escape from the Inquisition, without being retaken! escape too from the Castle, in which he was placed for greater security!—was ever such a thing heard of? Certainly this was a triumph for the nineteenth century of which the sixteenth could not boast. I shall treat then concerning my escape; not only of the fact itself, but of the causes that rendered it possible to be effected. I shall show the motives that induced the French to restore me to liberty; and the manner in which they granted what I had full right to demand at their hands.

A few pages will be given to the transactions of the French with regard to myself, which I shall accurately detail, in order that no future historian may deceive the world by a false account.

But before my departure from the Inquisition, there are two circumstances on which I shall dwell more at large, under the impression that those persons for whom I chiefly write, will be greatly interested in a minute account of all that took place on those occasions. I refer to my examination before the Judge of the Inquisition, and my conference with the Theologian of the same establishment, who was sent to endeavour by his arguments to bring me back to the Church of Rome. How such an idea ever got into their heads I cannot imagine. They knew that I had abjured their system in consequence of a thorough conviction of its falsity. They knew that for ten years I had studied the subject night and day. They were not ignorant that such attempts had been made before, and that they had always proved unsuccessful. Papal Rome had had to lament the defeat of many of her champions, who had leagued together to overcome me.

I was greatly surprised to see this Theologian, and still more so to hear that he had been sent by the Cardinal Vicar, by order of the Pope. Our conference, then, which took place privately, in a corner of the rich saloon of Julio Romano, in the Castle of St. Angelo, is now destined to become public, and I shall with great satisfaction undertake the office of making it so, in order that not only all that passed between us may be known, but that the manner of it may also be understood.[2]

The Romish priests always expect that persons placed in the Inquisition will lose courage, and become unable to exert any strength of mind. And this persuasion they naturally indulge in, from the established fact, that the major part of those who are incarcerated within its walls do become enfeebled, even to wasting away, and begin to implore compassion. But they do not call to mind how many others are to be found in the annals of the same Inquisition, who have displayed the most heroic fortitude, have resisted all the vain arguments of their fallen and corrupt Church; and, full of zeal, have opposed the truths of the Bible to their decrees, the Gospel to tradition, the true Word of God to the vain conceits of men.

My imprisonment was also intended to deprive me of the benefit of any communication with my friends. Such were the orders issued from the first, and they continued in full force throughout the whole period of my confinement; the gaolers were threatened with punishment if they allowed the least communication with me whatever. Nevertheless, though how it happened I cannot tell, I certainly was visited by many. Meanwhile, I enjoyed full liberty of mind, and was too sensible of the importance of my mission to rest from the work of God. Within those walls I not only served as a witness of the Truth, I was also an expounder of it. With my Bible in hand, I discoursed of religion to all who came into my presence; satisfied, each time, that I was exalting the name of Christ, in casting down that of the Pope; and that I was building up again the pure religion of our fathers, on the ruins of the superstitions introduced by the priests. I was full of faith in the declaration of the Lord that Babylon should be destroyed, that a voice should cry: "Come out of her, my people, that ye be not partakers of her sins, and that ye receive not of her plagues."[3]

This voice, I repeated to myself, shall be mine; I will execute the command of the Eternal Judge, I will warn my brethren. Yes, I will warn them in the name of God, and in the power of Christ, to take vengeance on this shameless harlot.

"Reward her even as she has rewarded you, and double unto her double, according to her works: in the cup which she hath filled, fill to her double. How much she hath glorified herself, and lived deliciously, so much torment and sorrow give her; for she saith in her heart, I sit a queen, and am no widow, and shall see no sorrow. Therefore shall her plagues come in one day; death, and mourning, and famine; and she shall be utterly burned with fire: for strong is the Lord God who judgeth her. And the kings of the earth, who have committed fornication and lived deliciously with her, shall bewail her, and lament for her."[4]

In this manner I communed with myself, and thus I made known my sentiments to others. Neither did my opinions remain confined within the walls of my prison; frequently they made their way abroad, without being conveyed by any messenger from myself; nor was I permitted to approach any stranger from without. I mention this lest any one should be compromised, among those who are at present under the clutches of that barbarous tribunal.

May what I have to relate tend to the glory of God, and to the welfare of souls; and may it lead to the shame and dishonour of those instruments of wickedness, whose business it is to do the work of Satan. Those who do not blush at their evil deeds will have to endure the disgrace of hearing themselves spoken of with reproach; and perhaps on this account alone they may be induced to desist from the commission of further offence. I do not altogether despair of producing some salutary effect in them, through the means of this publication: if nothing further, it will at least strike their minds, enter into their hearts, and may possibly, as I sincerely desire, lead them back to a state of moral health.

My story will be told with simplicity, and my observations given with freedom. My chief care will be to give no just cause for reproach. If many, as will probably be the case, differ from me, it will give me little concern. If they should be my friends, I shall request them to specify their objections—I might, perhaps, sometimes profit by them. At any rate I deem it expedient to open my whole mind to my readers, and to disclose, in all sincerity, what I believe in matters of religion; in order that no one may be mistaken in me, and that with regard to the tendency of my mind and operations there may not be two opinions. So that, should my name survive the tomb, posterity may know that it was I who preached religious reformation to my native country.

If I had published this declaration before I fell a second time into the hands of the Roman Inquisition, I should have been spared the trouble of making so many explanations to the Pope and the Cardinals, with respect to my change of opinions. They would then have had a more clear and definite idea of what existed in the interior of my mind, and would not have deceived themselves with the hope that I was not so attached to the truth as to resist their artifices as firmly as, through the grace of God, I was enabled to do. And they would then necessarily have had a less confident hope that, through their instigations, that return which St. Peter speaks of in his Second Epistle (chap. ii. ver. 22,) might have taken place; a return, which the Theologians of the Inquisition would have denominated a wonderful one, to the arms of the Holy Mother, the Church of Rome.

## FOOTNOTES:

[2] A complete account of my conference with Dr. Theiner will form the subject of a future work.

[3] Rev. xviii. 4.

[4] Rev. xviii. 6-9.

# CHAPTER III
# MY CREED

The first time that I was laid hold of by the Inquisition, I blamed myself for not disclosing more fully what my belief was at that period. Already for several years, I had received the doctrines of the Bible: I had become a theologian of the true primitive Church. I cannot, however, say that as yet I was a firm believer, since I had not abiding in me the spirit of the Gospel of Christ; which is neither the fruit of our reading, nor the work of our own intellect, but is given us immediately from God. I was a Christian in mind, but not in heart. If Christianity, as some suppose, were a mere opinion, a belief, it would suffice, in order to become a Christian, to admit the truth of the Scriptures. The absurdity of which is manifest, from the consideration that, in this case, the first Christian would have been no other than the devil, since he was the first to acknowledge the truth of Christianity. I understood and acknowledged the truth, although I was not yet fully actuated by it; I possessed the understanding of faith, but not faith itself; I could instruct others in its precepts, but was not myself capable of obeying them. This, I apprehend, was a state necessary for me to undergo, preparatory to the great change—as the state of the chrysalis is essential to the production of the butterfly. I stood midway between the old and the new man: the old man was already buried, but the new man had not yet come to life.

What, then, would have been my profession of faith, at this period? That of a theologian, who draws his arguments from the Bible; that of a man who, aware not only of the errors of others, but of his own also, renounces, condemns, and endeavours to get rid of them, by every possible means. This profession of faith I had not yet publicly avowed, but in many ways it might have been surmised; and putting together the various opinions I had already made known, it was not difficult to form a pretty correct idea as to the whole of my religious persuasions. I by no means wanted the courage—I wanted only a fitting opportunity to declare myself.

Every action, to be well performed, ought to be done in its proper time and place. The true reason, therefore, why I had not avowed my full sentiments was, that a fitting opportunity had not yet presented itself.

But Rome was not ignorant of my real opinions. Surrounded as I was with spies, although leading a private life in Naples, separated from the Dominicans, apart from society, and buried among my books, the Papal

Court still found no difficulty in becoming acquainted with my state of mind, and was displeased thereat; and since there appeared but little hope that I should retrace my steps, it would have been very glad had I, at that time, come so far forward as to afford a pretence for my apprehension.

The Inquisition, ever since the year 1833, had been endeavouring, by means of its emissaries, to discover in my conduct some ground for accusation. But either through want of ability, or from not being so malicious as it required, they brought nothing against me that the Holy Office could take hold of. Their accusations, as far as I could learn, were vague, uncertain, and frequently contradictory. Among my accusers were two cardinals. One of them stated that during all the time I had lived with him, (I think it was during Lent, in 1835,) although he had studied my character with great attention, he never could make me out satisfactorily; that he had listened to above forty of my sermons, and never found in them a single expression to which he could object;—but that in my private conversation he had often detected much bitterness against the Court of Rome, and, in many points, direct opposition to the Council of Trent; and that, although not himself altogether a disciple of Bellarmine, he felt shocked at the severity of my attacks upon that celebrated writer: neither, he continued, did I spare the other two historians and annalists of the Church of Rome, Orsi and Baronio; that I spoke highly of Fra Paolo Sarpi to Cardinal Pallavicino; that I ridiculed the sanctity of Gregory VII., and went so far as to say that it would be well to take the opinion of the Countess Matilda on that point. The other cardinal who accused me, expressed himself as follows:—

"I have nothing to say against Father Achilli myself, but my vicar has told me that he is unstable in his faith. I think him a dangerous character: it would be best to make a friend of him, by kind treatment. I see no middle path; we must either make him a bishop, or shut him up in the Inquisition."

This worthy cardinal was generally considered to be rather deficient in judgment. I am of a contrary opinion. Indeed, when I read his letter, among other documents respecting my cause in the Inquisition, I judged him to be more crafty than many of his brethren.[5]

Among other accusations brought against me, there was one written by two Dominicans, who had formerly been my pupils in theology; and these friars deposed that I manifested a continual spirit of opposition to many of the doctrines of the Church of Rome, and that they entertained but little doubt that I should shortly renounce it altogether,—which, indeed, I had already done. I was also accused, by them, of paying no respect to authority. Another Dominican asserted that I did not believe in the power of the keys to absolve the penitent; and that I explained in a perfectly new manner the words of Christ addressed to Peter: "And I will give unto thee the keys of the kingdom of heaven," &c.;[6] that my explanation, he continued, was as follows:—"I will give unto thee," signifies a promise that Jesus Christ makes to Peter, and not a power which he confers upon him, as the Church of Rome asserts. "The keys" signify knowledge, whereby we unlock and arrive at the mysteries of science, &c. "Of the kingdom of heaven," signifies of my church upon earth; on which account we say in our prayers, "Thy kingdom come." Thus, "I will give unto thee the keys of the kingdom of heaven," means, I promise to give unto thee the knowledge of my church; that is to say, to place thee within it, to give thee fully to understand its principles and its doctrines, and the spirit with which it is animated. That the following passage, "Whatsoever *thou* shalt bind on earth shall be bound in heaven; and whatsoever *thou* shalt loose on earth shall be loosed in heaven," is to be interpreted by another, "Whatsoever *ye* shall bind on earth shall be bound in heaven; and whatsoever *ye* shall loose on earth shall be loosed in heaven."[7] And this, again, by the following, "Whosesoever sins *ye* remit, they are remitted unto them; and whosesoever sins *ye* retain, they are retained."[8] "Ye"—it being no longer said to Peter alone, but to all the apostles; yea, to all the disciples also, which includes all believers. Wherefore St. Augustine exclaims, "What is said to St. Peter is said to all:" *Quod dictum est Petro dictum est omnibus.* To you believers, what ye bind shall be securely bound, and what ye loose shall be entirely loosed.

This interpretation had given such great uneasiness to the poor friar, that he found it necessary to disburthen his conscience, by relating the whole to the Inquisitors. I do not recollect on what occasion, or in what place, I told him all this: it is, however, perfectly true; and I imagine, in his own mind, the friar did not disagree with me; though he found it extremely difficult to reconcile it with the tenets of the Church of Rome, which preach that Jesus Christ, in these words, confers upon Peter, and upon him alone, the authority of the keys; by which is to be understood the power of excommunication, and of absolution, to whomsoever he thinks proper, and for whatever cause he may judge expedient; and that this power is still possessed by the heirs of St. Peter, the popes of Rome.

My opinions on these heads were extremely unpalatable to the Church of Rome; and the more so from the consequences that might attach to them. Other accusations were also preferred against me, with reference to the famous dogma of Transubstantiation. It was asserted that I did not appear to believe in the literal sense of the words of Christ, respecting the bread and wine of the Last Supper.

All this, however, was very imperfectly related by my accuser, so that I think no great effect was produced by his disclosures on the minds of the reverend Inquisitors.

Much clearer was the account of a poor nun, written, as she set forth, at the instigation of her confessor. With great simplicity, she related a conversation she had held with me in the confessional, respecting the two sacraments, which entirely occupied the spiritual thoughts of this poor sister, Confession, and the Holy Supper. With respect to the first, she stated, that of all the confessors she had ever heard of, I had the most strange and singular method. I would listen, she said, with the greatest patience, to the disclosure, not only of her sins, but of her thoughts and feelings as well; in short, of all her deficiencies; and that I was very earnest in directing her conscience with respect to what she ought to do, according to the dictates of the Spirit; but that when we were arrived at that point when I ought to have given her absolution, I invariably turned my back, saying that it belonged to God alone to give absolution for sins committed against himself; that we can only absolve each other for the offences we may have mutually committed against each other; and that the priest and the bishop can, in the name of the church, absolve such sins as are committed against the church, but nothing further.

"One day, I said to him," added the nun, "'I believe that Confession, as the church teaches, is a sacrament instituted by Christ for the remission of all sins whatsoever. Is it not so?'—'I think not,' replied he, 'because I do not find any passage in the Holy Scriptures where the institution of this sacrament is spoken of.'

"'And the injunction of St. James,' I said, '"Confess your sins to one another?"'

"'They are of the same signification as those that follow, "and pray one for another." Do you imagine that only nuns and monks are to pray for the remainder of mankind? "Confess your sins to one another," signifies that it is your duty to confess to me the sins you have committed against me; and I, on the other hand, will do as much towards you, if ever I should offend you.'

"'Then it is unnecessary that I should reveal to a confessor the sins I may have committed against the laws of God?'

"'Not only unnecessary, but the practice is pernicious, if you believe that the confessor can, on the part of God, pardon you. We read that this power is granted by God to his Christ, who says, "But, that ye may know that the Son of man hath power on earth to forgive sins," &c. God can delegate to another, in an extraordinary mission, authority to announce to others that he has pardoned them, as we read in the case of Nathan, with respect to David. But whom do we ever read of, that was appointed by God to act as a confessor, and to give absolution in his stead? Jesus Christ has given to believers the power to remit their own offences, entirely, and for ever; and this he has done because he is constituted the Head of the Church, that is to say, of the people who are believers; to which people God has promised remission of sins, through faith in Jesus Christ.'

"'Then,' said I to him," continued the nun, "'how shall I be assured that my sins are forgiven me, unless a prophet is sent to tell me so, as he was to David?'

"'Oh! you will know it,' replied he, 'through evidence of your own faith, if you can truly say to yourself, "I believe in the remission of sins." Is not faith more convincing than words? Man's words may deceive you, but not the word of God. If you were to hear from me, what you have so often heard from others, "I absolve you from your sins," what assurance would you have, that you were really absolved? What am I, but a sinner, like yourself? Do you apply for health to a sick man, or for wealth to a poor one? Oh! how is it possible that you can prefer to be so continually deceived? Poor deluded being, come out of this darkness, and open your eyes to the light.'

"'Then,' I replied, 'my father, according to your idea, I ought never to confess to any one. How, then, could I partake of the Holy Supper?'

"'St. Paul,' he returned, 'has said, "Let a man examine himself, and so let him eat of that bread and drink of that cup." St. Paul nowhere tells us that it is first necessary to confess to a priest.'"

Here terminated the first part of her account, which was entirely confined to Confession. The second part related to the Communion, and was as follows:—

"One day I was at confession: my heaviest crime was a want of faith in the sacrament of the Holy Supper. I accused myself of having entertained doubts as to the real presence of Christ in the Eucharist.—'What do you understand by the real presence?' demanded he.

"'The substance presented before us of the body, blood, soul, and divinity of Jesus Christ.'

"'If such be your opinion, you are deceived,' he pursued; 'this substance cannot exist in the bread and wine. You know that this sacrament is instituted by Christ, to eat and to drink. Hence the precept, "Eat and drink;" and, again, the penalty for non-observance: "If ye eat not of this bread and drink not of this cup, ye have no life in you." Understand well that the body of Christ was not made to be eaten, nor his blood to be drunk. The natural body of Christ was offered in sacrifice once only,[9] which is enough for our sanctification, if you believe St. Paul speaks the truth.'

"'I believe it, indeed,' replied I, 'but I also wish to believe in the Holy Mother, the Church of Rome.'

"'My good daughter,' he said, 'if these two should be opposed to each other, to which of them would you give credence,—to St. Paul, or to the Church of Rome?'

"'I should certainly be more inclined to believe St. Paul, since he speaks through Divine inspiration.'

"'The case is plain then,—St. Paul and the Church of Rome are in opposition. The apostle calls that which we eat in the sacrament, bread, and that which we drink, wine; whereas the Church of Rome pretends that the bread and the wine vanish away, at the appearance of the body and blood of Christ.'

"'But then,' I rejoined, 'where is the sacrament; where is the communion of the body and blood of Christ?'

"'Clearly in the bread and in the cup. You believe St. Paul—listen to his words: "The cup of blessing which we bless, is it not the communion of the blood of Christ? The bread which we break, is it not the communion of the body of Christ?"'[10]

"To be candid," added the nun, "this doctrine led me away for a time; and in communicating in future, I intended to eat of the bread, and to conjoin myself by faith only, to our Lord Jesus Christ. From which period I could no longer adore the sacrament, for I could not help saying to myself, This is merely bread; it can have no particular signification shut up there;— and so all my devout prayers to this same sacrament were suddenly put an end to. I experienced a sort of repugnance in bending my knee, as I passed before the altar; 'If it be merely bread,' I thought, 'it is an act of idolatry to worship it;' and at length I felt shocked to see others prostrate, and adoring this bread, and offering up prayers to it, as if it were God. Afterwards, I confess, I experienced much suffering when other confessors undertook to lead me back to my old belief. It was necessary to prohibit me from thinking on the words of St. Paul, of which no one was able to give me a satisfactory explanation; unless I should call the reply of a certain reverend father (to whom I confided my difficulty) a satisfactory one, when he assured me that he thought it wiser not to trouble his head about such matters, lest he should have to find the best argument and the most satisfactory explanation within the walls of the Inquisition."

This poor nun, who was at that time converted by my arguments, was afterwards compelled to denounce me to the Inquisition, which she had done through fear of being herself shut up in it, had she refused; as it obtains possession of the greater part of its victims by threatening those who will not denounce them, with imprisonment themselves. And I have no doubt that she was so threatened more than once.

From these and similar accusations was my process got up, before the Inquisition, in the year 1842. Here then was my profession of faith, warranted on very respectable authority. I was very glad to see an account of it; and, to say the truth, I felt not a little proud of it. I hastily put together these few notices, and hid them for future use. I was annoyed that I had not time to read more of the voluminous process, and to extract from it other portions. I should perhaps have found a complete series of accusations, which might have completely laid open my entire Christian belief. In fact, there were denunciations with respect to what I had taught in the schools, in the confessional, and in the pulpit. Doubtless the opportunity was not lost of accusing me of frequently controverting the doctrines of Thomas Aquinas, respecting the pretended propitiatory sacrifice of the Mass, the number of the Sacraments, the value of Indulgences, the torments of Purgatory, and other doctrines of that time, handed down to us as dogmas of religion.

If these accusations were joined to others, which I saw in the volume at the Inquisition, chiefly from Naples, with respect to my preaching, then indeed there could have been nothing wanting to satisfy the Holy Office that I was a heretic, in every sense of the word, and richly merited to be consigned to the flames.

The Dominicans, to whom, in honour of their founder,[11] has hitherto been granted the great privilege of being the chief agents in the Inquisition, hold Thomas Aquinas and his doctrines in the highest esteem and veneration, insomuch that their principal school is called after his name. There is no degree of praise that they have not lavished on their master, on whom they have even bestowed the title of *Angelic*; and they have represented him, as all the world knows, with a radiant sun in his breast, as symbolic of his wisdom, and a dove at his ear, to indicate the presence of the Holy Spirit, revealing to him the truth. Among other pleasant stories recorded of him, is one which relates that the crucifix addressed him in a set speech, in approbation of his doctrine, saying, "O Thomas, thou hast written well concerning me!" The Dominicans swear to follow implicitly the theological and philosophical views of Thomas Aquinas; and it is indispensably requisite to take an oath to that effect, before admission into their colleges. At the present juncture, all who do not agree with the Jesuits, flock to the schools of the Dominicans. Indeed, I am of opinion that these two parties divide among themselves the whole Church of Rome: those who are not Jesuits, or Molinists, are Dominicans, or Thomasines. Other schools of theology are of little account, and are scarcely known, having no followers beyond the immediate establishments; such as the Benedictines, the Augustines, the Carmelites, and others.

Brought up myself in this school of Aquinas, I was early imbued with his doctrines. Five years I studied the writings of this author, so celebrated for learning and scholastic subtlety. Unquestionably, Thomas Aquinas was not the original framer of the Romish doctrines: they were already produced, and he did no more than defend and explain them. The most ingenious of theologians, he possessed a rare faculty of persuasion; so that if instead of the doctrines he undertook to defend, he had had others placed before him, still more opposed to the truth, he would equally well have reconciled them at once to the Holy Scriptures, and to the teaching of Aristotle. In his *Summa Theologiæ* is to be found all that can be most interesting to Rome, except *il diritto nuovo* of the Council of Trent. I have always admired the ingenuity of this writer, but very early I experienced considerable difficulty with respect to some of his theories.

Having completed my course of study, I was appointed, in my twenty-fourth year, to the duty of teaching. The first book on which I had to display my ability was this very *Summa Theologiæ* of Thomas Aquinas. Many opinions were formed as to how I should acquit myself on the occasion. It was predicted by some who had heard me strongly object to various points in the Thomasine doctrines, that I should not prove very faithful to them. The General of the Dominicans hesitated to confide to me a school belonging to the order, after he had heard that in my examination I had shown but little respect for the scholastic doctrines; and he wrote to a certain cardinal, who had sought to engage my services, as professor of theology, in a seminary: "I would willingly accede to the request of your Eminence, with respect to the Lecturer Achilli, were I not obliged, for certain reasons, to examine him a little further as to his orthodoxy."[12] After the lapse of a year, however, he granted me permission to officiate at Viterbo, where, for a considerable length of time, I was professor of various sciences, at the Seminary and Bishop's College, as I was also of theology, in the College of the Dominicans.

My labours in these situations obtained for me, from the very beginning, considerable reputation, and not a few friends gathered round me. Still I had many enemies, and chiefly among the friars,—a class of gentry who to a very little good, adjoin a large share of evil. Few among them are respectable in character; the major part of them being lazy vagabonds, who, to avoid every species of exertion, either physical or mental, and to pass their whole lives in sloth and ignorance, adopt the frock and cowl, which at once authorize them to receive food, clothes, and lodging, without any trouble or labour on their part. Altogether they constitute the worst part of society, and only serve to demoralize it by their bad example. As I could never endure them, and shunned all intercourse with them, it was natural that I should incur their hatred and censure.

It appeared that those among the friars who disliked me, feared me no less; since in all their attempted persecutions, they studiously avoided coming forward and avowing their hostility. However this may be, out of the cloister I was equally beloved and protected. Many bishops had a regard for me, and several cardinals. Pope Gregory XVI. looked upon me with a favourable eye, and spoke of me to the general of my order; and his predecessor, Leo XII., had recommended me to the Master of the Sacred Palace, as his Vicar, in the year 1827.

In the mean while my enemies grew more and more uneasy every day, and were more and more disappointed. Did they attack me on one side? They were speedily put to confusion. On the other? It frequently happened they inflicted injury on themselves alone. Often, I believe, they despaired altogether of accomplishing their evil intentions towards me. One only method remained, by means of which, secretly and securely, and without danger of being discovered by myself or my protectors, they might effect their object; and this was the Inquisition: for in that place no one, not even the dearest friend, can afford protection or support. There every accusation has to be fully entered into. The accuser gives his name to the tribunal, which for its own part affects to be ignorant of it. The same with the witnesses. Rarely does it happen that they are examined a second time. Their first deposition is sufficient.

They began in this manner with respect to myself, in order to undermine the edifice they were determined to destroy; and the first attack against me was made at Viterbo, in concert with certain parties in Rome, and some of the Dominicans from Naples, who were also invited to lend their assistance.

But observe the foolishness and blindness of men! They who wielded this powerful weapon against me, thought to destroy me with it; instead of which, they were the means of giving me fresh life. They undertook to explain to others my profession of faith, which I had not yet been able to make out clearly to myself. They reared the structure in the most solemn manner, before the Inquisition, that they themselves might no longer doubt, and that the memory of my conversion from Papacy to pure Christianity, which began about the year 1830, from which epoch the earliest of my accusations are dated, might for ever be preserved. May the Lord be praised!

Why do not my present enemies publish these facts in the manner in which they took place? I should like to see the secret accusations against me openly detailed. Instead of falsely framing charges of immorality which never existed, let them state my real crimes. They might show "that in point of religious belief I could not depart from the Holy Scriptures; that my Christianity did not extend beyond the Bible; that I was greatly opposed to the later doctrines of the Roman Church; that my theology had existed eighteen centuries, neither more nor less; and that every article that did not conform itself to this old theology, I neither owned for doctrine, nor for Christianity." Such was the epitome with which a Dominican friar of Naples wound up a lengthened declamation, to prove that I was, reader, guess what—a *Neoterico*—a *Novatore*.

To say the truth, if the Commissioner of the Inquisition had communicated to me the substance of the above, I should have leaped for joy. But in the opinion of the friar, these premises were terrific. A heretic, according to the Bible! A *Novatore*, according to primitive Christianity! These titles were for me a source of pride and gratification. The Inquisitor thought it far better that I should not be made acquainted with the charges. He did not foresee that I might read them without his permission. But since I had read them, and retained them perfectly in my memory, it frequently happened that I made use of them, in my replies to him. For example, when he asked me *Quid sentis de fide*? I remember my answer was:

"To those who are good Latin scholars, this question may be considered in three points of view: you might intend to ask me what I think concerning faith? or, what do I think I ought to believe? or, lastly, what is it that I do believe? I will readily reply to all these points. 1st, What do I think concerning faith? That it is a gift from God, by which we are made believers in the truths that He has revealed.—2d, What do I think I ought to believe? The truth alone; which He has revealed to us, according to what is written in the authentic book of Divine Revelation, and interpreted according to the spirit and common sense of Christendom.—3d, What is it that I do believe? The answer is already given."

"Then," rejoined the Inquisitor, "you believe nothing but what you find written in the Bible?"

"Certainly."

"And you think that all that was said and done by Jesus Christ, is recorded in that book? How is it then that St. John tells us, that if that had been the case, the whole world would not have contained the books that would have been written?"[13]

"I am glad, Father Inquisitor, to hear you quote a text from the Evangelist, which, if I interpret it aright, leads us to infer that Jesus did many other things which we do not know; and not, as you imagine, that we know them from other sources; and that, as they are told to us from these sources, so we ought to believe them. I do not believe, Father Inquisitor, more than I find written, because I know that to be sufficient; I am satisfied that I am not deceived; and besides, I believe that no one should add to what is written from Divine inspiration. You have quoted St. John, I now quote him in my turn, and I select that passage in which, speaking of his Revelation, he affirms as follows:—

"'If any man shall add unto these things, God shall add unto him the plagues that are written in this book: and if any man shall take away from the words of the book of this prophecy, God shall take away his part, out of the book of life.'[14]

"Is it not clear, from this, that we are instructed neither to add to, nor to take away from, what is written? The faith, therefore, that I profess, is the same that was defined by Jesus Christ himself, emanating from him eighteen centuries ago. This law was never abrogated in order to engraft new doctrines upon the old, or to make us falsify our original belief. Are you of opinion, Father Inquisitor, that we can possess a different faith from our forefathers? I speak of those early Christians, who, in this very country, renounced idolatry to follow Christ; of those very men to whom the apostle addressed the invaluable testimony: 'Your faith is spoken of throughout the whole world!' In all other matters I am willing to go with the nineteenth century; but as regards religion, I do not depart from the first. I do not know, Father Inquisitor, what your opinion is, but I am firm in the belief that all Christians ought to be similarly minded; and that the Church should return to its first state, both as regards discipline and faith."

Such then, at that time, was my profession of faith; in which I was continually, through the operation of various circumstances, being perfected; not a little assisted by the machinations of my enemies themselves. It is true, I had not yet sufficient courage to seek for occasions of trial; but on their occurrence, I invariably experienced such grace and favour from God, that in no instance was the opportunity lost of deriving due profit from them. And since it has been ordained by Providence that I should bear solemn testimony in favour of the pure and true religion of Christ, and publicly make avowal of my faith before men, and before God, so it was expedient that I should, in the first instance, make declaration of it in the face of my enemies, and of that very tribunal before which so many had sacrificed their lives, in defence of the same holy cause.

I did not at that time perceive the lofty designs of this all-wise Providence: my eyes were not open to behold the hidden destiny which, nevertheless, was in store for me. I walked in darkness, and only knew that I should not lose my way, because I was assured that a Divine hand would be my protection and my guide.

At present, however, through the mercy of the Lord, I see my way more clearly. By his power I have been snatched from the abyss of perdition, delivered from the malice of my enemies, and conducted to a land where there is liberty of belief, and where man lives honourably, in obedience to the laws of truth and justice.

My first step, on finding myself a free man in a free country, was to make a full and unqualified declaration of my religious faith, that there might not remain the least shadow of doubt, as to my entire secession from the Church of Rome.

Every one acquainted with me knows that I never attempt to disguise what I feel; should prudence occasionally enjoin me to be silent, it is only for a very short time that I can listen to her dictates. My energy increases before an opposing barrier, until, like a rushing torrent, it levels and destroys every object it meets with. Thus, no sooner did an outlet present itself for the manifestation of my opinions, than they eagerly pressed forward, and swept away all opposition that stood in their way.

I was full of wrath against the Church of the priests, ever since I discovered the deceit in which I had been educated; and still more so, on account of having myself been instrumental in propagating her doctrines and her errors. This wrath I had hitherto been obliged to restrain within my own breast; but when I arrived in Corfu, in the year 1842, I found an opportunity for giving way to it, of which I quickly availed myself. My tongue was not idle, and my pen was more active still.

I regret that I have not kept copies of several letters I wrote at that time to divers cardinals at Rome, which, although full of stern reproof, were written without bitterness, and in a conciliatory spirit; and I still remember them with pleasure, because I know that they evinced how strong my feelings were upon the subject.[15]

I shall, however, present to my readers, in the Appendix to this work, copies of two letters which I wrote about the same period to Pope Gregory XVI., as well as of one which I subsequently addressed to his successor Pius IX.

## FOOTNOTES:

[5] On one occasion I was left alone by the Inquisitor, above an hour, in one of the apartments of the Holy Office, while he was preparing my process. He had left on the table a bundle of papers, containing the correspondence of the Inquisition with its agents, and from which my accusations were drawn: I therefore deemed myself at full liberty to peruse these documents, and obtained from them much important matter, relating to my own affairs.

[6] Matt. xvi. 19.

[7] Matt. xviii. 18.

[8] John xx. 23.

[9] Heb. x. 10.

[10] I Cor. x. 16.

[11] Domenico di Guzman was the first Inquisitor, under Innocent III. (1215), to whom he suggested the great project of destroying, by an armed force, all the Protestants of that period, chiefly known under the denominations of Albigenses and Valdenses. This friar, in conjunction with the pope, founded an order of knights, whom he frequently led on himself, and who were renowned for their massacre of these good Christians, who, retaining the Gospel, rejected the new doctrines of the Fourth Council of the Lateran.

[12] Letter from Father Velzi to Cardinal Galeffi (1825).

[13] John xxi. 25.

[14] Rev. xxi. 19.

[15] Since the publication of my first Edition, I have discovered among my papers a copy of one of these letters, which will be found in the Appendix. It is addressed to Cardinal Lambruschini, at that time Secretary of State, on occasion of his having urgently required of the Papal Consul, at Corfù, that he should endeavour to induce the Ionian Government to have me sent out of the country. As, however, my real motive for quitting Rome was well known, the Cardinal's remonstrance only served to render the Government more determined to protect me.

# CHAPTER IV
# THE INQUISITION IN THE NINETEENTH CENTURY

We are now in the middle of the nineteenth century, and still the Inquisition is actually and potentially in existence. This abominable institution, the history of which is a mass of atrocious crimes, committed by the priests of the Church of Rome, in the name of God and of His Christ, is still in existence in Rome and in the Roman States, with the Pope at its head.

I have heard of some avowed or concealed papists, belonging to Great Britain, who, on occasion of the public demonstrations that took place in the principal cities of the kingdom, on account of my liberation, had the boldness to deny that I had ever been incarcerated in the Inquisition at all; or that any such establishment existed in Rome, at the present period. I shall not take up my own time, or that of my readers, in arguing with these persons, any more than I should with those who might deny that it was noon-day, when the sun was in its zenith.

In the month of April, 1850, during my stay in Dublin, an immense number of people, of all ranks and classes, attended the meetings that were held in my favour, to express their joy in seeing me, and the satisfaction they experienced in hearing me. The whole body of papists were considerably annoyed on the occasion, and not knowing in what manner to put a stop to the proceedings, some of them took it into their heads to spread a report through the city, affirming that I was not the Dr. Achilli, imprisoned by the Inquisition, but an impostor, who assumed his name. This poor invention, however, was not very likely to serve them, as it would have been easy for me to prove my identity. In like manner, any one who should persist in denying the present existence of the Inquisition in Rome, would soon find his statement refuted and held up to ridicule. And this being granted, can any one attempt to justify the conduct of the Church of Rome in permitting it?

I do not know what to think of the audacity of a certain writer, unquestionably not an ordinary personage, who published an article in the "Dublin Review" (July 1850), entitled "The Inquisition;" the object of which was to persuade the world that, after all, this Inquisition, respecting which so much *unjust clamour* (!) had been raised, contained nothing but what might *honestly* be considered *necessary*, for the *present state of society*, and the *interests of religion*. Every religion, it was stated, had been intolerant. "What by us," it said, "in the present day, is denominated intolerance, entered into the very spirit of the Jewish religion." (P. 423.) The learned writer, who, to his shame, is an Englishman, and at this present time a cardinal, leads the reader to the conclusion that the Almighty himself, the founder of the Jewish religion, has countenanced intolerance.

He then proceeds to observe: "Of the five great religions which divided the Gentile world—the Greek, the Roman, the Egyptian, the Persian, and the Indian—there is not one which can claim exemption from the charge." (*Ib.*) His inference, therefore, is, that it is no wonder that Christianity also is in a similar state; and this involves the farther conclusion that Christianity itself, in this respect, is a system of religion similar to these five great religious systems which divided the pagan world. This is the doctrine held out to us by a Cardinal Archbishop! According to him, Christianity, like the preceding religions, has always been more or less intolerant. With respect to papacy, it is most true that in practice it has always been more or less so, but in theory it has been always the same. In fact, Thomas Aquinas, the leading theologian and doctor of the Church of Rome, lays down the following doctrine, which his Eminence, and others of his school, seem very ready to act upon. "It is," says he, "much more grievous to corrupt faith, which is the source and life of the soul, than to corrupt money, which only tends to the relief of the body. Hence, if coiners and other malefactors are justly put to death, by the secular authority, much more may heretics not only be excommunicated, but put to death."[16]

For example, if you, reader, a Christian of intelligent mind, should deny that the bread and the wine, in consequence of a few words uttered over them, should cease to be bread and wine—you, in that case, have corrupted the faith of the Thomasine school, which is that of the Church of Rome; the reverend Inquisitor therefore speedily lays hold of you, with sufficient argument before him to condemn you to death, for the glory of God.

These barbarities were formerly common in Spain and Italy; but now!!—Is the theory of the Church of Rome, you ask, still in favour of these practices? I answer, it is not possible for Cardinal Wiseman to renounce this doctrine, and at the same time remain consistent to his principles. Is it not manifestly a contradiction? It is his duty,[17] then, as a Roman Catholic, and an Archbishop, to condemn you to death, whenever he may have the power so to do, if you refuse to believe that the bread and the wine, over which a priest has breathed the words, "*Hoc est corpus meum*," have not, forthwith, ceased to be bread and wine. Yes, his Eminence, faithful to his oath, and sanctioned by the theological and legal decision of the Thomasine doctors, must of necessity consign you to the flames. Are flames no longer resorted to, as attracting too vividly the attention of the public? It matters not; poison will get rid of a heretic equally well, and more secretly.

The reverend Jesuits, Busembau, Sa, Escobar, and others, readily gave their vote to that effect. When, in the year 1842, I was for the first time delivered over to the Inquisition, the General of the Dominicans, the oldest of the Inquisitors,[18] exclaimed before the council: "This heretic," speaking of myself, "we had better burn him alive." Such was the humanity of one who had grown grey among the corruptions and evil practices of his profession! His proposition, however, was not seconded, it being the first time I had been accused; but what might not have been my fate, if this old man had been living, and appointed to judge me in the year 1850? In fact, I heard last year, whilst I was in Rome, that another of these precious theologians, less fierce and furious than the Dominican, suggested a more moderate proceeding, in the following terms:—

"I should advise that Achilli be so dealt with as to prevent the possibility of his ever troubling us any more."[19] This, unquestionably, evinced no intention of setting me at liberty. And at a later period, after I had written my letters to the Pope, and published many other things in opposition to the Romish doctrines, the same *monsignore*, speaking of me to one of his adherents, who was more my friend than his, observed:

"I was right in the advice I gave in 1842, that Achilli should be so dealt with as to prevent the possibility of his ever troubling us any more. Had it been followed, we should not have had the present annoyance. And who knows what worse he may not have in store for us?"

I am indeed much indebted to this *monsignore*: I hope to do far better yet for the true Church of Christ.

What, then, is the Inquisition of the nineteenth century? The same system of intolerance which prevailed in the barbarous ages. That which raised the Crusade, and roused all Europe to arms at the voice of a monk,[20] and of a hermit.[21] That which—in the name of a God of peace, manifested on earth by Christ, who, through love for sinners, gave himself to be crucified—brought slaughter on the Albigenses and the Waldenses; filled France with desolation, under Domenico di Guzman, and raised in Spain the funeral pile and the scaffold, devastating the fair kingdoms of Granada and Castile, through the assistance of those detestable monks, Raimond de Pennafort, Peter Arbues, and Cardinal Torquemada. The same system which, to its eternal infamy, registers in the annals of France the fatal 24th of August, and the 5th of November, in those of England. The same which at this moment flourishes in Rome; which has never yet been either worn out or modified, and which, in the jargon of the priests, is still called "the Holy, Roman, Universal, Apostolic Inquisition." Holy, as the place where Christ was crucified is holy; Apostolic, because Judas Iscariot was the first Inquisitor; Roman and Universal, because from Rome it extends over all the world.

It is denied by some that the Inquisition, which exists in Rome, as its centre, is extended throughout the world by means of the missionaries. The Roman Inquisition and the Roman Propaganda are nevertheless in close connexion with each other. Every bishop who is sent *in partibus infidelium*, is an Inquisitor, charged to discover, through the means of his missionaries, whatever is done or said by others, in reference to Rome, with the obligation to make his report secretly. The apostolic nuncios are all Inquisitors, as also are the apostolic vicars.

Here, then, we see the Roman Inquisition extending into the most remote countries. In India, for example—who would ever believe that the Inquisition was at work there? So far from Rome! in the dominions of the English! The bare assertion would meet with ridicule. "Oh! the Inquisition in India! No, no, we cannot believe that. In name, indeed, it may be there, but never in actual reality." Fortunately, however, I have a letter by me, which I received in this country in March last. The original has been seen by many persons; among others, by Sir Culling E. Eardley, through whom, indeed, I received it. It came to hand very opportunely. It is written in English, and, if not elegant in its phraseology, it is at least sincere, and to be depended upon. It is as follows:—

"Dear and Reverend Sir,—I hope you will excuse me, if I, who am a stranger to you, take the liberty to address you the present letter. But the same God who delivered you from the brutal hands of your persecutors, (for which I congratulate you,) has given me courage to rise from my lethargy in which I was; and, kneeling before His presence, I heard a voice, saying, Write to Mr. A. [Achilli] for advice, and fly again from this Babylon. Therefore, full of confidence, I take the pen, in order to relate to you all my story.

"I am a Roman Catholic priest, and, as soon as I was ordained, being very anxious to preach the gospel to the poor Hindoos, I left Rome, on the 2d of March, 1840, being then twenty-three years of age, and was sent by *Propaganda Fide* to India; and there, being able to speak the English language, I was appointed, by the Roman Catholic bishop of Bombay, as military chaplain, and was sent to a military camp at Belgaum, where I was a very zealous and bigoted Roman Catholic priest, till God was pleased to open my eyes in the following manner:

"A Protestant clergyman of the Church of Scotland, named Taylor, celebrated the marriage ceremony to two Catholics; and this hurt my feeling very much; therefore I thought it my duty to write him a letter in very impolite[22] manner, as is the custom of all Roman Catholic priests to do, to which he answered very kindly, and sent me also some Protestant books to read;—of course I refused to read them, and I returned them to him. But God put into his heart to call, as he did, on me. He spoke to me a new language, which I had never before heard;—it was the language of a true Christian—(how sinner is justified before God). This language, by the grace of God, touched my heart in such a manner that I took a Protestant book and began to read. It was 'The Spirit of the Papacy,' which opened my eyes, and I began to perceive the errors of the Church of Rome. Then, quite another man, I opened the Holy Bible, and confirmed myself that the Catholic religion is in perfect contradiction to the word of God, and that the Protestant Church was the Church in which God called me; therefore I opened my mind to the Rev. Mr. Jackson, who was the military Protestant chaplain at Belgaum, and a great friend of mine. He advised me to write to Dr. Carr, bishop of Bombay, which I did; and his lordship was pleased to answer me in a very polite manner, begging me to write my sentiments about the real presence of our Lord Jesus Christ in the Sacrament, and a treatise on the spiritual power of the Pope, which I also did; and then he wrote to me to go to Bombay, where I embraced the Protestant religion; that is to say, the pure religion of the Gospel.

"A Spanish Jesuit priest, named Francis Xavier Serra, whom I never saw before, called on me, in a secular dress; and, speaking the Italian language well, he told me that he was an Italian layman, and having heard that I was an Italian too, he called on me: but he did not mention anything about religion, saying he did not care about it;—and he was very kind to me. He called on me four or five times; till one day, being a very agreeable evening, he begged me to take a round with him, which I did. And we went near the Catholic church, and to my great surprise, I was taken by four men, and forced to go to the vicar-general, where they forced me to write a letter to the Protestant minister, Mr. Valentine, in whose house I lived, stating my intention to return to the Catholic religion; which I am very sorry to say I did. They then closed me in a room, till Sunday; when the vicar took me by force to the pulpit, and dictated to me what I was to say to the congregation; and he obliged me to declare that I left the Catholic religion for worldly motives; which was quite contrary to my sentiments. When night came, they took me from the room in which I was closed, and delivered me to a captain of a French ship, as a prisoner; with the order to take care of me to Marseilles, where he delivered me to the bishop; who, with a French priest, sent me to Rome. From Rome I was sent, as a punishment, to a convent at Perugia, where I remained for five years, till I got again my liberty, and returned to Rome; this was in November 1848.

"I am sure, Sir, you are not surprised to hear the treachery made to me at Bombay by that Jesuit, and by the vicar. Besides, you must know that the vicar, whose name is Father Michele Antonio, for his bad character, had been put in gaol for six months, by the British Government at Bombay.

"Now, Sir, I live in a most miserable estate of mind, being from my heart a Protestant, yet I am obliged to observe the Roman Catholic forms; which is quite contrary to my feelings. I am very sorry that I had not in India the Christian courage which you have demonstrated just now in Rome: but you must know that they threatened me with brutal menaces, and that I was too young.

"I am at present firmly resolved to fly from this Babylon, and embrace again the pure doctrine of the Gospel; to remain in the faith, by the grace of God, till my death, and to preach it throughout the world....

"I have the honour &c.
"Your Brother in Jesus Christ,

"N. N."

"Rome, the 26th Feb. 1850."

This adventure at Bombay proves that the Inquisition is not only in existence, but sufficiently daring to carry on its operations even within the British dominions: and we see the manner in which it acts. In Bombay, the recantation of this poor priest is all that is known (as an English missionary, who was there at the time, told me): it was said, indeed, that he had since left the country; but no one knew of the treachery of the Jesuit, or of the tricks of the apostolic vicar.

Similar events occur, more or less frequently, in various parts of the world; most commonly in the Levant; since the Turkish governor does not grant his protection to foreigners, and the obliging consuls of Austria, France, and Naples generally have the complaisance to arrest whomsoever the bishops require, and send them to Rome. It is notorious that in Constantinople, in the year 1847, an Armenian priest, D. Giovanne Keosse, although an Ottoman subject and born in Constantinople, was seized in the night by four bullies from the Austrian Embassy, and hurried into a steamer, to be conveyed as a prisoner to Marseilles, and thence to Rome, to be handed over to the Inquisition. And all this took place by order of the Armenian Catholic Bishop.

This Keosse, who was confined in a cabin on board the steamer, found means to effect his escape, by slipping through the window, into a boat, while the vessel was disembarking a part of its passengers and goods at Smyrna. He subsequently put himself under the protection of the American consul; and the Austrian, finding himself discovered, gave up the affair, and so it ended. Keosse, however, did not feel at all sure of his safety from the grasp of the Inquisition, so long as he remained under the Ottoman Government; and being advised to go to Malta, he went there without delay, and there he remains at the present period.[23] This affair of Keosse was much talked about; several journals took it up; and some went so far as to insult the Embassy, for acting in the character of Inquisitors.

I certainly think these gentlemen must be ashamed of themselves for having lent their aid to the Inquisition of Rome; pretty much in the same manner as the French have reason to blush for having lent six chasseurs of Vincennes, to effect my imprisonment in the same place. But such is the witchcraft of this renowned harlot, that, almost without being aware of it, "all nations have drunk of the wine of the wrath of her fornication, and the kings of the earth have committed fornication with her."[24]

We have seen constitutional Austria and republican France degrade themselves so far as to bombard our cities, to replace upon the throne—whom?—the head of the Inquisition! And Spain, that has shown so much determination in resisting priestcraft, monkery, and the dominion of the Inquisition, she also hastened to Rome,—and for what purpose? To assist in the restoration of the papacy!

But let us inquire what is the Inquisition of the present day in Rome. It is the very same that was instituted at the Council of Verona, to burn Arnold of Brescia; the same that was established, at the third Council of the Lateran, to sanction the slaughter of the Albigenses and the Waldenses, the massacre of the people, the destruction of the city; the same that was confirmed at the Council of Constance, to burn alive two holy men, John Huss and Jerome of Prague; that which at Florence, subjected Savonarola to the torture; and at Rome condemned Aonio Paleario, and Pietro Carnesecchi. It is the self-same Inquisition with that of Pope Caraffa, and of Fr. Michele Ghislieri, who built the palace called the *Holy Office*, where so many victims fell a sacrifice to its barbarity, and where at the present moment the Roman Inquisition still exists. Its laws are always the same. *The Black Book*, or *Praxis Sacræ Romanæ Inquisitionis*, is always the model for that which is to succeed it. This book is a large manuscript volume, in folio, and is carefully preserved by the head of the Inquisition. It is called, *Libro Nero, the Black Book,* because it has a cover of that colour; or, as an Inquisitor explained to me, *Libro Necro,* which, in the Greek language, signifies "the book of the dead."

In this book is the criminal code, with all the punishments for every supposed crime; also the mode of conducting the trial, so as to elicit the guilt of the accused; and the manner of receiving the accusations. I had this book in my hand, on one occasion, as I have related above, and read therein the proceedings relative to my own case; and I moreover saw in this same volume, some very astounding particulars: for example, in the list of punishments, I read concerning the bit, or as it is called by us the *mordacchia*; which is a very simple contrivance to confine the tongue, and compress it between two cylinders, composed of iron and wood, and furnished with spikes. This horrible instrument not only wounds the tongue and occasions excessive pain, but also, from the swelling it produces, frequently places the sufferer in danger of suffocation. This torture is generally had recourse to in cases considered as blasphemy against God, the Virgin, the Saints, or the Pope. So that, according to the Inquisition, it is as great a crime to speak in disparagement of a pope, who may be a very detestable character, as to blaspheme the holy name of God. Be that as it may, this torture has been in use till the present period; and to say nothing of the exhibitions of the same nature which were displayed in Romagna, in the time of Gregory XVI., by the Inquisitor Ancarani—in Umbria, by Stefanelli, Salua, and others, we may admire the inquisitorial zeal of Cardinal Ferretti, the cousin of his present holiness, who condescended more than once to employ these means, when he was Bishop of Rieti and Fermo.

Every one knows how the Holy Inquisition has surpassed every other tribunal by its exquisite ingenuity in torturing human nature. Must I bring examples from the Inquisition of Spain? That of Rome has her own to answer for as well. Through the mercy of Heaven, the former has come to an end; but that of Rome is still in full vigour.

I do not propose to myself to speak of the Inquisition of times past, but of what exists in Rome at the present moment: I shall therefore assert that the laws of this institution being in no respect changed, neither can the institution itself be said to have undergone any alteration. The present race of priests who are now in power, are too much afraid of the popular indignation to let loose all their inquisitoria fury, which might even occasion a revolt, if they were not to restrain it; the whole world, moreover, would cry out against them; a crusade would be raised against the Inquisition itself, and for a little temporary gratification, much power would be endangered.

This is the true reason why the severity of its penalties is in some degree relaxed at the present time, but they still remain unaltered in its code.

Concerning the method of conducting a process, I read in the *Libro Necro* as follows: "With respect to the examination, and the duty of the examiners—either the prisoner confesses, and he is proved guilty from his own confession, or he does not confess, and is equally guilty on the evidence of witnesses. If a prisoner confesses the whole of what he is accused of, he is unquestionably guilty of the whole; but if he confesses only a part, he ought still to be regarded as guilty of the whole; since what he has confessed proves him to be capable of guilt, as to the other points of accusation. And here the precept is to be kept in view, 'no one is obliged to condemn himself,' *nemo tenetur prodere seipsum*. Nevertheless, the judge should do all in his power to induce the culprit to confess, since confession tends to the glory of God. And as the respect due to the glory of God requires that no one particular should be omitted, not even a mere attempt; so the judge is bound to put in force, not only the ordinary means which the Inquisition affords, but whatever may enter into his thoughts, as fitting to lead to a confession. Bodily torture has ever been found the most salutary and efficient means of leading to spiritual repentance. Therefore, the choice of the most befitting mode of torture is left to the Judge of the Inquisition, who determines according to the age, the sex, and the constitution of the party. He will be prudent in its use, always being mindful, at the same time, to procure what is required from it—the confession of the delinquent. If, notwithstanding all the means employed, the unfortunate wretch still denies his guilt, he is to be considered as a victim of the devil; and, as such, deserves no compassion from the servants of God, nor the pity or indulgence of holy mother Church: he is a son of perdition. Let him perish, then, among the damned, and let his place be no longer found among the living."

This most astounding page is followed by another, in which is given the mode of obtaining a conviction. Various means are pointed out to establish the guilt of the prisoner, and to declare him deserving the condemnation of the tribunal. For example, Titius is accused of having eaten meat on Friday or Saturday. The Inquisition does not permit the name of the accused to appear, neither those of the witnesses. The accusation is laid that Titius has eaten meat in the house of Caius. Sempronius is the accuser, and he summons the family of Caius to give evidence; but, as these have been accomplices in the same affair, they cannot be induced to depose against Titius; perhaps other witnesses may be brought, who may be equally incompetent. In which case the wary judge endeavours to draw from the prisoner himself sufficient to inculpate him. He will first inquire respecting several other families the points which he wishes to know with regard to that of Caius. He will try to learn at what other houses Titius has been accustomed to eat, in order to know concerning the house of Caius, where the meat was eaten. The accusation sets forth that on such a day, at such an hour, Titius went to the house of Caius, where the whole family were present, and that all sat down to table, &c. &c. If Titius admits all the circumstantial matters brought forward by the accuser, with respect to time, place, and persons, but is silent, or denies entirely the only crime imputed to him, he stands convicted: the accuser has no necessity to bring forward witnesses: judgment is pronounced.

This practice is still employed by the Inquisition. In the year 1842, I was accused of having spoken, in a certain house, against the worship of saints. If the judge had made my accusation known (as is the case in all other tribunals throughout the world), saying to me: You are accused of having, in such a house, spoken of such and such matters, in the presence of so and so,—I should have known my accuser by the part he would take in the question. But instead of interrogating me in a straightforward manner, I was made to give a description of the house in question, together with that of several other houses; to describe the persons belonging to it, and many other persons at the same time; to discuss the real subject of accusation, mixed up with other irrelevant matters, in order to mislead me as much as possible, and prevent me from gaining any insight whatever of the points of which I was accused, or of the persons who had accused me. Whether I confessed or not, I was to be declared guilty, or, as they term it, *reo convinto*.

With regard to these denunciations, the Inquisition declares that, in matters of offences against religion, it is the positive and bounden duty of every one to become an accuser. Children may and ought to accuse their parents, wives their husbands, and servants their masters. The law is, according to the decrees of several popes, that whoever becomes acquainted with any offence committed against religion, whether from his own knowledge, or from hearsay, is bound, within fifteen days, to bring forward his accusation before an inquisitor, or the vicar of the Holy Office; or, where these are not present, before a bishop. The crime, whatever it may be, not only attaches to the principal and the accomplices, but also to every one who knows of it and does not reveal it. So that if you, for example, dear reader, should unfortunately belong to the Church of the Inquisition, you would be obliged to accuse not only me, who address you, but all those who, together with yourself, listen to me: and whoever knows that you have listened to my discourses, although he himself may never have heard me, is under the obligation to denounce you to the Inquisition. The punishment for non-observance of this duty is excommunication, which excludes the party subject to it from the benefit of all the sacraments, and shuts him out from the kingdom of heaven. Moreover, besides excommunication, he is liable to be imprisoned in the Inquisition, and to suffer such other punishment as may be deemed necessary. Even the very Cardinals, and the Inquisitors themselves, are not exempt from this obligation; the Pope himself has followed the example. My letters to Gregory XVI. were immediately forwarded to the Inquisition, by his own hand. I have reason to believe that Pius IX. did the same when I wrote to him. All this we may overlook: but that a wife should be obliged to accuse her own husband, or a mother her children, is too dreadful to think of.

I will here relate a fact which it always pains me to recall to mind; and which, until the present occasion, I have never before spoken about. During my residence at Viterbo, my native town, where I was public professor and teacher in the College of *Gradi*, I was one day applied to by a lady of prepossessing appearance, whom I then saw for the first time. She requested, with much eagerness, to see me in the sacristy; and as I entered the apartment where she was waiting for me, she begged the sacristan to leave us alone, and suddenly closing the door, presented a moving spectacle to my eyes. Throwing off her bonnet, and letting loose in a moment her long and beautiful tresses, the lady fell upon her knees before me, and gave vent to her grief in abundance of sighs and tears. On my endeavouring to encourage her, and to persuade her to rise and unfold her mind to me, she at length, in a voice broken by sobs, thus addressed me:

"No, father, I will never rise from this posture, unless you first promise to pardon me my heavy transgression." (Although much younger than herself, she addressed me as her father.)

"Signora," replied I, "it belongs to God to pardon our transgressions. If you have in any way injured me, so far I can forgive you; but I confess I have no cause of complaint against you, with whom, indeed, I have not even the pleasure of being acquainted."

"I have been guilty of a great sin, for which no priest will grant me absolution, unless you will beforehand remit it to me."

"You must explain yourself more fully; as yet I have no idea of what you allude to."

"It is now nearly a year since I received absolution from my confessor; and the last few days he has entirely forbid me his presence, telling me that I am damned. I have tried others, and all tell me the same thing. One, however, has lately informed me, that if I wished to be saved and pardoned, I must apply to you, who, after the Pope, are the only one who can grant me absolution."

"Signora, there is some mistake here, explain yourself: of what description is your sin?"

"It is a sin against the Holy Office."[25]

"Well, but I have nothing to do with the Holy Office."

"How? are not you Father Achilli, the Vicar of the Holy Office?"

"You have been misinformed, Signora; I am Achilli, the deputy master of the Holy Palace, not Office: you may see my name, with this title, prefixed to all works that are printed here, in lieu of that of the master himself. I assure you that neither my principal nor myself have any authority in cases that regard the Inquisition."

The good lady hereupon rose from her knees, arranged her hair, wiped the tears from her eyes, and asked leave to relate her case to me; and, having sat down, began as follows:—

"It is not quite a year since, that I was going, about the time of Easter, according to my usual custom, to confess my sins to my parish priest. He, being well acquainted with myself and all my family, began to interrogate me respecting my son, the only one I have, a young man twenty-four years of age, full of patriotic ardour, but with little respect for the priests. It happened that I observed to the curate that, notwithstanding my remonstrances, my son was in the habit of saying that the business of a priest was a complete deception, and that the head of all the impostors was the Pope himself. Would I had never told him! The curate would hear no further. 'It is your duty,' said he, 'to denounce your son to the Inquisition.' Imagine what I felt at this intimation! To be the accuser of my own son! 'Such is the case,' persisted he, 'there is no help for it—I cannot absolve you, neither can any one else until the thing is done.' And, indeed, from every one else I have had the same refusal. It will soon be twelve months since I have received absolution; and in this present year many misfortunes have befallen me. Ten days ago I tried again, and promised, in order that I might receive absolution, that I would denounce my son; but it was all in vain, until I had actually done so. I inquired then to whom I ought to go, to prefer the accusation. And I was told to the Bishop, or the Vicar of the Holy Office, and they named yourself to me. Twice already have I been here, with the intention of doing what was required of me, and as often have I recollected that I was a mother, and was overwhelmed with horror at the idea. On Sunday last I came to your church, to pray to the Virgin, the mother of Christ, to aid me through this difficulty; and when I had recited the rosary in her honour, I turned to pray also to the Son, saying: 'O Lord Jesus, thou wert also accused before the chief priests, by a traitorous disciple; but thou didst not permit that thy Mother should take part in that accusation. Behold, then, I also am a mother; and although my son is a sinner, whilst thou wert most just, do not, I implore thee, require that his own mother should be his accuser.' Whilst I was making this prayer the preaching began. I inquired the preacher's name, and they told me yours. I feigned to pay attention to the discourse, but I was wholly occupied in looking at you, and reflecting, with many sighs, that I was under the obligation to accuse to you my own child. In the midst of my agitation a thought suddenly relieved me; I did not see the Inquisitor in your countenance. Young, animated, and with marks of sensibility, it seemed that you would not be too harsh with my son; I thought I would intreat you first to correct him yourself, to reprimand, and to threaten him, without inflicting actual punishment upon him."

I shall not recapitulate my injunctions to this poor woman, to tranquillize her mind with respect to having to denounce her son. I advised her to change her confessor, and to be silent with regard to him—anyhow she was not in fault. And if confession, I further remarked, be a sacrament that pardons sins, it can never be made a means of unwarrantably obtaining information as to the words or deeds of another.

But had I really been Vicar of the Holy Office, what would have been my duty in this matter? To receive the accusation of a mother against her own son. An unheard-of enormity! She naturally would have made it in grief and tears, and I should have had to offer her consolation. And since this horrible act of treason has the pretence of religion about it, I should have employed the aid of religion to persuade her that the sacrifice she made was most acceptable to God. Perhaps, to act my part better, I might have alluded to the sacrifice demanded of Abraham, or Jephtha; or cited some apposite texts from Scripture, to calm and silence the remorse of conscience she must have experienced on account of the iniquity of bringing her child before the Inquisition.

Now let us see what is done by the Inquisitors. In what is called the Holy Office, everything is allowable that tends to their own purposes. To gain possession of a secret no means are to be disregarded; not even those against our very nature. For a father and a mother to reveal the thoughts of their own children, so trustingly confided to them,—a revelation which may lead to their death,—is so great a crime that we cannot imagine one more base. And yet the Inquisition not only sanctions, but enjoins it to be done, daily. And this most infamous Inquisition, a hundred times destroyed, and as often renewed, still exists in Rome, as in the barbarous ages; the only difference being, that the same iniquities are at present practised there with a little more secrecy and caution than formerly: and this for the sake of prudence, that the Holy See may not be subjected to the animadversions and censure of the world at large.

## FOOTNOTES:

[16] St. Thom. 2d. 9: xi. art. 3.

[17] The bishops swear to observe the laws of the Inquisition.

[18] Father Ancarani, an Inquisitor of forty-five years standing.

[19] This most reverend personage is a man of mild temper, apparently incapable of cruelty. He was at that time one of the Counsellors of the Inquisition.

[20] Bernard of Chiaravalle.

[21] Peter the Hermit.

[22] As the style does not interfere with the sense, it has not been deemed necessary to correct the foreign idioms in this letter.

[23] We have lately learned that this worthy has again entered the Romish Church. It appears that even while he was employed in the Malta College, he was negotiating with Rome for his pardon; on what precise terms is not known, but certainly on condition of abjuring Protestantism, and declaring himself its adversary. It is said he is now at the Propaganda.

[24] Rev. xviii. 3.

[25] Every offence of which the Inquisition takes cognisance is called "an offence against the Holy Office."

# CHAPTER V
# THE SUBTLETY OF THE INQUISITION

The case of this poor woman, obliged to denounce her son, is in accordance with both the old and new regulations of the Inquisition; and the manner in which it was endeavoured to be enforced is of common occurrence. Many other means are also in use among the artifices of this Holy Office, to induce persons to betray their friends. A wife, however, who is called upon to accuse her husband, has to encounter still more difficulty than a mother under the obligation to accuse her children. Indeed, such a circumstance would never take place, if the husband could discover that it was the intention of his wife to lay open his secret thoughts before so horrible a tribunal, the consequence of which would be speedy arrest, torture, and condemnation!! The difficulty of this case could not escape the observation of the Roman Court. If it was known as a certainty, in even a single instance, that a wife, to oblige a priest, had betrayed her own husband, and that the priest had made use of the confessional to induce the woman to the commission of such an act, would any husband calmly see his wife going to confession, and not apprehend that between her and the confessor some plot might be hatching against him? A single doubt, a mere suspicion, would be enough to sow discord between a married pair; and as in Italy the physical temperament is sufficiently ardent easily to fall into excesses, it might happen that, through the agency of the priest, the husband might beat, repudiate, or even murder his wife.

How then is it to be managed that the wife shall betray her husband with the least chance of his discovering her treachery? The best method is, that she should be instructed by her confessor to go to another town, where she is not known, and there make her disclosure; keeping it secret that she is the wife of the accused, and concealing his real name, till the confessor has disclosed the affair to the Inquisition, which alone knows all the intricacies of the proceedings. And since, moreover, it might happen that the husband might know that his wife, under a false pretence, had gone to another place to see the Inquisitor, or the Bishop's Vicar, the Inquisition grants to other persons the privilege of receiving an accusation; constituting them Sub-Inquisitors for that single case, under the pledge of inviolable secrecy. This arrangement is not merely imaginary, but really takes place; and in confirmation of it, I will here, for the first time, relate another fact which happened to myself.

In the year 1832 I was living at Viterbo, occupied with many duties, which precluded me from the enjoyment of a moment's leisure. In the Civic College I was, during seven years, Professor of Logic, Metaphysics, and Ethics; in the College di Gradi, during five years, I was chief Professor of Theology; in the Bishop's Seminary, I was Professor of the Holy Scriptures, which chair was founded by myself, and ceased on my departure, after I had held it for two years. I was Sub-Master of the Sacred Palace three years under Cardinal Velzi, and three years under the most Reverend Father Buttaoni; I was also yearly Preacher at the Church di Gradi, and Superior of the Monastery, with the title of Grand Vicar. And, lastly, I was Confessor to the Apostolic Delegate, who is the governing Prelate of the province; and as such I was in the habit of receiving many applications from all classes of people, who had recourse to me, to obtain favour or justice from the delegate.

One day, when I was very busy, a lady was announced, who, without sending in her name, earnestly desired to see me. I imagined she only came with some request concerning the delegate, and therefore sent word that I was too much engaged at that moment to be able to see her. The lady persisted, and I sent the same excuse. At last, finding that I was firm, the lady handed a letter to the lay-brother, sealed with a large seal, and directed to "The Very Reverend Father, Professor G. Achilli, Gradi, Viterbo." The seal was that of the Roman Inquisition, signed by the Commissary-General. The letter was as follows:—

"Very Reverend Father,—The Sacred Congregation of the Most Eminent and Reverend Cardinals, in their sitting of Wednesday, the ... have desired me to hand over to you the enclosed form of denunciation, according to which you will have the goodness to examine and interrogate the lady who is the bearer of it; avoiding to ask of her name, the place she comes from, and her connexion with the party accused; all which are already known to the Sacred Congregation. For this purpose I am authorized to invest you with all necessary authority on this particular occasion, and for this time only. I recommend to you all necessary prudence, and to be mindful of the inviolable secrecy due to the Holy Office, the slightest breach of which is punished with ecclesiastic censure, and is finally referred to the Pope.

"You will have the goodness to send back, with all diligence, after the performance of this duty, not only the formula of questions, with the answers to them, but also the present letter, of which no copy is to be taken.

"May the Lord prosper you."

"Rome, from the Palace of the Holy Office, March 1832."

When I had finished reading the letter, I felt a curiosity to see this mysterious visitor. I therefore descended to the apartment where she was waiting for me, and I saw a lady, about thirty years of age, well dressed, and in a style that announced her to belong to the wealthier class: her accent showed that she came from another part of the country. She received me with some degree of consternation in her manner, and replied to me half trembling, and with downcast eyes, and evident anxiety.

"Signora, I have received a letter through you; the contents must be known to you. Will you inform me in what manner you obtained it?"

"From my confessor: I do not know whether directly from Rome, or through the bishop."

"Can you make it convenient to prefer your accusation another time?"

"I beseech you, let me do so at present, since to-morrow I am obliged to return home."

I considered with myself whether I could not find some excuse for not acting in this business, and so avoid all trouble by sending the Signora away; or whether I had not better sacrifice a little time to receive the accusation, and hear what it was about.

"Well, then," said I, "let us to business. I should imagine it would not occupy much time—what is your opinion?"

I then sat down before a table, and unfolded the formulary of questions, which were comprised in a printed sheet. I looked over the paper, to ascertain its tenor, and of what it treated. I thought no more of the lady; my mind was entirely occupied in considering how I should proceed, when a deep sigh aroused me, and made me turn my eyes towards her. She began to weep outright.

"What is the matter, Signora?—why do you weep?"

Tears and sobs were her only reply. I endeavoured to speak comfort to her.

"Signora, do not weep; calm yourself: reveal the cause of your affliction, and you may find relief. If you disclose your mind to me, I may, in my turn, say something that will console you; but if you do nothing but shed tears, I must send some other person to attend to you, for I have business which I cannot postpone."

She grew calmer by degrees, and I began my task. The formula was in Latin; I had to translate it into Italian: her own answers were to be written down exactly.

I was displeased to see the act begin. "In the name of God," &c.: I felt also unwilling to put my own name at the head of the document, which said, "Before me, A. B., a certain woman presented herself." I had, nevertheless, a great desire to know the whole affair, and was, in some measure, pleased that the Inquisition had, on this occasion, required my services. I had always abhorred the Holy Office, and had intended, even from my earliest youth, to expose its iniquity, as far as it was possible for me to do so, whenever an occasion should occur. "The present is a good opportunity," I said to myself, "to get at the mysteries of the Inquisition. I shall doubtless learn some curious matters, which may be useful to me hereafter."

"Now, Signora, you must remember that it is your duty to declare the truth. I suppose it is no trifling affair that has induced you to denounce a person to the Inquisition;—above all, I desire to know what may have been your motives?"

"To save me from a hell."

"Sometimes it happens that in seeking to avoid one hell, we may fall into another; that in endeavouring to silence a scruple, we may incur remorse; and that the means we take to save the soul of another may endanger our own. Tell me, from what kind of hell do you seek to be delivered by this act?"

"The hell that I experience in entering a church. It is not every one who goes there that finds it a Paradise. God is there, Jesus Christ, the most holy Madonna, saints, angels, and holy water. It is there we are baptized, confess, and receive the grace of God. I alone participate in none of these ordinances in the church; therefore it has become hateful to me, and the priests are odious in my sight."

"And how does all this happen?"

"Father, it is as I say. You will understand it all. Relieve me from this load, and I shall hope to be able afterwards to make peace with God and the saints, and be delivered from this hell."

"Well, what is the deposition—the accusation you have to make?"

"Allow me, father, to relate my story from the beginning. I cannot tell you by halves."

So saying she remained thoughtful a few moments, and then exclaimed:

"I hardly know where to begin.—I would inform you—but—"

"Courage,—relate the affair simply as it is. I wish not to know either more or less than you choose to tell me. For example, I ask neither your name, your place of residence, nor what connexion you have with the party accused."

"Ah! Father, these are the express conditions on which I consented to disclose what I have to unfold. Shame forbids me to reveal either my name, my residence, or my connexions; since, were you ever to visit the town where I, with my family, reside, you would recollect a deed of which I am sure you cannot approve. And where would be the use of concealing the place of my residence, and telling you the name of the party whom I am to accuse? It is too well known that you should not yourself immediately recognise it. Oh, is it possible that at this price alone I am to recover my peace!—at this, and at no other, to be admitted anew to the privilege of confession, and the benefit of the other sacraments! That to be a Christian, I must consent to betray another!—to betray the person whom in all the world I best love!—enjoined to do so, both by Divine and human laws?"

As she concluded, she arose, and I observed that with the fingers of her right hand she pressed upon her left, and turned round a ring that was there, on the annular finger. She then resumed:

"Where then shall we in future hope to place confidence?—how trust in the sacredness of vows pledged at the altar? Can God be in contradiction to Himself? Are there two sets of laws, the one natural and the other contrary to nature? and are they both obligatory? Ought I, at the same time, both to love and to hate? Oh! what would *he* say if he knew what occupies me at this moment? And can I return joyfully to him, who little suspects what I am doing, to still live with him, and call him by the tenderest names, until the day comes, or perhaps the night, when the officers of justice shall secretly enter the house, apprehend, and take him away—and to what place? To the dungeons of the Holy Office! And who would have placed him there? I, myself, by the very act I am going to commit! But if I do not do so, I am in a state of perdition, since there will be no longer pardon or absolution for me! Excommunication, from which no one can deliver me, will be my fate! And he also will be excommunicated! His soul will be for ever lost, unless it be purified in the Inquisition!—Both of us to lose all hope of salvation and eternal life! And that, because we refuse to make fitting sacrifice on earth! These, Father, are the thoughts that agitate me, that divide my soul, that have led me here, and that have since sealed my lips. What ought I to do?—what reveal? I am miserable, because I listen at once to the flesh and the spirit; and whichever way I force myself to act, I am always divided against myself. Oh! why are not you, who are called fathers, husbands as well? then, as other men, you would have wives to love; and you would better comprehend these matters, and would see the value of the text, 'Do not to others what ye would not that men should do unto you.'"

"Let us come to an end, Signora. You have promised the Inquisition to make an accusation, and that as a matter of duty, or rather, from scruples of conscience. When you made this promise, you no doubt imagined you did what was right."

"No, Father, I do not deceive myself; I never thought I was doing right. In every point of view I considered I was doing wrong. Nevertheless, I judged it necessary; as it is necessary to have an arm or a foot cut off, that is in a state of gangrene. I looked upon it as a castigation from the Almighty; as if my house had been burned, or a heavy beam had fallen on my shoulders. I thought that God was angry with me on account of my sins, and that to appease Him I must sacrifice to Him what was most dear to me. I have often felt as if I should not survive so dire an event; the mere idea of it is afflicting to me beyond expression. Father, I am here to make a sacrifice of myself upon the altar, I regret to say it, of the Inquisition."

"And do you desire, Signora, that I should be the priest on the occasion? It is an office I have never performed. My hand is more ready to be stretched out for good than evil. I should feel remorse in sacrificing you. I thought that you were come to make your deposition voluntarily, or your own free-will; and even in that case I should have had some hesitation in receiving it: I repeat, I have never undertaken the office of an Inquisitor. In the present instance, I will by no means lend my aid to an act of violence. I am a minister of a God of Peace, of Christ, who died for our sins; and it is on condition of believing in what He has done for us that we obtain pardon. I do not find that any sacrifice is required of us, to be reconciled to God, unless it be the sacrifice of our spirit on the altar of faith. 'A humble and a contrite heart,' says David, 'O God, thou wilt not despise.' I find throughout the whole of the Bible a continual invitation to seek God; and to find Him there is but one way, which is Jesus Christ. He has said, 'I am the Way, the Truth, and the Life: no man cometh to the Father but by me.' Moreover, He says to us, 'Come unto me, all ye that labour and are heavy laden, and I will give you rest.' And this is more particularly addressed to sinners, whose duty it is to go to Christ, and it is ours to endeavour to invite, to lead, to bring them to Him. Do you understand me, Signora?—to Him, and to Him alone, and not to the Inquisition."

"Ah! my Father," here exclaimed the Signora; "what balm you pour into my wounds! Your last words have restored me to life. It is to Christ then, and not to the Inquisition, that I shall trust my husband. Yes, my husband it is whom I am called upon to accuse, because he had spoken ill of the Pope, the Bishop, and the Priests; and had on one occasion declared that if he could be assured that the Pope was St. Peter himself, he would nevertheless spit in his face if he could. I told my confessor of this, not to accuse my husband, but to learn what course I had better pursue with him; adding, that at times he was so excited as scarcely to know the meaning of the words he uttered: but, without further inquiry, my confessor enjoined me to denounce him to the Inquisition. Finally, however, he proposed that I should do so to the Bishop; but as I would consent to neither proposition, he obtained permission from Rome that I should come to you at Viterbo, to prefer my accusation, without disclosing my name, or that the party accused was my husband. But you have shown me how far better it is that I should recommend him to the love of Christ, than to the wrath of the Inquisition. It appears that you agree with me, that in religion there cannot be any law contrary to nature. Oh, how often have I repeated on this occasion, what my husband so constantly asserts, that the priests have a religion and a morality contrary to nature! To compel a wife to accuse her husband! Is it not a demoralization? A bad wife may do so through motives of revenge; a good one would rather accuse herself. It is a base thing, in any case, to accuse a person secretly, without giving him any opportunity of exculpation, or allowing him to know who is his accuser. It is a crime that no moral duty can justify. Even the contemplation of such a step has driven me to the brink of self-destruction. But my confessor assured me that, in that case, both my husband and myself would be undoubtedly damned. And in confirmation of this, I once read, in some old work, a story of a certain woman who had refused, before her death, to make one of these disclosures; and in consequence, not only was her soul condemned to the torments of hell, but her body also found no rest in the grave, being continually forced to leave it, until, being conjured with holy water to declare the cause of its disquiet, it replied that it was so punished because it had not obeyed the injunction it had received, to accuse certain heretics to the Inquisition; but as all present earnestly prayed to the Madonna, it was granted to this unhappy body to return to life, for the space of half an hour, that it might prefer its accusation to the Inquisition; after which, it died anew."

"And do you believe this story?"

"I was unwilling to do so, but the Priest showed me that the book was printed *con licenza de' superiori*. To tell the whole truth, my idea was, to obey our Holy Church, in this barbarous law, and then to commit suicide, leaving behind me a letter to my husband, explaining the motives that had led me to the act. But God be praised, I shall now neither accuse him, nor put an end to my own existence. You have doubly saved my life, in saving my honour and my conscience. God will reward you for the charity you have shown me. I shall return to my home and to my family. But what must I say to my confessor?"

"Leave him altogether. He must never know what has passed between us. Signora, I have prevented you from betraying your husband, and you tell me I have restored you to life. Will you then betray me? I do not think so. God be with you; I shall immediately burn these papers from the Inquisition, along with the letter you have brought me; and their contents will be buried in your breast."

"Oh! yes, there they shall remain, and with a lasting recollection of yourself. Farewell."

"Farewell."

In relating this story I have not hesitated about going into particulars, since no one now can injure the good lady, who is gone to her eternal rest. She lived a few years after this adventure, and wrote to me occasionally. She died like a good Christian, loving Jesus her Redeemer, and believing in his good tidings, and detesting, with all her heart, the errors of the Church of Rome. In one of her letters she told me that her old confessor, a few months after her visit to me, came to her to inquire whether she had delivered the letter from the Inquisition; and that, fearing to compromise me, she was puzzled to find an answer. She did not so much regard her own danger, and therefore replied as follows:—"Signore, do not talk to me any more of this business: Father Achilli has too much good sense to trouble his head at all about the Inquisition: consequently, the letter found its way into the fire. What would you have me do more? For a woman I think I have done quite enough." This answer, which did not involve any falsehood, left the confessor in doubt, without furnishing him with the means of injuring either of us. He subsequently interrogated her again on this point, and all the reply he obtained was: "I know nothing about it; I have told you not to talk to me about it any more." I was myself questioned on the subject ten years afterwards, at the time I was in the Inquisition; and I got out of the affair by saying, as was the fact, that I had never received any accusation from the lady—with respect to the letter itself I was silent.

But what cruelty, what malignity does not this case reveal! To pervert the natural feelings of the heart, so as to induce a wife not only to accuse her husband, but to spy out his most secret thoughts, the very inmost of his mind, and to disclose what might peril his very life! I have only given one instance, but I could relate many more of the same character. The wife of a bricklayer, whose name I never knew, about the same time, came to me at Viterbo, to accuse her husband by order of her confessor. She came from Vitorchiano, a fief of the Roman Senate. I sent her away, however, telling her I had nothing to do with the Inquisition. Several came to me from other parts—no fewer than four or five; and all these were wives, who had come to denounce their husbands to the Inquisition. I took care to give them all the same answer. And if so many cases of this sort came to my own knowledge, how many more must there have been, who applied to the Vicars themselves, or to the Inquisitors of the Holy Office!

In my time, there was a report that in Ancona two Inquisitors had seduced certain wives and daughters, in order to induce them to accuse their respective husbands and fathers. In the year 1842, in the month of September, having left the Roman States, I was at Ancona, from which place I embarked for Corfu. And it was during my stay in the former place, that an Inquisitor endeavoured to persuade two virtuous girls to accuse their uncle of some alleged profanation, in order to have a pretext for his imprisonment. The Inquisitor was angry with this honest man, because he had forbidden him his house; and thought, by throwing him into prison, to be able at all hours to visit the nieces, imagining they were favourably disposed towards him. But they were much better than he was; they threatened him with publishing his dishonest proposals, and so the matter ended. This same Inquisitor is famous for his persecution of the Jews. His edict against them, published in 1843, is known to all the world. In it all the Jews under his jurisdiction—that is, not only those of Ancona, who are very numerous, but those also of Pesaro, Osimo, Sinigaglia, Loretto, &c.—are ordered, within the term of three months, to sell all their possessions in land or houses, under penalty of confiscation; within eight days to abandon all their shops outside the Ghetto;[26] and within three days to dismiss from their houses all their Christian servants, both male and female, even the nurses of their children. They were prohibited to sleep a single night out of the Ghetto; to take a single meal, or to hold any communication with a Christian. Nay, to the shame and disgrace of the Inquisition be it spoken, these children of Israel and of Judah were even prohibited from singing the Psalms of David, in their service for the burial of their dead.

That so precious a document might not be lost, I took care to have it reprinted at Corfu, from the authentic copy that was sent to me by the Secretary of the Lord High Commissioner; and, as my readers will easily believe, I wrote my observations upon it pretty strongly, not only as to its author, but also as to the whole tribe of the *Inquisitori*.[27] I was desirous of knowing what was generally thought to be the reason of the publication of this edict. A letter from Ancona on the subject, stated as follows:—

"The Father Inquisitor is a person of very licentious habits, and at the same time extremely greedy of money. He became offended with our women (the Jewesses) because they would not listen to his propositions;

he allured, he threatened, but could never render them subservient to his desires. At length he took a fresh occasion of offence against us, because we refused to pay him a considerable sum of money which he claimed, and not for the first time; saying that his predecessor had had many such donations, that it was for that reason he had looked upon us favourably, and that, if we did not make him similar acknowledgments, we need not expect any service or consideration from him. After due deliberation upon the matter, however, it was resolved that we should not give him any thing; and now see what has happened!"

The predecessor of this personage is well known to everybody, as having extorted as much money as he possibly could, brought many respectable persons into trouble, seduced many women, and finally fled from his situation, to seek an asylum in Tuscany.

The Inquisitor of Ancona does not act differently from his brethren. Any one who wished to write a history, not of the Inquisition, but of the actual Inquisitors in the Roman States, need only take the trouble to ask what is thought of them from Rome to Bologna; in Umbria, La Marca, Romagna; in short, wherever there is an Inquisitor or a Vicar of the Holy Office—and he will hear some extraordinary stories, which would disgrace the most scandalous chronicle.

Rome takes no notice of these reports, and winks, as the saying is, at personal immorality, to obtain that which constitutes her moral code—wealth and dominion. For dealing in immoral acts, immoral agents are necessary. Would an honest man do for an Inquisitor? Would a follower of Christ, who said, speaking of man and wife, "Whom God hath joined, let no man put asunder,"—would he sow discord between them, and demoralize the wife, to make her betray in the basest manner her own husband? Does not an Inquisitor require to be one whose heart is hardened against every gentle and social feeling, so that he may not hesitate to commit barbarities which are unknown among the most savage nations?

Are the torments which are employed at the present day at the Inquisition all a fiction? It requires the impudence of an Inquisitor, or of the Archbishop of Westminster, to deny their existence. I have myself heard these evil-minded persons lament and complain that their victims were treated with too much lenity.

"What is it you desire?" I inquired of the Inquisitor of Spoleto.

"That which St. Thomas Aquinas says," answered he: "death to all the heretics."

Hand over then to one of these people a person, however respectable; give him up to one of the Inquisitors (he who quoted St. Thomas Aquinas to me was made an Archbishop;)—give up, I say, the present Archbishop of Canterbury, amiable and pious as he is, to one of these rabid Inquisitors: he must either deny his faith or be burned alive. Is my statement false? Am I doting? Is not this the spirit that invariably actuates the Inquisitors? And not the Inquisitors only, but all those who in any way defile themselves with the Inquisition, such as Bishops and their Vicars, and all those who defend it, as the Papists do. There is the renowned Cardinal Wiseman, the Archbishop of Westminster, according to the Pope's creation; the same who has had the assurance to censure me from his pulpit, and to publish an infamous article in the *Dublin Review*, in which he has raked together, as on a dunghill, every species of filth from the sons of Ignatius Loyola; nor is there lie or calumny that he has not made use of against me. Well, then, suppose I were to be handed over to the tender mercy of this Cardinal, and he had full power to dispose of me as he chose, without fear of losing his character in the eyes of the nation to which by parentage, more than by merit, he belongs; what do you imagine he would do with me? Should I not have to undergo some death more terrible than ordinary? Would not a council be held with the reverend fathers of the Company of Loyola, the same who have suggested the abominable calumnies above alluded to, in order to invent some refined method of putting me out of the world? I feel persuaded that if I were condemned by the Inquisition to be burned alive, my calumniator would have great pleasure in building up my funeral pile, and setting fire to it with his own hands; or, should strangulation be preferred, that he would, with equal readiness, tighten the cord around my neck: and all for the honour and glory of the Inquisition, of which, according to his oath, he is a true and faithful servant.

And since we are on this subject, allow me to relate a fact concerning myself, which strongly evinces the subtlety of the Inquisition, according to the practice of the Jesuits, in availing themselves, in foreign parts, of the assistance of Bishops and dignified personages.

Every one knows how miraculously I escaped a second time from the horrors of the Inquisition. All those who had any feeling rejoiced at it; and such as met with me expressed their satisfaction by kindness and polite attentions. In the month of January, 1850, I was at Paris, and was visited by a vast number of persons of every class, not only Protestants, but Catholics also, who expressed the interest they took in my recovered liberty. I waited upon the government ministers, and others who had assisted me, to thank them for their services; but they interrupted me by assuring me that they had done no more than follow the impulse of their own hearts and the dictates of humanity; that they had merely performed a duty; and were rejoiced to think that their interference had so well succeeded, that instead of being shut up in the prisons of the Inquisition, I was at liberty to walk about the streets of Paris as I thought proper.

In the midst of this universal pleasure, which appeared to animate all I met, and which was responded to by the public journals, I exclaimed to one of my friends:

"Observe how the voice of the whole people is with me; not a word is uttered on the contrary side, except by the journal of the Jesuits, which, to my credit be it spoken, thinks proper to abuse me in a foolish, senseless article, full of contradiction, written in the vulgarest language of the streets, or of their own sacristy, and only worthy of contempt."

One day a friend came to tell me that it appeared the Jesuits had employed some other party to vilify me.

"It is impossible," I observed, "that such an office should be undertaken by an honest and well-bred Frenchman. To insult a person who has miraculously escaped from the Inquisition! No; a true-hearted Frenchman would no more undertake such a task than he would seek to persecute one who had escaped from shipwreck or from fire, or who had evaded the hand of an assassin. To insult one freed from the Inquisition might be allowable in a Jesuit, but never in a Frenchman. What a surprise it would be to him to read, in the *Messager de la Semaine*, an abusive article against me, full of falsehood and calumny!"

"But you ought to reply to it," I was told; "these are no Jesuits who write, but members of the Assembly, and others who call themselves gentlemen." "I do not answer those," I replied, "who lie for the pleasure of lying and calumniating. Such writers may reply to themselves."

My friends took some trouble to discover the writer of this article, and ascertained it to proceed from the pen of a diplomatist, M. de Corcelles, the ex-minister at Rome, who had endeavoured to negotiate the return of Pius IX., but without success, and given such proofs of his devotion to the Jesuits and other priests at Rome. This M. de Corcelles, after having by his subtlety contrived the French plot against Rome herself, and tarnished the honour of his nation by a thousand falsehoods, has returned thus disgracefully to Paris, and has had the baseness to accept the task from the Jesuits themselves, of writing a miserable article against me, as mean and as black as their own garb.

It was a brilliant idea of the Inquisition to get a French diplomatist, a member of the National Assembly, to vouch for their lies; and here M.

de Corcelles came forward. To strengthen his assertions, it was thought necessary to look out for some one in England also, who would corroborate them; and after six months' diligent search, as they could find no other, and were anxious not to lose more time, they got the recently created Cardinal Archbishop of Westminster to take up the pen against me. This second production was even more abusive than the first. The bishop had far less sense of shame about him than the member of the National Assembly, particularly when he had the cardinal's hat in view. It is related of Cardinal Pallavicino, the celebrated Jesuit, that being chosen by the Court of Rome to write the history of the Council of Trent, in opposition to that of Paolo Sarpi, on which occasion he was promised the rank of cardinal, the poor man suffered grievously in his mind, on account of the number of lies he had to invent; and sending for a red cap, the insignia of his future dignity, he shook it in his hand, and placing it on his head, exclaimed with bitter sighs: "Ah! how much I endure on your account!" *Oh! quanta pro te patior!* In like manner Dr. Wiseman, at the sight of the red hat, and all that pertains to the cardinalate, has judged it expedient to make a sacrifice of honour and truth, and to rake up the most offensive matters, to present them to his co-religionists in the British isles. The indecency and revolting nature of this article shows to what an extent the immorality and mendacity of a bishop of the Church of Rome may proceed. The documents laid before the British Consul at Rome by my friends, whilst I was in prison, proving the falsehood of the accusations laid to my charge at Viterbo, might equally be brought forward in my justification against the slander of this titled Minister of the Gospel; but it rebuts itself, in its very exaggeration. Moreover, every one who knows me knows also that I was held in high estimation by the Church of Rome, until the very day when I was handed over to the Inquisition. I had never been the subject of complaint or reproof, much less of punishment. I was on good terms with all the bishops until that time, and appointed by them to preach and to hear confessions. Indeed, I should have blamed myself had they been dissatisfied. Have I not many letters from them requesting my services? Was I not appointed to preach, during Lent, before the Court of Naples? In good sooth, it requires the brazen impudence of a *Monsignore*, to lie so openly and so basely.

See now the work of the Inquisition. It says to its coadjutor, "You shall have a cardinal's hat, if you raise an outcry, right or wrong, against the heretic Achilli. But you must not call him a heretic, because that term in England would not avail you; no, you must assert that he believes in nothing whatsoever; above all, you must say that he is an immoral man, addicted to all sorts of licentious habits, (a common case, you well know, in such as take the oath of celibacy). Say of him whatever evil comes into your head; no matter about time or place. Say a great deal, that a part at least may be believed. Relate suppositions as facts, and comment on your own statements. Cry out loudly, raise reports, and give them publicity. Stick at nothing; hazard whatever may tend to discredit your adversary. In this way you will weaken his endeavours. What can he do to vindicate himself? Does he bring you into court? Shall you have to pay a fine?—Double the amount will be raised to pay it. Are you thrown into prison?—Call to mind the martyr of Turin. In short, earn a cardinal's hat"!!

The temptation is too powerful for a bishop of the Church of Rome. It is in this manner that the Inquisition manages its affairs throughout the whole world, and works so as to gain its ends, by promises and threats, by fraud and subterfuge.

### FOOTNOTES:

[26] The Ghetto is a part of the city, enclosed within walls, in which the Jews are confined. It exists in every city of the Roman States.

[27] See the Edict from this Inquisitor in the Appendix, together with my observations upon it.

# CHAPTER VI
# THE PROTEUS-LIKE CHARACTER OF THE INQUISITION, BOTH IN ANCIENT AND MODERN TIMES

When I asserted that the Inquisition had never undergone any change, that as it existed in the time of its founder, Innocent III., so it continued in the days of its renowned legislator, Paul IV., and in those of the fierce persecutors of good Christians, Pius V. and Gregory XII., and that we find it still preserving the same character, in our own time, under Gregory XVI. and Pius IX., I did not intend to lead my readers to suppose that it invariably, after having arranged its plans and established its system of laws, carried on its operations with the same uniform regularity; and in undeviating exactitude pursued its unchanging course, however baleful, with the steady progress of a planet in its orbit, without ever deviating from it in the smallest possible degree. No, such was not the idea I intended to give. In its spirit it has always been the same, and its laws have never undergone any change; but nothing is more varied, more uncertain, more changeable, than the manner in which it has acted to attain its purposes. With the same spirit and the same laws, the Inquisition of Rome is, nevertheless, different from that of Spain, and the Inquisition of the nineteenth century greatly varies from that of the three preceding centuries. The slaughter of the Albigenses and the Waldenses, that of the Moors, and the massacre of St. Bartholomew, are events, so similar to each other, that whoever has read of the first is little astonished at the second or the third. But between the perpetration of these acts it was expedient that at least the period of a century should intervene, in order that the people might have time to recover from the shock they had experienced, and be induced to receive fresh arguments in favour of a repetition of the same enormity. In the meanwhile a thousand other events took place of a totally different character. For example, Pius V., while he was burning his heretics in Rome, or drowning them in the Lagoons of Venice, while he persecuted the Moors in Spain, and sent his bands to destroy the Jews, made himself patron of the Knights of St. John of Jerusalem, who, after having been driven out of Rhodes, were dispersed abroad in various parts; he obtained for them the island of Malta; and lavished his bounty upon them with unsparing hand, in order that they might fortify themselves on that rock. Now what did these Knights of Malta become? The pirates of the Inquisition, founded by Dominic di Guzman. Yes; these crusaders, who assumed to themselves the title of Christian Knights, ended by becoming a pack of plundering blood-hounds, ever on the alert to hunt out their victims, and who, even now, do not blush to acknowledge themselves as the *Familiars* of the Inquisition; though so dishonourable do they know their trade to be, that they are obliged to carry it on under the mask of secrecy. But these heroes who still keep up the empty title of Knights of Malta, ingloriously end their degenerate career in the ante-chambers of the Vatican, as the Pope's guards; for the Holy Office, when they are too old for more active service, no longer takes any care of them, nor does it allow them the smallest pension. Many Roman institutions have in the same manner flourished and fallen away; others, although useless, still continue, through a difficulty in getting rid of them.

It is now about four centuries since Rome instituted monkish and knightly orders for the service of the Inquisition. The necessity for them was first found out after the Council of Constance, and increased after that of Trent. Martin V. was too dissipated to trouble himself much about it, but his successor, Pius II., who had witnessed the death of John Huss and Jerome of Prague, and who clearly saw the danger that threatened the Church of Rome, in the spirit and the voice that arose from the ashes of those holy men, felt himself called upon, in the year 1459, to institute an order of knighthood to be called after the name of Jesus, whose employment should be to war against the Turks, for in those days all were so called, who did not venerate the Church of Rome. Accordingly under such pretext they undertook to wage war against heretics of every description, whom, according to the Christian charity of the popes, it was their duty to exterminate. This order was not pleasing to Paul II. and was consequently abolished: but Alexander VI., that well-known monster of profligacy and crime, raised up a fresh body of knights, for the service of the Inquisition, which he placed under the protection of St. George, in the year 1492. These heroes could do no less than imitate the example of their unprincipled founder, and, in a very short time, gained for themselves an undesirable renown, for their deeds of the most abominable licentiousness. The succeeding Pope, however, laid them on the shelf. Leo X., in the year 1520, came forward with a new order of knights, under the patronage of St. Peter. It is well known that this pope lost no opportunity of putting this favourite saint of his forward, on all occasions where money was to be made of him. It was for the building of the church that bears his name that indulgences were sent for sale, into Germany and Switzerland. The new knights limited their services to the collecting of money for St. Peter, that is to say, for the Pope; this degraded order, however, soon died of decline. Paul III. felt more than any one the evils that were likely to arise from the Council of Trent, and the danger of what was called "reviving heresy:" in order therefore, to give greater activity to the Inquisition, he founded an order of chivalry, under the title of St. George of Ravenna, in the year 1538, the nominal duty of which was to war against heretics, but its real object was to renew the sanguinary scenes acted under Innocent III., and to repeat in Germany the slaughters of Dauphiny, Languedoc and Navarre. Fortunately, however, this pope became involved in a dispute respecting the celebrated exchange of the duchy of Parma and Plaisance, in favour of his natural son, Peter Lewis Farnese, and consequently, the Knights of St. George had to pacify the minds of those who were offended at such robbery and injustice; but it was found that this single order was not sufficiently powerful for the purpose, wherefore another was created in 1542, called the Order of the Lily, in order to reward such as readily submitted to the Papal authority in that matter.

But in the meanwhile the Reformers gained ground; Luther in Germany, and Zwinglius in Switzerland, made great progress. Paul III. had need of a society to oppose them; his knights were no longer equal to the task— it was impossible to resist, by force of arms, so rapid and wide-spreading an influence. Charles V., if he did not openly declare himself a reformer, was but little favourable to Rome; and Duke Frederic of Saxony, the most esteemed prince in Germany, was an open convert to Protestantism. It appeared necessary, therefore, that a society should be formed, which should present itself to the world as a religious body, to act in favour of the Holy See. A Spanish knight, weary of the occupation of war, and disgusted at the treachery of his mistress, had at that time offered up his sword on the altar of the Virgin, and devoted himself to her service, and he soon proved himself a fit champion for the necessities of the times. This Spanish knight was no other than Ignatius Loyola, who came to Rome in the year 1540, and became the founder of a religious order which, for the purpose of captivating the imagination of the whole Christian world, and to gain universal homage, assumed the title of *The Company of Jesus!* Every one would have thought that this order would have been of the same description as that which was founded a short time before by Gaetano Tiene, and that which soon afterwards owed its origin to Giuseppe Calassanzio. Now it is the deceptive policy of the Inquisition to make it appear that these knightly orders are for the purpose of defending Christians from the attacks of infidels; and also for the education of youth. But without doubt, the sole object of this grand piece of machinery is entirely the upholding of the papacy; indeed, the whole body of knights, as well as of friars, are nothing more nor less than servants of the Pope. In illustration of this fact, we read in the history of Pius IV., that in the year 1560, he founded an order of knighthood, under the title of St. John Lateran, and that the principal duty these heroes had to perform was that of carrying His Holiness on their shoulders, seated in his chair of state, with the privilege of kissing his most sacred foot, both before and after the ceremony. In subjecting his nobles to this degrading office, the Pope wisely considered that he was preparing them for the performance of any servile act that the future exigencies of His Holiness might require. The Roman people, however, turned the cross-bearing knights into ridicule, calling them Knights of the Foot, and the Pope saw with dissatisfaction that the order did not prosper. He determined, therefore, to invest them with fresh dignity, and decreed that every knight in service should also enjoy the title of Count Palatine, with the privilege of creating doctors in every department of science. This succeeded for a time; the knightly Counts were content to submit their shoulders to the sacred burden, and kiss the foot they carried; but the sarcasms of the Romans proved more powerful than the titles and honours of the Pope; the knights began greatly to disrelish their occupation, insomuch that the successor of Paul was obliged to stipend his titled porters still more liberally, or run the risk of not being carried at all.

Another curious fact connected with our subject may here be related. Pope Sixtus V. had, or pretended to have, a firm belief in the miracle of the Holy House of Loretto, which was stated to have occurred shortly before his time. Now many persons, with the Bishop of Recanati, a town a little way from Loretto, at their head, absolutely denied that such an event as that the house should have flown through the air, from Nazareth to Dalmatia, and finally to Loretto, had ever taken place. But the Pope was determined to uphold the truth of the miracle, and created an order of knights expressly to maintain and defend its authenticity; this was in the year 1586, and the order was named after the town of Loretto. Every knight, therefore, was bound to draw his sword in its defence, and to challenge to single combat whoever should venture to impugn its veracity. They were chiefly selected from the inhabitants of the province signalized by the event. This order continued in existence about a century, after which lapse of time, as no one appeared to think it worth his while to contend with Rome on the subject of the imposture, it was considered as useless, and was no longer kept up.

While these knightly orders were instituted on one hand, on the other, many fresh monastic bodies were established, under new denominations, and with different dresses; all, however, were employed by the Church of Rome to uphold her doctrines and her practice, even to fanaticism. If they were not both equally injurious to society, the only difference was that the one was dreaded from its open use of the sword, whilst the other excited fear from its secret machinations; as servants to the Inquisition they were all obedient alike.

And now a word or two with respect to these secret machinations which hitherto, it seems, people have been afraid to talk about. The monks, whether to their credit or not I leave others to decide, have proved themselves more doughty champions than the knights; inasmuch as the latter could never stand against ridicule, whereas the former have braved and overcome it; they have even derived strength from it: their disciples, moreover, are expressly taught to despise it, and through a long course of years a generation of men has been trained up, who are appalled by no dangers or difficulties, and are capable of confronting every obstacle, in the service of Rome.

The first experiment under this audacious system was made in the 13th century, when that knave Innocent III. bestowed on his church the renowned Order of St. Francis of Assisi. This holy brotherhood understood better than any other in the whole world how to live well at the public expense, without any possessions of their own, and without ever incurring labour or fatigue. The first principle they inculcate in their order is, that there is no disgrace in the act of begging. *Fratres nostri non erubescant.* Clothed with a coarse garment, bound round their waist with cord, with sandalled feet and shaven crowns, dirty and greasy, they are truly as lawful objects of ridicule, to all who behold them, as the grossest cynic was to the enlightened Athenians. Little, however, do they regard it; there are even among them not a few who imagine they present an engaging appearance in their strange garb, and pretend they would not exchange it for the gayer costume of the cavaliers. The Franciscans attach so much importance to their dress, that their rules enjoin the penalty of excommunication to any one who lays aside the holy vestment, or cuts off the sacred beard. It is considered a mortal sin for a *Capuchin* to assume the guise of a *Zoccolante*, and *vice versâ*. This prohibition is equally in force with respect to all the monkish orders, and the neglect of it is considered as a species of apostasy.

When human beings are reduced to such fanaticism, both in principle and in practice, it is not to be wondered at if they are capable of any crime they may imagine it their duty to commit. The obedience a monk owes to his superior is more absolute than that of the soldier to his commanding officer, inasmuch as it wears the cloak of religion; the monk considers himself a spiritual soldier, and his obedience is based in superstition. Moreover, every monastic institution is a secret society, and a true monk should have the genius of a conspirator. He should love his own order before any other, and be ready to shed his blood in its defence. Every institution has its own particular saints. The Franciscan sees in St. Francis and St. Anthony the first saints in the whole world, the most favoured by the Virgin Mary, and the most fruitful in miracles; and on the other hand, the Dominican considers his St. Dominic and St. Vincent the paragons, the *ne plus ultra* of all sanctity and miracle-working. St. Dominic is not merely termed holy, he is denominated the most holy; *Sanctissimus Pater Dominicus*. Take one of these worthies, then, stolid by nature and rendered more so by his education, and place before him any sort of disgraceful work, and see if the Church of Rome will not be fully satisfied with her disciple.

From these societies the subtle and busy instruments for the extension of the Papal power have been selected; and by their means has Rome preserved her influence over the conscience, and extended her work of proselytism.

The knights, on the contrary, enjoyed too much liberty to remain long in the service of the priests. It was, therefore, often contemplated to unite the knightly with the monastic life; thus the Knights of St. John of Jerusalem considered themselves partly a military and partly a monastic order. Many professed chastity, poverty and obedience, and sometimes a fourth vow was added, that of making war against the infidels. But all this was insufficient to bring them completely under subjection; a life of still greater mortification was necessary, in order to humiliate and degrade the individual, and render him a mere automaton; and this was a life purely monastic. Whoever professes it, if he be sincere, ought to possess no faculty of willing or understanding, apart from that of his superiors; to whatever order he belongs he must bring himself to the persuasion that there is no hope for him in the mercy of heaven, unless he be obedient to them; who alone, according to the Romish doctrine, are responsible for his acts. At the last dread tribunal he believes it will only be demanded of him, has he been obedient?—this is all he has to look to; he who gives the order is alone answerable for its justice or its iniquity. Such is the teaching that these degraded beings are accustomed to receive. What its results are we need only look round those countries where it is most extensively carried on, to determine.

Now these so-called superiors ascend by regular degrees, and at their head is the Pope himself. An order emanating from him, quickly extends, by means of these subordinates, into any direction he chooses, through all its ramifications. Every one knows that his ministers amount to several hundreds of thousands, all belonging to the same system, sworn to obedience, and ready to undertake whatever may be required of them.

I will frankly confess my own private opinion of this organization. Doubtless it was planned by men of consummate ability. It is a diabolical invention to effect the greatest possible mischief. And such was the intention of the three or four popes who had a hand in its formation. Providentially for society, the succeeding ones were men of inferior genius, and did not see all its advantages. With respect to the present time, I should imagine there is little danger, as these gentry no longer enjoy the same credit as they did formerly. Moreover, in those countries where papistical doctrines predominate, the monks are held in the greatest disrepute: at least it is so in Italy, where they are well known; and I believe the case is the same in Spain. With respect to France, it is a matter of regret that they have renewed their former influence in that country, which, since the revolution of 1850, has become the reproach of Europe. Who would have believed that she would not only grant an asylum to Jesuits, but also become their defender and their partizan? It is, however, to be hoped that such a state of things cannot last long; and that this nation may at length recover from her delirium. This hope is founded on the conviction that he cannot in reality but detest the Papacy, which, at the present juncture, actually excites in the people no other sentiment than infidelity in everything pertaining to religion.

Now, with regard to England, so great was the enthusiasm of her Reformation in the fourteenth century, and such was the spirit of the people, and so firm their laws, that Rome had no longer any hope of regaining the country she had lost. Had it not been for Ireland, she would as soon have thought of establishing her empire in Jerusalem and Antioch, as in London or Edinburgh. Nevertheless, her hopes once more revived, on perceiving the good effects of her operations in 1829. The Emancipation Bill, in the estimation of Rome, opened the door for her return into England; and it was conjectured that in about thirty years, by adopting every possible means, the "good old times," such as they were in the early part of the reign of Henry VIII., might return.

The plan was no secret; in fact, about the same time the Jesuits renewed their operations. Pius VIII. was pope; a good old man enough in private life, but a great stickler for the Council of Trent. It was a serious grief to him that this *sacro-santo* Council was not law to the whole world. He was what the Romans call a good Canonist; indeed he was of opinion that the Canon Laws were the greatest possible blessing that the bounty of the Deity had ever bestowed upon mankind. And if such were his real opinion, independent of any personal interest or bias, no doubt he meant well in maintaining it. The Catholic Emancipation Act, therefore, quickly inspired him with the consolatory idea, that he should soon be able to introduce the Canon Laws of the Council of Trent into this kingdom, which, according to his view, was already preparing a return to Rome.

The Congregation of the Propaganda at the same time naturally fostered the idea of establishing a hierarchy of bishops and archbishops, in order to govern the Church of England according to the Romish laws. The project was a daring one, but there was work to do beforehand. Every colonist, before he plants, begins by preparing the soil. In like manner England had to be prepared to receive a Romish hierarchy. I imagine it was in the policy of Pius VIII. to prepare this ground in a better manner than it has been done by Pius IX. With another ten years of Jesuitical labour, their attempt would probably have obtained a better result, at least according to their own opinion; but it has pleased the Lord to confound their councils.

In what does this work of preparation consist? The grand secret of the Inquisition, the labour of the Jesuits, is to employ every means in their power that is most likely to secure their end. All the world knows that in the moral code of the Jesuits, which is also that of the Court of Rome, it is maintained that, provided the end sought be a holy and religious one, of which they make themselves the sole judge, ALL *means* whatever are good and lawful; and the reason, according to the doctrine of Thomas Aquinas, is, that our actions take their character from the end we have in view. Now the means employed to prepare England to receive the ecclesiastical hierarchy, with the Council of Trent, and the Canon Laws, on which her conversion depends,—the means, I say, are truth or falsehood, as may best serve; promises and threats, secret gifts, and hidden treachery; exaggerated praises to their friends, and the foulest calumny to those they believe to be their enemies. These are the means which the Inquisition invariably employs, in order to gain its end.

With respect to preparing England for the late *coup de main*, it was deemed expedient to arrange a grand Jesuitical mission to the two universities of Oxford and Cambridge. How well this mission succeeded, it is needless for me to bring proof. It is an acknowledged fact, that a number of clergymen of the Church of England have seceded to the Church of Rome since the year 1829. The rise and progress of Tractarianism and Puseyism, and the actual state of affairs, must be well known to all my readers. How many good-hearted people in England are now lamenting over the wounds that have been inflicted on their unhappy Church! God grant that they may one day,—and that day no distant one,—be healed!

Let us now inquire what the Roman Propaganda has achieved in this country from the year 1829 to 1850. It established, in the first instance, four apostolic vicariates, and subsequently, four others. The first four were entitled, "the district of London, the Western, the Central or Midland, and the Northern District:" the other four were established in the year 1840, and received the names of "the Eastern, Welsh, Lancaster, and York Districts."

The eight bishops attached to these districts carried on their operations under the immediate directions and superintendence of the Propaganda—the principal organ of the Inquisition; and their schemes went on quietly enough, until some among them, more ambitious than the rest, and not calculating the danger there might be of losing all the fruits of their previous labour, took advantage of the Pope's weakness, and the ignorance of the greater portion of the cardinals, and hurried matters on to the termination of the plot which was not originally intended to explode so soon. The effect of this precipitation, however, has been to render their measures for the conversion of England altogether abortive. Providence, in its all-wise purposes, influenced a certain Doctor Wiseman, whose ambition of being created a cardinal had long tormented his soul, to lead the weak mind of Pius IX. to commit the egregious blunder which has ruined the whole scheme laboured at by the Romish Church, and the poor Jesuits, with so much toil and perseverance, to bring to perfection.

I call it ruining the whole scheme, since the object was to go on secretly with the work, until the fit opportunity should arrive, when all the preparations should be complete, and men's minds sufficiently prepared for the *denouement*. If they could have continued their Jesuitical operations at the two universities for another ten years, the doctrines of the English clergy, and the Liturgy of the Church of England would have become altogether papistic. These delightful Tractarians, full of affection for the sister church, as they term that of Rome—full of admiration for the magnificence of her rites and ceremonies—impressed with respect for her worldly authority, and with veneration for her assumed apostolic succession, would readily have bowed to auricular confession, and would have admitted their belief in the real presence, and consequently in the efficacy of the sacrifice of the mass. As to the vow of celibacy, there were hopes held out that the Pope might be induced to modify it; so that there should no longer be any obstacle in the way of a complete fusion of the two churches, provided his holiness would recognise the English hierarchy. Such, until the present outbreak, were the dreams of the Puseyites.

But instead of all this, the whole affair is lost through the folly of the Pope and the ambition of Dr. Wiseman! An injudicious bull, in an unlucky moment, gave premature existence to the famous hierarchy; and, to complete the blunder, elevated the primate to the rank of cardinal. Not even in any Catholic country can Rome create a cardinal without the consent of the monarch, neither can she send bishops without the permission of the government: otherwise, they would be speedily sent back. In other Protestant countries, the affair is settled by treaty; but no such precaution exists with respect to England: still no pope, who had a grain of sense, would ever have dared to send to it, in so unlooked-for a moment, and without any previous notice, a batch of twelve bishops, with a cardinal at their head! Could a greater insult be offered, or a mark of more supreme contempt? By it the Pope has turned the English Government into ridicule, ignored the Anglican Church, and declared that he alone is the spiritual head of the country, and that he will govern it accordingly. It is, therefore, assuredly the part of England to give the Pope a proper reply to his arrogance, and not only to show a just resentment of the present insult, but at the same time to prevent its ever occurring again.

Now what has been the conduct of the Inquisition with respect to England? What has the cabal of Jesuits been about? Whenever Rome expects to meet with opposition, she invariably has recourse to indirect means to gain her ends. For example, it is her object to overthrow the Church of England. She conducts her operations in a twofold manner,—by endeavouring to pervert its ministers, and by exciting them to hostilities against the Dissenters. Indeed, the conflicting spirit between the two parties is greatly aggravated by the increasing corruption of the clergy. Within the last twenty years the Church of England has experienced immense losses, without knowing from what part her enemy assailed her. And now that the Jesuitism is discovered, what attempts are not made to conceal its existence! Up to 1850 it was the fashion for the clergy of the High Church party to profess Puseyism. I have frequently been shocked by hearing sermons from reverends and right reverends, openly in favour of Romish doctrines. At the present moment, however, they are all ashamed of having appeared to favour them. The bishops, who at first boldly advocated Tractarianism, both in doctrine and practice, are now as zealous in opposing it, and the journals are full of their correspondence with such of their clergy as have publicly been accused of Puseyism.

All this is most skilfully turned to account by the Jesuit Propaganda, who regularly correspond with, and receive their instructions from, the Inquisition at Rome. The English bishops, without being aware of it, have in their train their missionary from Rome, who, although he may not belong, *ipso facto*, to the company of Ignatius Loyola, is nevertheless in essence a rank Jesuit; and may probably be one of their own clergy, nay, even their own private secretary. Who shall say such emissaries are not to be found also in the public offices of the Government, nay, in the very court of her Majesty, the Queen of these realms? The Jesuits find their way into the highest society in the kingdom, introduced by foreign ministers, who place them in families as tutors and teachers of languages. I myself know several Italians who profess to teach, who call themselves liberals, in fact, who state that they are my intimates; and with such pretences they get into respectable families with whom I am acquainted, who consequently trust to them, receive them into their houses, invite them to their tables, and allow them to converse with their children. Many of these are Jesuits, or their friends, who are recommended by them. It is to be noted that among the Italians at present in London, who teach their own language, the partisans of the Jesuits are they who are the most encouraged, get the most pupils, and receive the highest payment. So that it frequently happens that the worthless and the ignorant find abundance of employment, whilst the deserving and the learned starve, for want of anything to do.

The Jesuits secretly spread the most atrocious calumnies against those who oppose them, whilst others they load with extravagant praise. For example, there are a few Italians here in London, who, like myself, have, through conviction of its errors, abandoned the Church of the Popes and the Jesuits. We are all of us loaded with abuse, and persecuted in every possible manner; I in particular am the butt for all their shafts. According to their representations, I have been guilty of all imaginable crimes, but of these crimes no proof whatever is offered; even witnesses suborned for the purpose have failed to establish them. For my own part, I have treated my slanderers with disdainful silence; others, however, have taken up my cause. A Cardinal, who is at the head of these calumniators, has had the lie publicly given to him. Any but a Cardinal or a Jesuit would have been indignant at such an accusation.

I mention these things to show what is the work of the Inquisition now going on in this country. Here they cannot imprison men, or torture them, or burn them alive; still they have lies, calumnies, and treachery to resort to; they sow discord among families, separate friends, and everywhere foment dissension and strife. They are unable to destroy Protestantism in England, but they excite the various religious sects to wage war among themselves, and then declare, in the face of all Europe, that the Protestants of England and Scotland endeavour to destroy each other. How often have I heard it said in Italy, "Oh! the Protestants cannot exist much longer; they are perpetually at variance among themselves; they will be ruined by their own dissensions." But the Divine Providence will protect them from this fate, however artfully their enemies endeavour to keep their disagreements alive. Still all this discord has considerably weakened the Reformers, and retarded their progress; and if the Jesuits have not succeeded in attaining their desired object, it is not because their plans were not well arranged, or their mode of carrying them out effective, but simply because the Almighty has willed it otherwise.

It is curious to observe with what malignant artifice they arrange the threads of their meshes. True followers of the Inquisition, they feign to be strenuous advocates for liberty, and are the first to call out for it. What was the plea for Catholic Emancipation?—religious liberty. Unquestionably the Inquisition desires to have religious liberty in England, in Scotland, and in Ireland; and to obtain it, pays court to, and unites with the dissenters, who being desirous of the same privileges, naturally join their votes against the party that opposes them. But does the Inquisition desire to see the same religious liberty in Italy, in Spain, or in Germany? No indeed: throughout the whole of the continent it cements itself in the strictest bonds of union with every government that oppresses the people. It sits by the throne of the Emperor of Austria, by the side of kings and queens, and even of presidents of republics. But in England, on the contrary, it flies from the Houses of Parliament, and the palaces of royalty, and betakes itself to the manufactories of Manchester, Birmingham, Liverpool, Bristol, and Sheffield. Upon the continent it employs every possible means to be absolute, in spite of the people, while in the British dominions it associates with, and makes friends of the discontented and rebellious of every denomination, crying, "Brethren, we are an oppressed people; they who oppress us, oppress you also. A luxurious and extravagant court, a weak and improvident ministry, and a parliament where our masters are our representatives; these are our tyrants and yours. We are loaded with taxes, which are continually on the increase. Scarcely can the working man find the means of existence. The Church swallows up all our profits, and serves no other purpose than to foment scandal and division. Let us unite our forces, and attack our adversaries. Liberty is the people's right." Such is the language of the Jesuits to the Chartists, and such the proclamations of Dr. Wiseman and Co. in their appeal "to the good sense of the people of England."

With whom did the liberal party in parliament vote? was it not with the Catholics? It would scarcely be believed in Italy, that the Jesuits could induce the liberals of this country to join with them under the idea of gaining greater liberty, when their real object was to re-establish among them, as far as it was possible, the power of the Inquisition, even under the mask of freedom.

It was the Inquisition that, under Gregory XVI., bestowed a benediction in Muscovy on the troops of the Czar against the unfortunate Poles, and which, under Pius IX., celebrated the defeat of the Hungarians by the armies of Austria and Russia. The same Inquisition, which is capable of any enormity, is at the present moment on the point of exciting the ignorant and desperate rabble of Ireland against the British parliament. It would not surprise me to see ere long the affair of the *Sonderbund* of Switzerland renewed in Ireland and in England, occasioned by a few wretched bishops, as it took place in the former country on account of a few unworthy Jesuits.

The real object of all this disturbance is to introduce into the country the government of Rome. All might have been prevented in the year 1815, when the *Protestant powers* made such haste to reseat the Pope on the throne, and a still better opportunity was neglected in the year 1849, when, the Romans having legitimately deposed the Pope from the government, after his desertion of his people, foreign powers were allowed to invade the country, and to bombard Rome and two other principal cities of the state, to restore to him his justly forfeited temporal power. And could not this invasion have been prevented? And why was it not done? Was it not an offence against the Almighty? And will it not be visited, sooner or later, with the punishment due to it? This question naturally suggests itself to the minds of those who now, in virtue of their faith, feel themselves called upon not only to resist and to protest against it, but also to place every possible impediment to the further progress of the Inquisition of Rome.

# CHAPTER VII
# THE JESUITS

The term Jesuit has various significations. It generally means the followers of Ignatius Loyola, who profess the rules of the Company; and also those who are in strict friendship with them, who eat their bread and are supported by them, and who are always anxious to ingratiate themselves in their favour. These may be considered the Acolytes of the Jesuits. Moreover, some are called Jesuits who are even opposed to the sect of Loyola, and are averse to any connexion whatever with its members; but who still think and act according to the principles of the Jesuits; they are equally subtle and ambitious, intriguing, time-serving, deceitful, and hypocritical, in every respect, as are the Jesuits themselves. The world is full of such persons, and they are called Jesuits, because they are in reality of the same school as the sons of Loyola, whose doctrines and maxims they follow, although they do not profess to be his disciples. It would be as ridiculous to see a soldier or a statesman, for example, in the dress of a Jesuit, as it was to see the Emperor Charles V. in that of a friar; but what would you say on hearing that Jesuitism was more nourishing among society at large, than even in the Company itself? Would you not smile to see the present members of the French Assembly marching as in a procession, each with a Jesuit by his side? Father A. for example, with M. de Montalembert; Father B. and M. de Corcelles; Father C. and General Oudinot, the bombarder of Rome; until we come to the last couple, Father Rootan, and the President of the Republic, Louis Bonaparte! This sight might make you smile; but the thought it would inspire, would kindle, as it does in me, a sentiment of indignation.

In this work I shall have occasion to speak of every description of Jesuit. Meanwhile, I have a few remarks to offer with respect to these sons of Ignatius. What part do they take in the Inquisition? The most active and the most influential. They are its right hand. Without their aid the twelve Cardinal Inquisitors would sit in vain; their long and secret meetings every Wednesday throughout the year, in the great hall of the Minerva, would tend to no effect. Of what service would be the weekly congregation of about seventy members of the Inquisition, held in the great hall of the Holy Office, at the Vatican, every Monday, without the zeal and unwearied activity of the Jesuits? Apparently they are nothing; in reality, everything. Among the servants of the Holy Office a Jesuit is never to be found; rarely among their coadjutors. A Jesuit is never seen entering the Palace of the Holy Office, or in conversation with an Inquisitor. It might even be imagined that the Reverend Fathers were opposed to the institution, or at least that they shunned all relation and intercourse with it. And so studiously do they keep up this appearance, that many persons actually believe that the Jesuits have nothing whatever to do with the Inquisition. Indeed, I was at one time of the same opinion, till I was fully enlightened on the subject by a Jesuit himself, and, what is more, a worthy Jesuit too! one who had been my tutor in the *Belles Lettres*, in the College at Viterbo, and whom I met again at Tivoli, in September, 1833.

I was there in the discharge of my duty as Visitor of the Dominicans, and at the same time availing myself of the salubrity of the climate, which was beneficial to my health. Accordingly, I was accustomed to walk every day for some hours in the country. The good Jesuit was soon aware of my regularity in this habit, and as the time I selected was invariably the last two hours of the day, he proposed to me to become my companion on these occasions. I believe it was the first time that a Jesuit had been seen walking abroad in company with a Dominican. My former master had become my friend; and although I had never at all liked the society of the sons of Loyola, yet I found this one, and another or two of a similar description, to be honest and worthy men, who, to their misfortune, had adopted the robe of the Jesuits. I was visited almost daily by my friend, who came either alone or in company with a lay brother; we walked out together, and entered into familiar conversation. One day we spoke about the Inquisition. We were alone, in that beautiful grove of olives which crowns the pleasant hill on which stands the town of Tivoli, so well known to Horace.

"How does it happen," said he to me, "that you have never been embroiled with the Inquisition? Some time ago I was told that you were Vicar of the Holy Office; but I have since, on better authority, learned that you were merely Vicar of the Sacred Palace. And I was glad that it was so,—it would have grieved me much to have heard that you were an agent of the Inquisition."

"Oh! I had neither inclination nor ability for the office: treachery, deceit, and malice are the necessary qualifications for its agents. An Inquisitor must be suspicious, prone to judge amiss, to convert shadows into substance, and to see everything in the darkest colours. In the eyes of an Inquisitor every individual is evil, and deserving of punishment. How could I be led to form injurious opinions respecting my brethren, when I am naturally disposed to see things in a charitable point of view, and as far as possible to make excuses for others? An Inquisitor, besides, is one who is lost to all sentiments of humanity, without heart or feeling, and more indifferent than a stoic. God preserve me from the temptation of ever connecting myself in the slightest degree with the Inquisition."

"As far as I see, then, it appears you have never entertained the least desire for such an office, I give you joy. The Inquisition is injurious to the Dominicans, who are prompted by an insane ambition to become Inquisitors, and this entails on them the hatred of the whole world. The Franciscans are too prudent to connect themselves with it. The Jesuits, more cunning than the rest, act as the monkey did when he made use of the cat's paw to get the chestnuts."

"How! do the Jesuits meddle with the Inquisition?"

"My dear friend, is it new to you? What would the Inquisition be without the Jesuits? The Dominicans may call themselves Inquisitors; but they could not even decline the noun *Inquisition*, unless the Jesuits taught them. In fact, what do the Inquisitors search out? They sit still to receive denunciations. The Holy Office would be but badly supported if it depended solely on the exertions and abilities of its own immediate officials. Unquestionably, St. Dominic, with his cloudy intellect, was an Inquisitor; Peter of Verona, commonly called Peter the Martyr, was more efficient, but his imprudence cost him his life. I marvel much that a similar fate did not befall Domenico di Guzman! He slew, and caused to be slain, many more than Peter of Verona ever did; of a ruddy complexion, fierce and sanguinary, he was equally imprudent as his disciple. Far otherwise was Ignatius Loyola; cautious and wary in all his operations, and, although a soldier, averse to exposing himself to danger, he cautioned his followers to use the utmost prudence in carrying out their measures, and by no means to expose themselves foolishly to public odium or indignation. I say foolishly, because what, after all, is the amount of profit, to those who are in the service of the Inquisition? You, who are a Dominican, understand this better than I do."

"Oh! it is next to nothing. Our Inquisitors in Umbria and Romagna receive from the Holy Office in Rome, under the head of 'vestment money,' the paltry sum of three *scudi* (about 13s. 6d.) a month; which they have no means of increasing, unless they can occasionally pick up a trifle by saying a few masses. The monastery allows them no other advantage than the ordinary diet of the friars. Besides, it not unfrequently happens that, on account of the Inquisitors claiming exemption from the duties of the monastery, the prior deprives them of what he grants to the other members. In a visit I once made to the Monasteries of Spoleto, Foligno, Perugia, and other places, I found the Priors and the Inquisitors in open dispute with each other. The Priors complained that the Inquisitors refused to sing in the choir; and the Inquisitors, on the other hand, were indignant that they had not enough to eat, nor any wood to burn during the winter."

"They were not denied what was wanted for an *auto-da-fé*. I suppose: but continue your recital."

"Well, these disputes were settled by the Provincial and by myself, and it was arranged that the Inquisitors should thenceforth sing in the choir, and be subject to the Prior, as to all the duties of the monastery; the Prior, on the other hand, was to be considered under the obligation of treating the Inquisitors with civility, and allowing them the same advantages as were enjoyed by the rest of the brotherhood. At Spoleto, the Inquisitor not being inclined to take his dinner at the usual hour with the rest of the community, the Prior frequently obliged him to go without any at all. The Inquisitor complained to the General of the Order at Rome, and he wrote me word to accommodate the matter between the parties. It was proposed that a certain sum should be allowed by the Prior, for the dinner and supper of the Inquisitor. Fifteen *baiocchi* (sevenpence halfpenny) were all that was offered by the liberal-minded Prior for the daily expenses of the Inquisitor, and it was not without much trouble that I got the sum raised to seventeen baiocchi and a half. I mention this matter to show how little profit accrues to an Inquisitor, if the duties of his office are honestly discharged. An Inquisitor once told me in confidence, that he found it necessary, in order to live, to abstract a little money occasionally from the office, by augmenting, in his accounts with it, the amount of his expenses. Another lost his situation at Perugia, because it was discovered that he had regularly charged double for the maintenance of the prisoners under his care; and another, at Faenza, seized upon a poor shoemaker, and imprisoned him, that he might be obliged to work for him; and when he wanted his clothes to be mended, he laid hold of some tailor, whom he shut up till they were done, on pretence that he indulged in a habit of profane swearing."

"What a shame! How base they become! How degraded is that faith which requires the support of such a race! The office itself is too degrading to be exercised by any person of probity or honour. At one time the Inquisition was greatly enriched by fines and confiscations; and many spontaneous offerings were made to it by the rich, who freely opened their purses to get out of trouble. Money also came in from numerous patents: in short, the Inquisition was enabled to allow a good salary even to its clerks. But the times are altered; the Holy Office has lost its credit, and consequently its officials are bankrupts."

"But how," I suggested, "have the Jesuits become connected with the Inquisition? We have departed from our original question."

"Doubtless you imagine that the Holy Office is engaged in taking notice of crimes or offences against religion. It is true, when such cases occur, they proceed according to rule. But you are not to conclude that such is the sole occupation on which above seventy counsellors, and twelve cardinals, with the pope at their head, are engaged in the weekly meetings. If it be necessary to punish, as they say, all who deserve it, they ought to begin with unbelievers; in that case they would find many among the cardinals themselves who have no belief whatever; and the same infidelity descends throughout every class of society. But it never happens that any of them are subjected to punishment; on the contrary, only those heretics are the objects of attack, who are unbelievers merely as to some of the doctrines of Rome, although firm in their faith as regards the doctrines of Christ and of his apostles. Of these, however, few allow themselves to be seized by the Inquisition. An Italian who changes his creed generally contrives, before the fact gets known, to make a pilgrimage to Geneva,[28] and the Holy Office has to delay its vengeance till its victim can be arrested. Were the Inquisition to have no other care than to look after heretics, it would be the same as if the Jesuits were to have nothing else to do than to attend to their schools for young boys; in which case two-thirds of the Order might well be dispensed with. It is well known that at Rome everything opposed to clerical government is considered as heresy, and excommunicated accordingly; but real heresy is the last subject to be thought of, or attended to. The principal object of the Inquisition is to possess itself, by every means in its power, of the secrets of every class of society. Consequently, its agents enter the domestic circle, observe every action, listen to every conversation, and would, if possible, become acquainted with the most hidden thoughts. It is, in fact, the police, not only of Rome, but of all Italy; indeed it may be said of the whole world. Now the Dominicans, even with the assistance of the priests, would be altogether unequal to this task, were not the Jesuits themselves the secret officials of this police. The mere government spy is seldom enabled to arrive at the exact truth: it is difficult for him to get at the secrets of a family; he is met with counter operations; schemes are laid expressly to deceive him, and he is frequently put to considerable trouble and inconvenience to ferret out an affair, without obtaining any final success. For a long time the Italians, and more especially the Romans, have learned the art of playing upon the credulity of the spies, and making them believe things quite contrary to truth. But nothing of this sort takes place with the Jesuits, to whom no door is closed, no curtain drawn, no veil or shadow cast over secret or mystery. What they cannot learn from the men, they ascertain from the women; what the father will not disclose, the son will reveal; and what the master of the house may be desirous to hide, the servant may bring to light. The spy has need of frequent and lengthened research; whereas the Jesuit arrives at the fact at once. As has been before observed, the spy is deceived by false statements, which is not the case with the Jesuit. The confessional leads to many important discoveries; and where this is insufficient, much is learned even from the children in the schools. The police daily sends forth its numerous spies, who disperse themselves throughout the whole of Rome, and pursue their investigations, not only by day, but by night also. Frequently, overcome with the fatigue that the incessant labour of one day has produced, they are obliged to devote the whole of the succeeding one to a complete state of rest. It is different with us Jesuits. You know the church of the *Gesu*. Every morning at break of day, as the doors are opened, twelve Reverend Fathers ascend the steps of the sacred edifice, dressed in their robes and surplices, and seat themselves in their confessional chairs. Who are they who present themselves at that early hour, to give an account of their sins? Servants of both sexes, and all the old men and women who are stirring betimes in the morning, shopkeepers and workpeople; all those, in short, who are better acquainted with other people's business than with their own. So that in less than an hour all the transactions and gossip of the city are related at these twelve confessionals; from whence, at the termination of the audience, they are taken home, as you may imagine, to be examined, discussed, and, with due caution, registered as *cases of conscience*, &c.

"What is done in the church of the *Gesu*, is also done in that of St. Ignatius, of St. Andrew on the Monte Cavallo, of St. Vitale, and the other churches belonging to the Fathers of the Company. Frequently a fact, or a conversation, that is half ascertained in one place, is fully disclosed and confirmed in another. The cleverest among our body have the office of confronting those they desire to examine; and every day they go from house to house, collecting whatever intelligence of interest may present itself. In this manner we become acquainted with the most minute and secret affairs of the city. But our exertions do not end here. We have our nocturnal oratories, as that of the Caravita in Rome, whither the *élite* of good society generally resort. We have besides, as you know, our courses of spiritual exercises, which are always well attended; the conferences for the scrupulous, where they worm everything out of them; friendly visitations, which are never deficient in supplying information; and of which there are always a vast abundance over the whole country. Every one who is desirous of place or office, applies to us. It is impossible to be more courteous or zealous than we are in proffering our services, and what we ask of the government for our friends, we naturally succeed in obtaining. Moreover, we supply families with servants, and change them when required: consequently, every one is obliged by us, and entirely devoted to us.

"What I have told you respecting Rome is equally true with regard to all other places, wherever we are to be found; in Naples, Turin, Genoa, Modena, Verona, or anywhere else. Look, for instance, at this little town of Tivoli. No one stirs a foot in it but we are aware of it; and we have no occasion to go out of our houses for information. I myself have been here seven years; I have never ascended the staircase of any house in the place, and yet I am well acquainted with the affairs of every family that resides here; what they are doing, what they are talking about, what their intentions are, even to the most minute matters: in proof of which, the next time we are walking out together, ask any question of me respecting any person we may chance to meet, and you shall have copious information."

We were here interrupted in our conversation by two other Jesuits, who were returning from their walk, and who accompanied us home.

The next day we met again. My companion was accompanied by a youth, who had, I believe, the charge of a school. He was also a Jesuit, and on terms of strict intimacy with my friend. We passed through the town with but little conversation: the two Jesuits, with their eyes bent to the ground, appeared to take no notice of the passers-by; yet I observed they never failed to see when they were saluted, nor did they ever omit to return the salutation. As soon as we were fairly out of the town, we began to enter into familiar conversation.

"Well," observed my friend, "what do you think of our discourse of yesterday?"

"To tell you the truth, I was greatly surprised at what you told me."

"You would perhaps be pleased if I made the experiment I talked of."

"Oh, I am fully persuaded of the accuracy of your assertions. Besides, I am but little interested in the concerns of this place. Nevertheless, I will not refuse your offer. But tell me, in the meanwhile, how is it that the Jesuits, who perform such services for the Church, are never raised to places of dignity or profit in it?"

"If we had any desire that way, we should soon obtain what we wished for. We who have the power of disposing of these situations to others, might easily choose for ourselves. Had any other person than yourself asked the question, I should have given him the answer which our Institution puts into our mouths—'A Jesuit is sworn to aspire to no ecclesiastical dignity; nor can he accept any, without a special dispensation from the pope.' But this reply will not be sufficient for you, to whom I have disclosed so many of our secrets. I tell you, then, that we should never succeed in our undertaking of supporting the Church of Rome, unless we kept ourselves aloof from all her honours and dignities. A man once placed high in the Church has finished his career. A bishop and a cardinal serve very well to make a splendid appearance, and that is all. In the human body, the head governs the members; but in the moral body of the Church, the case is reversed, and the more active and influential members govern the head. Thus the bishop is not the moving power in his diocese, it is his vicar or his confessor. In like manner, it is his theologians, and not the cardinal, who sway the congregation; he says Yes, or No, as they direct him. The theologians and the confessors, then, are really at the head of affairs, and not the cardinal or the bishop. The pope himself is subject to the same regulation. I smile when I hear of the pope's holding a secret consistory. The Romans believe that he is then actually himself engaged with his cardinals in the discussion of important matters; whereas the true secret consistory is held by the General of the Jesuits and his counsellors; and it is by them that everything is discussed and decided. Now, all this could not be done, were we not simple monks, and open to no ambition but that of serving the Holy See."

At this moment some ladies passed us, whom the Jesuits were the first to salute by taking off their hats: but from the coolness with which the civility was acknowledged, I saw there was very little friendship between the parties.

"Can you tell me," said I to my friend, "who these ladies are?"

"O yes, I can tell you not only their names, but their ages too, if you desire it."

"Have you ever been in company with them?"

"Never; but that does not prevent me from being able to furnish you with every minute particular in their biography."

Whereupon he entered into so many details concerning the history of these ladies, that I was astonished at the extent of his information; but I was still more surprised to hear the younger Jesuit contribute his share as well, and even correct some points which the other had advanced. I had the curiosity to inquire how long this youth had been in Tivoli, and discovered that he was a Pole, and had only been six months in the place.

A priest came by, next, and respecting him also we had a full and minute account. Afterwards the Princess Santacroce passed in her carriage; my two Jesuits made her a profound reverence, and the elder of them entertained me with the history of the lady, till we reached home.

The following day I thought I would engage my chronicler on some other interesting matters, and I led the subject to Rome and the Cardinals.

"You are acquainted," I said to him, "with the major part of the Roman cardinals, especially, I suppose, with such as are friendly to the Holy Office."

"I know them all, both friends and enemies, if not personally, at least by reputation; and of every one of them I could, if you wished it, give all the circumstances of their lives, from their birth to the present day. You may rest assured that a Jesuit, after ten years' experience, unless he chance to be a stupid fellow, in which case he is soon expelled from the Society, ought to know far more than the most expert and practised officer of police. For my own part, I am conscious that I possess a certain dexterity in these matters; and it is on this account that I have been sent into various places, and entrusted with so many commissions. I cannot, however, imagine why they have kept me seven years in Tivoli, doing nothing but what my office as professor of moral theology requires, to settle cases of conscience. Still they have given me my degree (*il grado*),[29] and I imagine I shall shortly be called to Rome, to attend to other matters."

"To be one of the twelve who every morning at an early hour occupy the confessionals at the *Gesu*!!"

The Jesuit smiled significantly, as much as to say, "I believe so."

"But tell me, my dear master," I rejoined, "would you not be more useful in other matters? How well you could impart instruction in Greek and Roman literature, not only my testimony, but that of all your other pupils, might be brought forward to prove. You direct the studies of youth with so much judgment! Besides, that is an occupation, as I understand it, worthy of a Jesuit. But to go about spying into other people's affairs, to serve the Inquisition and the Court of Rome, is an employment that God may perhaps pardon you for exercising, but society never will."

"My dear friend," replied he, "such is the price at which we are admitted into the Society of Jesuits. It is necessary to do many things to which we may be naturally averse, many things contrary to our nature, and even to our conscience." (And here a sigh betrayed the anxiety he felt.) "You will perhaps ask, why I remained among the Jesuits, before I had received my degree? I can understand the question. But you, who are now a theologian and a preacher, turn to the 7th chapter of the Epistle of St. Paul to the Romans, where the apostle laments his own state, speaking of himself: 'For the good that I would, I do not; but the evil which I would not, that I do;' and concludes with that memorable exclamation, 'wretched man that I am! who shall deliver me from the body of this death?' I can assure you that more than once I have proposed to myself to quit the Society while I had yet power to do so; and then a thousand thoughts came into my mind:—What will they say of me, if I leave the Society which hitherto has been as a mother to me? I shall have to endure the remorse of one who, as it is written, 'has put his hand to the plough, and has looked back;' and on account of my dereliction I shall be adjudged unworthy of the kingdom of heaven!

I desired so much to become a Jesuit, that I abandoned, as you know, my chair at the Sapienza, and gave up my inheritance to my brothers; I bade adieu to all the world, and buried myself in this cloak, which I have now worn for fifteen years. How was it possible to retrace my steps, to disclaim my own words, to give the lie to myself? Ah, my friend, I pray you may never repent having assumed your present habit, that you may never experience the regret I have endured! But all this has passed away. I am now a Jesuit, fixed in my vocation. In taking my last vows, I have sworn to die in my Order. Nothing can now alter my determination."

After this conversation several days passed without my friend's making his appearance; and I dared not inquire after him, fearing he might possibly have repented of the confidence he had reposed in me, and be desirous of breaking off our intimacy at once. I was however mistaken. He still retained his regard for me; but that which would have been commendable in any one else, was, it appears, in a Jesuit, a fault, a weakness, and contrary to the rules of the Order. The aged spiritual director of the establishment had found the conduct of my friend to be very reprehensible. This old man was not himself the Superior, but the superintendent; he was one of the assistants of the General of the Order, and usually resided at Tivoli, where he was well known as the celebrated Father Sineo. He was the oracle of the Society, and was consulted in all matters of importance. He generally inhabited an apartment secluded from the rest; like those idols of the Church of Rome which are withdrawn from the light of day, and shut up in obscure places, to inspire more veneration; or if placed in a niche, they are covered with a curtain, to guard them from the profane eyes of the multitude; who would go crazy, in their senseless adoration, if they saw them always before their eyes. In like manner, this Father Sineo lived at Tivoli, like the cuckoo in the fable, who delivered his oracular sayings from his hole in the rock, to those who went to consult him.

Now, this Reverend Father, seeing the intimacy that subsisted between my friend and myself, and fearing that he might disclose some of the secrets of the Company to me, summoned him into his presence, and told him that it was not befitting that a Jesuit should be seen more than once, in public company with a stranger to the Order; that our friendship might degenerate into familiarity, and so on into mutual confidence, to the danger of the betrayal of the secrets of the Institution. That, in fact, the General of the Order had learned that we were every day walking out together; and although this might not in itself be objectionable, still his Reverence advised him to break off such a public display. My good Jesuit had consequently to make a further sacrifice, and deprive himself of this little solace; he wrote to me on the occasion, assuring me that it was not from any diminution of friendship on his part if he could not meet me as usual.

I understood all this perfectly well, and continued my accustomed walks alone. Still my Jesuit was not forbidden to talk with me in private, and it was not long before he came to pay me a visit; when I expressed to him my satisfaction that our conversation had not been overheard.

"Oh!" replied he, "Father Sineo would not in that case have let me off so easily. Without doubt, I should have been immediately sent away."

"I trust they would have done you no further injury," I observed.

"The Jesuits are not like the friars and the nuns," he replied, "among whom those who transgress have to submit to a public penance; for instance, a Capuchin who cuts off his beard is obliged to eat with the cats,[30] until it grows again. But with the Jesuit it frequently happens that no one knows he is undergoing punishment; and he himself only perceives he has incurred the displeasure of his Superior, by finding himself constantly and most ingeniously thwarted in all his inclinations and wishes. In some cases the offender is made to change his residence, to leave his country, and to travel into Asia or America. Moreover, if a Jesuit commits any great crime, his offence is concealed, in order that no scandal may attach to the Company; for it desires, more than any other body, to be esteemed irreprehensible; as if its members were gifted with the privilege of impeccability. It is moreover always expected that a Jesuit thus protected by his Company, should consider himself bound to expiate his crime by the greatest possible show of repentance; after which he is again taken into favour. Generally, those who are sent into foreign countries are not allowed to return, until they have signalized themselves in some praiseworthy manner. It is considered a great favour to be called to Rome: as it is also a heavy punishment to be banished from it. For my own part, I have many times requested to be sent to some foreign country, but I never could obtain my wish. To tell the truth, I should much prefer a mission to England. I differ from my brethren in that respect; although a Roman, the air of Rome, and more particularly of the Vatican, is too oppressive for my liking."

"Well, for my part," said I, "I never could understand what business Jesuits can have either in England, or in the United States."

"Still," replied he, "there are many in both those countries, and many more will follow. It is our desire and our hope, to obtain the same influence in England that we have in Italy. Protestantism in that country already inclines greatly towards Catholicism, and will do so still more, in proportion as the Jesuits gain ground there.

"Our success would be yet more rapid were we not impeded by other priests and monks, who, in their ignorant fanaticism, imprudently attack the Protestants, and thus only strengthen their opposition to the Church of Rome. We, on the other hand, have the art of introducing ourselves among them without exciting attention; consequently, without creating suspicion or alarm. Apparently occupied with our own affairs, we appear to take no notice of those of other people. We readily associate with them, sit at their tables, and converse on general topics; we never oppose or contradict what they may advance. Do they talk of the Bible? we are ready to talk on the same subject. We always, however, have some strong arguments in reserve, for which most of them are not prepared; scholastic doctrines, which the Bible does not disavow, and which are received with great willingness. So that while, on one hand, we lament that there should be an Episcopacy separate from Rome, we talk largely, on the other, on the important doctrine that the Bishops are the successors of the Apostles; and thus prepare the way for the conclusion, that the Pope is the successor of St. Peter. In fact, you will find, that in consequence of this doctrine of Apostolic succession, the Episcopalians generally entertain a respect for the Chair of St. Peter, in which the chief of the Bishops is seated.

"The principle being admitted, the consequence naturally follows. And it is to be noted, that if any one speaks slightingly of the Roman Episcopacy, the Bishop of London is the first person to reprove him; and moreover, the English Episcopacy calls that of Rome her sister. It is not so, however, with the Presbyterians and other sects. The Church of England retains the two Sacraments of Baptism and the Holy Supper; both of which, according to their belief, and according to ours also, confer sanctifying grace, (*gratiam sanctificantem,*) not only *ex opere operato*, but also *ex opere operantis*, and thus the minister becomes an advocate, *sine qua non*, for justification in Baptism, and for the real presence in the Eucharist. Should a doubt be expressed as to the sacred character of the minister, or as to the efficacy of the consecration of a bishop, as practised in their Church; should their white robes, or their Book of Prayer be criticised, the same outcry is raised by them, as would be raised by the sandalled friar, if you ridiculed his tunic, or his legends of St. Francis.

"The state of the case is this: Missionaries in general are imprudent, and begin by depreciating points which their opponents most especially hold in reverence. We, on the contrary, take care to inform them that these matters, inasmuch as they are traditions of greater or less antiquity, are deserving of consideration; and the more so, as they come near the traditions of the Apostolic Church of Rome.

"Do you think the Episcopalian clergy would ever consent to change their book of prayer? We might as soon be expected to give up our mass-book and breviary. They cannot therefore blame us if we are tenacious in keeping to our ritual, liturgy, and other ecclesiastical observances.

"In the Church of Rome there are canons, whose office we ourselves deem objectionable; those, for instance, who, for a sum of money, often of considerable amount, make it their business to pray for other people, (heaven knows what sort of prayers are those they mutter in the choir.) Well, in the English Church, every bishop has his canons, who have the *negotium in otio*, and *otium in negotio*, to go every day into the choir, to repeat twice a-day the same service; and for this easy task they are well paid in good English pounds sterling. Suppose now, a canon from St. Peter's at Rome should present himself at the Cathedral of St. Paul's, or at Westminster Abbey, you would find that the reverend canons there would receive him with more courtesy than they would show to either Luther or Calvin.

"Observe now," he continued, "our method of proceeding in England. We get acquainted with the Episcopalians; our time would be lost with others; and while we praise their doctrines, we endeavour to show how near they are to our own. We compare the respective Churches, their bishops with ours, the canons with the laws of discipline, the Mass-book with the Prayer-book, the robe with the surplice, and so on. The only point on which we cannot assimilate, is our celibacy, and their matrimony; and here we argue that as that is a matter of discipline, the Church might alter it, should it be deemed expedient to do so; the pope having the power to dispense with the observance.

"If any one complains that with us the cup is not given to the laity, we observe that this, too, might easily be arranged, if there were no other difficulty. But the clergy of the Reformed Church of the present day, both ministers and bishops, have for the most part an idea that the Reformation has taken away much which might have been retained. They begin to be sensible of a certain dryness in their worship, without either an image, or the cross; no one knows why the mitre has been taken from the bishop, and the gown from the priest. We observe to them, that it would not be amiss to restore those customs which are harmless. And thus by degrees, in some churches, we see images set up over the communion table, which give it the appearance of an altar. And if an image is not allowed, at least a handsome cross may be painted and gilded, before which the minister, as he passes, may make his obeisance. The mitre which the bishops no longer wear on their heads, in sign of jurisdiction, is transferred to their coat of arms, their carriages, and their plate; and seeing it thus painted and engraved, the desire naturally arises in the breast of some of them to wear it also.

"Our priests are wedded to their collar, the English ministers to their white cravat. If we had the courage to show ourselves in London in our gowns, I would wager that they also would wish to be clothed in the long black garb, close to the throat, with a single row of buttons."[31]

"It appears then," said I, "that your mission to the British Isles is exclusively to convert their Episcopalian ministers to the Church of Rome?"

"Not them exclusively, but principally, as being the most accessible. We do not however altogether lose our time whilst looking after the sectarians also. In fact, some of us take the Presbyterians, and those who are called Dissenters, under our especial care. In ingratiating ourselves with the Episcopalians, they become sufficiently friendly to evince no great displeasure against us, if we now and then succeed in leading away one or two of them from their faith. In short, we have nothing to fear from them, either in England or in Scotland: so long as we handle them gently, they never turn against us. But it is very different with the Presbyterians, the Baptists, the Methodists, the Independents, and others of a similar class; we cannot deceive them into a belief that their opinions approximate to ours; everything regarding papacy they hold in such abhorrence, that, as they express it, they would rather enter into a league with the arch-fiend himself than with us. How then do we proceed with them? I have already said it is in vain to think of overcoming them by argument. Our efforts are directed to sow enmity between them and the Episcopalians. And from this we derive a double advantage; they cease to trouble themselves respecting us, and endeavour to annoy their adversaries. The result of the whole is, that the Episcopalians (I speak more particularly of the most zealous) end by preferring us to the Dissenters, and will one day or other bestow on us privileges that will be denied to the latter.[32] Thus from their mutual discord we gain an increase of power."

"The plan is worthy of the Jesuits," I replied; "but do you think it will succeed? Will they not ultimately become aware of your intentions? and may it not happen that all parties, Episcopalians, Presbyterians, Baptists, Dissenters and others may unite, and direct their hostilities against yourselves?"

"In that case our mission would terminate, as it would no longer be possible for our Church to maintain its establishments in that country. We must, to use the common phrase, shut up shop. But such a union is impossible. You might sooner expect the dog to be in friendship with the cat, the wolf and the lamb to feed together, or the fox and the goose to share the same meal, than that these different sects should harmonize together. I do not speak so much of the people as of their different ministers. They are always disputing among themselves, frequently on very trivial matters; and we gain ground from their dissensions. It is our business, therefore, to add fuel to the flame of their controversy. Should they relax ever so little, we endeavour to invent some new cause for debate, and to engage in it the most influential and wealthy individuals. It would be a sad affair for us were a religious alliance to take place in England—if the Bishop of the Established Church, for example, gave the hand of fellowship to the Scotch Presbyterian and the Dissenter; the reproach of Protestantism, on account of its division, would then be taken away, and the cause would present a new aspect to the Catholic world!

"I can tell you, moreover, that the desire to become Protestant would then extend even into Italy, which at present smiles at the disputes between the ministers of various denominations in England; similar to the quarrels which once prevailed in Italy between the different orders of monks, as to whether the robes of the minister should be white or black, and as to their specific form—for an Episcopalian would never preach his sermon in a Geneva cloak, neither would a Presbyterian pray to God from the liturgy of the Church of England;—whether the sermon should be written or extempore; whether the prayers should be offered up standing or kneeling; whether the organ should accompany the choir or not; and other points not worth enumerating, but which not unfrequently become state questions.

"You know the great political axiom, 'Divide and conquer.' As long as we can keep the Reformation divided, it will never be strong enough to attack us. In its early period it could do so, because then it was united. Those were terrible times for the Church of Rome! All her means and all her soldiers were then put in requisition. Paul the Third, in this very town of Tivoli, in the year 1540, saw that an other Order was necessary to save the bark of St. Peter from shipwreck; another body of soldiers, who should receive secret instructions how to combat against Protestantism; by dividing, and putting it in opposition to itself. It was for this especial object that the Jesuits were instituted. Think how much it must have cost to accomplish their purpose without discovery! The disclosure of their proceedings would involve some frightful particulars.

"If the Protestants could be persuaded that their weakness is occasioned by their dissensions, and that the best mode they could adopt would be to unite, and make common cause against us, they most certainly might, with the means they possess, combat the Roman Catholic faith so effectually, that it would fall even in Rome itself. It is on this account that we are so vigilant with respect to England. The people there are capable of every thing when once roused. Woe to us if they take it into their heads to recommence a religious war! I dread lest it should take place. It is one of my especial precautions that no imprudence on the part of Rome should compel the people to such a necessity. Rome has united the throne and the altar; the royal sceptre with the crosier of the bishop. Nothing is spoken of but the divine rights of religion and of the state. And in the meanwhile the patience of the people, who are oppressed, tormented, and rendered miserable, is worn out: their insupportable yoke is imposed on them in the name of God, of Christ. What might not be expected to take place were they to become aware of the treachery of the priests? What could restrain them from open rebellion, from bursting their bonds, from throwing off their yoke?

"The present moment is favourable for Protestantism to gain proselytes, should it be so inclined, which however certainly will not be the case; not that every Protestant does not desire to see all the world reformed, beginning with Rome herself; but because when the period arrives, when political discord shall smooth the way for Protestantism in Italy, and when a helping hand would be sufficient to effect the change which the Italians themselves would assist in procuring, in that very moment, the most fatal for Rome, the English and Scotch Protestants would lose their object, in perplexing the Italians with the question whether their new Church should be Episcopalian or Presbyterian. It is well for us that such is the character of that people, and there is no question that we should do all in our power to preserve it. Woe to Rome if she does not watch over England, and woe to Catholicism if the Jesuits give up their important mission."

"My dear master, you have greatly enlightened my mind on these matters. I should never have imagined such a mode of proceeding. Have you ever yourself been in England, and become acquainted with these Protestants?"

"No, I have never yet visited England; but we Jesuits know everything concerning a country, without having ourselves been in it, since all we possess is common to the whole Company, from the clothes we wear even to our very knowledge and ideas. Whatever we know, we are obliged mutually to communicate to each other. Thus we put into circulation the capital of thought and information which each individual brings to the common stock, taking care not to let it get abroad."

"Are you of opinion, then, that England will make an advance towards the Church of Rome?"

"It depends entirely on the industry of the Jesuits. If Rome confides the task exclusively to us, you may rest assured some bold stroke will be effected ere long; and that, too, without England being aware of our manœuvres. She is, you know, an exceedingly rich country, and consequently strong and powerful. Now it is natural that those who are conscious of strength should fear no danger; so England in consequence of her wealth is liable to no fear, and takes no measures of prevention for the future. We already enjoy a considerable degree of liberty there, and shall have still more in a short time.

"The bishops rolling in their riches, and proud of a numerous clergy dependent upon them, believe themselves sufficiently strong and secure; they sleep in their imaginary safety, and amuse themselves by looking at us, who every now and then are raising some church or other in their own immediate vicinity. One of these prelates, I believe the Bishop of Manchester,[33] a little while ago, went about saying, 'Ah, these poor Jesuits! they go everywhere trying and trying, and they effect nothing.' Let his Lordship wait a little longer, and then he will be able to judge more correctly, not only as to what we have been doing, but what we intend to do."

"But where are the funds for all these expenses?"

"Where? Everywhere—every country in which we carry on our operations is made to furnish us with the necessary expenses. And if it sometimes happens that we incur, in any particular place, an expense before we have collected the money, we consider it as a loan, to be repaid to us, with usury. Now, what we spend in England, is all English money; we have the art of obtaining it even from the Protestants themselves. Instigated by curiosity, they come to our churches, to witness our ceremonies, and seldom go away without leaving behind them more than we gain from the Catholics themselves."

"How fearful is the power exercised by your Company! How formidable to society; and how much more so from its secrecy! Take care that you be not discovered."

"Discovered! and suppose we were? How many times have we not been driven out of France, and have we not always re-entered it? In England, indeed, we have never been proscribed, in consequence of the principle which we ourselves preach there,—political and religious toleration. For my own part, I only fear for our situation in Italy, for we, being on the side of the sovereigns, if anything should ever endanger their stability, should be the first to fall; and our ruin would precede that of the sovereigns. Should it occur in our time that the Jesuits are banished from Rome, bear in mind, that whoever the pope may be, he too will find it necessary before long to fly.[34] But in England we shall never incur the risk of being banished, therefore it is that we increase and multiply there so abundantly. We have establishments, schools, and all that we desire to have; and these good Protestants themselves furnish us the means. If it should please Providence that we should live long enough to meet again at some future period, you will recollect what I have foretold; at any rate, let it be according to the will of God. Adieu, my good friend. I must return to our convent, where Father Sineo is expecting me."

## FOOTNOTES:

[28] A common expression in Italy to denote that a person has become Protestant.

[29] An expression among the Jesuits to denote that the party is admitted to the last profession; that is, that he has taken the solemn vow, in virtue of which he can never in future be expelled from the Society.

[30] To eat with the cats, *mangiare co' gatti*. This curious punishment is literally put into practice in the Capuchin monasteries. The culprit sits on the ground in common with the cats, of which there are always plenty in these houses, and is not even allowed to defend his plate against any attacks his feline companions may venture to make upon it.

[31] This prophecy has come to pass.

[32] Here likewise the Jesuit has proved himself a true prophet.

[33] The good Jesuit probably meant the Bishop of Chester, in whose diocese Manchester is situated.

[34] The Jesuit was again correct in his prediction.

# CHAPTER VIII
# THE DOMINICANS, AND MY LIFE AMONG THEM

Whoever speaks of the Inquisition, immediately recalls to mind the race of monks who appear to be, even from their origin, the primary agents of this terrible institution.

These monks are called Dominicans, from the name of their founder; and it was by the advice of Pope Innocent III. that their Order was instituted. They called themselves Preachers, because they went to different cities preaching; not, however, the Gospel of Christ, but the rosary of the Virgin Mary; the most absurd system of prayer that the Christian world has ever yet had: a system, indeed, diametrically opposed to the doctrine of Christ, who says: "But when ye pray, use not vain repetitions ... after this manner, therefore, pray ye: Our Father, &c."

Now the rosary is a repetition of fifteen *Pater Nosters*, with one hundred and fifty *Ave Marias*, and it is said that the Virgin herself taught this stupid form of devotion to Domenico di Guzman. The fact, however, is certain, that he was the promoter of it, leaving it as an heritage to his followers.

The rosary was the Marseillaise hymn of the Crusaders, when, headed by St. Dominic, they ravaged the provinces of Languedoc, Narbonne, and Dauphiny, to exterminate the heretics, as they called those true Christians who would not subject themselves to the dominion of the pope.

The Order of the Dominicans can boast of many men of great talent; yet they allowed themselves to be seduced from the primitive mode of worship, and to become in their turn seducers, to perpetuate this absurd system. It is from them that every thing most foolish and malignant in the barbarous ages, both in Spain and Italy, has been continued down to our own times. A multitude of fanatics started up on the same field, who, at first, called themselves monks, or hermits; then friars or brothers; afterwards, regular clergy; in order to distinguish themselves from those who call themselves priests, after the Greek *presbiteros*, or elders.

In every age there has been a rivalry and emulation between all these parties, to serve the papal cause; always, however, first taking good care of themselves. It therefore happens, that those in whom the love of that system has prevailed over the love of themselves, have advanced to the highest distinctions in the Romish Church; while, on the contrary, those in whom the love of themselves has been the dominant passion, have remained behind, and are held in little consideration; like the Monks of San Francesco d'Assisi.

Among all these various parties, I think the Dominicans hold a middle rank; though not the most active, they are by no means the most idle or most selfish of the ecclesiastical orders: they are zealous in things belonging to the Church, and have many theologians and preceptors among them; some of whom are ambitious of appearing eloquent in set sermons, studied for the purpose.

The Inquisitors also occupy themselves in preaching; not that they wish to instruct the Christian world, but because it is the only means of procuring them money; of which they are perpetually in want; less, however, for their personal necessities, than for their personal vices.

The Dominicans are known to be rich, and to lead an easy life. Their dress is the most becoming, or, I should say, the least unbecoming of all the tunics, capes, hoods, cowls, gowns, and scarfs, that form the monkish garb; and certainly, their mode of life is less irrational than that of the other orders: still they are full of hypocrisy and deceit. They have a code of laws; but although they swear to obey them all, they do not observe half of them. The Superior of the monastery has power to dispense with the observance of any of them, on the slightest pretext. According to their rules, they ought all to dress in woollen only, restrict themselves to meagre diet, rise in the night to pray, and so forth. They do nothing of the kind, however; and so far, I do not blame them: but they are wrong in practising so many deceptions. They profess never to eat meat in the refectory, or room for their common meals; and it is true, that in the refectory itself they do not eat it; but there is another room near it, which they call by another name, where they eat it constantly. On Good Friday they are commanded by their rules to eat bread and drink water. At the dinner hour they all go together into the refectory, to eat bread and drink water: but having done so, for the sake of appearance, they go one after the other into another room, where a good dinner is prepared for them all. I do not blame them for enjoying it, but I blame them for first feigning an abstinence, which none of them intend to keep. When I made a profession of these rules, at the age of seventeen, I was totally unacquainted with such pharisaical deceptions. I looked upon the Dominicans as a noble order, where propriety of life was observed; and, above all, I was pleased that the sciences and literature were studied among them, and that professors and preachers came to teach them.

The first year, called the year of noviciate, which is the time given for deliberation, passed away without my seeing what was going on, for I was kept apart from all the other monks. Nevertheless, I was twice strongly tempted to renounce my career, but some friends I had in the monastery prevailed upon me to remain. Unhappily, however, the eye becomes accustomed to see deformities, the ear to hear follies, and the mind to stupefy itself by the habits it contracts; thus, after some time, I became a monk, and attached to the system; for as I believed Domenico di Guzman to be a great saint, so also I believed his Order to be a useful and respectable institution.

Being by nature frank and sincere, I could not endure false and lying practices; but it may easily be imagined that these people can readily find distinctions and subtleties, to render their professions in plausible accordance with their deeds. Besides evil example goes a great way. There were persons in the monastery whom I much esteemed; and seeing them live in ease and apparent sanctity, I tranquillized my mind, in order to associate myself to the same system. Moreover, I led a life of study: at the age of sixteen I had completed not only the courses of natural philosophy, mathematics, natural history, and experimental philosophy, but also those of civil and criminal law. All this was before I entered the monastery of the Dominicans; they were therefore rather proud of me; partly because I was the only one who was thus distinguished, and partly because they hoped by my example to attract others to recruit their fraternity.

I professed the institution of the Dominicans, with the view of being freed from every distraction, and enabled first to perfect myself in the sciences, and afterwards to teach them to others. I preferred this task to every other, and it was a passion with me to learn all that was worthy of being learnt. The hours of the day were insufficient for this desire, and during several years I accustomed myself to pass two whole nights, every week, in reading and writing.

My most delightful study was that of the classics, both ancient and modern; but I felt it necessary to apply myself to the sciences, especially to logic, for which I had much taste. I studied the philosophy of the Peripatetics, in order to become acquainted with it, though I did not teach it; also the theology of the Schoolmen, to purify it from the dross by which it is defiled. All that I acquired of these sciences was by studying books, as I learned nothing from the teaching of preceptors, which was at that time inconsiderable among the Dominicans.

I must confess that I was at this time well contented with my condition, and would not have changed it for any other, because it enabled me to satisfy my desire of learning. I had all the comforts of life necessary for a student, and amply sufficient leisure, uninterrupted by any thing either to trouble me or distract my attention. I had, in short, retirement, quietude, and an abundance of books. I thought also that I should have had learned conversation, but in this I was mistaken.

The life of the Dominicans is intended for the cultivation of the sciences; and the design, not only of Domenico di Guzman himself, but of the succeeding heads of the Order, appears to have been to form an institution of learned men devoted to the service of the Romish Church.

The privileges accorded by the laws of the Order to any individual who cultivates the study of the sciences, and, moreover, the honours granted to it by the popes, corroborate this design. The doctor, or Master of Theology, as he is called, enjoys many distinctions and advantages: his degree is equal to that of the principal universities, and the same as that of the Sorbonne and of Salamanca. With the Dominicans the road which leads to this academical rank is long and difficult, while in the other Orders, and from the class of priests, the path is easy and short. A doctor of Theology, among the Dominicans, is chosen from the class of professors after many rigid examinations, and a course of lectures which last twelve years: but once elected, he is free from all the inconveniences of a monastic life, and enjoys every comfort and honour. Happy, then, is he who can attain to this high rank! The number, however, is very limited; hence arise endless disputes and intrigues to obtain admittance into it.

*Il Maestro Domenicano* is generally considered a personage of much importance; he would not abandon this way of living for any other employment; and if he accepted it, he would consider himself unhappy, in having given up his cherished idleness.

It is related of Friar Orsini, a Dominican, who in his youth was made cardinal and bishop of Benevento, and in his old age was elected pope under the title of Benedict XIII., that one day being with his fellow-monks in the monastery of the Minerva, he said: "If I had not been removed from my office of lecturer to my Order, I should now have been a *Padre Maestro;*" thus manifesting that his elevation to the papal chair was regarded by him as a loss.

At the age of thirty I was a *Maestro*, to which high rank no one had ever before attained so early. My having taught many different things at the same time, was of use to me; as during the seven years of my lecturing I occupied three chairs at once; viz. those of theology, Holy Scripture, and philosophy. The head of the Order was anxious to advance me to this degree, as he wished to promote me to the post of Rector, or Principal of the Minerva, which is the highest of all that the Order has to bestow.

The Dominicans endeavoured still more studiously to make me a devotee to the Romish system, as they perceived I was departing from it more and more every day; and they thought the best means for accomplishing their ends would be to appoint me to offices of importance, at the same time holding out delusive promises of even higher dignities. This is the net by which they entrap many, but I was one of the few who did not allow themselves to be ensnared: on the contrary, I several times entreated the General of the Order to allow me to remain in peace with my occupations at Viterbo, in the exercise of which I desired to live and die; but he obstinately refused to comply with my request, and ordered me to renounce my professorships and repair to Rome. The Bishop of Viterbo interested himself for me, in order that I might not be compelled to leave the place against my will; and he adopted every method, both of persuasion and entreaty, on the occasion: but the General was no friend to the bishop, whose mediation therefore only served to strengthen him the more in his determination to withdraw me from Viterbo, and bring me to Rome. At last I could resist no longer, and was obliged to surrender my two professorships into the hands of the bishop, who reluctantly accepted my resignation, at the same time muttering strong expressions of resentment against the General of the Dominicans.

It was thus that I was forced, at the close of 1833, to quit Viterbo, having first received a thousand proofs of friendship from the bishop, the *Prelato Governatore*, and all classes of the inhabitants.

There was one crafty man, however, who, whilst he caressed me openly, used to calumniate and injure me behind my back, of which I in my own unsuspecting nature was not for some time aware. This man, a certain M. Spalletti, noted for his villainous character, was vicar to the bishop; by much intrigue he afterwards succeeded in getting himself made Bishop of Sutri and Nepi, but he finished his career by being driven away by the inhabitants, loaded with crime. This man hated me because I was a friend of the delegate's, who for many good reasons was opposed to him. After my departure, Spalletti began to raise various reports against me, by means of his acolytes. He also made use of some Dominican monks, who, through jealousy, were displeased with my advancement; as well as of certain persons whom I had reproved whilst residing in Viterbo. All these were unfriendly to me, and conspired with Spalletti against me. But the good Monsignor Sisti, governor of the province, discovered this secret conspiracy, and he one day called Spalletti to him, and gave him to understand that he was able to frustrate all his designs. Spalletti, finding himself discovered, denied having entertained any, and declared himself to be one of my best friends.

I was told of these evil reports, but I took no more notice of them than as if they had been concerning a stranger; for I endeavour neither to glory in applause, nor to suffer depression from false and injurious accusations. I feel as acutely as any one the force of injustice; but having made a solemn vow not to revenge it, I leave it to the Almighty: the only relief I seek to my feelings is the consciousness of my innocence; and I have generally had the gratification of seeing some friend, almost as if inspired by Providence, take up my cause, to the confusion of my adversary. In the affair with Spalletti, I had for my defenders, not only the *Prelato Governatore*, but also the most respectable persons in Viterbo. The Cardinal Gamberini, to whom I made some complaint about the conduct of the vicar of Viterbo, said to me, "Leave the unhappy man who calumniates you to himself; he is in such discredit with all good people, that being slandered by him is rather an honour than otherwise."

I went to Rome, in obedience to the General of the Order, and when he saw me he said:

"I am very glad you are about to begin a new career; for it will confer great honours upon you, whilst it will also be of the highest utility to the Order."

In the course of a few days, he presented me to some cardinals, by whom I was received with the most friendly welcome. The Cardinal de Gregorio predicted that I should become Master of the Sacred Palace, and afterwards a cardinal. Cardinal Polidori, also, said to me, "I wish this new charge may give you the opportunity of acquiring much knowledge, and that the Lord may grant you, at the same time, much humility." Some days after, the General said to me,—

"The pope wishes to see you, and has ordered me to conduct you to him to-morrow."

I had known Pope Gregory well, from the time when he was Abbot of St. Romualdo. I had gone several times to see him, and he always used to give me a good reception, presenting me with chocolate and books, as the monks are in the habit of doing. I had also visited him when he was created Cardinal; and, finally, I had waited upon him when he was Pope, being presented to him by Padre Velzi, Master of the Sacred Palace, as *Vicario del Magistero*. Behold me now again before him: the pope granted us a private audience, and was in a very good humour.

"Holy Father," said the General, Jabalot, "I present to you the new Rector of the College of the Minerva."

"Oh! my dear Achilli," said the pope. "I rejoice, *Padre Generale*, that you have made so young a Rector."

And here he said some very flattering things of me; that he had known me ever since 1825, and had always esteemed me; with many other compliments of the like nature. He then recommended me to the General, and turning to me said, —

"Now that you are in Rome, I shall have the pleasure of seeing you again; come whenever you like, and on Thursday mornings especially, you will find me more at liberty; go to my *cameriere*, and he will introduce you at once, without taking you the round of the ante-chambers."

The General was quite pleased with this reception, and said to me confidentially, —

"The pope wished me to call you to Rome, and from what he has told me, it appears that he has much good-will towards you; indeed, he certainly has a great partiality for you."

Soon after he said, —

"The pope speaks of you with much interest, and has great hopes of you. I therefore feel more and more delighted that I have brought you to Rome, and I hope you also will be well pleased at my having done so. I have been wishing for the last two years to have you at the Minerva; recollect when you came here, at the beginning of 1831, to graduate,[35] how I then said to you that I required you in Rome, and I offered you some employments; but you declined my proposals, and preferred returning to Viterbo. You know that whoever seeks for preferment, must reside principally in Rome; and your spirit, your talents, and the many friends you have among the most illustrious personages, as well as the interest the pope takes in your welfare, guarantee to you the highest honours and dignities in the Church."

"*Padre Generale*", I replied, "if this ambition to attain to high rank and dignity existed in my mind, I should then feel the necessity of remaining in Rome; but if I desire to attend to the service of my ministry, then it appears to me that I can be useful anywhere. Besides, as most talented men crowd into Rome, it is well, I think, that some like myself, assuming for argument's sake that I possess the qualifications you are pleased to attribute to me, should be dispersed here and there, in different parts of the country. I assure you, *Padre Generale*, that if I had not been compelled by you, I should not have left Viterbo, where I believe I was very useful; at any rate, I should have preferred going elsewhere, instead of coming to Rome. I do not know why this climate feels so heavy to me, and why it depresses my spirits, but so it is. I will, moreover, tell you frankly that the monastery of the Minerva has for me something repulsive; and from the time I left it in 1826, I never had any desire to return."

"Then you do not like Rome?"

"On the contrary, *Padre Generale*, I like Rome very much; you know that I am a Roman, although born in Viterbo, and God knows how I love this unhappy city! But it is precisely because I love it, that I cannot live in it: something that I cannot describe makes me suffer while I remain in Rome, but I feel it less when I am anywhere else."

"I do not understand what you mean."

"Well then, *Padre Generale*, I must explain. Do not you see the corrupt state of this city? Does it not appear as if you were in Babylon, when you go to the Court of the Pope and Cardinals? And of what does the clergy of Rome consist? Is it not of a number of ambitious men, who serve in the Church, only through their avidity to acquire a higher grade, and who endeavour by every species of intrigue to frustrate the designs of each other? You may see this in every class, and in every order, from the College of the Cardinals to the Capuchin monastery. What is the monastery of the Minerva, to which you have now so eagerly called me, thinking to ensure my happiness? An asylum for discontented persons, each one of whom is trying to rise above the other; every lecturer wishes to be *maestro*, and every monk longs to be the Superior. From this ambition arise discord and artifice, murmurings and backbitings, often generating the blackest calumnies. The monastery of the Minerva is odious to me, because here more than elsewhere the monks quarrel with each other; and the scandal of their disagreements has spread throughout the monasteries of the provinces, and causes the greatest disorders."

"From what you say it appears you are not contented with your present situation; you are like the Israelites who sighed after the leeks and onions of Egypt."

"I confess to you, *Padre Generale*, that with your permission, and that of the pope, I should be most delighted either to return to Viterbo, or to leave Rome, and go to any other city, to do all you wish."

"Well! this is curious! What a pretty figure I should make, undoing all that I have done! What would the pope say? What would the cardinals whom we have visited say? Even the monks would find something to say, if you were no longer the Rector whom I have appointed."

"As to the monks, you need not trouble yourself about them: they have already murmured enough that I am placed here. Accustomed as they have been to see only aged men called to the office, they do not like my being where I am; they would indeed be very glad if I remained no longer. I could easily, through the aid of the pope or the cardinals, find means to resign, without any blame accruing to your reverence."

At this moment we were interrupted. Several days passed before I again saw the Superior, who then received me with great coldness. This man had, as is well known, a remarkable talent for preaching, so that he passed for the finest orator of his time. The Jesuit Finetti and the Franciscan Pacifico of Brescia were certainly inferior to him. Proud of the applause he continually received, Father Jabalot daily expected to be elevated to the dignity of the purple, so much so that amongst his friends he himself spoke of it as certain and near at hand. Father Velzi, another Dominican, the *Maestro* of the Sacred Palace, had been created a cardinal a short time before; everything, therefore, encouraged our General in the belief that he too was one *"infieri,"* for so in Rome are those called who are about to be made cardinals, or who so flatter themselves. Consequently, he immediately assumed an air of dignity and patronage. Such was this Father Jabalot; bulky in person, gentle in his manners, he was already prepared for the cardinal's hat. To those who congratulated him he mildly answered with downcast eyes, and a modest smile of internal approbation; and when any one spoke of his high attainments, of his claims to the office, of the ornament he would be to the sacred purple, *"Stavasi tutto umile in tanta gloria,"* —he was humble amid so great glory.

The good friar was well aware that I was not one of those who pay court to cardinals, real or expectant. He knew very well that he could not make a tool of me to advance his ambition; that on the contrary, eschewing all ambitious views myself, I should have been a continual thorn in his side; in fact, he saw he had gained nothing by having brought me to Rome; and I think he repented having done so. However that might be, he was determined to try a last expedient. "Perhaps," said he, "you do not like to be the principal of a college, since the office is one of very great responsibility; and accustomed as you are to have your time at your own disposal, you may find it too great a confinement. If this be all your difficulty, I can easily rectify that point; I have other posts to offer you, which perhaps you may like better: for instance, the office of librarian at the *Casanatense* is vacant, and I can give it you, if you would like it; in fact the pope, only the other day, speaking of you, told me that he should be pleased to see you in that post. I am persuaded he would be delighted if I mentioned to him that you had made the exchange. You shall have three days to turn it over in your mind, and then you can give me your answer."

"My answer," I replied, "is ready this moment, if you will permit me to give it; I have no need of ruminating on the matter to come to a decision. It is not the office of Principal that is the difficulty with me; on the contrary, that is the very one in which I feel I could do some good. But I find it impossible to live in this Roman monastery, where there is nothing but opposition, contrariety, and dissension. Suppose, for a moment, I should wish to reform any abuses that might exist in the college, I should be sure to encounter a war of persecution, as has ever been the case. My predecessor has not yet recovered from the effects of his attempt in that way. Above all, there is one thing in which I feel the great necessity of alteration, and that is, in the course of study. We are barbarians with our scholastic theology; it is that of the middle ages; it is horrible! Aristotle is taken as the expositor of the Bible; his works, with those of Pietro Lombardo, are the two text books of Thomas Aquinas. In Christian schools the apostle should explain the philosopher. The famous motto of the Platonists, '*Ipse dixit*,' has its counterpart in the motto of the Thomasines, '*Ut ait philosophus et Magister sententiarum*.' Now, Father General, does this appear to you to be the proper way to explain theology, which is the science of reasoning upon, and drawing conclusions from, the principles of Divine Revelation,—that is to say, from the Holy Scriptures, since there is no other revelation than what they set forth?"

"But our Order has always held this system of instruction; our theology has always been that of St. Thomas Aquinas, which is authorized by the Church; and whoso has ever deviated from his doctrine, said Pope John XXII., has always been suspected as to his faith (*fuit semper de fide suspectus*). How would you think then of introducing any reform in such matters? Certainly, all the lecturers and masters would to a man rise against it. For my part, I cannot see why the system hitherto adopted should not be still pursued: our Order has been always distinguished for its theologians, and this distinction they derive from the study of the 'Summa Theologiæ' of St. Thomas Aquinas. Take this from them, and it would be like taking the sun from the universe; all would be darkness."

"Father General, I knew that this would be a sore subject; and though I could sustain some weight of odium, if I thought I could do any good, I see I should not be seconded, and therefore I should labour in vain. For this reason have I deemed it unadvisable to open my mouth on the subject; for it is written: *Non effundas sermonem ubi non est auditus*. My voice would be as '*the voice of one crying in the wilderness*.' Perhaps the time is not yet come; perhaps I am not the instrument destined for such a work; or perhaps it is to be brought about in some other way. I feel that the monastery of Minerva is no longer the abode for me, and that Rome itself is no longer the place in which I can dwell. I hope that you will, for my own justification, make these reasons known. Let it be clearly understood that my not remaining at the Minerva, or in Rome at all, has depended on myself alone."

"And the pope?"

"I will undertake to excuse myself to him. And he is so good a man that I am sure he will not find the arguments I shall lay before him unreasonable."

"Of course you will speak to him of the theology of St. Thomas Aquinas!——"

"Oh! as to that, we have often talked together on the subject when he was simple *Padre Abate Cappellari* of St. Romualdo; and perhaps he was really the first who made me take this view of the subject. Believe me, Father General, I am no innovator; nor is this a novelty; it is a thing that has been long desired, according to the exigencies of times and persons. The sentiments I have expressed are those which the favourers of scholastic theology have often endeavoured to smother, but which they have never been able to extinguish; and now it seems to me they are ready to break forth anew. Theology, such as it is at present among us, can no longer stand; and the reason, Father General, is, because it is not so ancient as it ought to be. In matters of religion there are neither discoveries nor novelties; that which was established in the beginning, that same should remain for ever. Can the Bible ever become old or obsolete? To me it appears that it cannot; and yet, in the twelfth and thirteenth centuries, an attempt was made to remodel and modernise it in some particulars. This work of the dark ages must be destroyed, and the original system renewed. And what I call reform, is not a novelty, as some imagine, but simply a return to the ancient religion."

"Let this discourse go no further; for I fear if others should hear it, they may conceive a bad opinion of you. This, you very well know, is the constant cry of heretics; they want a reform in the Church, but it is not their office to effect it; it is that of the pope alone, as sole head of the Church. It is always dangerous to speak of reform, for it invariably savours of heresy: and at any rate I would not advise you to give utterance to such sentiments, especially in Rome."

Father Jabalot was one of those blind followers of the doctrines of Rome, who, between Christ and the pope, would rather have decided for the latter than for the former. Leo XII., speaking of him used to say, that he thought Father Jabalot one of the most ambitious men in the world; that is to say, most ambitious to serve the papal chair. He could not, therefore, well agree with me, who saw in the past nothing but a system of corrupted faith and relaxed Christian morality. In his eyes the pope was infallible; a dogma which, in our age, every Roman theologian, who is not an actual fanatic, is ashamed of sustaining. It was impossible to reason with such a man upon theology, because he always preferred believing whatever was most preposterous, foolish, and least credible. His was a weak mind in a robust body. Such a man being the head of the Order, was one of my principal reasons for not wishing to reside in Rome; especially in an office which would have brought me into perpetual collision with him. On the contrary, from that moment, I was incessantly contriving how I might withdraw from the whole race of friars, who had now become odious to me. Their superstitions, on the one hand, and their irregularities, on the other, every day diminished my esteem and attachment to the Order. Truly, it required much to make me dislike those whom before I had sincerely loved; and yet this work, by Divine mercy, was perfecting in my soul.

I had long dissented from the Romish doctrines, but was still bound by certain ties of friendship—perhaps the force of habit, and the prejudices of education, had much to do in the matter—so that it appeared very difficult to take the resolute step which should entirely separate me from all and everything with which I had so long been closely connected. And yet that Providence, which governeth all things, at length effected even this.

Rome did all she could to attach me to her side; but in this point, I, who at any other time would have been most docile, now remained inflexible.

"It appears to me incredible," said a friend of mine, "that neither pope, cardinals, nor generals of orders, have eloquence enough to persuade you to stay in Rome, to be loaded with honours and dignities."

Father Velzi, the *Maestro* of the Sacred Palace, having some little time before been created Cardinal, and sent as bishop to Monte Fiascone, it was my office, as his vicar, in the discharge of my duty, to be in the midst of all the festivities which are customary on these occasions; and, moreover, to accompany the new Cardinal to his diocese, and to attend upon him. Viterbo being in the immediate vicinity of Monte Fiascone, I often divided my time between the two; and was but too happy to render every service to my excellent friend, who frequently asked me to pass some days with him.

I had a great regard for this man on account of his worthy qualities; with all he was obliging; for me he evinced a particular friendship. I was entirely in his confidence, and he occasionally in mine. Our conversations were very interesting, and the most perfect familiarity existed between us when we were together. Though a cardinal, he assumed no superiority over me, but, as is customary with the Italians, as with the French, in cases of intimacy, addressed me in the second person singular.

Cardinal Velzi was by no means a friend of the Father General Jabalot; consequently, these two friars divided the Order into two parties. As may be imagined, I was on Velzi's side; without, however, making enemies on the other, for some of whom I had a great friendship, and especially for the good old Father Brocchetti, who was then the Provincial. But, as happens in all party matters, and above all among monks, I was frequently reproved by both.

"What says your Brocchetti?" Velzi would ask, smiling.

"Well, what is your Cardinal doing?" Brocchetti and Jabalot would inquire, ironically. I had more than once endeavoured to unite these conflicting spirits, but always in vain. I could never induce Brocchetti to dine with the Cardinal, or the Cardinal to write a friendly letter to the Provincial. These dissensions were chiefly fomented by Buttaoni, the *Maestro* of the Sacred Palace, and Degola, secretary of the Congregation of the Index, who, holding everything from Velzi, were opposed to Jabalot; and on the other side, by some foolish monks, who, aspiring to certain petty appointments in the gift of the General, paid exclusive court to him.

It appeared as if Father Jabalot wished to gain me over by offering me the rectorship of the Minerva. He now prevented me, as much as was in his power, from visiting Cardinal Velzi as often as I could have wished; moreover, the distance I was from him, and the nature of my employment, which kept me occupied every day in the week, rendered my opportunities of seeing him comparatively rare.

"You have not much time now to pay your visits to Cardinal Velzi," said my good old friend, Brocchetti, to me one day. I could not thereupon forbear reflecting with regret, how two men of talent were, so to say, lost! Here were two most excellent individuals, hating and carping at each other, without any reason. And so it often happens, that for the slightest causes, inveterate enmities are nourished, whence the most deplorable consequences frequently spring.

I had now given my decided opinion, not only against the office of principal, but against any other which would require me to reside in Rome, and especially in that Pandemonium, the Minerva, with the Father General Jabalot.

There were, likewise, other motives which urged me to leave Rome; and those were, my aversion to the government of Pope Gregory and his Cardinal Lambruschini. The prisons were full of honest citizens, who had sacrificed their best interests for the love of their country; hundreds of good men were in exile, and their wives and children were pining in misery, exposed to every insult and derision. These and similar atrocities moved my indignation, and frequently made me speak against the government. It was a miserable sight at that time in Rome, to behold the acts of tyranny and oppression that were daily exercised; and it was beyond endurance to hear the insulting answers which the pope and certain cardinals gave to those who craved grace or justice. We see indeed at the present moment what the *Gregorian* school of domination is capable of.

Though reared among monks, I still felt myself a citizen, and hated the government as much as the most zealous lover of his country could do. Hence, it would have been impossible for me to remain in Rome without exposing myself to the persecutions of the police, by the animadversions I should continually have been tempted to make.

One day I was summoned into the presence of Cardinal Galeffi, chancellor of the Roman university, who offered me a chair at the Sapienza. Here was a new difficulty for me! Still the same question of staying in Rome, and residing in the monastery of the Minerva; every hope and comfort vanished at the thought of these two evils. I was also offered the choice of two professorships in the university of Macerata, namely that of Holy Scripture, vacant by the resignation of Professor Matteucci, or that of theology, which Professor Borgetti would have ceded to me.

Macerata is a pretty city, the capital of La Marcadi, Ancona. I preferred this locality to that of Rome, and was just upon the point of making arrangements accordingly, and of declining the offers of the General of the Dominicans, and of Cardinal Galeffi; but can any one with impunity renounce even the honours of the Church of Rome? The renunciation is always suspected. I had before me the example of Father Giovanni da Capistrano, ex-general of the Franciscans, a highly respectable character, whether as regarded his learning or his holy life. He had more than any one served the Church of Rome, but had twice refused to be made a bishop, and had shown himself indifferent as to the honour of a cardinal's hat, which the pope seemed willing to confer upon him. Aged, and worn out by fatigue and study, he wished to leave the turmoil of Rome, and pass the remainder of his life in retirement. He refused certain offices proposed to him by Cardinal Galeffi, saying, "I have served your Eminences long enough; I have need to think a little of myself; pray leave me in peace, and I will pray for you." The cardinal insisted, and the good old man (as he himself says in his apology) began to lose patience, and finally gave an answer that seemed somewhat abrupt to the Cardinal, who pronounced it offensive to the Roman Church, viz. to the pope and cardinals. This was sufficient—poor Capistrano, in spite of his grey hairs, was cast into the prison of the Inquisition, and after three years' hard treatment in the "Holy Office" in Rome, was condemned to perpetual incarceration in a monastery. This event made me determine to extricate myself from this web of obliging offers, which were as so many snares and fetters to my feet.

The thought of Capistrano being in the Inquisition made me tremble, and Cardinal Galeffi alarmed me. I saw no other means of escape than by quitting Rome; and yet this was to be done with judgment; my plan, therefore, was not to accept any appointment, and at the same time to find something which might justify my absence.

Cardinal Velzi sent for me at this period to Monte Fiascone, to stay a few months in order to assist him in putting his seminary in order. This occupation was agreeable to me, because I myself had proposed a new plan of instruction, which in less time than had hitherto been required would have produced better scholars, in various branches of learning. I omit other offers I had from several bishops, who were my friends; but I may observe that Cardinal Micara wanted me at Frascati, and Cardinal de Gregorio wished to have me for Penitentiary at Santa Maria Maggiore.

About this time the Father General Jabalot died suddenly, and Padre Olivieri, commissary-general of the Inquisition, was appointed to the office. This man formed a third party in the Order, being little friendly towards Jabalot, and a decided enemy to Velzi. Olivieri was an example of what a man of little talent, but of laborious habits, can accomplish. He was slow and dull of comprehension, yet, by dint of application to books, he had made himself master of the Hebrew, Syriac, Greek, and Arabic languages: he understood German, and read the English newspapers daily, and all this without masters, by indefatigable study day and night. Of the Hebrew and Chaldee languages he had been for some years professor in the Sapienza at Rome, and of the Greek elsewhere. Indeed, I never saw his equal for tenacity of purpose in anything he undertook; he was capable of sitting day and night over a single volume. On one occasion, having returned on foot from Turin to Rome, in 1815, as soon as he came to the Minerva, tired, hungry, and covered with dust, the first thing he asked for was the Timæus of Plato, in Greek, to examine certain passages which he had recollected as he was walking. Such was the singular character now elected Father General of the Dominicans. The storm lowered more and more; the government of the Order was bound up with that of the Inquisition, and whoever was not friendly to that institution was sure to be persecuted.

These changes happened between Easter and Pentecost, 1834. I had preached the Lent sermons at Monte Fiascone, whither the worthy Cardinal Velzi had invited me.

"O my good Achilli," said he to me one day, "I perceive that this Order of ours will become a real disorder. The Father General Jabalot was a weak man; he has allowed a world of abuses to be introduced. The Father General Olivieri is an austere and obstinate man, and one who knows nothing of the government of a fraternity, however small; besides which, accustomed for years only to the cells and dungeons of the Inquisition, a heartless being such as he is will, I foresee, destroy every good regulation, and finish by ruining everything. I advise you by all the friendship I entertain for you, not to remain in Rome, nor to accept any appointment which obliges you to reside in the Minerva. Keep aloof till we see how things are likely to go on; if you like to come here, my house, my seminary, and everything you may desire, shall be at your disposal."

A letter from the Father General Olivieri now called me to Rome. On my arrival he saluted me as rector of the Minerva, and spoke to me of certain arrangements he had made with regard to the collegians and professors. Prudence forbade my showing any opposition at that moment, and suggested the expediency of my letting him say and do whatever he thought fit, till an opportunity should present itself of getting quit of my embarrassing situation, and leaving Rome altogether. Meanwhile he charged me with several occupations, in proof of his particular esteem; making me privy to certain important secrets, and submitting to me the decision of some of the affairs of the Order. One of the most important of these was in the monastery of Santa Sabina, upon the Aventine Hill in Rome, in which at that time was the general noviciate of two provinces, the Roman and the Lombard. This monastery was immediately under the General, and he elected me as visitor in his place. This was an appointment I could not refuse; and since I had accepted it, it became me to fulfil it with all due care and exactitude.

The superior of the monastery of Santa Sabina, Fra Savoldello, a Venetian, was one of the most extraordinary men I had ever seen among the Dominicans. He had under him two other strange beings, little inferior to himself in eccentricity; and these were as his arms, wherewith to work the machine which was to transform innocent, docile, good young men, apt and easy to be trained in all that is right, into malicious, headstrong, ill-educated monks, capable of no one thing useful to themselves or to society. Such was the spirit of that noviciate, as ordered by the late Father General Jabalot.

As soon as these monks saw me, they resolved, as they knew me well, to hide as much as possible from me, and whispered in the ears of the young men that they must not reveal anything relative to the establishment. But I, seeing the embarrassment of the heads of the monastery, easily imagined their malice, and therefore gave orders that the novices should be brought before me immediately, one by one in succession; and not in a body, as the prior had proposed. I also requested both the prior and the novice master to leave the room. The first of these poor creatures who was introduced began to weep, and said:

"I thought the life of a monk was a very different thing to what I have found it. I thought I was to serve God, and to prepare myself for the ministry of the holy Church; I imagined I should have to study useful things, to instruct my mind; and above all, I fancied a cloistral life was one of peace and tranquillity; that the brethren respected and loved one another. I entered these walls with no other feelings or sentiments, and for my own part, I have always endeavoured to practise the duties they inculcate: but I am sorry to say this is not the system which I find here; the laws are good, but they are not put in practice; everything is governed by the caprice of the superior, who often gives contrary orders, and makes us lose our time in things of no value. Instead of useful books, to form the mind and make men of us, they put into our hands none but ascetic works, calculated to make us bigots. The lives of the saints, abounding with the greatest absurdities, are what they perpetually give us to read, and their conversation is only on austerities and miracles. I therefore come to say that this life will not do for me; and I beg my parents may be informed of it, that they may take me away. I wish to get out of this place as soon as possible, for it is worse than a prison—it is a perfect hell."

"My good child," said I, "there is no difficulty in your leaving immediately, as you are not professed. I myself will take care that your relations shall be made acquainted with your wish, in order that they may send you a change of clothes, and take you home. But tell me, why are you so troubled as to weep? Perhaps you are afraid of me, or have some other occasion for fear."

"Oh no, I am not afraid of you; you have not a surly threatening face; and besides, I know that all the youths like you. If you were our superior, I should not take this step; since I am not so much discontented with the Order, or with a monastic life; but I feel I cannot live with such a race of beings as there is here. I love religion, not bigotry; good people, not fanatics."

"Then you have something to say against the local superiors! Speak out."

"Oh no, I will not say anything, because well I cannot, and ill I will not speak of them."

I endeavoured to persuade him to try his vocation a little longer. I told him all superiors were not like Savoldello and his agents; that, once out, he would find better people, and more liberty as his years increased; but nevertheless, if such were his feelings, if he did not feel the same vocation in him, he had better return to his former way of life. Which he did accordingly.

The second had been trained by Savoldello, and replied to my questions in a manner which led me to suppose that everything was well conducted; others were in the same story; but one was so witty, and so well exposed the whole by-play of these wretched friars, that I must quote some of his conversation with me. Upon being asked if he had anything to say, he replied,——

"I have plenty to say; but I cannot speak."

"Why?"

"Because my mouth is shut, like that of a newly-made cardinal."[36]

"And who has shut your mouth?"

"Our pope, the novice master."

"Oh! if that be all, I am superior to him, and can open it again: so I command you to speak."

"There is a difficulty in doing so, nevertheless; in obeying you, and not him, I shall expose myself to persecution from him, which would be terrible; and you could not remove the penance he would enjoin."

"I promise you, in the name of the Father General, to protect you against any persecution from him. You know that the General can change the master; and I can tell you thus much, that it is very probable he will change him, unless he does his duty."

"In that case I will speak. You must know the prior, the novice master, and the *Procuratore* all join in persecuting us. Nevertheless, we frequently hear them quarrelling among themselves; and only the other day I thought they would have come to blows: when, however, there is a question of some new rigour,—or observance, as they term it,—that is to say, some fresh torment or vexation for us, then they are in perfect harmony with each other. We are tired of this system, which forms neither the Christian nor the man, but the hypocrite and the animal. All politeness, all decency among them is banished. They are filthy in their persons, and would wish us to be the same. Cleanliness and neatness, they call worldly-minded foppery. For my part, I never thought that to be a monk it was necessary to be a dirty sloven. And then both prior and master do nothing but send us to hell. On every little disobedience they cry out, 'You'll go to hell.' If we speak a word in the hours of silence, if we raise our hoods, if we look about us in the least, if ever we laugh,—'to hell with us;' I say nothing about singing—there is then no hell bad enough."

"Tell me, what do your masters teach you? what do they point out to you as the way of salvation? and in what, according to them, does the Christian life consist?"

"The master says that to be saved we have only to imitate the patriarch St. Dominic, be devout to the Madonna, and observe the rules of the Order; and then we shall be the best Christians in the world, because these lead to perfection."

"Does he ever speak of Christ?"

"Scarcely ever; he gives us the lives of the saints of the Order to read; and recounts to us the miracles done by them."

My visit to the monastery of Santa Sabina had the effect of making some quit the habit, and others open their eyes to a better mode of life. The General made some changes in the plans, but not such as I pointed out to him. In short, the same system was practised everywhere by monastic bigotry, and what the followers of it desired least of all was to reform themselves.

The institution of monastic fraternities was a bad thing from the very commencement: they were devised about the beginning of the thirteenth century, by that knave, Innocent III., who commissioned the wild fanatics, Domenico di Gusman and Francesco di Assisi, to establish, as to them seemed best, a body of idle fellows especially calculated to maintain the cause of popery; principally in Italy, and from thence to propagate their doctrines over all the world. Hence these two orders have ever been rivals. If one had a saint in a particular branch, the other wanted one directly. For example: the Dominicans lauded to the skies the doctrines of their dear Thomas Aquinas, whom they call the angelic doctor; and behold, the Franciscans immediately cry up their Bonaventura da Bagnorea, whom they dub the seraphic: so the Franciscan order chose to have a *thaumaturgus* (a grand miracle worker), in the friar Antonio da Lisbona, or da Padova; and the Dominicans, not to be behind-hand with their rival brethren, immediately exalted Fra Vincenzo Ferreri to the same dignity.

Whoever wants to see how far the art of publishing fables as things divine has gone, let him read the lives of these two, let him compare one with the other, and see which could draw the longest bow.

As the Franciscans preach up their Antonio, as the greatest saint in heaven, so do the Dominicans exalt their Vincenzo, as having the power of Omnipotence itself in his hands; so as to work prodigies and miracles at the beck and call of any one, as a conjuror plays his tricks at the pleasure of his audience. St. Anthony, we are told, preached to the fishes when men would not listen to his discourses: St. Vincent, in order to convert an impenitent sinner, wrote a letter to the Holy Trinity, and received an answer. St. Anthony, to prove transubstantiation, made a hungry mule kneel before the Host, regardless of the food offered by its master: St. Vincent had only to ring the bell for any miracle that was called for. What Franciscan would not swear by the miracles of his St. Anthony? and what Dominican would not be filled with wonder and faith at the recounting of the miracles of his St. Vincent? In fact, they adore him, under the figure of a youthful friar, with a flame on his head (as represented of the apostles at Pentecost), an open book in his left hand, two wings on his back, and his feet in the act of rising, or dancing; by which they intend to represent the angel who is spoken of in the tenth chapter of the Revelation. Indeed, they assert, that one day he flew from his pulpit round the church, and then, having ordered a corpse to be brought to him, he restored it to life, and asked it who he, St. Vincent, was; upon which, the resuscitated body replied, "Thou art the angel of the Apocalypse:" and, so saying, he died once more.[37]

Now such follies (which I know not that I ever believed, and which I certainly had then rejected) form the food of all the self-styled devout. Could I live among such? Every day I felt my soul further alienated from them and their system. In fact I remained a friar solely to combat against friars. They were already aware that I was no longer one of them, and they feared in me a potent adversary.

The Father General Olivieri called me one day, to communicate to me, as he said, an important measure. Brocchetti, the provincial, was with him.

"When I sent you to Santa Sabina," he said, "it was not only the wants of that monastery which I had in my mind, but those of several others, which I and the provincial had thought of sending you to visit. They are the monasteries of the Roman province along the line that terminates with Terracina on one side, and Lucca on the other. It will be a journey of some months, which the Father Provincial can hardly undertake, on account of his health and infirmities. He is willing to be represented by you, and I give my assent and approbation to the measure. This journey is very pleasant in fine weather. The Father Provincial will accompany you a part of the way, and the rest you will go alone."

I received this announcement with pleasure; not because I had again to be mixed up with monks, their intrigues, and their immoralities, but because it afforded the prospect of my getting out of Rome, in which I could no longer bear to reside. As soon as Brocchetti had gone out of the room, Father Olivieri added:

"You know Brocchetti is old, and his head does not serve him so well now; he is not so capable of conducting the business of the provinces. I have begged of him to let you have the management, not only of the visitations, but also of the direction of the monasteries, and the government of the province. He will remain in office *pro formâ*, and you will in reality act as provincial. So you will learn what may be your own office in future."

"I accept, willingly, this new charge," I replied, "to serve the Order, and to do what is agreeable to you, Father General, and to my good friend, the Provincial, Brocchetti, whom I revere as a father. With him I am certain I shall perfectly agree, and I hope I shall meet your wishes also. Such a charge is fraught with difficulties, but I am not of a nature to be daunted by them. On principle, I hate evil; I have pity on those who commit it, and I do all I can to lead them back to good. I am a sworn enemy to hypocrisy, and I would it were banished from society. I could never agree with that axiom of St. Bernard's: 'Would that my brethren were hypocrites!' *Utinam fratres mei hypocritæ essent!* No; rather would I there was not a hypocrite on the face of the earth; for hypocrites are liars who falsify the things of Christ, under the cloak of religion. We have many who pursue this system, and I assure you, Father General, that I shall make it my especial care to mortify and expose them: certainly, I will persecute these Jesuits."

At these words, the Father General laughed heartily. "You are right," said he; "persecute all the Jesuits you find among the Dominicans."

Our visit began with the monasteries of the "Campagna Romana;" thence we went into Umbria and Tuscany: returning, we visited those of Patrimonio di S. Pietro. To some of them the good Brocchetti accompanied me; but this he only did for a little relaxation, for he did not mix himself up in any business whatsoever; and, with the exception of making a short discourse at the opening and closing of each visit, he did nothing. The rest was left to me. I acted as visitor, with full authority; so much so, that many things I did not even think it necessary to mention to him. The good old man was daily at his prayers. Oh, what a holy man he would have been if his head had not been full of popish errors! He prayed even during the night; but instead of praying to God, he was praying to the saints, and lavishing his affections upon the mother of Christ, instead of turning them to Christ himself. Whenever I found him in his room, he was always repeating his rosary and the office of the Blessed Virgin. Once there arose an argument between us about fasting, for which he was a great advocate.

"I think you do not much like fasting," said he.

"No; to say the truth, I do not. A moderate fast may be very well as a sanitary measure, but I do not think it equally good as a moral system; especially as those who practise it, generally attach so much importance to it. Is it not true, my good Father, that you, for instance, every time you fast, indulge yourself in the belief that you thereby *merit* the grace of God? and yet you teach me the doctrine of St. Paul, which says, grace is such, precisely because it has no merit of works. Grace is a gratuitous gift. If, then, our justification be by grace, it cannot be by works. What will render you justified before God? certainly not your own works, but the works of Christ, the Just One, imputed to us, the unjust, by faith in Him alone. This is my doctrine, and I know it to be yours also. But yet you trouble yourself about works, and attach merit to the exercise of them. I do that which my faith suggests, and I attach no importance thereto. Precisely as a servant who does his duty obeys his master, and performs his will, without pretending that the master is therefore his debtor. Who dare say to the Lord: 'Here are my works, now give me thy gracious gifts?' I should be ashamed to offer to the Lord my fast, as a thing acceptable to Him, when the Scripture tells us that all the works of our righteousness are before the Lord as filthy rags: I endeavour to do what faith inspires, and to do it for duty's sake; and from no other motive."

Father Brocchetti was a great admirer of the Thomasine school, and inclining a little to Jansenism. He was a firm upholder of the doctrine of St. Paul to the Romans and the Galatians, that we are justified by grace through faith. Often, when we have been conversing together on religion, has he repeated these words to me:—

"Remember that grand maxim, which our school has always maintained against the Jesuits, 'We are justified by grace, through faith.' This is what does honour to the Dominicans, who follow the doctrine of St. Augustine and St. Thomas."

I observed to him that the force of this truth came from St. Paul; and that, if we had not had it through Divine revelation, we should not have been bound to believe it.

"I am not obliged to believe Thomas, or Augustine," I added, "but I am obliged to believe Paul."

The good old man was silent at these observations, and seemed to receive them with approbation. He often read the Bible, but never allowed himself any other than the Vulgate, with the notes. He disliked the Italian version; but one day finding me reading the New Testament, translated by Martini: he took it from me, smiling, and said, "Let us make an exchange;" at the same time giving me a Latin version of the Vulgate. As he read the Bible himself, so he recommended others to read it, but always with the notes of the Roman Theologians, drawn from the Holy Fathers.

This visitation kept me employed from the summer of 1834, till February in the next year. My old friend accompanied me as long as the fine weather continued; when it began to break up, he returned to winter quarters, to take care of his health.

I had now all the burden on my own shoulders; I had to provide for the wants of several monasteries, and to hear the complaints of the monks. I had to connect spiritual with worldly interests; external strictness with interior comfort; to reconcile contending minds; to settle differences, and harmonize discord; to rouse the slothful; to excite emulation in sacred things; to inculcate a love of study, and an observance of the rules; and to correct the vicious with mildness.

Every one will remember the name of Domenico Abbo, who was condemned ten years after the period I am speaking of, for enormous crimes, to be beheaded in the Castle of St. Angelo, at Rome.[38] He was at this time a Dominican friar, Superior and Reader at the little monastery of Nepi, near Rome. I had heard several reports against him, and I went to verify the matter. I found him culpable in many things, and I advised him to renounce his present offices, and to retire to another monastery; repent of his evil ways, and lead a better life; he denied the whole, and turned against me, uttering the bitterest threats. I then suspended him from his ministry, removed him from office, and ordered him to leave in a few days. He appealed to the bishop, the provincial, the general, and got up a certificate from certain persons in the neighbourhood, to prove his good conduct: he even sent some of his friends to intercede with me for pardon, but I could not relax my decree towards one so incorrigibly bad, and I insisted upon his leaving the monastery. He accordingly went to Rome, quitted the Dominican Order, put on the dress of a priest, and was on the point of being made a prelate, through the protection of Cardinal Lambruschini, and the favour of Pope Gregory, then ignorant of the extent of his wickedness; but the Divine justice had prepared to make an example of him. He was guilty of the most enormous and detestable crimes. The facts became public—the people took part against him, and the government was obliged to act promptly in order to calm the popular tumult. One tribunal condemned him to death; another confirmed the sentence; Cardinal Lambruschini was afraid for his own safety; the Pope was obliged to consent, and the wretched man's head rolled on the scaffold. He on that occasion had moved a strong party against me, saying I had persecuted him because he was not of my way of thinking. He excited hatred in many towards me, but I thought no more of him, and the affair, melancholy enough in itself, passed away.

This visitation made me acquainted with many things of which I was before ignorant, but which certainly were anything but virtues, either in a Christian, or a citizen; and on my return to Rome, I made known to several persons the effect my visit to the monasteries had produced upon my mind.

Meanwhile, I had been sent for by the Cardinal Archbishop of Capua, as preacher of the Lent Sermons in his cathedral. The Father General allowed me to accept the invitation, on condition that I should return immediately, and enter upon my new office. Accordingly I went to Naples, in February 1835; certainly not with the intention of returning to Rome, but, on the contrary, with that of speedily emancipating myself from monkish thraldom.

## FOOTNOTES:

[35] L'Esame ad gradus. *The Dominicans so call the examination for the degree of Doctor of Theology.*

[36] Alluding to the ceremony in the creation of a cardinal, in which the pope first shuts the cardinal's mouth and then opens it.

[37] Teoli: Life of Vincenzo Perreri. Rome, 1825; Naples, 1837.

[38] The translator of these pages was residing at Rome at the period of this man's apprehension, and was credibly informed that the statement of the cruelties; and atrocities he had practised towards a boy, an orphan nephew, were so appalling, as to draw tears from the eyes of Gregory XVI., then reigning Pontiff.

# CHAPTER IX
# MY CONVERSION

The aversion which from this time I conceived for everything savouring of Romanism,—pope, cardinals, bishops, priests, and friars,—proceeded, no doubt, from the change which for several years had been working in my mind. I already was no longer a papist, for I had long ceased to believe in many doctrines which are matters of faith in the Romish Church. I will now state how this was brought about.

While holding the head professorship of theology, in the college of Santa Maria di Gradi, at Viterbo, and advocating and teaching, with great zeal, the Romish doctrine, a very nourishing school, not only of Dominican students, of which the college consisted, but likewise of other friars and priests, used daily to attend my lectures, and be present at our *circolo*, or "circle," as we call our meeting for scholastic exercise, when a theological proposition is given, and defended by a professor and a student, while other professors and students raise objections. The exercise is in Latin, and in the logical form of reasoning as held by Aristotle.

I had ordered that this exercise should take place three times a-week; the theological lectures were five in number during that period, and it sometimes fell to my turn to defend, while the others objected. One day I was defending the doctrine of transubstantiation; one of the best disciples in the school, whose name I feel a pleasure in mentioning—Father Baldassare Conti, a Roman, who afterwards filled the professor's chair of theology in the Minerva, at Rome, with much honour, was on my side.

The question was, "Whether the bread and wine in the sacrament of the Eucharist are, in virtue of the words of consecration, actually and substantially changed into the body and blood of Christ, together with his soul and his divinity." We maintained the affirmative, and three or four others, with fictitious earnestness, denied the proposition; advancing arguments which they had the precaution to assure us beforehand were all borrowed from the heretics. The contest went off, as it invariably did; we were, of course, right, and our opponents wrong. The reasoning of my good and clever Conti, and that which I contributed myself, were the *ne plus ultra*, for the school, and even elicited uproarious applause. The heretics were discomfited, the Roman Catholics triumphant. We were the two heroes who had gained the battle, the laurel crown alone was wanting. Who after our arguments could possibly have doubted a doctrine so boldly asserted, so powerfully demonstrated? Who would have dared to have sided with the heretics, viz. with those who denied transubstantiation? I believe not a shadow of doubt entered the mind of any one excepting myself. In the midst of this universal satisfaction, I alone remained unconvinced. To me, the answers to the objections appeared feeble and inadequate. I was disquieted within me. I asked the young Conti how he was pleased with the "circle?" whether any of our answers seemed to him to want weight?

"I am pleased with the arguments I brought forward," he replied, "and still more so with those that you yourself advanced. Indeed, I am not aware that more could possibly have been said. But after all, the matter is a mystery which cannot be explained by reasoning; faith must come to our aid. Henry Moore, a celebrated Englishman, has well observed, as Erasmus relates, *Crede quod habes, et habes*,—'Believe you receive, and you do receive.'"

Of course, it was not proper for me to infect the young student with my doubts; he was better pleased in having discovered, as he fancied, the mystery of that religious impossibility than an alchymist would have been in finding the philosopher's stone.

I had none in whom I could confide. My colleague and friend, Professor Borg, was a man who would rather have renounced his reason, or doubted of his very existence, than have denied a dogma of faith; besides which, he was of opinion that such points ought not to be too freely discussed.

"What did you think of our controversy?" said I.

"All went off well," he replied; "he is an excellent young man, that Conti. What he said pleased me very much; and very true is that famous verse of Salomone Fiorentino with which he concluded:

> Vedi che in fronte ha scritto: adora e taci."

It would evidently have been useless to enter upon any discussion with such a man as my good friend Borg; I therefore came to the conclusion that I had better study the thing by myself, and endeavour to ascertain the real truth.

It is this important question which so many have racked their brains to understand in the Romish sense. The matter resolves itself simply into this: Are the words, "This is my body," "This is my blood," to be understood in a literal sense? Every one must see the absurdity of it. The least consideration will show that Christ said these words in the same sense as he said on another occasion, "I am the bread that came down from heaven," and no one ever supposed that *He* was actually bread, and subsequently changed, or transubstantiated. A little examination was sufficient to shake my belief in that doctrine which I had hitherto professed. Would Jesus Christ have told us things that were impossible to be? Now it is impossible, absolutely impossible, that what is bread should at one and the same time be His body; and that what is wine should be contemporaneously His blood. This cannot be, either simultaneously or successively. The Church of Rome saw the first to be an absurdity, and therefore held to the second. But how can the body of Christ become bread, and His blood wine, if such change be not in accordance with the laws of nature? Could Christ deceive us? Now it is not true that bread and wine, according to nature, have ceased to exist in the sacrament; for we see they do exist; that which we see, touch, and taste, is natural bread and wine. Can there be faith against nature? And yet that is against nature, which neither is nor can be: whatever is, must be according to nature's laws. There may be substances of a higher nature, and subject to superior laws than those with which we are acquainted; but they can never exist in contradiction to those laws, since nature herself, in that case, would be destroyed. Therefore, what is bread and wine cannot be not bread and wine; God, omnipotent as he is, cannot order it otherwise. But the sacrament, after consecration, remains natural bread and wine; therefore it is not the substance of the body and blood of Christ.

And what, I should like to know, would be the use of this pretended transubstantiation? Would it merely be that the faithful might, materially, eat the body and drink the blood of Christ? Now who does not see that this so-called eating and drinking of Christ is entirely metaphorical?

"The kingdom of God is not meat and drink,"[39] said St. Paul; "It is the Spirit that quickeneth, the flesh profiteth nothing."

"The words that I speak unto you, they are spirit, and they are life,"[40] said Christ.

The expressions, to eat and drink, signify to believe; to identify oneself with; as also to accept anything with pleasure. "Kill, and eat,"[41] said the Spirit to Peter; in the vision at Joppa, figuring under the unclean animals, the Gentiles. Now, all this Peter well understood, and never imagined he was to eat those animals, much less the Gentiles that he might fall in with; but to convert and receive them into the communion of the Christian faith.

Why, then, should we eat Christ? To believe in Him—to unite ourselves to Him? But this is entirely the work of the Spirit, and has nothing whatever to do with matter; on the contrary, everything material is repugnant to this union of faith. Corporeal substance may be a type, a figure of the spiritual, but nothing more. Baptismal water is the outward and visible sign of the spiritual and purifying grace, because, as the former cleanses the body from impurity, so does the latter wash away the stain of sin from the soul. In the same manner as bread and wine are the common daily food of the body, and as through them we receive nourishment and strength, so the body and blood of Christ, immolated and shed for us, are the continual aliment of our faith, which gives vigour to our souls, and is the substance of our spiritual life and salvation.

The words of Christ are truly divine; full of truth and wisdom. The interpretation of the Romanists is a grovelling human conception; full of error, falsehood, and absurdity. Christ could not better symbolise the effect of his passion and death; and we cannot more grossly abuse it, than by attributing to a sinful priest the virtue and power of the Saviour: with the additional enormity, that what Christ has been pleased to do once, a wretched priest pretends to be able to repeat as often as he chooses. The doctrine of transubstantiation, considered in relation to Christ himself, is a falsity and an absurdity; considered as regards so many thousands of wicked priests, it is an impiety and an abomination.

Thus did I reason with myself, and became fully convinced that such was not the meaning of Christ's words; that such was not the Christian faith; that such was not the belief of our fathers: and that thousands of Christian doctors, in all ages, have refuted this doctrine of transubstantiation, the author of which was *Eutichus*, a heretic, whose dogma was presented to the Church by Pope Innocent III. who had it confirmed by the Council of Lateran (1215).

In consequence of this reasoning, I already disbelieved in the virtue of the Mass; which can only be a propitiatory sacrifice, so far as it presents a true and living Christ, to be immolated each time it is celebrated. Take away the doctrine of transubstantiation, and the mass, in its grand essential, is nothing but a lie; a solemn imposture; an actual sacrilegious assault against Christ; who being now glorious, according to our faith, is also impassible; and as such, can neither be "broken" nor eaten by us. To eat Christ! the bare mention of such a thing is blasphemy. Far less was the crime of those who crucified the Lord; for they knew not that he was Christ. What should we have said to those, who, associated with Christ, and hearing from his own lips the words which we read in St. John vi. 53, "Verily, verily, I say unto you, Except ye eat the flesh of the Son of man, and drink his blood, ye have no life in you," had straightway, from literal acceptation of them, begun actually to eat His body and drink His blood? Which of his disciples would not have exclaimed against such an act of barbarity? And yet they would not have been more guilty than the theologians of the Romish Church.

From this time, in saying mass I was no longer a Christophagus;[42] I had ceased to believe in what I did. What then, in reality, was the act I performed? I know not. I was like Luther, and many others, who no longer believed the mass, who had rejected its doctrine, and learnedly refuted its errors, but still continued to celebrate it. I said it, indeed, as seldom as possible; always with a bad grace, as if under compulsion, and frequently I could not restrain my sighs. I was, moreover, ashamed of saying it in the presence of sensible and intelligent persons; as if afraid of their censure for performing an act, in the efficacy or virtue of which I no longer believed. I contrived, too, to say it at those hours when there were the fewest persons in the church, and at the most secluded altars. I always refused solemn masses. In short, the mass, which for others was a delightful service, had become for me a very painful one. I endeavoured sometimes to regard it as a simple prayer, leaving out the idea of a sacrifice or sacrament; but this was impossible when what is termed the offertory was to take place, and still more so at the time of the consecration and elevation of the host and the chalice. Although I myself was no longer an adorer of the bread and wine, yet at my mass there never failed to be some who adored, believing in their transubstantiation, and therefore I could not help looking upon myself as the agent of that idolatry.

Thus, I consider that the dogma which constitutes the mass, with its double element of transubstantiation and propitiatory sacrifice, is the most fatal of Romish doctrines, the most detestable of all heresies, and the most abominable of all practices. Around this, as their sun, revolves all the rest of the papal system. The power which, according to this doctrine, the priest has of fabricating in a moment, not one, but as many Christs as he pleases, and of offering them to God, as victims of a sacrifice which in itself is enough to atone for the sins of all, and to take out of purgatory by them, as many souls as he pleases;—this pretended power, I say, is the occasion of so much pride in the priests, as to make them think themselves privileged persons, sacred and unapproachable; and to consider their head, the pope, holy, infallible, and having all authority in heaven and in earth.

In disbelieving the doctrine, I denied the power. To me friars, priests, and prelates all savoured of imposture; and the more I advanced in spiritual light, the more I felt myself adverse to such hypocrisy. The pope daily became more abominable in my eyes. In him, or rather in his ambition, I saw a Lucifer, who, after having seduced himself, had power to seduce others; thus causing the fall of myriads of shining stars from heaven to hell.

Many say, "I believe so, because the pope so believes; if the pope errs, I must err with him; if he were to call virtue vice, and vice virtue, I must be his echo, and in all and through all follow him." Such is the language of the

Jesuits, from Bellarmine to Father Perrone. "O ye foolish ones, who hath bewitched you?"

As my creed changed, so did my conversation. Lenient to the laity, I was severe towards ecclesiastics; for the former I was full of compassion, for the latter I had only reproof: their vices were become insufferable to me; with their example continually before me, I endeavoured to be as opposite to them as possible. They for the most part were unoccupied and idle; I made it a rule to keep myself constantly employed: they were generally given to gluttony; I was habitually temperate: they were heedless, imprudent, dissipated; inquisitive after other people's affairs, and intriguers in private houses: I never interfered in what did not concern me, and was an enemy to the intrigues and cabals in which they took so much satisfaction.

"Why do you scarcely ever go to hear confessions?" asked one of those friars who delight in hearing them continually.

"Because you and your fraternity, not knowing how to employ your time better, pass the whole day in listening to the business of others," answered I. "There is no reason that I should follow your example; on the contrary, I do what you do not; I study to learn, that I may be able to teach others: in short, I endeavour to be useful to my fellow-creatures, in every way I can."

"Why do you so seldom attend choir?" was the inquiry of one of those Epicurean friars, who had he not had the exercise of chanting psalms, and singing at the top of his voice, would probably have had no means of digesting his dinner, and preparing his stomach for supper.

"Because," I replied, "I have so many other corporeal employments, that I am in no need of this."

"But prayer? that is a duty we all owe to the Almighty?"

"No doubt prayer pleases me when made in spirit and in truth. But to be in spirit it should be free; not attached of necessity to the Psalms of David. What have you said or done, by reciting three, six, nine, or a dozen psalms in Latin? What have you achieved? I am sure you do not know yourself. If you go to ask something from the superior of a convent, your first care is that your petition should be at any rate intelligible, and have a meaning. When you were in your own family, and had any favour to request of your father, I presume you asked simply for what you wanted. You certainly did not begin by reciting poetry, or singing in Latin. And is not God, our first, our true, real, and heavenly Father? Why then do we pray to Him in psalms? The most we can do is to sing them in his honour and praise; but prayer, real prayer, should be in our mother tongue; clear, expressive, and simple. My good brother, he who doth otherwise, erreth; following false traditions, and transgressing the commandments of the Lord. Remember what Christ says, 'But when ye pray, use not vain repetitions, as the heathen do: for they think that they shall be heard for their much speaking.'[43] And observe the preceding verses. 'And when thou prayest, thou shalt not be as the hypocrites are: for they love to pray standing in the synagogues, and in the corners of the streets; that they may be seen of men. Verily I say unto you, They have their reward. But thou, when thou prayest, enter into thy closet, and when thou hast shut thy door, pray to thy Father which is in secret; and thy Father which seeth in secret shall reward thee openly.'

"These are the reasons why I come to choir so seldom. I prefer offering my prayers unto the Lord, in the seclusion of my chamber. I fear that reproof of Jesus Christ:

"'Ye hypocrites, well did Esaias prophesy of you, saying, This people draweth nigh unto me with their mouth, and honoureth me with their lips: but their heart is far from me. But in vain do they worship me, teaching for doctrines the commandments of men.'"[44]

These, and similar lessons, did I give to my companions in profession, and as I perceived truths myself, so did I endeavour to impart them to others.

Towards the end of my residence at Viterbo, I was made superior of the monastery di Gradi, and also of two convents of Dominican Nuns. I had for some time seen things in a new light, with a view to reform; I saw not much, or clearly, as yet, but sufficient, nevertheless, to place me far out of the common sphere. In Lent, 1833, certain friars came to me to ask permission to eat meat, on account of slight indisposition; and I was very lenient with them. The nuns came with the same request, and I willingly granted them all they required. The rumour got abroad that I allowed everybody to eat meat. Amongst the monks was a good old man, the *Padre maestro* Linares, who moreover was the confessor to the nuns. One evening he came to my rooms, and said, that he ought to address me with every respect; but that, as the oldest of the house, a master of theology, and not to fail in his duty, he felt compelled to represent to me the complaints of certain religious monks and nuns, subject to my jurisdiction, which complaints were chiefly touching the numerous dispensations I had granted for eating meat that Lent. "At this rate," said the worthy father, "the precept of fasting would be rendered null and void, were liberty accorded to every one not to observe it;" (which was true enough.) "I think," added he, "that many of those to whom you have granted the dispensation to eat meat, might have abstained without much inconvenience."

"I think so too;" I replied, "but I wished to save them even this little inconvenience. In short, they asked for what they wished, and I granted it to them: I did not feel their pulse, or look at their tongue, like a physician; I supposed they wished to eat meat, and I gave the permission, precisely in the same manner as I should have wished it to be granted to me, had I asked it of my superiors."

"Ah! you must not be so indulgent. This is a question of an observance of a divine institution—Lent!"

"I think, on the contrary, I ought to be as indulgent on this point as possible, bearing in mind the words of our Lord, 'And he called the multitude, and said unto them, Hear, and understand: not that which goeth into the mouth defileth a man; but that which cometh out of the mouth, this defileth a man.'[45]

"Strive as you can, my good Father, to prove that Lent is of divine institution, with all due deference, I cannot agree with you. I find no ordinance of the kind instituted by the Lord; of Him indeed it is written, that He fasted 'forty days and forty nights;' and it appears that He took nothing during that time; but He has not taught us to do it *now*. Our Lent is not therefore an imitation of Christ's fasting; with us it principally consists in abstaining from certain meats, and eating less of others. Both one and the other are human institutions in Christianity; they are precepts of the Church, and articles of tradition. To eat somewhat less at certain times, for us, who generally live quite well enough, I consider a very good sanitary principle, and as such I recommend it occasionally; but not so the abstaining from meat altogether; which is often prejudicial to health; and, moreover, what is substituted for it by the Roman regime is unwholesome, and to many very injurious."

"But we are commanded to keep Lent."

"Granted; and I am authorized to dispense with the keeping of it, by those who require it of me; and I do so with pleasure, and without much importunity."

In this manner I was frequently led into a discussion upon the various doctrines of the Church of Rome, which one by one glided from my belief in an incomprehensible manner; insomuch that my very disbelief seemed to be the effect of inspiration.

Frequently the decisions of my understanding were the promptings of my heart. I was called by an internal voice in my soul to that which I did contrary to the teaching of the Church. For instance, I became displeased with myself whenever I went to confession. I as yet knew nothing of the contrary doctrine, and yet I felt within me a conviction that the practice of confessing one's sins to a fellow-man, was not, neither ever could be, enough to form a positive command upon; particularly one of such rigour: I felt all this before I was well persuaded of its truth.

It is not possible, said I to myself, that this command should be of apostolic date. I had not yet fully examined the question, but had already decided it in my own breast. On this point, however, I ventured not to speak to others. In fact, I altogether left off confessing. I remember the last time that I related my offences to a priest, I felt as much repugnance in doing so as the most timid child could have experienced. My penitentiary was a certain Doctor Semeria, formerly a Dominican, but then living in Viterbo, as a simple priest: a man learned in many sciences, and one who had been professor of theology; but that which redounded to his credit in my eyes, was his goodness of character; his Christian simplicity, and his gravity of demeanour; which obtained for him universal love and esteem. My friend, while I was yet a child, was my confidant; he knew all my secrets when I chose him for confessor; I did nothing without consulting him. To such an one I had no difficulty in opening my heart, and disclosing all the operations of my mind; but I found that I could not do it truly and fully, unless in familiar conversation. The trust I had in him vanished in the formality of confession. More than once, in the course of it, I have been obliged to interrupt myself, and rise from my knees, because in that attitude I lost confidence in my friend, who, perceiving my embarrassment, would often kindly forestall me, and say, "Let us converse without restraint."

Confession had at length become so odious to me, that I could no longer bear it myself, nor endure the practice of it in others. People were continually wanting to confess to me, and I always found some pretext for not hearing them. From the earliest period of my ministry I had been obliged to apply myself to this branch of duty. I was not yet twenty-four, when I was sent, by the Bishop of Viterbo, to confess even nuns. In 1830 I was appointed by Cardinal Gazola, Bishop of Monte Fiascone, to officiate for a month as confessor and preacher in two of his monasteries. The good old man chose me for his own confessor likewise, (I shall have occasion to speak of him again;) Cardinal Gamberini would have me, afterwards, at Orvieto. This man, reputed a first-rate lawyer, was made prelate, then Bishop of Orvieto, afterwards cardinal, and lastly, Minister of the Interior in Rome. He had never been a theologian himself, nor was he much their friend, but a sworn enemy of the Casuists. The priests in the neighbourhood were all ignorant men; his own Theologian, for every bishop has to appoint one, was anything but what his title and office required.

"I wish to confess myself to you," the Cardinal said to me, one day; "I trust you will not deny me this favour."

"To say the truth, your Eminence, I do not like to confess any one who has nothing but his sins to communicate to me; I have so many of my own, that I hardly like to be burdened with those of other people. A confession of sins makes me melancholy, and I feel that I am not performing my proper duty in receiving it. Excuse the comparison, but I really feel like an actor reciting his part; and this is a part I know but imperfectly. If sometimes I am forced to play it, I do so as well as I can, but it is painful to me to listen to a catalogue of the failings and infirmities of other people."

"But I know that you do confess the common people, and even nuns; why then will you not confess a bishop?"

"It is true, I am more ready to confess the common people, and I have great patience also with the nuns; although I am so little interested about their sins, that when they recount them to me I never speak; letting them go on without interruption: and when they have finished, I make but few observations, directing them to ask pardon of God, who alone can absolve and pardon. I then dwell a little on the incidents of their life, good or bad as they may be, and especially on their peculiar habits; taking occasion to instil into them the moral precepts of the Gospel, correcting their faults, and exhorting them to walk in the way of virtue. Now, such schooling as this, of which both the people and nuns stand in need, and which I adopt in the confessional, your Eminence does not require."

"If everybody thought like you, we poor cardinals and bishops should find no one to shrive us."

"So much the better; you would then confess to God, who alone is able to remit sins. Does your Eminence imagine that the holy fathers ever dreamt of confessing? Bishop Fenelon says that he sought throughout the whole of their biography, and examined the minutest detail of their lives, and their pious and religious practices, and found not one single word about confession. 'We must therefore conclude,' he adds, 'that confession was not in use at that epoch.'"

"But those fathers were saints, and therefore did not require it."

"Saints, I agree, as far as holy life goes, far more so than we are; but your Eminence, I suppose, would not infer that they were without sin; for you must remember it is written, 'If we say that we have no sin, we deceive ourselves, and the truth is not in us. If we confess our sins, He is faithful and just to forgive us our sins, and to cleanse us from all unrighteousness.

If we say that we have not sinned, we make him a liar, and his word is not in us.'"[46]

"Well, St. John here says that we ought to confess our sins; and this is precisely what I wish to do."

"I consider that the Evangelist here speaks of confessing to God those sins committed against God; in the same manner as St. James speaks of confessing to men those sins especially committed against men, when he says, 'Confess your faults one to another.' Thus, for instance, if I should offend your Eminence, I know I am in duty bound to come and acknowledge my offence, and implore forgiveness; and your Eminence knows equally well what is written: 'If thy brother trespass against thee ... and if he repent, forgive him: and if he trespass against thee seven times in a day, and seven times in a day turn again to thee, saying, I repent, thou shalt forgive him.'[47] Such is the law of confession according to the Gospel; clear, and sufficiently easy for the comprehension of the meanest capacity. Now, we must not confound these laws with those of the Council of Lateran under Innocent III., and of the last Council of Trent. According to the Gospel of Jesus Christ, we are only obliged to confess our sins to God; according to the Canons and the Decretals we ought to reveal them also to a priest, called a confessor."

This conversation entered deeply into the mind of the Cardinal, and I believe produced a good effect; since, some years after, when I met with him in Rome, he said to me, "I remember well our conference at Orvieto, touching Confession; and the more I have reflected upon it, the more true I have found it." Certain it is, that from that time such were my sentiments; for which reason I desisted from Confession, and counselled others to do the same, so far as their sins alone were concerned. The case was widely different when I had to exercise my ministry; not as regarded authority, with which I did not consider myself invested, but for the sake of charity and friendship—then I fulfilled it most willingly. I was the friend of all those who came to confide their secrets to me, and to receive counsel and advice; and I exercised this duty with the greater pleasure the more I saw they were in want of it. I was particularly attentive to the instruction of the young men, but as to bigots, I drove them from my confessional.

During the time of my ministry in the Romish Church, I have confessed a vast number of persons—I should think many thousands, and of all classes. At first I did so, in the firm belief that in virtue of the power conferred upon me by the bishop, I really had authority to pardon sins; and subsequently, my persuasion was that Confession, made to a priest, as a sacrament, had the efficacy of obtaining pardon from God, and that the words of the Absolution were a declaration to that effect. In the first case, I acted, if not according to the doctrine of the Bible, at least in accordance with the tenets of the Roman Church. But in the second, I acted neither in agreement with the Bible, nor with the Church of Rome. Under this conviction, then, it was that I at last omitted the form of Absolution, as being unquestionably anti-scriptural, and limited myself to a prayer, muttered between the teeth, according to the usual mode of giving absolution; and in which I asked God to regard the faith of those penitent people, granting to them pardon of their sins, through the merits of Jesus Christ.

Yet even then I found occasion to accuse myself; since those who had made their confession to me, believed that they went away absolved, through the efficacy of my ministry. They were deceived, therefore, in consequence of my silence; yet, on the other hand, if I had spoken out, and explained my sentiments, they would have been scandalized and offended at my not conforming to the usual custom. I found, therefore, that the better way was to give up the so-called Confessional, wherein, as the people imagine, the priest becomes invested with the authority of a forgiver of sins; and to those who asked me to listen to them, I proposed any place, excepting the confessional, where we could both sit down, and have our conversation without any show of hypocrisy. This system I began in Rome, and followed also in Naples; confessing many persons, and even nuns, at the grating of the parlours; or rather, I held a conference with them on their moral and religious wants; terminating with a prayer to God, that He would pardon their sins, through the blood of our Lord.

This system, however, could not be continued without my coming under the notice of the Inquisition. In fact, when I was called to answer to the charges against me, I was accused of having acted with contempt towards religion—*in spretum religionis*—since I had not observed the laws and ordinances of the Church. At last I was tired of living in the midst of opposition. My conscience daily alienated me more and more from the practices of popery, whilst my soul expanded to the convictions of pure Christianity. I had taken an aversion to image worship, to the adoration of relics, the patronage of saints, and their whole catalogue of miracles. In Viterbo, I had often ridiculed the history of the monastery di Gradi, in which it is asserted, that in or about the year 1220, while St. Domenico di Guzman was on his way through those parts, staying in the house of Cardinal Capoccio, bishop of that city, Mary, the Mother of Jesus, one night appeared to both the cardinal and the saint, and conducted them in spirit to the site of the present church of the monastery di Gradi, where at that time stood a forest; and here, addressing the two holy men, she said, "It is my desire to have a convent established in this place for my dear brethren the *Predicatori*, [Preachers,] where I shall be honoured, and my rosary preached up by them." So saying, she burnt a circle in the wood with a lighted torch, marking out the boundary of the future building. Now, as the vision appeared to each of them, in the morning they compared notes, and setting out together to the wood, found there a circle actually marked out by fire. This history, which is entered in the chronicles of the monastery, is received by the monks as a fifth gospel. Was it possible that I should longer give credence to such a story?

There is also, in Viterbo, another monastery of Dominican monks, called *La Madonna della Quercia*; the history of which is, that an image painted on a tile, and placed in an oak-tree, in the midst of a wood, began performing miracles about the commencement of the fifteenth century. Devout supplicants thronged from all parts, and the graces that were bestowed, and the miracles that were performed, according to report, surpassed the most sanguine expectations. Thousands were said to have been healed of various infirmities; thousands to have received, in various ways, assistance from Providence; in dangers, in persecutions, in recovering lost property, and in retrieving their honour. But the greatest and most astounding miracles of all were those performed on persons who had been blind from their birth, and instantaneously recovered their sight, by the virtue of that same picture; and on others who eight days after death had returned to life.

These fables I had believed in, for a time, as true. Blind, like the rest, because born in the land of darkness, I also, at one time, used to go and pray to the image *della Quercia* (of the oak). One miracle, however, is certain, and that, too, the work of no other than this so-called "Madonna," (a horrible figure of a woman with a child in her arms,) namely, the enormous riches which rained down upon the *Frati* for more than three centuries in consequence of it.

The monastery is very large, with a magnificent church, in the *Bramante* style, and surrounded by houses inhabited by the servants and husbandmen, with their families, who cultivate the immense extent of land belonging to the fraternity, which brings in every year a considerable revenue.

There is a book upon these pretended miracles of the *"Madonna della Quercia,"* printed more than a hundred years ago, which relates them with the utmost minuteness of detail. This book is sold to the devotees who are continually going to the monastery in order to pour their money into the treasury; and after I began to disbelieve the influence of its vaunted Madonna, I named it the Book of Industry. It is written in the worst possible style, and is full of grammatical errors.

"Why do you not correct it?" said Father Pastori, who was at that time the Superior of the monastery; "why do you not revise it, and render it more readable? If you were to arrange the stories in proper order, and dress them up in flowery language, it would be perused with pleasure, and would tend to increase the number of devout worshippers of our Madonna."

"Believe me, I should like very much to correct it as it ought to be; but I am afraid, in this case, it would be much less readable than at present."

"How so?"

"Because out of three hundred pages there would not remain one."

Upon this the old fellow began to grow angry. I will not here repeat how many threats he thundered out against me for daring, as he said, the displeasure of the *Madonna della Quercia*. Little evil, however, has as yet befallen me, that I can trace to this cause.

One day this same old man, who, to say the truth, after all had really a partiality for me, was holding a conversation with me and some others, among whom was Cardinal Velzi, who, as well as myself, belonged to that monastery, at least, to that section or family, though neither of us resided there.

"I have been thinking," said Father Pastori, "of some way of reviving the worship of our holy Madonna; it is very much on the decline; what do you think we should do to awaken the dormant devotion of the people in the neighbourhood? I remember when I was a young man, that all the province of Patrimonio and Umbria, as far as La Marca, used to send pilgrims, votive offerings, wax candles, money for masses, and quantities of other offerings. Now, there is scarcely anything brought, even at the two fairs, and all the rest of the year we receive nothing at all. It is evident that the people no longer think of us, and that their piety is becoming lukewarm. I wish, therefore, to rekindle their devotion to the Madonna, and I think the best way of doing so would be, to send about, through all the neighbourhood, the large picture of the Virgin, with all the miracles inscribed around it; but as the engraving is not a very good one, I have thought of ordering another upon the same plan. What do you say to my idea?"

The Cardinal shrugged his shoulders, and neither said yes nor no. I was silent also.

"Well, I say, what do you think of it? The present engraving was executed more than two hundred years ago, and was retouched about one hundred years since. It is now high time to have a new one, for it seems to have lost its efficacy."

"I know very well," said Cardinal Velzi, "that these things pass current among the people, as matters of pious belief; but the fact is, there are too many of them in Southern Italy. I proscribed many similar observances within my own jurisdiction, when I was master of the sacred palace; besides, these miracles are not sufficiently attested."

"Your Eminence will doubtless recollect," added I, "how both of us, two years ago, prohibited the image of the Madonna of the Augustines of Viterbo, which was surrounded with a legion of devils, crying out, 'To hell with Viterbo.' This story is said to have originated at the beginning of the fifteenth century, when one day a letter issued forth from the sacred image, commanding the devils to quit the precincts of the city, and to follow the said letter as far as it should go. Off went the letter, and away went the devils; the letter fell to the ground about a mile distant, and the devils all sank into the earth on the very same spot; in perpetual memory of which event, even to this day bubbles up a well of boiling sulphureous water, in the identical place, which is said to take its rise from hell.[48] This Madonna has ever since enjoyed the title of *Liberatrix*, or Deliverer. I had frequent disputes with the Prior of the Augustines on this head, and threatened to seize all his pictures, if he made a trade of selling them. The only defence he could make was, that the engraving was ancient, of the same epoch as that of the *Madonna della Quercia*; and I recollect answering that I did not approve of the image *della Quercia* either, and that, for my part, I should do everything I could to prevent the circulation of that also: what then do you think I should do if I saw the image *della Quercia*, with all its pretended miracles around it, restored? Oh! do not entertain any such idea, my dear Father Pastori. I shall be obliged to oppose it, and I am glad to see that our friend the cardinal is of the same opinion with myself. And now, since we are upon this topic, let me, as a son of the monastery, give you another piece of advice. This church of ours has latterly become so filthy and disgusting, with its wooden and *papier maché* statues, its exhibition of heads, arms, legs, and every other part of the body, presented as votive offerings for all kinds of pretended cures, that, what with them, and the miserably painted tablets, broken blunderbusses, rusty daggers, and other objects, which disfigure the walls from top to bottom, any person of good sense would be ready to rush out of the place at the mere sight of them. I should propose, therefore, to take down all these things, whitewash the walls, which is very much wanted, and put all these votive offerings, or monuments of brigandism and superstition, into two or three large rooms adjoining the Church, so as to form a kind of museum of curiosities, for such as may feel inclined to inspect it."

The good old man could here no longer contain himself; but broke out into violent indignation, exclaiming that I was an innovator, a man whose opinions were of the most dangerous description, &c. The Cardinal, however, interposed between us, and so the matter ended.

By this time the change in my manner of thinking began to be publicly talked about. I was represented as not being one of those bigoted *Frati* who give credence to every religious lie, under the cloak of "holy faith;" that I was no great votary of saints and relics, and disbelieved all their miracles. Many other circumstances occurred to establish this opinion of me, one or two of which I will briefly relate.

I was requested to write the religious life of Santa Rosa, the patron saint of Viterbo.[49] This, however, I declined, on the plea that Santa Rosa would not be over-well pleased with my work; upon which the task was separately undertaken by my friend Dr. Selli and my uncle Dr. Mencarini. The former produced a small treatise of little or no importance, and I allowed it to circulate; the latter set to work in good earnest, and forwarded a large volume to the "censor." Now, this uncle of mine had been a second father to me, and was a man whom, of all others, I loved and respected. He was versed in many sciences, a man of refined learning, and a professor of natural philosophy; he was, moreover, a man who shone in society, a sincere friend, a benefactor to his country, and was universally esteemed and beloved.

I was surprised to see so large a volume on so trivial a subject as the life of a poor baker's daughter; though she certainly showed a great deal of talent in the part she took in the political disputes between the Guelfs and Ghibellines, which occurred in her time; and as she was on the pope's side, that is, for the liberty of the "commune," (for popes were liberals in those days,) she joined in the cry against the Emperor Frederic II., she was consequently persecuted by the imperialists, and ran through all the country, declaiming against them. She died at the early age of eighteen; poor but honoured, and highly eulogized by her fellow-citizens. The ignorance of the times attributed to her the power of working miracles, and superstition "dubbed" her a saint. There is no doubt she was a very excellent young woman, and as such, and on no other account, do I honour her memory. I dare say my uncle thought much as I did on the matter; but he got so bewildered with the mass of materials which various earlier biographers had collected together, that he did little more than copy what he found in their works, without giving himself the trouble of investigating their authenticity.

There are not in the whole world such *bonâ fide* liars as the writers of the lives of saints; for "the glory of God"[50] they allow themselves every species of invention and exaggeration. Can a lie ever tend to promote the glory of God? It is a principle I have never acted upon in any case. My uncle was deceived by a parcel of old impostors, and it was for me to undeceive him.

"Now," said I to him one day, "do you believe all you have written?"

"No," he replied; "I was disgusted with a great many things; but I thought it my duty to write, or rather to repeat them, because, having been asserted so long ago, they are now known and believed by everybody."

"Now, my dear uncle, do not say by everybody, for there are ourselves in this very place, who believe nothing about them; and who knows how many others may not have the same good sense? Why should we, then, seek to deceive the ingenuous and simple-minded, particularly the young, who would no longer read the old trash about this said St. Rosa, unless it were dressed up in the pleasing garb of a good style, and written with a show of historical erudition? Is it not a pity—nay, a sin?"

"But if I were not to relate what has been already written and handed down, what would there be to make a life of?"

"Little, I grant; my friend; little, but good. I should give the simple truth. This same Rosa was a very worthy creature, and a woman of spirit for the age in which she lived; full of courage, and loved her country as much as any one. The priests represent her as devoted to the pope; but I, on the contrary, maintain that she was devoted chiefly to politics, and only in a secondary degree to matters of religion. In fact, the people of Viterbo were almost all *Patareni*;[51] and yet, between the pope and the emperor, they held most to the pope, because he did not, like the Emperor, threaten the liberty of the commune, by imposing upon them any particular code of laws, but allowed the people to govern themselves by their own institutions. In short, to me the actions of St. Rosa appear so entirely mixed up with the political events of her time, that if I were writing her life, I should connect it with the history of that period, merely as an episode."

"And who would you get to read it?"

"Everybody, except a few bigots; but perhaps it is for them you are writing?"

These remarks appeared so far to influence my good uncle, that he began to correct his great volume, which soon became reduced to half its size, but gained double in value. Still, I regret to say, that some stories were left which would have been far better away. The truth of the matter is, that although I no longer believed in the miracles of Rome's catalogued saints myself, yet I had not as yet acquired sufficient courage to wage a war of extermination against them. I was more severe with another relation of mine, Dr. Nicola

Grispigni, who had written the life of Lucia di Narni, a bigot, beatified by Rome. He was at that time Professor of Rhetoric in the college at Viterbo, and is now Bishop of Poggio Mirteto, in Sabina. He too had followed the old biographies, and without any selection, had dressed up their worn-out falsehoods in elegant modern phraseology. The manuscript was sent to Rome, and duly approved, with the *nihil obstat* from two theological censors, and the *imprimatur* from the master of the sacred palace; and, as a matter of course, was about to be printed, when by chance it fell under my notice. Never in my whole life had I seen such a tissue of gross falsehoods. I immediately stopped the printing of it, and referred it again to the master of the palace, and received his authority to make all the corrections I might think necessary previous to its publication.

"My dear Dr. Nicola," said I to him, "where on earth did you find all the nonsense that you have put together in this volume?"

"In the biographies of the Beatified[52] Lucia, and especially in that written by a very reverend Dominican, under the approbation of the master of the sacred palace."

"I am delighted to hear it, but these relations are all evidently untrue, and some of them are absolutely immoral. Such, for instance, is that which states that a wife, in consequence of some vow, refused conjugal duty to her husband,—a thing quite at variance with sound morality. Here now is a story invented by some one in the first instance, repeated by others, and now related again by yourself; and which, having once more escaped the eyes of the censor, would have been in print in a very short time. Had I not happened to have seen it, the religious world would again have been regaled with the same lies and the same imposture! And what is all this nonsense about angels descending from heaven to minister to your *Beata!* and all the saints, and the Madonna, the mother of Jesus, coming down to hold conversation with her! Away with all these fables; we have already too many of them; they disgust even the most simple-minded. Religion holds such falsehoods in abhorrence; they are called *pious*, whereas they ought rather to be termed *impious* beliefs. For it is highly impious to mix falsehood with truth in order to mislead the understanding and deprave the heart. You surely are not so simple as to believe everything that is printed *con licenza dei Superiori*, under which authority you have admitted all these foolish stories about Beata Lucia. At any rate I cannot allow the reprinting of them. Revise your book, purge it of such ridiculous matter, and I will then give it my approval."

My friend was easily guided, and having left out what he considered the most difficult to swallow, the work was finished; but after all I was too indulgent, and allowed much to remain which ought to have been expunged: the fact is, as I said before, although I saw what my duty was, I had not then the moral courage to act entirely up to it, a courage which is the particular gift of God's grace.

My reformation must have been the immediate work of God, and therefore from Him I felt myself destined to receive the perception and knowledge of the truth. St. Paul gloried in having received the Gospel not from men, but from God, through whose command he also received authority to preach it. His reform was instantaneous, as was his conversion, and they are wonderful in our eyes. A gradual conversion and a progressive reformation are not so astonishing. The lightning flash amid the darkness of night affects the senses in a far greater degree than the opening dawn that gradually brightens into day. I imagined I had already received the full day-light of truth, whereas it was only that of the morning star, the sweet harbinger of a brighter day. What shall I say then of my entire conversion? God alone knoweth. My understanding unquestionably began to be illuminated about that time, but the conversion of my heart took place at a much later period. I began to be aware that we are not saved by our own merits, but by the merits of Christ; I knew, moreover, that those merits are not imputed to us by the efficacy of the sacraments, but by virtue of faith. This, which I deem the only true system of salvation, I already taught in the schools, preached in the pulpit, and sustained in public, as well as in private conversation: therefore it was that I had incurred the hatred of the priesthood, and of the Jesuits of the Romish Church. But for all this I was not as yet converted at heart. So true it was, that I did not at that time even understand the difference between these two conversions. I was already a Protestant, but not yet sufficiently a Christian. My life had not undergone a formal and complete change, but only a partial amendment. My virtue arose from self-love, and not from faith. I had acquired some practice in the habit of well-doing, but was not yet guided by Divine inspiration. My heart had desires, but not affections. I spoke of Divine love, but did not yet experience it in my soul. Oh! what joy possessed me when I first began to feel its influence. Oh! how delightful is the life of a believer. He lives by faith. He may vacillate for a moment, but he soon returns to the principle that forms the system of his life. The believer, far from considering himself infallible or sinless, feels, on the contrary, the weakness of his nature, trembles for his safety, and incessantly humbles himself before God. True faith does not attribute to man strength that he does not possess. Peter was weak when he believed himself to be strong. Jesus Christ said to the Apostles, "All ye shall be offended, because of me this night."[53] And what was Peter's reply? "Although all shall be offended, yet will not I." And lo! Peter the believer, who esteemed himself stronger than all his brethren, and vaunted himself accordingly, met with the severest humiliation. Who would say with Cephas, "If I should die with thee, I will not deny thee in any wise?" To such a one the reply is ready: "Verily I say unto thee, That this night, before the cock crow, thou shalt deny me thrice."[54]

So true it is that conversion is the work of faith, and this comes by grace. In me faith has been awakened after much experience, accompanied by conviction in the understanding, and affection in the heart. I thank the Lord, who has made me a believer through His grace; and so much the more do I thank Him, as He has given me this grace for the conversion of others. I felt the necessity of my giving up a system which I had found defective in so many points, and experienced a strong desire to assist others in getting out of the same mire. I could no longer hide the truths I had discovered. I seemed a traitor to myself, to my duty, and to the will of God, in concealing my enlightenment; while on the other hand, I saw the danger of publicly acknowledging it. The only way was, to communicate my principles in secret. But the Inquisition is a tremendous power, it possesses every possible means of discovering the most hidden secrets; and in that part of Italy where its laws are in vigour, nothing is concealed from its penetration.

I began my mission in the manner I have related, and the Inquisition soon commenced its proceedings against me. More than once did its officers try to circumvent me, and arrest my progress; but the beneficent hand of Providence was over me, and guided and protected me; so that I never feared anything. No one knew better than I did the artifices of that diabolical tribunal, and the means it employed to hunt out its object. And yet I was not afraid; I felt a certain secret assurance in my mind of my final success. I accordingly quietly pursued the path that Providence and the hand of the Lord had opened out to me, knowing not where my steps might lead me. I was like a man blindfolded, but led by a faithful friend; sure of His care and love, I willingly abandoned myself to His direction.

I will now state what happened to me on leaving Rome in 1835, as well as what took place after my departure from Italy, in 1842. All which will fully explain the complete history of my conversion; which, while it has been to me the most fortunate event of my whole life, will also, I hope, prove the commencement of an era in the history of Italy which my fellow-countrymen have been expecting and looking for during the last 300 years.

I look upon this circumstance as the first link of a long chain, that is one day to be completed. My individual conversion and reformation will, it is to be hoped, be the means of effecting that of many others; how or in what manner, I am unable to judge; certainly not as calculated upon in the popish sanhedrin, but according to the secret arrangements of the Most High. I read in this conversion of mine a most extraordinary event: Rome did all she could to retain me as her defender, as a theologian qualified in every respect to serve her purposes; and I, on the contrary, against the inclination of the natural man, did all in my power to show how much I despised her service, and her flattering offers,—indifferent alike to her honours and her gifts; drawing down upon myself her eternal odium and vengeance. Still I must acknowledge, that it was not myself, but a secret spirit within me, that resisted; overruling my natural inclinations, and preventing my being led away by the proffered allurements of ambition and wealth. I began to look without apprehension on my position with respect to the Church, and my duties connected with it. The dormant idea of Hierarchy had faded from my mind, and that of Community occupied its place. I required not the assistance of the pope to understand the Bible; I looked to the Saviour alone to elevate my soul towards God. It had now become impossible for me to remain any longer under so vile a subjection. Higher aspirations came over me; I was led into other paths, through the adorable dispositions of that Providence by whom the destinies of all men are ordained; the same which, after having permitted for all-wise ends the abomination of popery to dominate during so many ages in Italy, seems now to will its destruction. So may it be. Amen.

## FOOTNOTES:

[39] Rom. xiv. 17.
[40] St. John vi. 63.
[41] Acts x. 13.
[42] Christ-eater.
[43] Matt. vi. 7.
[44] Matt. xv. 7-9.
[45] Matt. xv. 10, 11.
[46] 1 John i. 8, 9, 10, c. v. 16.
[47] Luke xvii. 3.

[48] This is the famous Bullicame of Viterbo, a thermal spring, which existed many years before this famous Madonna. Dante makes mention of it.

[49] Every town in Italy has its patron saint, besides several subordinate ones. Naples has its St. Januarius, and about fifty subalterns.

[50] *Ad majorem Dei gloriam,* is the motto of the Jesuits.

[51] A class of heretics so called.

[52] *Beata* is a degree below Saint, as Bachelor of Arts is below Master.

[53] Mark xiv. 27.

[54] Matt. xxvi. 34.

# CHAPTER X
# MY FAREWELL TO ROME

In the month of February, 1835, I had so arranged my affairs that nothing stood in the way of my projected departure from the Eternal City. I hesitated some time, between two separate modes of accomplishing my purpose; a sudden flight, or the more regular way of setting out in due form and with the permission of the appointed authorities. The former would put an immediate end to all my embarrassment, and give me my complete liberty at once. I was at first disposed to adopt this method, but subsequently abandoned it, on reflecting that I should thereby give occasion to a great deal of discussion with respect to my reasons for so suddenly leaving Rome; more especially as I had never yet publicly given any idea that I was at all dissatisfied with her doctrines, or that I differed in opinion with the monks, or had quitted that faith which I had hitherto advocated to the world with so much applause. It only remained to me, therefore, to adopt the latter plan, which, in a quieter and more convenient way, would suit my purpose, and excite no troublesome inquiries. Accordingly, after due deliberation, I arranged all my plans and left the result to Providence.

Cardinal Serra di Cassano had requested me to preach during Lent, in his archiepiscopal church at Capua. I accepted the duty, and forwarded to the good Father General Olivieri my resignation of the post he had conferred on me; which he was pleased to accept, on condition that, as soon as my duties at Capua were over, I should return to Rome, where, he gave me to understand, fresh promotion awaited me. I made him no promise, merely hinting that it was possible I might return, unless God should think fit to order my steps elsewhere. He did not appear to comprehend my meaning, and my projects were confined within my own breast.

"I hope," said he to me, "you will present yourself to the pope. Cardinal Polidori told me that he wished to see you. I think it would be as well for you to keep up the etiquette in these matters."

"As you wish me to do so, most reverend father, I will go to the pope; but, to tell you the truth, I thought I might dispense with the ceremony."

"Why you know the pope has a regard for you; he frequently inquires after you; and it was only the other day he was talking of a dinner given by

Cardinal Velzi at the Villa Salara, where he said he met you and Cardinal Castiglioni, before he became Pius VIII."

"I certainly remember that dinner, and the conversation I then held with Cardinal Cappellari, now Pope Gregory. He spoke very forcibly concerning truth, and his words will ever remain engraven on my memory; he extolled it as superior to everything, declared that it was God himself, that all truth proceeded from Him, and that all who obeyed the truth were the sons of God. He spoke of Jesus, the Christ, as the visible form of Truth, who being fully imbued with it, as St. John says, showed to the world that in Him, the Word, the *Logos*, the Divine Wisdom, was incarnate. He reminded me, that in His death, Christ bore witness to the truth; and we cannot better follow Him, and become like unto Him, than by a veneration for, and a strict obedience to the truth. And here, placing his hand on my shoulder, he added, 'My dear friend, ever advocate the truth; live for it, combat for it, even die for it, and God will be your reward.' This holy advice I listened to as if it came from an angel; at that moment I really believed him to be inspired. I remember also another remark he made. Cardinal Castiglioni had exhorted me to read Pallavicino's History of the Council of Trent; to which I replied, that I had already given it a perusal, as well as that by Friar Sarpi. 'Well then,' exclaimed the good old man, 'read Pallavicino again,' — and he thundered his words out so loudly, that some present thought he was angry with me. 'What's the matter with Castiglioni? asked Cappellari. 'He wishes me,' I replied, 'to read over and over again the History of the Council of Trent by Pallavicino.' 'He is so passionately fond of that history, that he advises every body to read it,' observed Cappellari; 'for my own part, I should like to see a third writer on the subject, who would give us the true account of that Council. But this work, which ought to be written in Rome, and from the archives of the Vatican, could never be published there.' 'Then,' observed I, 'the truth must not be spoken in Rome!' to which Cardinal Cappellari replied with a smile and a sigh."

Olivieri listened to me with profound attention, then wrung my hand, and recommended me anew to pay my respects to the pope.

There was at this time living in Rome a very respectable man, a certain Father Parchetti. He was well known to a great many people, but had few friends. His universal talent in all kinds of literature had gained him considerable reputation; he was of a liberal and kindly disposition, a keen investigator in all matters of science, and was more worthy of honours than he was ambitious in looking after them; he had, in fact, never received any promotion, simply because he despised it. Strict in his own habits of life, he was indulgent towards others: kind and charitable to the poor, and easy of access to all who were not themselves proud or overbearing. He was a great talker, and was sometimes sarcastic and even satirical in his speech, which arose from a naturally ardent temperament.

To the monk Cappellari he had been a friend, but to Pope Gregory he was an enemy. We had been acquainted with each other from my earliest youth; I never, however, talked about our friendship before other people, as he was in disgrace with the Court, and consequently his associates would have shared in the contempt bestowed upon him by their party. I had not at that time sufficient firmness to go against the tide, and boldly declare my opinion in his favour; but still I had a great regard for him, on account of his sincerity and truth; and I discovered in him so many estimable qualities, that I overlooked his trifling defects. He had frequently given me his counsel and advice. I had consulted him with respect to my scruples of conscience; I had laid before him my new theological views, and he had considerably enlightened me on the subject, and confirmed me more and more in my new opinions. I had recourse to him whenever I required advice. He first taught me what Rome really was—Rome, as influenced by priests and monks, by prelates and cardinals. Whoever wanted information respecting the papal court, applied to Father Parchetti, who knew the secret history of every one connected with it, and was perfectly well informed in the history of the Romish Church; his experience was of seventy years' standing, in the course of which time he had become well acquainted with everything that had happened in Rome, and every exact detail as to place, time, and person.

"Well," said I to him one day, "I am going to leave Rome. I thank you for your good advice as to keeping clear from the snares of office, and shunning ambition in my views. See how well I have eschewed everything of the kind! I am going to Naples, on the plea of having to preach at Capua during the ensuing Lent. I shall be heartily glad to leave this place; I most thoroughly detest it, or, rather, the people who govern in it, and sincerely hope never to return to it. I shall find some good reason or other to remain in Naples, when Lent is over; at any rate, I can petition for my secularization,[55] I shall then be at liberty; and in the quiet of private life, occupied entirely with my studies, I may hope to obtain tranquillity and peace."

"No, my friend," replied Parchetti, "do not hope for peace in Italy, under any circumstances. It is not enough that you keep quiet. You know full well, that among other evils to which those gentry who call themselves our masters are subject, is that of envy. Do you imagine they would let you rest? And suppose you quit the brotherhood of the monks, you would still be among the priests. Well, then, there is the bishop, and his vicars, and others of their set, who would load you with calumnies, and persecute you in a far greater degree than you have had to endure hitherto, and which your present strength would by no means enable you to support. Here there is no middle path; we must be either bigots or hypocrites, as they are, or become subject to their hatred and their malediction, and exposed to every danger and every evil, through their instrumentality. They have adopted as their motto, 'He who is not with us is against us;' and consequently, they reckon every one as their enemy who removes himself ever so little from their prejudices, their customs, and their society. He, moreover, who refuses to bend the knee before the idol of the Vatican, is, as you very well know, looked upon as a heretic: here, it is not God in whom we are to believe, but the pope. C—— and T—— are a couple of atheists; nevertheless, they were both made cardinals. But if you and I were to declare that we believed in the Bible, and in the Bible alone, we should be speedily handed over to the Inquisition, and there condemned as heretics—if, indeed they would do us so much honour; for they begin to be sensible that the term heretic is no longer one of so great reproach as formerly; but still, not to allow us to escape, they would give out that we were condemned for some offence or other against the civil laws, such as theft, adultery, and the like. There is poor Capistrano condemned to perpetual imprisonment in the dungeons of the Inquisition; I once asked one of the officials of the Holy Office what he had to say against such a respectable old man; 'He is a great scoundrel,' was the reply; and on my inquiring why he bestowed on him that epithet, 'Why,' rejoined he, 'because he is guilty of a great many crimes.' 'How?' I exclaimed; 'has he then robbed, borne false witness, or committed murder? But what an abominable thing it is to attribute crimes to so good a man as Capistrano! I will tell you what you yourselves are guilty of, and for which he has justly reproved you—the crime of Herod, who condemned John to death!' Now, listen to me, my dear friend: as long as you remain among either friars or priests, you will never enjoy a moment's tranquillity; but you cannot get out of their way whilst you stay in Italy. The first conclusion therefore is, that in this country you will never be at peace, since both friars and priests will unite to persecute you."

"And what, I pray you, is the second conclusion?"

"The second is, that as long as you continue in the priestly office you never can hope for rest in this country. It is not enough that you cease to be a friar, you must also cease to be a priest: both are equally bad; there is no choice between them; they uphold the same system, and the system itself is bad. You must renounce it altogether, if you would be at peace. But a great difficulty stands in the way; a great obstacle is to be overcome before this can be done; and it is this very obstacle that has hitherto prevented me, also, from shaking off this terrible slavery, which I have a hundred times desired to do. The difficulty I allude to is one which deprives an Italian of all courage; it is, that of being obliged to quit his native country; and for evermore to lose the idea of returning to it. Geneva, they say, is a fine city; and I have heard that in London, too, one may hope to find the means of subsistence. But another Italy we can never hope to see; and nothing, I fear, could compensate for its loss. I speak in a worldly point of view. Certainly, such a step requires courage. I can easily conceive that the first step is the grand difficulty; and, after all, a great deal is in our own imagination: but we Italians, like all southern nations, are swayed more by our imagination than by our senses; our understanding, indeed, may be said to feed upon it. Now, if you have more courage than, I confess, I possess, and can decide on taking the grand leap that will place you beyond Italy, I feel assured you will at length find peace, and become happy."

"This project of yours," I replied, "is the true, the only one; I have frequently entertained the same idea. But, as you observe, it presents a difficulty that appears insurmountable; to quit one's native country, to leave one's relatives behind us, to lose all one's property and one's means of subsistence, to reduce oneself to indigence, and undergo privations always more or less humiliating, is a sacrifice, my dear Parchetti, that a man is not always prepared or willing to make. There must be some great motive, or, to speak more correctly, some sudden impulse from above, similar to that which arrested Saul on his way to Damascus, to impel a man to do that concerning which he was before uncertain and irresolute. Perhaps the day may come when I shall myself be thus influenced; but at present I must proceed gradually, till I acquire greater experience; and I shall always submit to the will of God. As we are on this subject, however, tell me, Father Parchetti, and tell me sincerely for our old friendship's sake, what is your opinion of the Protestants? I speak of those of Geneva and London."

"You have chosen rather a dangerous subject to discuss in Rome; but, however, as we are alone, and no one can overhear us, I will speak out; and may it be for the glory of God and the advancement of truth! This is not the first time I have touched upon the argument between Protestantism and Romanism; and you know how excited I get on that topic, and how apt I am to forget the place I am in, and to whom I may be addressing myself. It has happened more than once that I have inveighed against the Holy Office in the presence of some of its officials, and have, in various public places, spoken pretty freely about Rome, likening her to Babylon, and Geneva to a second Jerusalem. It was fortunate for me that the Inquisition did not get hold of it. Since, however, I have up to the present day escaped being burnt alive, and since the ears of the public have become accustomed to my remarks, I do not imagine they will molest me, now that I am old. In fact, they content themselves with vilifying me in their own way; they call me a madman, a foul-mouthed fellow, who speaks ill of every body, and so on.

And in this manner they repay me for the attacks I make upon them, which I do not cease from doing in the cause of truth.

"But to return to our subject. Protestantism is early Christianity revived, which protests against and denounces later Christianity; that is to say, Romanism, or, more properly, Popery. Having given this definition, the truth of which it is impossible to deny, I proceed to observe that I consider the Protestants are right *de jure,* but that the Romanists arrogate that right to themselves *de facto.* I will explain myself more clearly. The Protestants have the Bible on their side; their doctrine is founded on its truths, and, fortified with them, they boldly challenge the Romanists to enter the field of controversy. But against these truths papistical arguments cannot stand. For this reason I maintain that the Protestants are right *de jure.* On the other hand, the Romanists boast of their traditions, a series of alleged facts more or less ancient, altogether irreconcilable with Scripture, but received on the authenticity of respectable men, whom their own Church has dubbed as saints and doctors. These traditions have given rise to various decisions in councils, and these again have occasioned the celebrated decretals of the popes, bulls, and pontifical constitutions, which serve as so many dogmas of faith with all the upholders of Romanism. And this is how they possess their right *de facto.*

"Now, these two parties are similar to two armies, which have been opposed to each other for the last three hundred years; but they are by no means of equal strength: I speak of human strength. The Protestants have gained over to their side many men of learning and sense, yet they have hitherto failed in their attempts to overthrow the papacy; they have, however, humbled it, and prevented it from domineering over the whole of the Christian world.

"Romanism is nevertheless content with its *de facto* power, which it upholds through the authority of its doctrines and the activity of its Propaganda. It has proclaimed to the vulgar herd, that the holy men who have worked miracles were all of them of its own Church; and this assurance is sufficient for those who have no better principle to guide them than the criterion of authority. It has, moreover, found means to send its missionaries to all parts of the world. The great secret of Rome is this—money to send out missionaries, and missionaries to send back money. Whoever sees the expenditure of the Propaganda 'Fidei,' praises the zeal of Rome, and imagines that the pope makes an immense sacrifice every year, to supply the wants of such an institution. How many bishops, vicars apostolic, friars, and missionary priests, derive incomes from the Propaganda! And who supplies all this money? Is it Rome? and where does it come from? Again, who maintains the Court of Rome, with all its crimes and all its caprices? who, if it is not the Propaganda? Look at the offices of Rome—the *Dateria*, the chancery, the office for briefs, the council, the bishops and regulars, the rites and indulgences, sacred relics, and the like; whence do all these derive support? Evidently from foreign parts. And what, in return for all this money and protection, does Rome send abroad? Indulgences and quackeries. Who are they who sustain the Court of Rome, and the papacy, in all its ambition—I will not say its honour, because it never had any—if they be not the Romanists abroad? and not only they, but even Protestants themselves, now, contribute to the coffers of the Romish Church. How willing are the English to pay at our festivals! and Rome wants nothing else, desires nothing but money. She thinks herself the first power in the world, and has gone so far as to insult and hold in derision the Protestants. They must be good people, indeed, to submit to it, for they have it in their power to make Rome tremble, and reduce her to dust.

"But to return to the subject of religion. The Protestants have only one defect, that of being divided among themselves, and often waging war upon each other. And now I will tell you a secret, that you cannot know as yet; but I do. It is one of the artifices of Catholic missionaries (especially the Jesuits) to sow discord as much as possible among the Protestants; because they can afterwards profit by it, by fishing in troubled water, according to the common saying. So long as the Protestants will moot the question, whether their Church should be Episcopalian or Presbyterian, and go on excommunicating each other, Roman priests and friars will make proselytes from each party. Now, these good Protestants do not see how this very question is settled *de facto*, without noise, or rumour, or division, by the Romanists. They have their priests and friars; the former governed by bishops, and consequently episcopalian; the latter (and in these I include monks and regular clergy, &c.) subject to their superiors, who are nothing more nor less than presbyters. Consequently, this set, which exceeds that of priests in numbers, is, in fact, Presbyterian. Priests and friars have also their disputes; and it is impossible there should not be disputes amongst any body of men whatsoever; but they are soon settled: for both parties have the Church between them in common, as well as the pulpit and the confessional. There is no difficulty in passing from one order to another, as you well know; and when they do, they change not only their habits, but their rites, forms of prayer, and every branch of discipline. I do not see why it should not be permitted to Protestants to do so likewise. But, above all, what I blame is, that the Episcopalians, for example, shut their churches against the Presbyterians. I here speak of the ministers; because the people themselves would care little about mere forms, provided they find in their pastors (whether Episcopalian or Presbyterian) that spirit, and knowledge, and zeal, that is according to faith in the Lord Jesus Christ."

"My dear, friend," I replied, "what you say is excellent. It never struck me before, and certainly books would never have imparted it to me. I thank you for the lesson, and again repeat, that though I quit with sorrow the one Rome I so much love, I do so execrating from my soul the other that I so much hate; and who can say whether you do not hate it even more than I do, and did not hate it long before I did; for you have known it longer and better than I have! But tell me another thing, (and may the blessing of God be with you!)—Do you think this wicked Rome—this Babylon, as you call it, and which St. John the Evangelist calls 'the great whore,' 'with whom the kings of the earth have committed fornication,'[56]—do you think it will always remain in such transgressions, or do you believe a day will come in which popish Rome will be reformed, and that we shall unite with the Protestants to form one only church; that is, one and the same body of believers in the pure doctrine of ancient Christianity? Tell me truly your opinion—do you prophesy that it will be so?"

"I will tell you what I think; but first I will say that which I believe. I believe that popish Rome will be destroyed. The eighteenth chapter of the Apocalypse strengthens me in this belief. I also think that papal Rome can in no way reform itself. Popes are bound hand and foot, so that they cannot move. Popery is become immovable—a petrifaction. Can she alter her creed to anything different from that composed by Pius IV.? She must first destroy the Council of Trent. Can the Latin Church return to the faith of the Greek Church, in all in which the latter is right? She must first destroy the Council of Florence. Can she, in short, be brought to approve the doctrine that the Reformers profess? and that, too, after having burnt as many of the Reformers themselves as she could get into her clutches? This outrage was first committed by the Council of Constance, by which those two holy men, John Huss and Jerome of Prague, were sentenced to be burnt alive! Would Rome, then, condemn the Council of Constance? The French, in one of their Gallic propositions,[57] (which, by-the-bye, is not prohibited,[58]) would come forward and say that the council is superior to the pope, and cannot be destroyed by him. So you see that Rome has deprived herself of every means of extrication, and shut the door upon the possibility of return.

"Papal Rome must therefore necessarily remain as she is, or cease to exist. But she will never die by her own hand, and she will make every possible struggle against any other that may be lifted up to give her her death-stroke; unless it be the hand of God, which, let us hope, will strike her so surely that she shall never raise her head again. So be it. Amen. And this may be the case even in our time. Do you not think, indeed, that she herself is hastening the moment, and that, as David says, she will fall into the pit she has dug for others?

"Yes, yes; the Lord blindeth those whom He wills to destroy. Rome is committing the greatest blunders every day, and does not know how to correct them. And the hour will come when she will make a last and fatal one. Can you guess what it will be?"

"Certainly not; but I should like to hear it from you."

"Listen, then, and remember it, because I shall not live to see it, although you may. I am already old, and the Lord will, most likely, soon take me to himself, before my eyes have seen the salvation of Italy.

"But now mark what I foretell. The war between Catholicism and Protestantism will be renewed. However improbable a religious war may appear, in these times of liberalism, it is nevertheless inevitable, and cannot be far distant. And Rome herself will be the exciting cause, inasmuch as the missionaries of the Propaganda, ignorant and blind as they are, and liars by profession, industriously circulate the report that through their labours all the world is about to be converted to papacy; that the Madonna and the saints are working miracles on every side. And so they will instigate Rome to commit some act of imprudence.

"Remember the case of Leo XII. who in 1824 created an Archbishopric of Grand Cairo; and, without any consultation with the Viceroy, appointed as archbishop that inefficient youth Cashiur, and gave him for vicar such a knave as Father Canestrari; sending them both to Alexandria, to make converts of all the Mussulmans, beginning with Mahomet Ali himself. The end of the affair was ridiculous enough, excepting for the condemnation of the poor Archbishop. But who can tell what was the real intention of Pope Leo and his advisers? Now what I foresee is this: the influence of Rome in the British Isles must produce its effect, which is that of converting many Protestants to our faith. If to the English and Irish missionaries which Rome has hitherto employed, those of Italy, and more especially the Jesuits, are united, proselytes cannot fail. In fact, they will be so numerous, and will excite so much interest, that Rome will be led to imagine that the time has arrived for her to take England by assault. Accordingly, the Pope will create Bishops and Archbishops, declaring the Protestant hierarchy completely null and abolished. England, not being prepared for this master-stroke of policy, will for the moment be too astonished to testify her sense of its audacity; but soon recollecting her former history, and conscious of her power, she will shake off the lethargy that has so long oppressed her, and permitted an enemy to enter into her house; and perceiving that not only is her substance wasted, but her rights usurped, and her Church outraged, she will do that which every person of sense would do, when conscious of having erred, of having been incautious, ill-advised, and imprudent: she will refuse to continue her vain indulgence, and will withdraw the hand of friendship from the Church of Rome,—she will institute new laws to prevent usurpation, and will drive away the aggressors, forcing them to restore what they have stolen: in short, she will destroy the nests of these crows,— the only method of preventing their increase,—and once more put them to flight, and banish them beyond her seas. England will do this the very day that Rome gives her sufficient provocation: and that day will be fatal in its results. Italy, wearied out with popery, will profit by the opportunity; all her strength will be exerted to break her old chains, and break them she will! The papacy will be destroyed in Italy by the Italians themselves; and the idol of the Vatican, before which the pagans of modern times have for so many ages bent the knee, will be driven into exile, an object of mockery and derision. Yes, 'the man of sin, the son of perdition,' who has seduced the world by his lies, will have the finger of scorn pointed at him by the whole world. This, my friend, is what I prophesy: when it comes to pass, recollect what my words have been."

These sentiments delivered by the good old man in the year 1835, now appear as if they had been dictated by inspiration.

One evening, Cardinal Polidori conducted me to the pope, who was in a very jovial humour. A Venetian priest, a friend of his Holiness, was present. The Cardinal conversed with the priest, whilst the pope took me aside, and, somewhat profanely, addressed me as follows:—

"What is the purport of this nocturnal visit? You follow the example of Nicodemus, who visited the Lord at night."

"His Eminence the Cardinal chose this time to present me. I am come to ask the blessing of your Holiness, before I set out for Capua, where I am summoned by the cardinal-archbishop to preach during Lent. The papal benediction will, I trust, be followed by the blessing of God."

"May the Lord bless you! After Easter, I hope you will return to Rome: is not that your intention?"

"I cannot promise. After so many years of fatigue, I need a little repose. I may perhaps visit Naples for a short period."

"Naples is a dangerous place to go to: its luxurious climate, its numerous attractions of every description, so powerfully enchant the mind that it is difficult to get away from their seductive influence. I hope you will not become a Neapolitan. But tell me, is there any particular reason why you are desirous to quit Rome? It appears to me that you are not quite satisfied with your situation here? Perhaps matters are not according to your mind at the Minerva. But the monks are not better at Naples than they are at Rome: I am of opinion that if you complain of them here, you will equally do so there."

"In that case, Holy Father, I should find means to separate myself from them altogether. Your Holiness would not withhold from me your permission to secularize,[59] as many others have done."

"And if that should not be sufficient?"

"God will provide for the rest."

I now began to be persuaded that my getting rid of my employments of Rome, of quitting the city, and even of abandoning the monks, would not be sufficient. Father Parchetti had foretold it all; the pope too seemed to be fully aware of my discontent, and to have a pretty good idea of what was to follow. Nevertheless, I had not yet learned to go boldly forward; I advanced in my onward path step by step, and passed through many states of sorrow and temptation. For example, though I already abhorred popery, I still continued to visit the pope, and even felt a veneration towards his person, which no doubt was the result of habit and early education. I detested the cardinals as a body, yet I was on friendly terms with several of them: there was no great harm in that. But with respect to the mass, although I was thoroughly persuaded of its imposture, and of the two great heresies in its doctrine, I still continued to perform it; certainly without devotion, yet with a show of earnestness: I very seldom celebrated it, but had not the courage to abandon it altogether. I became anxious and worn out, and felt a strong necessity to throw myself into the arms of a better faith, since my present one, so far from satisfying me, every day rendered me more and more wretched.

The importance I attached to this departure from Rome is worthy of remark. I seemed to be leaving it never more to return. On every former occasion of absence I had never thought it necessary to make parting visits to my friends; but now I sought out all my acquaintance to bid them farewell. Many days were consumed in parting and complimentary visits, which I had never before been accustomed to make. One day I was dining with Monsignore Cioja, the governor of St. Spirito, and two of that order of canons (which, I believe, is now abolished) were there. The discourse turned on Germany and England. One of these canons was a man of learning; not so the other: both of them, however, joined in the conversation.

"Do you not think Luther was in the wrong," said one of them to me, "in making himself the head of a church? And in England, what a farce it is to see the king placed at the head of religion!"

"You do not understand what you are talking about," replied I; "Luther never made himself the head of the Church; neither are the kings of England at the head of religion. Both the Lutherans and the Anglicans acknowledge no other head than Jesus Christ. He, as St. Paul asserts, is the sole Head of the Church. And for this reason, my dear canon, that a Church does not mean a body of priests or bishops, but a people and congregation of believers. It is very well that the bishops should have authority over the priests, and among all the bishops one must be the chief: in the Latin Church, the first, the head of the other bishops, is the patriarch of Rome; in the Greek Church it is the patriarch of Constantinople; in the Anglican Church there are two primates, who for the government of the Church, as regards worship, depend altogether on the king and the parliament. What do you consider objectionable in this?"

"That the king and the parliament," replied the other canon, "can understand nothing at all about ecclesiastical matters, as the bishops do; that the king of England and the parliament have never been addressed in the character or person of Peter, in the words, 'Feed my sheep;' that the king and the parliament have no apostolic succession—they do not belong to the hierarchy—consequently are not invested with any spiritual authority whatever."

"Allow me," I rejoined, "to make a few comments on your observations. You say, the kings of England and the parliament do not understand ecclesiastical matters. You imagine that the Protestant sovereigns are as uninformed in Church affairs, as the rulers of Roman Catholic countries, who require to consult their theologians on such points, (and these now-a-days are invariably Jesuits.) The sovereigns of England, of Prussia, of Hanover, of Wittemburgh, and other Protestant dominions in Germany, understand quite as much about religion as the pope and his cardinals.[60] The first study of Protestants, is the study of their Bible, in which they are all well read. In the British parliament there are men learned in every department of science; there are even bishops and their primates: in cases of difficulty it resolves itself into a council, in which religious questions, like others, are rationally argued, and brought to a settlement. No one among them pretends to infallibility; if the question before them is not made sufficiently clear in a first sitting, it is argued in a second, or in a third, until they are agreed upon it. There are no oracles in England or in Germany; these are for the benefit of Rome only: there are only believers; who, however are possessed of true Christian knowledge, and are under the guidance of the Lord. Now, it was to the believers that the words of Christ were spoken: 'Feed my sheep.' 'Peter' is not intended to denominate the person (his true name indeed was Simon), but it is an appellative; as when, for instance, I call you 'canon.' By Peter is to be understood every one who is a man of firmness and stability; in short, a believer. And for this reason it is that St. Augustine, alluding to these words of Christ to Peter, says more than once, 'What was addressed to Peter was addressed to all;' that is to say, to all believers. *Quod dictum est Petro, dictum est omnibus.* Therefore to you and to me, who are neither the Apostle Peter, nor his privileged successors; to us two, who are not even bishops, but simply believers, are the words of Christ spoken: 'Feed my sheep.' Do you see any difficulty now in this matter? If the sovereigns of England and the members of the parliament are in the true faith, have they not also the office of feeding the people committed to their charge?

"Can you define to me what is the nature of this apostolic succession, which is so much talked of in Rome? Is it a peculiar right of heirship which the apostles bequeathed you? And what, I ask, would be the nature of the bequest? The apostles were rich in faith, and consequently were full of the Holy Spirit and celestial gifts. As they had faith, they also possessed an understanding of the holy Word, and they had that Spirit which rendered their teaching infallible. Being full of faith they accomplished prodigies. But can you really believe that faith is transmitted by succession, and granted as a privilege to a particular class of men? According to your view, then, who would be the true successors of the apostles? The pope and his bishops? But are they grounded in faith, as the apostles were? If so, then truly are they their successors. But if, on the other hand, they are wanting in this faith, to which of the Apostles would they succeed? To that only one who was without faith; to Judas Iscariot.

"I can very well understand how Apostolic succession may take place among the true servants of the Lord—among those who live conformably to the Divine laws. Without doubt, this succession is bestowed on those zealous ministers of religion, who, in the midst of danger, difficulty, and privation, warm with holy charity for the salvation of others, bear to distant regions the name of Jesus Christ. Would you equally bestow the title on those fat priests, clothed in their rich gala dresses of various colours, who rise from their luxurious tables, glutted with the choicest viands, to repose on soft couches, or to seat themselves in their gilded coaches, and endeavour therein to digest their sumptuous meal?

"The apostolic succession through the laying-on of hands, is an idle dream; invented by priests, in order that the laity may not look at their vices, but at their dignity; and on account of that quality, at least, hold them in some sort of respect! Now I would propose, that if these persons are to be objects of public veneration, Judas Iscariot also, who was one of the chosen twelve, should be held in the same estimation by Rome.

"But let us return to the sovereign and parliament of England, who, according to your doctrine, ought to have no ecclesiastical jurisdiction, since they are not in the ecclesiastical hierarchy. That is to say, they are not of those for whom their mother requested of the Lord the highest offices in the church, saying, 'Grant that these my two sons may sit, the one on thy right hand, and the other on thy left, in thy kingdom.'[61] At that time it was that the first idea of a hierarchy arose among the followers of Christ. Concerning which project, however, I find no other approval on the part of our Lord than that contained in his subsequent words spoken to the apostles and to their successors: 'Ye know that the princes of the Gentiles exercise dominion over them, and they that are great exercise authority upon them. But it shall not be so among you: but whosoever will be great among you, let him be your minister; and whosoever will be chief among you, let him be your servant.'[62] Might not this, now, be the beginning of the ecclesiastical hierarchy?"

"St. Paul tells us that Jesus Christ himself 'gave some, apostles; and some, prophets; and some, evangelists; and some, pastors and teachers.'[63] Now here is sufficient gradation to form a hierarchy. And the apostle says, in another place, that there are in the Church of Christ 'diversities of gifts ... differences of administrations ... diversities of operations ... to one is given by the Spirit the word of wisdom; to another, the word of knowledge by the same Spirit; to another faith by the same Spirit; to another the gifts of healing by the same Spirit; ... to another prophecy; to another discerning of spirits; to another divers kinds of tongues; to another the interpretation of tongues;'[64] &c. Now all this being of ordination, implies an office and a ministry derived from another. And we call this a hierarchy."

"On the contrary, I find that all this is operated in the Church 'by the same Spirit,' and 'by the same Lord.' 'There are,' says St. Paul, 'diversities of operations, but it is the same God that worketh all in all.'[65] Do you find a hierarchy in the human body? You are aware that the apostle has likened the Church to the human body. Listen to, and consider his words. 'For us the body is one, and hath many members, and all the members of that one body, being many, are one body: so also is Christ.'[66] And so it also is with the Church of Christ."

"But is there not a hierarchy belonging to the Church in heaven? Equally, then there must be one in the Church upon earth."

"*Nego consequentiam et paritatem.* It is no reason that because it is so in heaven, it must be so upon earth. Besides, I know nothing concerning the hierarchy in the Church in heaven. If by Church you mean the assembling together of human spirits, who are blessed in the Lord, in my opinion, they are equal among themselves, and God himself is over them all. They have neither rank nor office; nor have I ever been able to suppose who was the greatest among them."

"Was not St. Michael the Archangel called the chief of the heavenly hierarchy?"

"In that case, he would belong to the hierarchy of the angels; not to that of men. But the Romish Church finds a hierarchy everywhere. I assure you, I know of none; there is none mentioned in the Bible. How is it, then, revealed to us?"

This argument was long and interesting. On quitting the house, we crossed the Piazza, and all three (the two canons and myself) went into the Church of St. Peter. Before leaving Rome, I appeared to myself to be under the necessity of paying a visit to this church, which every time I entered it inspired me with different sensations. I had never been so devout as to worship at what is called the tomb of St. Peter and St. Paul, because (I believe the first time I entered the place) I overheard a priest say, speaking of this tomb, "I, for my part, have no faith in the authenticity of this; and I have good reasons for doubting it: if, however, it were not credited, who would come here to visit and to pray to the holy reliques, and fulfil their vows of gifts and thanksgiving?" Ever after this, I looked upon the place where so many lamps are burning and so many people praying, with great indifference. I never either knelt or prayed there, but always turned another way. On the present occasion, my two priests knelt down to offer a short prayer to St. Peter;[67] I, without taking notice of them, occupied myself with looking up into the cupola, till they should have finished.

"What a prodigy of art!" exclaimed one of my companions. "This truly may be called a church! In the whole world there is not another like it. I should call it the temple, *per antonomasia*, like that of the Jews. What say you? It must have cost its weight in gold."

"I should rather call it '*Haceldama*,' or the field of blood,[68] since the price of it was not so much gold as it was blood."

"Truly," rejoined the other canon, "your remark is just: the field that the high priests purchased with the money of Judas, was so called. And St. Peter's was built with that derived from the sale of indulgences, sent into Germany by Leo X."

"Since we are on this subject," said the elder of my companions, turning himself towards me, "explain to me a little about these same indulgences. Is it true, as they say, that a plenary indulgence immediately introduces one into paradise?"

"No doctrine whatever," I replied, "is so completely incomprehensible to me as that of indulgences. According to what is stated concerning them, it would appear that the infinite merits of Jesus Christ, and of the saints, and of the Virgin Mary, are, by authority of the pope, bestowed on such individuals as perform certain prescribed works; one among which is the payment of a sum of money. Much has been written on the subject, as to the origin, nature, and effect of these indulgences; and all agree that there is in the Church a treasury or bank of these merits, and that the pope has the power to draw upon it, and dispose of it as he chooses. This is what is taught: it is of very little consequence whether theologians believe it or not, so long as the people do."

"You believe, then, that the theologians have no faith in indulgences?"

"I am certain they have not. Whoever attentively examines this doctrine finds it to be new, extravagant, and anti-scriptural. The early Christians knew nothing about it: there is no vestige of it in the writings of the fathers. How, indeed, can it be supposed that the pope has the power to apply the merits of Jesus Christ to a person who pays him a sum of money, or makes a pilgrimage, or prays before a particular image; or to one who persecutes the heretics, who delivers them up to the Inquisition, and does his utmost to have them burned alive? The Scripture teaches us that the merits of the passion and death of Christ are applicable to us through faith; not through the operation of any man, but from Jesus Christ himself, who is the only Head of the invisible Church, the only High Priest; as it is written of Him, He, 'because he continueth ever, hath an unchangeable priesthood. Wherefore he is able also to save them to the uttermost that come unto God by him, seeing he ever liveth to make intercession for them. For such an high priest became us, who is holy, harmless, undefiled, separate from sinners, and made higher than the heavens; Who needeth not daily, as those high priests, to offer up sacrifice, first for his own sins, and then for the people's: for this he did once, when he offered up himself.'[69] Such is the doctrine of St. Paul concerning the merits of Christ and their application. As to the merits of the Virgin Mary and other saints, I conceive the inventors of indulgences are altogether mistaken, since no human being whatsoever has any merit due to him for his good works, as it is written, 'So likewise ye, when ye shall have done all those things which are commanded you, say, We are unprofitable servants.'[70] Certainly, no one of them has any overplus to bestow, as a legacy to the Church of Rome."

"What doings are these!" exclaimed the canon, turning to his companion. "Who, after hearing even these few revelations, can believe any longer in the virtue of indulgences?"

"My dear friends," continued I, "there are many other things I could tell you, should I have the pleasure of meeting you again. It is useful to discuss these topics, in order to elucidate the truth; if you cannot do so with me, at least do so among yourselves. Do not be afraid of reading books that are called heretical. You know very well that in this country, whatever is not in accordance with their own doctrines, the priests condemn as heretical; and it frequently happens that these doctrines are nothing else but what regards the mitre and the belly, as Erasmus said."

This conversation was not without its good effects. My two canons began to open their eyes. Some years afterwards I met one of them at Naples, who told me of a work on the Bible which they had undertaken conjointly. Their views were truly Christian. May it be the will of God that through faith they may be regenerated into newness of life.

I continued to pay my parting visits, letting all my friends know that I was about to leave Rome.

"You intend," observed some of them, "to return to us, we hope."

"I cannot say," I replied; "I do not think my return probable."

"Oh! but you will though," said Monsignore Ubaldini, "a canon of St. Peter's assured me that you would return to Rome to be consecrated bishop. The pope told Monsignore Acton so, the other day, when he was speaking about you."

"May Heaven preserve me from such a misfortune! If I could have foreseen such an intention on the part of the pope, I should have done all in my power to have got out of the way of such a chastisement from God."

"How! do you call a bishopric a chastisement from God?"

"And can you esteem it otherwise? The office of a bishop, such as it is at present in the Romish Church, is altogether unscriptural. Read the Epistles of St. Paul to Timothy and to Titus, and compare what a bishop ought to be, with what he really is."

"Well, if you were to be made bishop, you might begin by giving a better example."

"Yes, and that would serve to send me more speedily to the Inquisition."

"How! a bishop, for doing his duty, would be sent to the Inquisition?"

"Unquestionably. The first duty of a bishop is to preach a 'sound doctrine;' and that would be sufficient to condemn him at once. The doctrine at present taught by the bishops is no longer that of the evangelists or the apostles, but that of decretals and canons. Do you imagine, my dear monsignore, that I could be brought to tamper with my conscience, so far as to preach differently to what I thought? Do you recollect what I said to you, when Monsignore Acton and yourself used to come to me in an evening to study theology: that the foundation of this science could be found in no other place than in the Holy Scriptures? We ought, therefore, as soon as ever we perceive that any doctrine which may be offered to us is in opposition to the Scriptures, immediately to reject it. This you admitted as a principle. We had none of us at that time made application of it, but we were quite resolved to do so, when necessity might require it. Well, this necessity presented itself to me the moment I became aware that certain doctrines in the Romish Church are opposed to Holy Scripture. You, too, may arrive at the same conclusion, if you will take the trouble to examine these matters for yourself."

"Oh! that is not very likely to happen. My practice is, to rely entirely on the authority of the Church of Rome, and so I am spared the trouble of any investigation."

This maxim of Monsignore Ubaldini's, I am sorry to say, is generally adopted by men of mere worldly wisdom in the Romish Church. They allege that they are themselves not competent to judge in questions between the Church and the Bible, which of the two has reason on its side, and that it is consequently better to avoid discussion, lest their conscience should be disturbed thereby. "We have no business," say they, "to call the Church to account for any of her acts; we are bound, on the contrary, to give an account if we have not obeyed her." This is their argument, which is full of sophistry and deceit.

Two opposite feelings at that time influenced my mind with respect to my leaving Rome. I was convinced of the necessity of separating myself from a class of persons whom I held in such aversion; I longed to escape altogether from the city that I considered was polluted by their presence; and I must frankly confess that I could not help condemning to the utmost the whole race of priests, and invoking the vengeance of Heaven upon the Vatican, hoping that I should myself one day see the people, blessed with the light of truth, and aware of their own rights, rise up against their oppressors. All this made me desirous to hasten my departure from Rome. On the other hand, I was about to quit the land of my affection: a Roman by birth,[71] I loved my native country, as I love it now, and as I ever shall love it, while life remains. How then could I tear myself away without grief of heart? In the midst of my desire to depart, I was overwhelmed with affliction; at one time I expressed my satisfaction, at another my grief, at the thought of going.

In walking through the streets, I met on every side, lordly priests, who seemed to be the masters of Rome; cardinals in their gilded coaches, whose looks denoted their desire to be saluted by the passers-by. But I turned aside from their path, and looked on the people; that beloved people, who are not made to be the slaves of priests; an intelligent people, full of genius and good sense, exceedingly amiable in conversation, uniting wit and elegance of diction with judgment and discernment in their mode of thinking; a people proud of their traditionary history, with a natural superiority about them which the priests have never been able to overrule.

How frequently have I heard one of the laity disputing with a priest, and very often having the best of the argument! How frequently have I stopped to admire their various costumes, especially on festivals; and to take pleasure in witnessing their gaiety!

One day, passing along the Lungara, in the Trastevere, I observed a number of persons, chiefly women, collected together around one of those mendicant friars who go about relating visions and miracles to the people, to induce them to bestow more liberal gifts and offerings on their saints and their Madonnas. He had a box in his hand, like those in which church money is generally collected, and was just then begging *baiocchi* for one of his saints. I had the curiosity to stop to hear what was going on between him and the people, who were joking and laughing around him.

"Uncle Friar,"[72] said one of the women, "what a glorious life you lead! We poor creatures must work hard to get through the day; our husbands have to sweat to gain a morsel of bread; and we are destitute of almost every comfort; but you, through the favour of St. Francis, can live in plenty, without a single care; you have nothing upon earth to do, but to come and tell your miracles to us, in the hope of drawing a little money out of our pockets, for you are never satisfied. Come, work us a miracle, if you can; persuade St. Francis, who has such wonderful power, to cause us to find a good purse of money when we return home: I promise to share it with you."

"It is a good joke," observed another woman, "for the friar to seek money of us poor folks. Let him go to the pope; he has got plenty."

"Would it not be better," said a fellow who was standing by, "for the friar to make our fortunes, by giving us the lucky numbers in the lottery? We could give him rare contributions then."

"Well!" said the friar, "let me go; I see it is of no use my staying here."

"No, no!" exclaimed several voices; "you shall not go without giving us the numbers."

"These friars," observed an old woman, "have dealings with the devil; they are sure to know what numbers will turn up prizes."[73]

"I think," said a boy, "that we had better take the old friar home, and keep him without victuals, till he tells us."

Another proposed that he should be taken to the *osteria*, and well plied with wine, in order to get the secret out of him.

The friar consented to this latter proposition, on the understanding that the wine was good. Accordingly, off they set in a pretty strong body; and no doubt they got merry enough.

This little incident led me to reflect on the cause of the idleness and immorality of the common people; and I saw clearly that it had its origin from the example of this odious class of society, which shuns all manner of employment, detesting industry, and everything tending to produce; while, on the other hand, it is greedy to consume: a parasitical race, living entirely at the expense of others, and on the fat of the land too, without ever troubling their heads about its cultivation. Oh! how I should like to root out these impostors, scandalous alike for their slothfulness, their ignorance, and their vices.

These idle drones are the real cause why, in the southern parts of Italy, we find our population so generally inert and sluggish. They see these friars, who, like the ravens in the parable, "sow not, neither reap," enjoy all the necessaries of life. Is it not very natural that they should look with an envious eye on such an easy lot, and endeavour as much as possible to make their own like it? Let us hope, for the welfare of my dear country, that this worthless race may be wholly extirpated; and that in future, if any one be determined to turn monk, or hermit, he may do so in the best manner he can; without coming to disturb others, who in the holy bands of matrimony obey the Divine laws—let him, I say, separate himself entirely from the world, and live in a wilderness at once; and renounce in good earnest, and not in deceitful words, the comforts and the pleasures of society.

I was on the point of departure from Rome, when I received a summons from Cardinal Falsacappa. I had never been particularly friendly with him, and did not know that he interested himself about me. I thanked him for having, as he said, spoken favourably of me to the pope, and also for his courteous expressions. But the principal object of his desiring to see me was to keep me at Rome, or at least to obtain a promise from me that I would return, as soon as my business at Capua was terminated.

"No," said I, "I cannot promise what I do not intend to perform. Indeed, to tell your Eminence the plain truth, I do not mean ever to return to Rome again, unless a wonderful miracle should take place."

"And what would that be?"

I was silent, to give him to understand that what I had in my mind was not to be spoken in the ear of a cardinal, without danger. And in fact his Eminence appeared to take my meaning perfectly well.

"I understand," said he; "it is not always prudent to speak out: confidence can only exist between friends. A cardinal is frequently to be pitied, since he inspires no confidence, and never enjoys the delights of friendship."

"And what more than you already possess, do your Eminences desire?"

"I ask of you, what is it that we really possess, that is so valuable? You who are intimate with so many cardinals know what their life is. Are there in the whole world men more sacrificed than we are? Loved by no one, not even by our nearest relatives, we are frequently hated by our own brethren; and are certain to incur the odium of all those who desire our favour, protection, or interest, and fail in their hopes. Our very servants are often our enemies: they spy out our faults and make them known to the public. Every one praises us to our face, even to adulation; behind our backs their censures amount to calumny. Does this appear to you an enviable life? I think a cardinal is more an object of compassion than of envy. Our only advantage is in the opportunity we occasionally have of doing good to others. And if we always availed ourselves of it, it would be well for us; otherwise, even that is a misfortune. I mention these things to give you my own idea of a life which many esteem as so fortunate and happy. I cannot, therefore, wish you may ever wear a cardinal's hat. Far better is a private life."

"I am glad to hear this from your Eminence. You are not the first cardinal who has made these complaints. Cardinal Velzi, among others, frequently exhorted me never to desire a dignity like his own, observing that he himself would gladly relinquish it. For my part, I make my bow to their Eminences, and do not trouble my head with their affairs."

"I understand—you have but little veneration for them. But I do not wish to assume the Cardinal over you. Consider me as a friend, and speak to me as such."

"Well, then, to a friend I should in all confidence say, that I leave Rome grieved at heart, on account of the abominable acts of the government, and the false and anti-scriptural character of the Church. I would say to a friend, that, having no longer any hope of seeing things mend, in so corrupted a system, my prayer was, that all that was incapable of being reformed might be cut off. All this I should say to a friend, though not to a cardinal. It would need no explanation, since the political and religious state of Rome is sufficiently notorious."

The good Cardinal sighed; he sought, however, to persuade me that under such circumstances a good man ought not to abandon his country, but rather remain in it, and endeavour to be of use. I convinced him, however, that the idea was altogether hopeless; that neither he nor I, even with the assistance of some few others, whom we might be able to rely upon, could do anything towards the reforming of that which was old and callous. It had been tried before, and without success, and the lives of those who made the attempt were sacrificed. And here, I remember the poor Cardinal threw his arms round my neck, almost weeping.

"All honest men, then," he exclaimed, "all real lovers of their country, will abandon us! Surely the wrath of God hangs over us.... May I be taken hence before I see the punishment that is preparing for this unhappy country!"

Such were the parting words of the good man, as he dismissed me from his presence. It is well known how he subsequently was the victim of his own philanthropy.[74]

I next visited Cardinal Micara, an old friend of mine, long before he found out that I was also intimate with Luigi da Bagnaja, his enemy and rival, but whom I esteemed for his many good qualities. I esteemed Micara also for his talents and his liberality, and above all things, I liked to hear him declaim against the Court of Rome. No cardinal was ever so severe as he was, against the vices and luxury of this court. He always himself, on gala days, appeared in his old shabby dark-coloured coach, drawn by very ordinary horses, and with servants in the plainest livery. He generally resided in the Capuchin monastery, where he dined with the monks, on the common fare. Being made Bishop of Frascati, he inhabited an apartment in the Seminary, and accustomed himself to the same table as the Professors. He would have been accounted an excellent man, in every respect, had he not retained too much of his early education in the cloister, which rendered him jealous, invidious, and censorious; faults too generally the result of an intercourse with the brotherhood.

The Cardinal was not much liked by his colleagues. I have frequently heard them openly abuse him. This, however, was by no means to his disadvantage; indeed, the common people, who instinctively hate the whole race of cardinals, liked him all the better on that account. Many of his sayings were in great repute among them, as well as many passages in his discourses before the pope and cardinals, in which he boldly denounced the manner of living among these "princes of the Church."

At length, having paid and received all my visits, I quitted Rome with a lacerated heart. I had never before experienced so much reluctance to absent myself as I felt on the present occasion. I seemed to have given up so many things! I could not express my sensations: I was like one who is obliged to leave his family at the very moment when they most require his assistance! I was separated from them in body, but present in spirit. My affections were divided between love for the people, and hatred for the priests. Yet, although I was overcome with grief, I did not despair. I remembered our Redeemer, who wept over Jerusalem; and my trust in the providence of the Almighty was a balm to my soul. A voice appeared to sound in my ears, with words of comfort to my heart—"Weep not, endure yet for a season, and you will witness the salvation of your country!"

"Farewell, Rome!" I exclaimed; "the land of my fathers, the country of my predilection. Thou hast had a glorious page in the annals of the world; thou hast enjoyed a state that no other land can boast, the memory of which will endure to all generations. But what now remains of all thy former grandeur? A melancholy recollection! On every side we behold the remains of thine opulence, thy beauty, and thy prosperity. Such was Rome! Her name only now remains: her existence is gone; but the name lives, and will long be preserved. Let us, however, hope she may yet revive; not the Rome of the Cæsars, but of the people; not the haunt of superstition, but the abode of truth. Alas! at the present moment, where is the boasted wisdom of the senate, the majesty of the people? A foolish government dishonours, an evil one persecutes us, and renders the descendants of heroes imbecile and depraved. Farewell, then, Rome of the priesthood! The mists from the Tiber are thickening around thee, and shutting out from thy sight the Vatican which has enslaved thee with its sorceries. Oh, my beloved Rome! a sun is arising in the east which shall gladden all around, and dispel the darkness of the horizon: a sun which shall not again be obscured."

Thus did I bid adieu to Rome. And what was to be my future destiny? I knew not. My going to Naples was a mere pretext to enable me to get away. I felt a strong impulse to extend my journey to a far greater distance. The idea of a more spiritual separation from Rome was also busy in my brain; a separation more complete than could be effected by any distance of sea or land; and for this, unconsciously to myself, everything was preparing. The ways of the Lord are different from our ways, they are the dispositions of that adorable Providence which regulates alike the most trifling and the most important actions of our lives.

## FOOTNOTES:

[55] The relinquishing of the religious habit and office, for that of the secular clergy.

[56] Rev. xvii. 2.

[57] A certain declaration of the clergy of France in relation to the infallibility of the pope.

[58] That is to say, not by the Holy Office in Rome.

[59] To quit the monastic life, and to live as a simple priest. See note to p. 189.

[60] It were devoutly to be wished the latter knew as much.

[61] Matt. xx. 21.

[62] Matt. xx. 25-27.

[63] Ephes. iv. 11.

[64] I Cor. xii.

[65] Ibid.

[66] Ibid.

[67] Many persons believe that the body of St. Paul lies under the church, in the Via Ostia; others are of opinion that it is buried by the side of St. Peter. The Romish Church favours both these beliefs.

[68] Matt. xxvii. 8.

[69] Hebrews vii. 24-27.

[70] Luke xvii. 10.

[71] My family is one of the oldest in Rome, and celebrated for its hostility to the popes, and the persecutions it has endured.

[72] A popular mode of addressing the friars at Rome and Naples: *Zi frate*, which is similar to *zii* (uncle).

[73] The prevalent idea throughout Italy is that priests and monks can name the numbers in the lottery that will come up prizes.

[74] He died of grief, in consequence of the treatment he experienced from Gregory XVI., who when the Cardinal was pleading before His Holiness the cause of some poor liberals who were sacrificed by the cruelty of Cardinal Lambruschini, the Pope harshly reproached him, saying, "Your Eminence must look to your own acts."

# CHAPTER XI
# NAPLES AND THE NEAPOLITANS

On quitting Rome I no longer thought of its material objects, its churches, and its palaces; but of its unworthy government, and its degraded race of priests and friars. As yet I had never visited Naples; I fancied to myself that in most respects it was less objectionable than Rome. I passed over the Pontine Marshes, that famous Maremma, on which Pope Pius VI. expended so large a sum, in order to drain it, and render it free from the malaria that infested it, but which still continues the same. I arrived at Capua, which town I was soon to revisit, to preach the Lent sermons; a vast number of priests were here mixed up with a few townspeople and soldiers. At length I reached the city of Naples, where, as every one knows, the eye wandering among the busy throngs that are perpetually hurrying through the streets, discovers, on every side, innumerable hats of priests and cowls of monks; and, what at first sight excites so much surprise, friars of every colour, order, and denomination; who pursue each other through the crowd, as regardless of the tumult as if they were in the seclusion of their own cloisters. "Well!" thought I to myself, "Rome is not the only place that is overstocked with these gentry; Naples has its full share of them as well."

Naples is an exceedingly fine city, abundantly enriched by nature, and endowed with every gift calculated to ameliorate the condition of man, and to improve society. In casting our eyes over this delightful country, where variety and harmony, beyond the reach of art, prevail on every side; where nature, often in other countries sparing of her bounty, here lavishes her utmost to produce the beautiful, the lovely, and the enchanting, we are called upon to acknowledge that it is a land especially gifted by Providence. As I then saw and enjoyed it, I blamed myself for not having visited it sooner, and I made a resolution to remain in it, until some weighty reason should determine me to the contrary.

As it wanted but a few days to Lent, I chose to remain *incognito* during that time, busying myself in studying the genius of the people, and the manners and habits of the various classes. The tumult of the city, at all hours, and in all parts, was equally novel and strange to me; as was likewise the great contrast I observed between those who were in authority, and those whose duty it was to obey: the first, full of importance, and proud of their privileges, assumed not merely an air of superiority, but of disdain and contempt for the lower classes; who, in their turn, aware of their necessities, and humiliated by their lot, betrayed in their countenances a sense of their utter degradation, and seemed themselves to authorize the slavery that debased them.

This moral deformity presented a strange contrast to the physical beauty that reigned on every side: the one inspiring satisfaction and delight, the other abhorrence and disgust. Naples itself is a paradise; but the Neapolitans, to what are they to be likened? Whatever they are, it is the government which has made them so. The people—and by the people I do not merely understand the lower orders, but even those who inhabit the court—have not a single fault that is not to be attributed to their rulers: the better they are by nature, the worse they become by their education. This evil is more apparent in the capital than in the provinces; an evident proof that the government and the court occasion the evil, and the consequent demoralization; in fact, it is with the king himself, who sets the example, that the whole mischief originates.

Suppose a lazzarone steals a handkerchief out of your pocket; might he not plead in excuse that others commit far greater robberies with impunity? Does not theft pervade every rank of society, even to royalty itself? What barefaced depredations are not made on the public purse, under the title of salaries and stipends, for duties which do not exist! Whatever vices prevail in the lower classes, are invariably to be found in a greater degree in the higher, and more especially in the court circle. Lying, which is so common a vice among the lower orders, is elevated to a science in the middle class, while among the nobility it is regarded as a grace and a sort of gallantry, and with the king and his ministers it is esteemed as an essential principle in the art of governing.

The wife who lies to her husband, and the children who do the same to their parents, encourage by their example the servants, who consequently lie to their masters; and all these persons are encouraged to do so by the priest, who, in his confessional, pardons, without any sort of hesitation, every species of falsehood of which they accuse themselves. Lying and thieving, which in all civilized countries are held in detestation, are in this unhappy land almost regarded as virtues. Blame is only attached to the practice when it is unskilfully performed, so as to bring disgrace upon the order of liars and thieves, *en masse*.

I reflected much on the lamentable condition of a people destined by nature to be virtuous rather than vicious; and I was moved at the consideration of the real cause of their misery. The immorality of the people is entirely owing to its government; that is to say, to its unjust laws and its corrupt magistrates. The police protects every description of iniquity, and leagues itself with malefactors. Money, the source of all evil, changes the face of everything. Both witness and judge are notoriously sold to the highest bidder; it is money, therefore, and not right, which decides a cause. For money, the police is either alert or otherwise; it either invents crimes, or conceals them. For money, the king grants pardons, and out of the sums so applied a large portion finds its way into the pockets of the confessor, and the servants about court. What wonder can there be then that the example of the ministers of religion, whose office it is to govern and to instruct, should be so generally followed? Money is, in reality, the god that is worshipped in Italy. Naples is the kingdom of the Church; Rome is the state. It is in Naples that the papistry of Rome is in the fullest vigour, and the poor Neapolitans furnish abundant proof of the iniquity of the system: they are the rowers of the pope's grand bark, and the king is at their head. The priests rule in every direction; they insinuate themselves in a thousand ways into every body's concerns, and, directly or indirectly, possess an influence over all. Through confession they obtain dominion over the very minds of men, and discover their most secret thoughts and intentions. Whoever would ascertain what priestcraft really is, and the mischief it occasions in Italy, let him go to Naples.

It was during Lent, in the year 1835, that I went to Capua, and was the guest of Cardinal Serra Cassano. He was an exceedingly polite man, but to myself his attention was more than ordinary. His attendants remarked to me that they had never known him so much at home with any one before, and that he addressed me as his dearest friend.

Every day I preached, both morning and evening; and I had also other duties assigned to me by the Cardinal: to draw up rules for monastic bodies, to lay down a plan of study for the seminary, to suggest measures of reform with respect to the clergy, &c. were what I had to attend to; besides which, he was in the habit of consulting me on other matters. Our conversation was unrestrained: and I frequently had the satisfaction of declaring the truth to one whose ears had hitherto been accustomed only to the voice of adulation, as he was exceedingly wealthy, and held a sort of court, in which his will was absolute. Did it happen that any one contradicted or offended him, even in a single instance, he was sure to visit the culprit with his indignation; and if he were in his service, he ran the risk of being immediately discharged. All his dependents, therefore, trembled before him, and watched with anxiety the expression of his eye. However much he might be in the wrong, his servile followers were obliged to say: "Your Eminence is in the right." He was like one of the feudal barons of the middle ages, with respect to the state and tyranny of his conduct. I was greatly amused at his extravagances; and as I did not fear him, I sacrificed nothing of my own independence in my demeanour towards him. No argument of any consequence took place between us, although I often endeavoured to lead the conversation to serious topics: in fact, he had not much head for subjects of high importance. All that I could do was, to present a few words of truth to him, in the simplest form, since he was incompetent to enter into any grave discussion. He disliked to talk of religion, but delighted to expatiate on the Church; on the dignity of bishops and cardinals; of the privileges of the clergy, of their immunities, &c. He was frequently at issue, nevertheless, with his clergy, and had many important lawsuits with the heads of the cathedral and the collegiate church. Consequently, he was generally disliked: it may, indeed, be averred that he was beloved by no one at Naples, not even by his own relations.

I relate these circumstances, which are well known to all his acquaintance, in order that the true character of these sons of the Church of Rome, in her last days, may be known. The Cardinal, who was a man of very slender ability, had already occupied the post of Apostolic Nuncio, at the Court of Bavaria, and had performed good service in that capacity for the Holy See; having obtained, as he himself told me, from that country large sums of money, by the sale of indulgences and papal dispensations. He had, moreover, executed many important commissions on the part of the Propaganda and the Inquisition; and even, on one occasion, had successfully resisted the power of the king, in his attempt to interfere in some ecclesiastical matters. "Your Majesty must recollect," said he, "that you are the subject of the Church." These few words, the Cardinal observed, were sufficient to stop the proceedings of his majesty.

In these matters he was adroit enough. His altercations with the King of Naples were perfectly amusing, and no one was more frank than he was in expressing his sentiments. But the worst of it was, that all his courageous efforts were directed either to matters of no importance whatever, or to support things decidedly wrong and bad. Never, in a single instance, that ever came to my knowledge at least, was there any subject discussed between the king and him, of a noble or useful nature; though he was continually perplexing his brains with government affairs, and censuring the ministers, or giving them his advice.

He took great delight in all private gossip, and Neapolitan jokes, which are often none of the most decent; and encouraged all dealers in satire, provided it was directed against classes he deemed fitting subjects for it; more especially against the monks, for whom he professed very little regard. With the pope or the cardinals, however, it was different: no one was permitted to censure them in his presence. Nevertheless, I often took the liberty of doing so myself, on which occasions I never failed to receive a gentle reproof.

"Ah! you are no friend to cardinals," said he to me one day.

"On the contrary," I replied, "I am so much their friend, that nothing would give me more pleasure than to introduce a real reform among them, and give them an opportunity of becoming estimable characters. The good Bishop Bartholomew de Martiribus, the primate of Hungary, was of the same opinion when he exclaimed before the Council of Trent: *Illustrissimi et Reverendissimi Cardinales indigent illustrissima et reverendissima reformatione*. [75] Three ages have elapsed since this exclamation was made, but nothing as yet has resulted from it. Who, indeed, can ever reform them, so long as they alone possess the privilege of doing so?"

"The pope, who is their superior, may reform them."

"And the pope himself, who is to reform him?"

"The Almighty."

"May it be so."

On my leaving Rome, Olivieri, the Father-General of the Dominicans, and head commissioner of the Inquisition, had deputed me to go to Mugnano, in the diocese of Nola, where the celebrated new saint, Philomena, the pretended worker of so many recent miracles, is held in great veneration. The Inquisition was not quite satisfied with the manner in which the priest Don Francesco di Lucia had exhibited these miracles to the public. This priest, it seems, was in possession of certain reliques, fragments of bones, which he had brought away from Rome in the year 1802, and subsequently enclosed within a little image of *papier maché*, originally a figure of Christ, such as are sold at Naples, to which he added a female mask and suitable garments, disposing the image in a sleeping attitude. Thus metamorphosed into a female, the worthy priest soon found a name for his saint, although no one could tell whether the bones had belonged to a male or a female.[76] Be that as it may, he was the first to celebrate their fame, and set up a sanctuary, in which such astonishing prodigies were soon said to be performed, that ignorant peasants came from all the neighbouring parts, to worship the new idol, bringing their offerings with them, and inducing other devout idolaters to do the same.

I was therefore authorized by the commissioner to reprove the priest, on account of the numerous tales he had spread abroad, respecting the life, death, and miracles of his wonderful saint. I was directed to inform him that not one of his boasted prodigies could be believed, since there was no evidence whatever of their having actually occurred; and that the Roman

Inquisition entirely disapproved of his conduct, and was on the point of condemning all the books he had published on the subject.

I undertook this office with considerable satisfaction, as I had for a long time been disgusted with all the fabulous stories of saints and miracles that inundated Italy and Europe, and were even introduced into the sermons of the missionaries of the Propaganda. Accordingly, during the Holy week, when I had no duty to perform, I took upon me to go to Mugnano, accompanied by Monsignor Angustoni, a preacher in the collegiate church of Santa Maria. Our arrival was hailed with great pleasure by Don Francesco, who, at the sight of us, flattered himself that two preachers from Capua had actually become followers of his saint. He accordingly began in his usual style to vaunt her perfections, and the wonders she had performed.

"See," said he to me, pointing to the image, "this saint is different from all other saints in existence. She knows beforehand the favours her devotees come to ask of her, and she shows in a decided manner whether she intends to grant their suit or not. A few days ago a bishop, I shall not tell his name, came to pay his respects to her; I saw at once that she was displeased at his visit, as she visibly changed countenance, and assumed a pale and sad aspect: whereas, on the very same day, when the Marchioness of Riso, from Naples, came here, her aspect was altogether different. I wish you could have seen how handsome she looked! The marchioness told me she had come to ask a favour, but that she found it was granted, even before she had arrived at Mugnano."

"I hope our visit will be equally acceptable to your saint," said I; "and that she will look favourably upon us, when you make us acquainted with her. I do not know whether my friend here has any boon to ask of her. For my own part, I require nothing at all from her saintship."

Before withdrawing the curtain that concealed his oracle from the common gaze, the priest showed us a piece of marble upon the altar, which, he said, having been accidentally broken in two pieces, the saint had miraculously joined, and made it as perfect as before. I however begged leave to point out to him that there were pretty evident marks of its having been cemented in the ordinary way, by mastic. He also showed me a little shrine, from which, as he assured me, the reliques of the saint, after having been carefully placed there by his own hands, suddenly disappeared; because the owner of it was not sufficiently devout. As I could allege nothing to the contrary, I made no remark, but merely smiled at his absurdity. Don Francesco now rang the great bell of the church, lighted the candles upon the altar, and assembled the people. Among them I particularly noticed twenty or thirty young girls, who were maintained at the expense of the priest, out of the money given to Saint Philomena; their office was to pray to the saint, in behalf of those persons who presented gifts to her.

These girls, with loud shrill voices, frequently raised to their extremest pitch, chanted the customary prayers, in the same style as the old women at Naples, in the chapel of St. Januarius, invoke the saint to perform his annual miracle of liquefying his own blood. Other girls tinkled the various bells belonging to the church, while Don Francesco, devoutly kneeling, exposed the sacred reliques. We, for our part, were lost in admiration, at beholding such solemn ceremonies, on so ridiculous an occasion as the appearance of a painted doll, dressed in female attire, with a few bones withinside, and called Saint Philomena.

"Oh! how beautiful she is," exclaimed Don Francesco, turning towards us. "Observe the charming colour of her cheeks; she is like a rose of Paradise!"

"Which is a good sign, I suppose, is it not?" I replied. "She must be greatly pleased with our visit."

"Undoubtedly she is," he returned, "and quite disposed to grant whatever you may ask of her."

"Is she then omnipotent?"

"Why, as to that, she is the daughter of the Omnipotent God, and dispenses all his favours; she keeps the treasury of the Divine grace, and to her friends she denies nothing; what she receives in heaven she freely bestows upon earth; she takes from the hand of God, and gives to us."

"Don Francesco," said I to him, "all this appears to me an idle dream; it agrees with no doctrine in theology. Christianity is not based on such superstitions, but on real facts. Who has told you that your saint is what you report her to be? Besides, what you affirm concerning her, is also affirmed of hundreds, nay, thousands of other saints, who are said to be equally powerful; all have access to the Divine treasury, all deal in miracles, prodigies, and conjurations alike. Besides, with so many saints to intercede for us, what becomes of the office of Jesus Christ, of whom it is said by John, that he intercedes for us, that he is our only advocate with the Father? Moreover, He himself says, 'Come unto me, all ye that labour, and are heavy laden, and I will give you rest.'[77] 'No man cometh unto the Father but by me.'[78] Now, it is clear that you, Don Francesco, have recourse to others than the Lord Jesus Christ, to gain admission to the Father. Take care you do not altogether mistake the way, and teach what is not true. For it is written, 'If the blind lead the blind, both shall fall into the ditch.'"[79]

Don Francesco appeared greatly disconcerted by so public a rebuke as this: it was what he so little expected. He concealed his embarrassment, however, as well as he could, and continued, but with less assurance, his account of Saint Philomena.

"See here," said he, "one cannot deny that her hair grows, or that she has moved her feet; they are more stretched out and curved than they were. She even changed her position a little time ago."

"She, do you say? tell me, do you mean the saint herself, or the pasteboard image? for I do not suppose you have operated the change, or transubstantiation, of the saint into *papier maché*, and *vice versâ*! What does it signify if the paper doll has become a little twisted by the changes in the temperature of the atmosphere? Are not the ropes of the church bells affected in the same way? do not they become longer when the weather is damp, and shorter when it is dry? These miracles of yours all arise from natural causes. Even suppose it otherwise, what benefit would it be to the Church if the image really moved itself about?[80] Divine miracles always have an important object, never being wrought but for purposes of exceeding utility. Do you ever read in the Bible about miracles, performed as it were in sport, or to satisfy vain curiosity, such as these of your saint? Religion has no need of such, and they do her no honour. I wish to heaven that we had never talked of the miracles of St. Anthony, of St. Vincent, and others, which are only derogatory to the excellence and the truth of those operated by the Saviour and his apostles. In the early days of Christianity there was a necessity for miracles, in order, as one of the Fathers expresses it, to water the new plants of the religion of Christ. Those plants are now strong and healthy, and have no need to be watered as they formerly were."

At these words I saw the priest evince great signs of dissatisfaction. He eyed me askance, his lip quivered with a sort of convulsive movement. It appeared that he had a reply ready for me, which he had probably been concocting all the time I had been lecturing him. I paused therefore to give him an opportunity of speaking.

"Then you have no faith in the miracles of St. Philomena?"

"What miracles do you mean? Those you have spoken of are no miracles at all. The operations of nature, even when most extraordinary, are not miracles. Miracles are above the power of nature, and contrary to her laws. All that you have brought forward is child's play, mere nonsense. As to the other marvels you tell me of—the instantaneous cures that have been effected, gifts and visions from heaven, angels appearing, and devils being put to flight—I hold them all to be pure inventions. You seem angry with me for discrediting your account; I hope you will be less so with the cardinals of the Inquisition, who, I can assure you, highly disapprove, as well as myself, of your wonderful relations, and hold them all as fables:

moreover, I have to inform you, which I do in the presence of Monsignor Angustoni, brother of the Pope's Sacristan, that the rebuke I have given you is at the special direction of the Commissioner-General of the Holy Office."

At these words the priest hung down his head, as one who already hears the judge pronouncing his sentence. I saw that he was effectually humbled, and therefore did not carry my reproof any further.

"My dear Don Francesco," I said, "the religion of Jesus Christ, which we both profess, is truth in its most luminous aspect; but it is as a mirror, which becomes sullied by human breath. If it be entirely from God, man can add nothing to it. It is our duty to receive it such as it is, without seeking to embellish it with our own inventions, however holy or spiritual they may appear to be. Grievous superstitions have in this manner been introduced into Christianity, If our venerable fathers of the early ages could return to this world, they would find so many abuses and falsehoods among us, that they would no longer recognise the holy spouse of Christ. Give up, therefore, these idle stories about Saint Philomena, which cause great injury to the simple-minded, in leading them to worship, instead of the Lord Jesus Christ, a created being, nay, even dead bones and a senseless image. May God pardon you the offence you have already committed!"

And what, it may be asked, was really the effect of my lecture on the mind of Don Francesco? I verily believe it had none whatsoever; since, as I afterwards understood, he continued his practices exactly in the same style, and I never heard that the Inquisition took any steps towards interfering with them. Perhaps he may have learned to accommodate his lies on the subject, according to the prescribed rules of the Holy Congregation of Rites, and consequently is no longer at variance with Rome. The miracles attributed to this saint have been trumpeted forth to all the world, and her worship, or rather idolatry, extends everywhere. The King of Naples, his whole family, and the members of his court, are among her most zealous supporters, and Don Alfonzo d'Avalos, the Court Grand-master of the ceremonies, has the honour of being her treasurer!

"What is your opinion with respect to this Saint Philomena?" inquired the Cardinal one day, as we were discoursing together.

"I think it is a gross piece of idolatry to worship her," I replied. "I reproved Don Francesco for his fanaticism pretty severely. But how is it possible to convince a priest? One might as well argue with a block of stone. To what a pass has religion come in this country of ours! to the worship of images and reliques; to the adoration of the Madonna and the saints! God, or Jesus Christ, serve only as names to cover or sanction this species of idolatry, under the title of the Christian religion. No, your Eminence, this is not Christianity, it has been corrupted by the priests altogether. And what are our bishops about? They shut their eyes to what is going on, regardless of their responsibility in these matters. Every shepherd is bound to take care of his flock; he who neglects this duty is a hireling, and unworthy of his charge. Now what is the Bishop of Nola about, while these impostures are being carried on in his diocese?"

"Why, they say they pull together in that respect; but I do not believe it," replied the Cardinal.

It is indeed notorious how the worship of saints increases, as well as the fame of their miracles. The priests and the bishops favour the practice alike. The Cardinal, although he appeared to disapprove of this affair of Saint Philomena, was only instigated by his desire to pay greater homage to other saints, whose repute he was more interested in advocating. But what can be advanced in favour of these proceedings, when it is seen that the greatest saint in the Romish Church is that of whom the greatest lies have been invented? They only are true saints, who, without any of these pretensions, died, according to the old Latin phrase, *in osculo domini*; they alone are those whom God acknowledges as such, and whom we may hope to meet in heaven.

During my stay at Capua, before the termination of Lent, a certain Monsignor Lasteria, Bishop of Zante and Cephalonia, came on a visit to Cardinal Serra. He was a native of Capua, and had formerly been the Cardinal's secretary. The object of his visit was, apparently, to solicit the good offices of the Cardinal with the Propaganda, to obtain leave for him to resign the bishopric he held; possibly with a view of obtaining a translation to some see in the dominions of the King of Naples. The Cardinal had broached the matter to the Propaganda some time before, but the grand difficulty appeared to be the providing another bishop for Zante and Cephalonia. I was applied to on the occasion, and asked if I knew of any fit person whom I could recommend to this bishopric, which was a difficult post to fill, as the Romish Church was there placed between the Anglican and the Greek Church. The Cardinal repeatedly urged me to name some one of my acquaintance, to present to the Propaganda, instead of Monsignor Lasteria.

I was wearied by these frequent applications, and one day briefly told his Eminence that I had neither a Titus, nor a Timothy to propose; hoping that after such an observation I should be no more troubled on the subject. But not many days after he came to seek me with a very satisfied and condescending air.

"I hope," said he, "that you will acknowledge the will of God in the proposition I am about to make you. The holy Father, on the recommendation of the secretary of the Propaganda, has signified his approval of your succeeding Monsignor Lasteria yourself, in the bishopric of these two Ionian Islands; and besides which he invests you with the office of Vicar Apostolic of Corfu. He observed, however, after having spoken very favourably of you, that he could not compel you to accept this office in a foreign country, but at any rate, if it did not please you, it need only be for a short time, as he should, himself, be better satisfied to have you in Rome."

"Many thanks to your Eminence, as well as to the Pope, and to the secretary of the Propaganda. This office, which in the time of the apostles was very desirable, according to the words of St. Paul to Timothy,[81] is now no longer so; at least, not in my eyes. Indeed, such as the episcopacy is in our day, I would counsel no man to accept it: far less would I accept it myself. My objection does not apply alone to the see of the Ionian Islands, but to every bishopric whatsoever, belonging to the Church of Rome. The laws and general usages connected with them are such that I could never conform myself to them, either as regards practice or precept. I wish it therefore to be understood that I do not refuse a poor bishopric, in the hope of obtaining a rich one; it is the dignity itself, the prelacy that I object to: what I consider therefore as a dangerous acquisition, I am by no means disposed to possess."

"Come, take three days to consider of it. Your refusal is too hasty, you ought to reflect before you decide. Offer up your prayers, these three days, to the Lord and the most holy Madonna, that they may enlighten you."

"Well, I will wait three days, and offer up my prayers to the Lord, and at the end of that time I will communicate the result to your eminence."

A few hours after the expiration of the allotted period, the Cardinal came to me again, to know my decision.

"Everything," I replied, "strengthens me in the resolution I have already expressed to your Eminence, of declining to accept the bishopric. I look at what is true in the office, and at what is false. The duty of a bishop is essentially that of a shepherd; as the one leads his flock to pasture, so the other conducts his people into the way of truth. But the shepherd has become the doctor. He has, and *very inappropriately*, assumed a command, an authority, a jurisdiction, a power which usurps dominion: yet He who said to Peter, 'Feed my sheep, feed my lambs,' also said to him, and to all the apostles, 'Ye know that the princes of the Gentiles exercise dominion over them, and they that are great exercise authority upon them. But it shall not be so among you.'[82] Now the office of a bishop at the present day is totally opposite to what it ought to be. By a bishop, we understand an ecclesiastic who, in consequence of possessing a dominion, has authority and a right to command; which right it is pretended he receives from Christ, through the apostles. But it is evident that the apostles themselves never had such right. And what are our present bishops? Shepherds? Would to God they led their flocks to the pastures of truth, to the holy Word! If any one in the present day were to fulfil his duty as bishop, according to the original signification of the office, he would soon be at issue with Rome, from whence all the scandal proceeds, and which stigmatizes as innovations any return to the customs and observances of the early times of Christianity."

"I have no more to say then. If you refuse, I will write and tell them they must choose another. Have you any one to propose?"

"There is at Rome, among the Dominicans, a missionary, one Father Hynes, an Irishman, who has lately come over from the United States, in the hope of obtaining promotion. He would be very fit for the Ionian Islands."

The next day the Cardinal came again with a letter in his hand. "I am going to send," said he, "your answer to Rome. I have stated that, for certain private reasons, you cannot accept the offer that has been made you. Am I right? Shall I send the letter? or do you think better of it?"

"I request your Eminence will forward the letter at once. And since you have already shown me so much kindness, I am encouraged to open my mind still further to you. I wish to send these two other letters to Rome; one to Cardinal Polidori, Prefect of the Congregation of Discipline, and the other to Monsignor Acton, the secretary, to request from the pope my secularization. I wish to quit the Order to which I belong: it brings me too much before the public. I have no ambitious desires, and would rather lead a quiet life, as a simple priest, without any office whatsoever in the Church. I feel myself called by God to preach according to his Word; and in the performance of that duty I would willingly spend the remainder of my existence. I should also resume the delivery of my scientific lectures. I have another strong reason for relinquishing this Order, in which I can never hope to enjoy any tranquillity, since with my own eyes I have witnessed the irregularities that are practised in the different monasteries I have visited. It has, moreover, the additional dishonour of having provoked the pope to dismiss the Father General Olivieri.[83] At Rome, in that most abominable monastery of the Minerva, all who have any good about them are sure to be persecuted, as was the case with my friend Brocchetti. I can no longer live among such people. I shall request my passport, and leave them."

"And where will you go?"

"I cannot tell: probably I shall remain some time in Naples, if they will leave me alone. I foresee a secret persecution hatching up against me. I shall live entirely to myself, if I am allowed to do so, and shall attend solely to study and preaching."

The Cardinal did all in his power to dissuade me. He averred I was tempted by the devil, that I was relinquishing a very desirable position, that I should give great offence at Rome, and only bring ruin on myself. He added, that he should immediately set about writing letters in opposition to mine, to throw all possible impediments in my way; and said many other things, just as they came into his head. I let him talk on, and pursued my own measures.

In this state of affairs I left Capua, with abundance of courteous expressions on the part of his Eminence, which it is needless to repeat. In a letter that he wrote to Cardinal Caracciolo, Archbishop of Naples, he reiterated all the personal compliments he had paid to me; of which letter the archbishop kindly sent me a copy; and I still preserve it among other papers.[84] Cardinal Serra, moreover, on my taking leave of him, made me some presents, and favoured me with two appointments—one to preach during Lent in 1837, in another of his churches; and the other to confess, *in perpetuo*, in the whole of his vast diocese, which he told me was a distinguished privilege that he never before had granted to any one.

This authority to pardon sins, which the bishops take upon themselves to grant, is a great abuse in the Church of Rome. It is a gross imposition, a monopoly, a very usurpation. I do not here enter into the question of auricular confession; I confine my remarks, for the present, to the privilege of granting absolution for sins, which the bishops confer on their friends. To myself it was given in its utmost latitude, for an unlimited period, and for every species of crime. In general, the power is not granted for any length of time. In Rome, it is seldom for more than six months, in Naples, for three only. When it is granted for a year, it may be annually renewed, on application to the bishop. It is seldom conceded without the party's being examined on the doctrine of casuistry at least, and never for every description of sin. Every bishop has his own list of reserved cases; that is to say, of some particular sins, not comprised in the general list of pardonable offences; and for these the confessor is obliged to seek the assistance of the bishop. There are some indeed, which the bishops themselves cannot absolve, the pope always reserving to himself, in these graver matters, the power of absolution; and the confessor is obliged on such occasions to apply to his holiness himself, who, in his turn, refers him to the grand penitentiary; since neither the pope nor any of the bishops receive a confession; which office is always confided to their inferiors; being considered one of far less dignity than that of consecrating a church, blessing a cemetery, or baptizing the bells.

It is a sure sign that a priest who is appointed confessor to a diocese, is a particular friend of the bishop, since, on the slightest disagreement between them, or the least feeling of ill will, he is forthwith suspended from his office. I must here observe that I always enjoyed the friendship of those prelates who from time to time granted me this great privilege in their several jurisdictions; since not a single one of them ever suspended me in the execution of my office, even at a time when I began to be suspected of entertaining heretical opinions. It was also an honourable distinction in my favour, that none of the bishops by whom I was appointed ever thought it necessary to subject me to the usual examination. Neither did I ever solicit the office, it having been invariably bestowed on me as a mark of their individual good will. I have a whole bundle of these diplomas, many bearing the signature of cardinals, and one from the Archbishop, the great chaplain of the King of Naples, for all the royal churches in the kingdom of the Two Sicilies. Some were presented to me out of compliment; as, for instance, by the Bishop of Nocera, on the occasion of his returning my visit to him, in the year 1836, when his first act was to present me with the office of confessor. The same also took place with the Archbishop of Sorrento, the first time I was in his company, which was at dinner in his own house. It is astonishing to see the exceeding politeness and courtesy with which these worthies bestow on their subordinates the power to pardon the most grievous offences against the Majesty of Heaven. Would they, with equal grace and condescension, have granted it for offences committed against themselves? A circumstance that took place between one of these dignitaries and myself, will throw a little light on the subject.

I went one day to Sorrento, to endeavour to promote a reconciliation between the archbishop and a poor priest of Meta, whom the archbishop had, for a number of years, hated and persecuted to such an extent as to create a great scandal through the whole diocese. The chief cause of offence complained of by the archbishop was, that the priest had written some satirical lines upon him, and had also spoken of him with little reverence. The priest had subsequently heartily repented of the act, and had in every possible manner implored forgiveness for the offence: he had written many letters in the humblest style, and had frequently got persons of character and respectability to intercede for him. It was, however, all in vain. The archbishop was obstinate, and persisted in holding the priest in suspension from the performance of all ecclesiastical duty within his diocese. The last hope remained with me, and out of compassion for the poor fellow, I undertook the task, as well as for regard towards the Archbishop, who, before being acquainted with me, had spoken of me with kindness; in return, therefore, I was equally anxious to be useful to him. My visit to him took place after we had exchanged two or three polite notes, and was apparently the result of a desire for greater mutual acquaintance, but, for my own part, my principal object was this affair of the priest. As the Archbishop had no idea of the kind, I waited for a favourable opportunity to introduce the subject, which soon presented itself on his Grace's bestowing on me the diploma of a Confessor.

"Then I am authorized, in virtue of this, to receive confessions of all offences committed against God, and to grant pardon and absolution to whoever repents?"

"Unquestionably; and, moreover, I invest you with power to do so, in all reserved cases, for the term of a year."

"This is certainly a very desirable power, and one for which I have for some time been particularly anxious. I can then absolve in those cases reserved for your Grace?"

"Yes; and for those referred to the Synod of the diocese."

"It is well; I shall then absolve whoever truly confesses, however great his sin may be."

"To be sure; it is to the greatest sinners that God extends the chiefest mercy, and we, as his ministers, should receive them with open arms," observed the Archbishop.

"How gracious the Lord is to pardon so freely," I continued; "I am lost in admiration whenever I reflect on the manner in which Jesus Christ pardoned the poor woman, and also the publican in the parable, immediately on his asking it. Alas! how difficult we find it to follow his blessed example! how reluctant we are to pardon those who have offended ourselves! notwithstanding Jesus Christ has told us, 'If ye forgive not men their trespasses, neither will your Father forgive your trespasses.'[85] And it avails us little if we do so once or twice, or even ten times; for Christ commanded Peter to forgive seventy times seven; which signifies to forgive without limitation; as it is written, 'If thy brother trespass against thee, rebuke him; and if he repent forgive him. And if he trespass against thee seven times in a day, and seven times in a day turn to thee, saying, I repent; thou shalt forgive him.'"[86]

At these words I fancied I perceived in the countenance of the Archbishop an acknowledgment of the sacred nature of this duty, and accordingly I thought it best to seize the opportunity without further preparation. "Monsignore," I exclaimed, "these divine assurances encourage the poor priest Lasteria to ask anew of your Grace pardon for the offence he acknowledges he has committed, and of which he now thoroughly repents."

"No," loudly roared out the Archbishop, "it is not true that he repents; he only feigns to do so, that I may be induced to pardon him. To all others I am willing, but to this person I can never extend that favour."

"Monsignore, the poor man came to me yesterday with tears in his eyes. 'I hope,' said he, 'that my Archbishop will at length consent to pardon me, for the love of God, and that the blessed God may also pardon him his sins. Oh! what comfort shall I experience if he restores me to his favour! if you obtain permission for me to go and make my peace with him, I shall then be content to die.'"

"I cannot receive him; neither will I pardon him, till I am thoroughly convinced of his repentance and humiliation."

"What then must he do?"

"Go into a monastery, and remain there till I recall him."

"And for what purpose?"

"To undergo penance."

"God makes no such condition to us. We should be badly off, if for every offence we had to undergo a suitable penance! If God pardons, on the sole consideration that Jesus Christ has made satisfaction for us, as faith teaches us to believe, can we find any excuse for not pardoning those for whom Christ has suffered? On what condition does Christ pardon our sins? What penance has he enjoined?"

"What! do you deny then that the Church has a right to impose penance?"

"I find that the custom is very much lessened. The question, however, at present, has nothing to do with the Church. It is altogether a personal offence, and you have yourself full power to remit——"

"No, no, I cannot remit, the offence has been too public."

"All the better. Your Excellence will grant the more public and solemn forgiveness."

"It appears to me that you are come here to preach me a sermon, rather than to pay me a visit."

"Exactly; it is the visit of a Preacher. Ought I to waste my time in vain speeches or idle compliments? I avail myself of the present opportunity to discuss an affair of equal importance to your Excellence and to the priest; and I declare it is for the regard I entertain for both parties that I interest myself in it. If the priest, on his part, has need of your pardon, it cannot be denied that it would be equally advantageous for your Excellence to grant it him, to put a stop to all the idle talk of the neighbourhood, as well as to the imprecations of the numerous relatives and friends of the priest, who form a large party in Meta and Sorrento."

"What a capital advocate you are!"

"Have I then gained my cause?"

"Tell your client to do as I have said—let him go into a monastery, and then he may send to me again, and I may perhaps take his petition into consideration. Now let us talk of something else."

In this way it was that the Archbishop closed the door upon all hope of reconciliation: he refused his brother the forgiveness which he asked of him for the love of God. A year after, the cholera put an end to his life.... How fearful are thy judgments, Lord! Here was a man who willingly pardoned all sins committed against God, but who knew not how to pardon a single fault against himself. Such is the character of the higher Clergy in the Romish Church; indulgent in the extreme to all those who do not stand in the way of their interests or their ambition, they are implacable in their hatred, and cruel and fierce in their vengeance.

No sooner had I taken up my abode in Naples, after the termination of my preaching at Capua, than I was exceedingly courted by the Bishops and the Superiors of the Order. I had on every side the offer of a pulpit in their churches. I chose before all others the Lent discourses for 1836, in the principal Church of the Dominicans, as a testimony of my good will towards them. In 1837 I was again engaged by the Cardinal of Capua. In 1838 I officiated for the Cardinal of Naples; and in 1839 I preached for the Papal Nuncio, in his church of St. James.

In this manner passed over the six years that I remained in Naples. My occupation was not confined to the city, it extended to the neighbouring parts. Besides the duty during Lent, every Sunday and Festival, throughout the year, I preached in various churches, and occasionally on other days of the week. I have frequently delivered two or three sermons in the course of the same day. A part only of these discourses was prepared beforehand, as it was impossible for me to write even one half of what I preached; but in general I found no difficulty in getting through my task, as I had accustomed myself from an early period to extempore delivery, which had now become easy and familiar to me; sometimes, however, not being exactly in the mood, I could not express myself with equal fluency as at others. Still I think it is the preferable mode for evangelical preaching, as notwithstanding a few trifling inconveniences, arising from occasional repetition and inexactitude, its simplicity presents a great advantage; since with regard to expression, the less it is studied, the more it is true, persuasive, and touching: moreover, he who is completely master of his subject need not fear that he will want words or proper arrangement; according to the opinion of Horace—

— —"Cui lecta potenter erit res,
Nec facundia deseret hunc, nec lucidus ordo."

My preaching was originally commenced, as is customary with all students in religion, with the study of rhetoric; and was limited by certain rules, which teach the manner of arranging the various parts of an oration: hence I at first experienced a sort of vain glory in my pursuit, and panted to acquire the fame of an eloquent orator; but I afterwards changed my style, when I became convinced that a sacred speaker ought to be governed rather by the influence of the Holy Spirit than by rules of art; I therefore applied myself more to prayer than to study, and my discourses became less brilliant, but more efficacious. Any one who had heard me preach at these different epochs would readily have perceived the change I speak of, though he might not have understood the reason of it. My first attempts aimed at great elegance of style, and I was ambitious to be thought an able writer. My sermons at the Court of Lucca were of this character: I was then about twenty years of age, and had not yet been ordained priest. Persons of high distinction were among my auditors; among whom I may reckon Lazaro Papi, the Marquess Cesare Lucchesini, Professor Gigliotti, and the famous personages, Teresa Bandettini and Costanza Moscheni. I was honoured with their friendship, and they approved of my pulpit-labours. Alas for me! How little at that time had I been educated in the school of the Redeemer! The favour of men was all I sought after. By degrees, however, I began to perceive that all this was vanity.

From Lucca I proceeded to Rome, and from thence to Viterbo. My preaching had much improved; it had less display, and was more suitable to its design. I reserved my flowers of eloquence for panygeric orations, (which in my then darkened state greatly occupied me,) and began to be more grave and sedate in my style. On my removal to Naples, these feelings increased, as I thought, more deeply on matters of true religion, and my sermons assumed an evangelical tone, which was agreeable to persons of talent; and I was perfectly indifferent as to the opinion of those who disliked it.

The last of my Lent duties, that at the church of St. Giacomo, at Naples, was the actual commencement of my new style. I gave a series of thirty-seven discourses, in which I not only avoided all papistic doctrines, but set forth those contained in the Scriptures themselves; such as justification by faith, the sole mediation of Christ, his only priesthood, and single sacrifice, &c. These were entirely new views in a country where nothing else was taught than the efficacy of works of merit, the intercession of saints, the pretended dignity of the priests, the great value of the mass applied to souls in purgatory, and the necessity of worshipping the Madonna.

I saw very clearly that my advocating anew the practice enjoined in the ancient and holy teaching of our forefathers, would excite the fiercest animosity against me. I began to hear it rumoured about that my sermons were more Protestant than Catholic; I received several anonymous letters on the subject; and as at that time I preached every Sunday in the church of St. Peter the Martyr, I saw many priests among my congregation, who had very much the look of spies. Notwithstanding all this, I stuck to my argument, and continued to preach in the same style the doctrine of early Christianity; bringing texts from Scripture alone, in support of my propositions, rarely citing the Fathers, and never the Theologians of the Romish Church.

The altered character of my discourses soon gave rise to many conferences among the bigots of the Neapolitan clergy, and to many letters from Rome. The Cardinal Archbishop asked me one day if it was true that these conferences and letters had reference to the new doctrines I was advocating.

"They are new," I replied, "in the same manner that the moon every fresh month is called new, though she is nevertheless as old as the world."

"But they assert that you no longer preach the necessity of good works, faith alone being sufficient."

"That is not exactly the case; I stated that works are not good, unless they are the fruits of faith, and that others are of no avail; as St. Paul says, 'Whatsoever is not of faith is sin,'[87] which signifies all disorder and deviation from the right road."

On another occasion the good Cardinal reproved me because I had asserted in one of my sermons, that the most beneficial mode of confession was that which was made to God; and the best penitence a sincere renewal of the heart, and a humble return to Him.

"It is very true," was my reply, "and if your Eminence calls upon me to prove it, I am ready to do so from the Holy Scriptures."

"There is no necessity: your proposition may be true, abstractedly considered—that is to say, viewed theoretically; but in practice you would not find it so useful."

"I understand; it would not be so useful to the priests and the confessors, but greatly more so to the people. If everybody was in the habit of confessing to God alone, what necessity would there be for such a host of priestly confessors? But the question is, not what we ourselves prefer, but what we ought to teach the people. I wish to God that every one would confess to his priest less, and to his God more; as our fathers had the grace to do in former times."

I paused, but the Cardinal, not having a reply ready, remained silent. I therefore continued:

"Your Eminence has already shown me so much kindness, that I am encouraged to lay open my mind more fully. Is it not a fact, that in no other place is there so great a herd of confessors as at Naples? What now is their real object? Your Eminence will tell me that it is to listen to a recital of sins, and to give absolution for them; but I maintain that their real object is to get money; and it is more notoriously the case in Naples than elsewhere. The predecessor of your Eminence, Cardinal Ruffo, when he conferred the office of Confessor on any one, used to say, 'There, my dear fellow, there's a good fifteen ducats a month for you, if you know how to go to work!'

"Now I happen to know that his hint was not thrown away: the least industrious among them get their fifteen ducats, and as to the others!—ask the confessors of the nuns what they gain by their business. I do not mean to say that they require payment for an absolution, that would be too barefaced. They do not sell, but they accept gifts; if not for themselves, for the souls in purgatory, or for some miraculous image, for which they require masses and other oblations. Is it not true that they impose, as a penance, the obligation to cause a number of masses to be celebrated? And to whose pecuniary benefit, if not the confessor's? And in cases of deathbeds, how vast is the speculation of these gentry! Let your Eminence look to the operations of the Jesuits in this line of business; to the Missionaries, to the Liguorini, to the Theatines, the Franciscans, the Dominicans, and other worthies of the same class, who despoil houses, impoverish families, and frequently turn mother and children out of doors, destitute and forlorn. These evils, as your Eminence knows far better than I do, are the results of the practice of confession. I would that your heart were equally pained as mine is, by the reflection. Although I have not the authority of a bishop in this place, still, if I were silent on the occasion, I should consider myself as guilty of favouring the practice. Much more is required of him who is in reality the pastor of this flock, who has assumed the office of watching over it, and to whom are addressed the words that were spoken to Timothy: 'I charge thee ... preach the Word; be instant in season, out of season; reprove, rebuke, exhort, with all longsuffering and doctrine.'"[88]

Cardinal Caracciolo wrung my hand, and exclaimed, with a sigh: "Oh! what a hard trial it is to be a bishop! What a burthen on one's shoulders! I see many evils in the Church, and would fain apply a remedy to them, but I know not how."

Naples, in point of religion, is an extraordinary country; the inhabitants themselves believe that they have more than the whole world besides; and such indeed would be the fact, if superstition were synonymous with religion. No people upon the whole earth are more superstitious. All the old superstitions of Greece and Rome have taken refuge among them. Idolatry is the foundation of their faith; they have no idea of worship without some statue or picture to bow down to. A God that is not visible to the eye is altogether unknown to them, or exists as a king whom no one is allowed to approach. The God of the Neapolitans has consequently a vast number of ministers, to whom supplication is made. At the time I am speaking of, they had no less than fifty Patron Saints, and I have no doubt the number is now greatly augmented. Every one of these saints has his own state ministers. At the head of them all is St. Januarius, who acts as their president. But this does not exclude St. Gaetano to be prayed to, as a sort of Minister of Finance, who is considered to be in the department of the Divine Providence. The ministry of Grace and Justice appear to be divided between St. Anthony, St. Vincent, and St. Andrew Avellino. The Jesuits endeavoured to foist St. Francis Xavier and St. Louis Gonzaga into this office as well, but they are not considered to have succeeded.

St. Januarius, who, like John Bull, may be looked upon as the prototype of his countrymen, both with respect to their good and bad qualities, has a sort of jealous feeling towards others, and more particularly towards the Jesuits; since it appears he considers them as likely to interfere with his dignity. He is sometimes thought to be a little vindictive, choleric and presumptuous; on which account the Neapolitans occasionally reprove him, and not over gently, in their devotions. I scarcely think a pure and spiritual religion would be possible in this country, where all is so material and so sensual. I have often considered the problem, and am inclined to doubt its practicability, at least with respect to the present generation. They are a people perpetually on the look-out for miracles, and consequently flock round their saints and their madonnas, since the priests assure them that they perform wonders in that way. In their belief, a religion without its daily stock of miracles is no religion at all. I have sometimes heard them discoursing together respecting the Protestant religion, and they have declared that they could not see how there could be a religion without saints to work miracles. They are a people who do not readily believe anything but what is incredible, and repugnant to common sense; so that the more improbable the miracle is, the more willingly it is credited. *Il prodigio o è grosso o è niente*, is a common saying with them; small doings are not worthy of great saints.

In the midst of this ignorant race, born and educated in the grossest errors and prejudices, there exists a class of persons who do not believe in the superstitions of the vulgar, as they call these pretended miracles of St. Januarius and other saints; neither in the inventions of purgatory and similar stories; having read in some book, or heard some one affirm, that they are no better than fables; but, unhappily, they also extend their unbelief to all that is related of Christ and of his Apostles, and in fact assert that all these writings might be tied together, and thrown into the fire, as old and worthless.

These are the learned, people of genius, who go to church merely to gratify the sight, or to delight the ear with harmony; and who kneel before the reliques and the images in a procession, for the sake of appearance, as they term it. They go to confession at Easter, to deceive the priest into a belief of their piety, and receive the communion that they may escape censure. As lying and hypocritical as they are unbelieving and immoral, they form a very extensive class, most injurious to society in a thousand different ways; chiefly because being, as they are, without faith in religious matters, they are equally void of it in social affairs: and being weak-minded, through continual falsehood, they are mean in all their undertakings; timid and pusillanimous, with a mixture of irritability and rashness. In morality they are monsters of depravity, and this miserable land abounds with such persons more at this present time than ever; in the face of its glorious sun it is covered with the thickest darkness.

Between these two extremes of the direst superstition and utter unbelief, is there for these people no middle path of religion, of pure early Christianity? God alone knows. I have sometimes persuaded myself that there must be such; I have again doubted, and again I have returned to my former hope—at any rate I will not despair of it. Christian charity, and trust in God's mercy and providence, alike forbid me so to do.

### FOOTNOTES:

[75] "The Most Illustrious and Most Reverend Cardinals require a most illustrious and a most reverend reformation."

[76] In the cemetery near to these bones, a broken stone was found, on which was to be read the following inscription:— *Lumena in Pace* ⚓ Fi ... Don Francesco, on the authority of the sacristan, had no doubt the word *Filumena* was signified by the Fi....

[77] Matt. xi. 28.

[78] John xiv. 6.

[79] Matt. xv. 14.

[80] The same question might be asked with respect to the late pretended miracle of the image of the Virgin at Rimini moving its eyes. A shameless imposture, honoured by Pio Nono with the institution of an annual festival in its commemoration!

[81] 1 Tim. iii. 1.

[82] Matt. xx. 25, 26.

[83] For six hundred years it had never happened that the General of the Order had been dismissed by the Pope. It was the contrivance of a few ambitious friars, among whom Monsignor O'Finan, Bishop of Killala, in Ireland, was the most active.

[84] See the letter in the Appendix.

[85] Matt, vi. 15.

[86] Luke xvii. 3, 4.

[87] Rom. xiv. 23.

[88] 2 Tim. iv. 1, 2.

# CHAPTER XII
# THE MONKS OF NAPLES

Separated from human ties, apart from the laws of nature, there is no race of beings, in my estimation, so useless to society, so immoral, and so absurd, in a religious point of view, as they who call themselves monks. The Jesuits are monks, as well as those instituted by St. Francis of Assisi; both have the same very small degree of worth, and the same defects. I used to believe that the monks reckoned among their virtues kindness, gentleness, humility, and moderation; I imagined that they were full of charity towards their neighbour; and believing nothing of them but what was good, I thought when I entered into their society I should be living among saints. Who would have supposed that all their imaginary virtues should fade before my eyes, from the moment I became bound to them by vows which prevented my return? Every day the pleasant delusion became less and less, and bitter experience continually operated to undeceive me, at various periods of my sojourn among them.

I had paid strict attention to the proceedings of the Dominicans, both in Rome and Tuscany; and from what I had observed I was led to form a resolution to escape from them, and to renounce their society for ever. The request I had made to the Court of Rome from Capua, with respect to my secularization, had at first been received with dissatisfaction; but finally, on my reiterated applications, backed by a letter from Cardinal Polidori, the Pope granted my petition in the terms in which it was made, and for the reason I had stated; which was that the Order had become odious and insufferable to me.

Monsignor Acton informed me that the permission was made out, and at my disposal. He besought me, however, on the score of our old friendship, not to put it in execution, but to wait and see whether I could not find in the city of Naples a better race of monks, with whom I might associate happily, and pass my future days in tranquillity. I also received letters to the same purpose, first from Cardinal Polidori, and afterwards from Cardinal Gamberini, both friends of mine, in which they urged me to delay my projected secularization, until I had assured myself that my repugnance to remain in the Order could not be overcome. Cardinal Polidori informed me that such appeared to be the wish of the Pope, who seemed anxious, he said, that I should not act upon the permission he had granted me, till I found myself absolutely obliged to do so.

The good Acton took a great interest in my behalf on this occasion; writing to the Cardinal Archbishop of Naples and to others, and also several times to the Apostolic Nuncio, now Cardinal Ferretti, who was equally kind in endeavouring to persuade me to seek an asylum among the monks of Naples, after leaving those of Rome.

"Are you not of opinion, yourself, Monsignore," said I to him, "that these monks of Naples are *birbanti*, (vagabonds,) as well as those of Rome?"

"Nay, I think they are worse," replied he. "But it is precisely on that account that you ought to stay among them. If we did not do all we could to keep a few good persons among this class of gentry, we should have a community of a character qualified to inspire us with fear, and to compromise us utterly. I believe the monks of Naples are more ignorant and more turbulent than any others; and I repeat, it is for that very reason I request you to place yourself among them, where you will be most useful, both through your example and your teaching."

"But they will drive me to despair."

"In that case, then, you must leave them."

"But why, in the mean time, should I be made to endure such a tribulation?"

"To do good; to be useful to your brethren, for the glory of God——"

"Well, be it so. I will consent to make the experiment, commending myself to Him."

In the meanwhile, the Dominican monks had had recourse to all their powers of persuasion to induce me to take up my abode among them. Solicited on one side to enter the monastery of St. Dominic, and on the other that of St. Peter the Martyr, I chose the latter. The monks could hardly show me civility enough in their demonstrations of friendship and regard. They even declared me *figlio di quel convento*,[89] and though I declared I had no desire for any situation beyond that of Preacher or Professor among them, they forced upon me the office of Vice-Prior, and subsequently that of Prior itself; and if I had not vigorously opposed the measure, they would even have elected me their Provincial.[90]

Behold me then once more domiciled among the monks; not, however, as one of their society, nor with the intention of remaining permanently among them. They were not aware that I had the Pope's *rescritto* [91] in my pocket, in virtue of which I could turn my back upon them whenever I chose; and I must acknowledge, the idea that I could do so was a source of great satisfaction to me; it rendered me more tolerant, and at the same time gave me courage to do my duty: indeed, I accepted the Priorate for no other reason than to be better enabled to be of service to the community. I began with looking into the state of their finances, and with augmenting their income. But my principal endeavour was to benefit their moral and religious condition, as far as I could hope to do so among a set of people who had been educated in principles diametrically opposed both to sound morality, and pure and true religion. Nevertheless, the ascendency I acquired over their minds, and the friendship they felt for me, greatly seconded my views; to say the truth, they were far more docile than I had anticipated, and if I had been at liberty to carry out my system as I could have wished, I do not doubt that I should have formed them into a good and regular community.

But there were in other monasteries, belonging to the same Order, many despicable monks, who united in their own persons every vice that can be found in human nature. These appeared to hate the faintest trace of honesty or virtue, and were always ready to plot, to calumniate, and to stick at nothing to promote their own interest. I frequently took occasion to reprove them, and threatened, more than once, to make public their infamous proceedings, unless they thought proper to desist from their practices. But all my remonstrances were in vain, and at length I lost my patience: I fought manfully against them for a long time, but the General of the Order, Ancarani, was on their side, and lent them his powerful protection: I therefore felt that I had nothing more to do than to hold out, to the end of my year of Priorate, and then to give in my *rescritto* to the proper officer; which I accordingly did, in the month of August, 1839, and finally separated myself from the Order.

A new epoch in my life now commenced. I had never really been a monk, although I had lived so long among them. I therefore gladly threw off my monk's dress, and relinquished all the titles it had conferred on me, except that of Doctor of Theology, which, as one not belonging to the Order, I considered I had a perfect right to retain; it being granted to persons who had acted as Professor in certain sciences, for a determinate period, and subsequently gone through an examination; both of which I had satisfactorily done.

This degree is equally open to the laity as the clergy, on the fulfilment of the necessary stipulations; and once conferred can never be taken away; not even on account of heresy, since it is a title not granted for a man's belief, but for his ability. The obligation to teach is not made a preliminary condition, it is a subsequent duty; and the doctrine of the Roman Church is, that even if the Doctors themselves go into perdition, they still retain their degrees. I do not feel proud of the title as it was when I received it; but I confess I do as it has been, since my embracing the reformed religion. In the first instance, all my labour was in favour of Rome; now my most strenuous endeavours are in opposition to her doctrines. But even up to that time I had always regarded myself as a Doctor of the Holy Scriptures, and they, and they only, have occasioned the change in the aspect of my degree.

But how, it may here be asked, did I, on my secularization, get over the monastic vows which, it has been alleged, I took? I must inform my readers, that the Dominicans, contrary to the practice of all other monastic bodies, in their religious profession make but one single vow, which is that of obedience. My profession, therefore, was nothing more than a promise to be obedient to the Superior of the Order, and was couched in the following terms: "I, brother Giovanni Giacinto Achilli, promise obedience to God, to the most blessed Virgin Mary, to the Patriarch St. Dominic, and to you, most reverend Father General of the Order of Preachers, according to the rules of St. Augustine, and the constitution of the Order of Preachers."

Now it cannot be urged against me that I promised more than I expressed. Had I belonged to any other Order I must have vowed three things: obedience, chastity, and poverty. The Dominicans require obedience only. Some theologians pretend that in this obedience everything else is included; but this is neither legal nor philosophical. No one is obliged to do more than he has promised, even when that promise is valid and pleasing to God; which I do not consider to be the case with respect to the vows of the cloister.

But when I obtained my secularization, the Pope, who can do everything, dispensed with my vow; and consequently released me from obedience to the Order of Dominicans. The only condition was that I, as priest, should continue subject to the bishop of the place I inhabited. I do not mention this because I desire to justify myself in the sight of Rome, for I consider that the vows of the Monastic Orders are impious in themselves, as being contrary to the laws of nature, and in opposition to the eternal decree of God: I only wish to state what at that time were my relations and my ties to that Church which I have now abandoned.

My relinquishing the Dominican Order was the signal for numerous desertions. Many of my friends were not slow to follow my example; among them I may mention two celebrated men, the Rev. Father Talia and the Rev. Father Borgetti; equally respected on account of their years and their learning, as for their personal probity. Neither will I conceal the name of another, for whom I had the sincerest regard; the Rev. Giovanni Martucci, who at that period, although very young, was Professor of Natural Philosophy.

These persons, disgusted, like myself, at the falsehood with which they were surrounded, no sooner saw me throw off the cloistral habit, than they, also, demanded their rescript, and quitted the Neapolitan brotherhood. The worthy old men wept for joy, that the Lord had graciously, before their death, liberated them from the society of the prevaricators.

I remember Father Talia, who was exceedingly esteemed among the clergy of Naples, expressed himself in the following terms before the Cardinal Archbishop:—

"I do not believe your Eminence will suppose that I am actuated by an overweening desire for liberty, in emancipating myself from the Order of these monks; I would rather persuade you that my doing so has been occasioned by the pure love of truth and virtue, which the monks altogether refuse either to acknowledge or to practise. Your Eminence may say that I am an old man, and as such might have been contented to finish the remainder of my days in the cloister; but I would observe that my spirit is not affected by age, and that before I terminate my earthly career, I, though old in body not in mind, would fain leave behind me to the youth of the present generation, an example of Christian courage; showing that when an institution becomes corrupt, it is one's duty to abandon it, early or late, as it may be; for as the homely proverb expresses it, 'Better late than never.'"

To this the Cardinal replied that he was willing to admit that the good Father had his own reasons for quitting the Dominican habit; that he could not suspect a man like him to be actuated by light-mindedness; and that his friendship towards him would always remain the same: insomuch that the good old man felt himself not a little comforted with these kind assurances.

The monks, however, and more particularly those to whom our desertion from the Order was a bitter reproof, were by no means humbled; on the contrary, they were exceedingly irritated at our proceedings, and set themselves to consider how they could most persecute and injure us; in which intent they were greatly encouraged by the assistance they derived from Rome; I mean from the head of the Order, which unfortunately was at that time represented by the Monk Angelo Ancarani, a man of the most dark and gloomy character that ever disgraced humanity. His history might all be told in these few words: he was, during forty-five years, an Inquisitor of the Holy Office.

We, meanwhile, united ourselves in stricter bonds of friendship; mutually aiding each other, and defending ourselves, as well as we could, from the continual attacks of our malicious adversaries, who never let a single day pass without some effort to annoy us, by their false and calumnious reports.

We exhorted each other to patience and endurance. Nevertheless our dear friend Martucci, although of a pacific disposition, and always ready to forgive, could not forbear exclaiming: "Oh, these wretched monks! never was there seen a race so perverse and evil-minded as they are!" And I likewise, who had proposed to myself to endure everything with fortitude and resignation, could not at all times bridle the indignation I felt at their malicious attacks.

The most infamous slanders were preferred against the two good old men, and the excellent Martucci; for my own part I had less to complain of. It appeared that they had a dread of my numerous friends, who always stood forward in my defence. Still, in a crafty and insidious manner, as is customary with the Jesuits, they endeavoured to ensnare me to my ruin. I was informed that such was their intention; but as I am naturally averse to think evil of any one, I could not persuade myself of the truth of the allegation. Indeed, I held the monks and the priests in so little esteem, that I fancied as I never troubled my head about them, they also were very ready to forget me, altogether.

I occupied a handsome house in the Toledo; had two good servants, plenty of books, such as were necessary in my general studies, and a small circle of most excellent friends. I had in other places been annoyed by idle visits from people I cared nothing about; I determined, therefore, to make myself a more rigid monk now, in my own house, than I had ever been in the monastery. In the midst of my favourite pursuits, enwrapt in the most delightful contemplations, undisturbed by the continuous roar of the city[92] without, while within an unbroken silence prevailed—feeling that I was in the midst of the busy world, but enjoying a pleasing solitude—I was tranquil and happy: as a man who rests after a wearisome labour, or a tired warrior, who tastes the blessing of peace. I sought after, I wished for nothing more than peace, and tranquillity of conscience. And I may truly say I possessed it, since God gave it to me; but my invidious enemies sought to deprive me of it. Oh, evil minded men! cease to persecute him who is protected by the providence of God.

Affairs were in this state when I received a kind visit from my uncle, Dr. Mencarini, of Viterbo; who, as he had a great regard for me, was desirous to assure himself of my well-being, after my secession from the monks. He proposed to me that I should return with him, and settle at Viterbo, where he assured me every one, from the Bishop down to the humblest labourer, would be glad to see me; but I had left Rome with the resolution to remove myself as far as possible from its walls; and I too soon found that Naples was not sufficiently distant to ensure my deliverance from the machinations of the city that I abhorred, and which had become my most bitter enemy.

I had often revolved in my mind the idea of abandoning Naples, and even of quitting Italy altogether if an occasion should present itself. But how could I hope to bring myself to such a determination, without the severest shock to my feelings? It appeared as if nothing short of absolute necessity could impel me to desert my native country. As yet, however, this necessity had not become evident to my judgment. I imagined I could continue to enjoy my newly awakened liberty of conscience, in the secrecy of my own breast; whereas of this very liberty the natural consequences were my emancipation from the cloister, my separation from Rome, and my withdrawal from all that had hitherto formed the duties of my ecclesiastical office!

Who was there that did not know that I had altogether given up the practice of confessing, while the bishops still continued to send me their diplomas, for the performance of that ceremony? As to the mass, I scarcely ever celebrated it; and after several months' neglect I remember I said it once, from the weak and unworthy motive, I blush to acknowledge, that it might not be supposed the bishop had forbidden me to do so. My preaching, too, afforded the most convincing proof that I was no longer in agreement with Rome. How then could I continue such a system in the Roman States or at Naples? How could I hope to remain unobserved, when so many eyes of monks and of priests were upon me?

I began to see how utterly impossible it was that my reformation might, as I had fancied, take place without its being publicly known, and consequently without its drawing down upon my head all the hatred and the persecution of Rome. I have since bitterly condemned this weakness in myself, as being contrary to the Spirit that had enlightened me. To a character naturally frank and open, deceit is detestable; and I might have known that without deceit, without disguising the truth, neither by the Church nor by the government should I have been permitted to continue in the country.

Perhaps the idea of this reconciling of adverse principles, or in other words, of serving "two masters," arose in my mind from seeing that many persons without any belief whatever, without observing any of the forms of religion, were permitted to live free and unmolested, not only in Naples; but even in Rome itself. In Naples there are many priests whose conversation is that of infidels, but who nevertheless celebrate the mass, and hear confessions; and many others who, having abandoned the mass, and every ecclesiastical rite, unblushingly live with other men's wives, and openly declare their unbelief. Nobody, however, takes any notice of them; the bishop does not consider it to be his duty, since having left the work of the ministry, they are in a certain degree independent of him; and the government makes it a rule not to interfere with priests, unless they are charged with civil offences; taking no cognizance of their morality, still less of their faith. I therefore naturally concluded that I, likewise, should be allowed to live quietly at Naples, provided I conducted myself as a good citizen, and professed the faith of a Christian. The fact is, that if I had believed in nothing at all, I should have given offence to no one; if I had even adopted the language of Voltaire, I should have merely raised a laugh; but in speaking the language of the Bible, I attacked the priesthood, and incurred its hatred and its persecution.

The case, I may say, is precisely the same at Rome; where for heretics, that is to say Protestants, there is the Inquisition always ready; but as for unbelievers and atheists, so long as they are obedient to the pope, and outwardly reverential towards the Church, they are rather favourites than otherwise, and nothing stands in their way of receiving a cardinal's hat. Well may she be called by St. John, "the mother of abominations!"

It was a providential circumstance that I had occasion to leave Naples, on account of some important business which called me to Rome in the year 1841. I set off with the intention of returning at the end of a fortnight; but He who is my Master and my Guide ordered otherwise: it was according to his good pleasure that whilst I was on the point of leaving Rome to return to Naples, I was arrested by an invisible enemy, and that enemy was the Inquisition.

I look upon this event as one of the most fortunate of my life; if it had not befallen me, I should certainly have returned to Naples, to the quiet comfort of a private life and a peaceful home; enjoying a little world of my own, in the middle of a great city, and living solely for myself. But this was too mean and limited a sphere to satisfy me; I felt that I was not destined to live for myself alone, intent only on my own gratification; but to be useful to others, to contribute to the wants of a people, and to lend my aid towards the salvation of a nation. I had an important mission to accomplish; I considered it was given to me by God. Was it in the power of man to take it away?

On hearing that the Inquisition had laid hold of me, the monks of Naples began to chant their hymn of victory: "He who made war against us," said they, "is fallen; he who branded us with dishonour is fallen, to rise no more. The Inquisition will root out from the earth the very memory of his name."

Thus they rejoiced over my apprehension. Two or three of them were in correspondence with the Holy Office, through the General, Ancarani, and communicated whatever malice came into their heads concerning me. But their accusations were so palpably gross and untrue, that Ancarani himself, skilled as he was in the art of fabricating a charge for the Inquisition, could not make use of them: one of his letters, relating to this business, fell into the hands of a friend of mine; it was to a certain Father Avezzana, a Dominican, belonging to the Monastery del Vomero, at Naples. Among other passages were the following:—"I fully believe all you say, but it must be related in a different manner for the cardinals to believe it.... You should endeavour, in stating a fact, to state it so as to make it tell; to have effect: another time consult with Father de Luca and Father Travaglini."

In May, 1848, when I came through Naples, on my way from Malta to London, and stopped there a few days, another friend showed me a letter from the same Ancarani, directed to a lady, evidently one of his *devotées*, since the letter began, "*Carissima* Figlia in Gesù Cristo," in which he prayed her to use her influence with the Marquess d'Andrea, Minister *del Culto*, to compel certain persons to depose against me; especially as to what occurred at the time of Lent, in the church of St. Giacomo, where the Marquess himself, and others of the ministry frequently came to hear me. It appeared, however, that d'Andrea did not trouble himself about the matter, if indeed the lady ever solicited him on the occasion. This letter my friend found between the leaves of a book which belonged to an ex-Dominican nun of the Montfort family.

I relate all this to show what kind of men these monks are, and how they act in concert with the Inquisition. In the conducting of my process, among the various documents relating to my cause that I was enabled to get a sight of, I saw many papers in their handwriting, and some in that of Ancarani's secretary, Father Spada, a Sicilian; who, although I do not believe him to be naturally a bad man, was capable of going to any extreme in the way of his business, even to the burning of heretics, if required by his patriarch, St. Dominic, or by any one who might be considered his representative.

Among other papers produced by the monks, I saw a letter from my uncle, Mencarini, written at Naples while he was staying in my house, addressed to the Bishop Scerra, at Rome. In this letter, which was couched in the most friendly terms, he spoke of the base and unworthy conduct of Ancarani, and several others among the brotherhood; all of whom he designated as instruments of the Inquisition: and he advised the Bishop, as Secretary to the Congregation of Discipline, to put a stop to such proceedings, lest I should be so far irritated by them as to make disclosures that might cover them with confusion. I believe this letter had been intercepted at the office, and had so fallen into the hands of Ancarani, who had it copied by his secretary; for I cannot suppose that the Bishop, who was so friendly towards my uncle and myself, would have had the weakness to send it—being strictly confidential—to be copied for the use of the Inquisition. If that were the case I should be obliged to class him with Ancarani himself, and with others, who, for right or wrong, have sold themselves to the Inquisition.

Another circumstance is worth relating. The two principal agents in my accusation were Ancarani and Cardinal Lambruschini.

"We ought to burn this heretic alive;" said Ancarani, at one of the sittings of the Inquisition: at another he was a little more moderate, and only suggested my being sent to the galleys for life. The Cardinal asserted that I was not only a heretic, but a conspirator as well. In a meeting of cardinals at the Holy Office, this dreamer assured their eminences and the pope, that he could bring proof that I was a heretic in religion, a Freemason, a Carbonaro, a member of a secret society, and I know not what besides.

Several of the cardinals who were personally acquainted with me, opposed his remarks; but he was obstinate in his assertions, declaring that he had papers in his possession, and expected others from Naples, which would prove the truth of what he advanced. It appears, he was furnished with the fabricated documents of the monks instigated by Ancarani, and expected to receive more of the same description. But above all he hoped to gain possession of my private papers; for which object he had directed the papal nuncio at Naples to make a diligent search in my own house, and to forward all that he could lay his hands upon to Rome.

The nuncio could not refuse the Secretary of State's order, but he was obliged to act through the agency of the police, which was refused, when it was understood I was in the hands of the Inquisition; for the Neapolitans have the greatest horror of that establishment, and, to their honour, would never allow of it among themselves; rising up in open revolt every time the pope or the bishops endeavoured to introduce it. It is an interesting fact, that the minister of police refused the pope's nuncio permission to break into my private dwelling, and possess himself of my papers. I have been assured that he said to the nuncio, "I have no charge to prefer against Signor Achilli; he has lived in Naples quietly, and in obedience to the laws, and has gained great credit as a preacher. The police has no reason to suspect him of belonging to any secret society."

Cardinal Lambruschini made but a sorry figure before the Inquisition after this event; I fancy he was not very ready to come forward any more with his papers and precious documents.

I have frequently had occasion to observe how remarkably all those who at that juncture sought to oppress and calumniate me, have come to shame and confusion, without any effort on my part towards hostility or revenge. God himself has defeated and humbled them, and covered them with infamy in the sight of mankind. Ancarani died loaded with execrations. Lambruschini is still, for his greater punishment, among the living. Many others from Naples, and other parts, who persecuted me, have been signally visited with the chastisement of the Almighty. To Him be all honour, glory, and praise. Amen.

## FOOTNOTES:

[89] "An adopted son of the monastery." A great mark of esteem and favour among the Dominicans, including many separate privileges.

[90] The head of all the religious houses of the same order in the province.

[91] An answer to a petition.

[92] Every one who has been at Naples knows how incessant is the noise and bustle of the Toledo.

# CHAPTER XIII
# MY EXILE

It was in the month of September, 1842, that I found myself beyond the walls of Rome, in the province of Sabina; in a fine country, near Nazzano, in the neighbourhood of Mount Soracte. I had chosen this situation as a commodious one, and sufficiently distant from the capital, to allow me to arrange and settle my affairs, previous to my final departure from Italy.

But how bitter was the thought that I was about to leave my native country! Nevertheless, I saw that it was necessary for my spiritual good I should do so, in order to follow with more advantage the path which had been assigned to me by the will of the Lord. In no part of Italy had I as yet been able to find a secure asylum, where I could hope to be safe from the attacks of the pope, his monks, and his Inquisition. Though I was set free from the prison of the Holy Office, for want of any definite charge being established against me, I was still under its strict surveillance. All my proceedings were watched, all my words noted; and I was committed to the especial care of spies, bishops, and similar agents of the government. I could not therefore be considered as at liberty, although no longer within the walls of a prison.

In the meantime, regardless of these annoyances, I continued to speak without any disguise, about my departure; of my separation from Rome, of my renouncing the Church, and of my voluntary exile. Indeed, before being released from the Holy Office, I had altogether given up my connexion with the Church of Rome; I had abdicated all right and privilege of serving it, and consequently was exonerated from all its obligations. I was desirous to avoid all future imputation as to retaining any of its honours, its dignities, or its gifts; and therefore I renounced them altogether. I knew that according to the faith of the Church, it might be imagined I must retain the effect of the unction imparted to the priesthood, by the imposition of hands. I revolved in my mind how I could best free myself from this as well; and I saw no better method than by altogether renouncing the doctrine, and publicly protesting against it.

Before leaving this part of the country, I judged it expedient to apply to Rome for my passport; not indeed so much out of absolute necessity, as from motives of convenience. My letter was addressed to one of the officials of the Inquisition, who called himself my friend. I received in reply an intimation that the cardinals were not aware of the necessity of my request; which was as much as to say, that being clear from all imputation, and entirely set at liberty, I was unquestionably free to go wherever I pleased. Some of the cardinals, indeed, suggested that I had better return to Rome, in order to make my peace with the Holy See. I received other letters, at the same time, full of dangerous flattery and enticing offers,—the more dangerous as they were made by my dearest friends, to whom it is always extremely difficult to reply in the negative.

"Well," I exclaimed to myself, "I must be firm in my resolution; the more I am pressed and solicited to remain, the more speedily shall my departure take place. As long as I am met with reproaches and annoyances, I have nothing to fear; but when the opposite measure of kindness and entreaty is adopted, I am too weak to resist; and I cannot look for a miracle in my favour, if I needlessly expose myself to danger. Onward, then, and let me depart, in the name of God."

But whither? In what part of the world should I seek an asylum? At Geneva? or at Malta? I at length determined for the Ionian Islands. Previous to my departure, I called upon all my friends in the neighbourhood, and I wrote farewell letters to others who were beyond my reach. I did not neglect to visit my relations; and, having provided myself with a servant, I set off for Ancona, stopping on the road in those towns where I chanced to find any of my acquaintance.

The Governor of Ancona, Monsignor Orfei, (now Bishop of Cesena), was an old friend of mine; consequently I did not hide from him the reason of my leaving Italy, or the place I had chosen for my retreat, which I had frequent occasion to discuss with him during the fortnight I remained in the place. I mention all this as a proof that I neither fled from my country, nor sought in any way to conceal myself; and that my going into exile was a matter of free choice, dictated by conscientious motives, and nothing else.

I left Ancona on the 4th of October, and two days afterwards reached Corfu. I was fortunate enough to get included in the passport of a family with which I travelled, without any separate mention being made of my name; this was a necessary precaution, to ensure me from molestation on the road. But at Corfu I was on free ground, protected by the laws, and under colours that owe no obedience to the pope.

Here, then, I blessed the Lord, and offered up my thanksgiving to Him, for having thus far preserved me from the jaws of the lion, and from the hands of those who sought to ensnare my soul. For the first time in my life I breathed the fresh air of true liberty—of that precious liberty of spirit which is granted to the children of God. I sought for a minister of the holy Evangelists; and soon became acquainted with the Reverend Isaac Lowndes, an independent minister, and Secretary to the Bible Society. I ran to him as a famished man would to obtain bread; I opened my whole mind to him; I chose him for my spiritual director; and he has always proved himself to be one of my best and most esteemed friends.

My stay at Corfu was marked by many events. The first was a persecution emanating from Rome, clumsily enough conducted by two emissaries of the Inquisition—the papal consul, and the curate of the Romish Church. The first of these had the boldness to present himself before the Lord High Commissioner of her Britannic Majesty, with a despatch from Cardinal Lambruschini, demanding my expulsion, as having been guilty of enormous crimes. Being asked, however, by the consul, to state the nature of one, at least, of these pretended crimes, he could not find in his pocket-dictionary any term suitable for his purpose. I was subsequently assured that the secretary of the Lord High Commissioner reproved him for his assurance. The second of these worthies contented himself with speaking all manner of evil of me, whom he hardly knew by sight. It appears that both of them had a miserable pittance allowed them, for which they amused themselves in inventing and promulgating their abominable falsehoods. I know that the director-general of the police, Captain Lawrence, twice summoned before him one of these detractors, a Neapolitan tailor, and severely reprimanded him; and I also know that this tailor confessed he had been paid for his slanders.

Several of the Maltese, who constitute the most vile and wretched part of the population of Corfu, had, at one time, taken it into their heads to follow me in the streets, with insulting and threatening words; and when some of my friends, who were more disgusted with it than I was myself, inquired as to the reason of their doing so, they replied that the curate had desired them. I might have called the curate to account for this, had I been vindictively disposed; but the case was otherwise.

I must now say a few words upon a subject which perhaps may by some be deemed foreign to "my dealings with Rome;" but still it is in some degree connected with the principal facts of my history. And at any rate, it will be a page devoted to the memory of two dear friends, whose loss I have not yet ceased to lament,—to Attilio and Emilio Bandiera, universally honoured and deplored by all good men, for the sacrifice they made for their country.

These noble, generous, pure, and high-minded youths, were compelled, in consequence of being betrayed, to resign their commissions in the Italian-

Austrian navy. They repaired to Corfu, at separate times; and, as I was already on friendly terms with both of them, they requested me to allow them to remain in my house, and partake of my table. For four months I had the pleasure of the society of Emilio, the youngest of the brothers; and for two months, that of Attilio. It is not my intention in this place to relate their history, since it is already well known, how at the head of a few Italians, they embarked from Corfu, and landed on the shores of Calabria, where, in a skirmish with the troops of the Bourbon king, they were taken prisoners; and, under I know not what barbarous laws, were, with seven others, put to death; their only crime being a devoted love for their country.

Who among the virtuous and the brave has not mourned their loss? And who among them would not have considered himself honoured in their friendship? None valued it more than myself, who was regarded by them as a brother; to whom they confided their parting injunctions, and who was a minister of the Church of which they had become members; the Italian Church, which I opened in Corfu, in March, 1844, with Emilio Bandiera at my side.

I have hitherto been silent before the public respecting these young men, whilst others have spoken of them, and written the history of their fate. But my silence was solely occasioned by knowing that the Jesuits and their followers, availing themselves of the well-known fact of our intimacy, had spread abroad the report that I was only interested in the success of religious reform so far as it might lead to a political one; that for religion itself I had no respect whatever, and only assumed the appearance of it to ingratiate myself with the English, whose money and protection I coveted; in proof of all this they brought forward my friendship and intimacy with the brothers Bandiera.

And here observe how far malice will lead men astray. The *Dublin Review*, in July, 1850, stigmatises me to the religious world, as a mere political adventurer, while to the political world it represents me as a religious enthusiast, changeable, inconsiderate, inexperienced, and an immoral person, and a hypocrite to boot.

As to the Jesuits themselves I care little about them or their opinions, except as they influence the minds of other people. Certain it is that, in consequence of their calumnious insinuations, the religious cause which I advocate, in the face of my country and before the whole world, has in some degree been impeded.

Before I was known, and had gained the confidence of my good brethren in the faith, it was no doubt an unfavourable circumstance in their eyes, that I was so closely associated with persons who appeared to have no other object in view than political alterations. I confess I had not, at that time, sufficient Christian fortitude to meet these insidious attacks; and, therefore, felt it prudent to be silent with respect to my beloved friends, the Bandiera, until I should have established my religious reputation on a firm basis, and have acquired the confidence of the public with respect to my Mission. Now, however, God be praised, I am so far advanced in the general estimation of the Christian world, that I may speak out, and reply, as is incumbent on me, to the calumnies with which I have been assailed.

If I was so united, so closely united with the brothers Bandiera, it was because religious reform was the most noble, the most sublime idea in their minds; and because they felt the necessity of destroying the abhorred Papacy, and restoring to their beloved country the ancient pure Christianity of our fathers. On this head their language and their ideas, as well as their faith, were similar to my own. The only difference between us was, that they had not themselves as yet put their hands to the work, beyond confiding in Him who knows how to bring it about by ways of His own.

A reform in the Church is not to be effected by force of arms, nor by clamour and sarcasms. Temperate argument, and mild persuasion, and virtuous example, are the proper means, and such as the Reformers of the sixteenth century employed. The arguments, moreover, require to be based upon the written Word, which among all religious sects is received as the touchstone of truth. Now, my young friends had not the boldness to consider themselves sufficiently well instructed in the Holy Word to enter into a theological discussion with the people, or a controversy with the priests of Rome. They were desirous of reform, and in the furtherance of it they were content that I should lead the way, declaring themselves my followers. They had the hope that, in various parts of Italy, conscientious priests might be found capable of being reformed themselves, and afterwards of conducing to the reformation of others. They had a great desire to see the Bible circulated; we sent several copies of the Diodati Edition, to friends at Venice, Trieste, Ancona, and other places, and they themselves always carried about with them one which I had formerly given them; we had frequent conversations together respecting the meaning of different passages; and Attilio, especially, carefully wrote out any particular view which might arise in our minds on our perusal of them.

Emilio Bandiera, speaking to an Italian, who professed that, for his own part, he cared nothing about religion, thus expressed himself in my hearing:—

"It is every man's duty to care about religion. He who makes a boast that he has none at all is to be held in abhorrence. I would never choose such a one as my friend—much less would I have a wife of such a character, or children, or even servants. Do you imagine that any society could possibly hold together, in the proper discharge of its mutual duties, without religion? What would a political reform avail you without it?"

On another occasion, when one of his countrymen asserted that, good or bad, he would never change his religion, Emilio observed:—

"Your words are devoid of sense. If the religion you profess be, in your estimation, good—keep it; watch over it, and defend it; if, on the other hand, it be not so good as you first thought, by all means change it forthwith; that is to say, get rid of your present false notions, and take up those better opinions which hitherto you have not had. It was so that our ancestors did, whether Gentiles or Jews; as soon as they perceived that their religion was no longer good, in obedience to the dictates of their conscience they adopted Christianity, which appeared to them the only true one."

Both the brothers had a high regard for truth, in its pure and simple form. I will here quote a passage from the note-book of Attilio:—"The most important truth must, of necessity, be religious truth: it is present with us at all periods of our life, and is connected with all our necessities. The influence of religion is universal, and I believe that, whoever has the folly to endeavour to escape it, is nevertheless pursued by it, in spite of himself. Every individual in society who is irreligious, has to endure a greater struggle than he is aware of, and the more obstinate he tries to be, the more he has to endure."

O blessed spirits! without doubt you were visited with heavenly consolation, at the extreme moment of your separation from this miserable life. You believed in the words of our glorious Redeemer; you confessed yourselves sinners before Him, since every living soul is such in His sight. But in the eyes of men ye were justified. It was neither interest nor ambition that led you into the midst of danger, but a disinterested love for your country and your fellow-men. He who judges of the merit of an enterprise by its success, may say that your prudence was at fault in undertaking it; but I am of a different opinion. I assert that you were in political matters what John Huss and Jerome of Prague were in those of religion, the precursors and the first martyrs. May the Lord bestow His blessing on your labours, by blessing also the labours of those who may follow in your steps!

The two brothers left Corfu with twenty followers. Above a hundred Italians remained in the Ionian Islands, all equally acquainted with what was going on, and in which all were interested. No opposition was made to their project of forming armed bands upon the mountains which traverse Italy, the chain of the Appenines beginning in Calabria, in order to strengthen the revolution which had become necessary for the country. The two Bandiera, Morro, Ricciotti, and Nardi, with a few others, were the first who offered themselves for the enterprise; and accordingly they set out to join the forces that were already on the mountains, expecting their arrival. A single night would have been sufficient to take them there, as the mountains extended to the sea-shore. But, unfortunately, three days were lost among the inhabited parts, and this delay was fatal to them.

Thus it was that they fell into the hands of the enemy; not by private treachery, as has been falsely and malignantly represented. What treachery could there be where there was no secrecy? Their intentions and their expedition were known from the first, to everybody, and twice they had an encounter with the King's troops. Yet, would it be believed that the desire to calumniate and injure me has pushed the writer of the article I have already alluded to, in the *Dublin Review*, so far as to make him dare to assert that I, their friend, their counsellor, their bosom-refuge in their hour of trouble—I it was, who tempted these valorous brothers into the battle field, and procured their capture and their death, in order that I might possess myself of their effects!

Had I been capable of harbouring the thought of such an enormous crime towards any human being whatever, towards them at any rate, I could have no motive for doing so; since they arrived at Corfu in so destitute a condition, that they were actually obliged to part with the few articles of dress they could spare, in order to supply themselves with the requisites for their expedition; this they stated in a letter to Mazzini, shortly before they left Corfu, which letter he published in his memoirs of them.

When my friends set out for Calabria, I also took my departure from Corfu to settle at Zante. It was understood between us that I should undertake in that place, where I could be free from interruption, a work connected with the religious reform of Italy, and it was settled that I should there receive communications and instructions from them, as to my future proceedings.

My exile was not similar to that of other emigrants who were left in peace by all parties. I had never given cause of offence to my government in political matters, but I had done so with respect to its religion. I had not designated the monarch as a knave, but I had stigmatized the Pope as an impostor: it would have been a small matter for me to unmask the character of a man who has always been a slave to ambition and self-interest; I rather chose the task of disclosing to the world the presumptuous iniquity of one who calls himself holy and infallible as God Himself; the Spiritual Father of all men; the Lord over all believers; placed above all; with the power to save and to destroy; to open heaven, and to close the gates of hell. Such a centre of blasphemy, such an exalted idol, I resolved to combat and overthrow; I felt an enmity towards this enemy of God, this falsifier of holy truth, this opposer of every moral and civil improvement: I determined to wage such an incessant warfare against him that he should finally be obliged to succumb, and while life remains to me I will continue so to do. Let the Jesuits, the Inquisition, the priests, and all their spies combine their efforts against me. I heed them not, neither do I fear them, however numerous they may be. The power of hell has no influence over those who are commissioned to preach the kingdom of heaven. Against them, as it is written, "the gates of hell shall not prevail."

# CHAPTER XIV
# THE ITALIAN CHURCH

When I left Rome, and threw myself as an exile into the Ionian Islands, I confess I had not at first a clear idea of the task that Providence had assigned me. Still I felt as if I was destined for some high purpose. I acknowledged the hand that was guiding me through new ways and unknown paths, and in my humble prayers to the Lord I repeated the words of the prophet: "Speak, Lord; for thy servant heareth."[93]

Often did I meditate on the designs of Providence. But how can man comprehend the ways of God? It was with me as with the great German Reformer Luther: he felt that he was in the hands of the Lord; he felt the necessity of obeying the voice which called on him to reform the Church; and he was obedient, without knowing what he performed. I, too, obeyed a divine call when I separated myself from Rome, and, renouncing her honours and her dignities, quitted Italy for a foreign land, where I knew not what awaited me from the hand of the Lord: I only knew that I was ready to execute His will.

And it was His will, I doubt not, that a work should be commenced, which will be the most important, the most illustrious of all the events of the present age—the religious reformation of Italy, the establishment of a new church, to be called the Italian Church; founded on the ancient doctrines of Christianity, with its original form of worship, and with no other novelty than the adoption of the language common to the country. For three centuries has there been a struggle for religious reform in Italy, which has occasioned the sacrifice of thousands of noble victims, burned by the Inquisition of Rome, drowned in the Lagoons of Venice, and hungered, poisoned, or strangled in the prisons of Naples, of Tuscany, of Piedmont, and of Lombardy.[94]

The popes, the true tyrants of their country, have uniformly endeavoured with all their might to arrest its progress; and they had the power so far to destroy it as to cut the tree down to the earth, leaving only the trunk and its living roots under the soil. This reform so necessary for the people, and so desired by all good men, now appears as the dawn of a brighter day than has ever yet arisen upon my beloved country. It derives not its name from men, but from the Divine Founder of our belief, and is consequently only known under the denomination of Christian Reform; and as being more particularly connected with Italy, and as the language of worship ought to be exclusively that of the country, so the Church which is to be the result, has received the title of the Italian Church.

The reformation that we advocate and preach, is not founded on novelty. We profess no other belief than what the Holy Scriptures distinctly and directly authorize; and we repudiate all that in later ages has been added by men. Our worship, therefore, goes back to the practice of primitive Christianity, pure, simple, and spiritual: adapted to the requirements and the devotion of the faithful; not bound by laws to any particular form, but varying according to the necessities of times, places, and persons. Our doctrine is in agreement with the Bible, and our forms are similar to those of the Reformed Evangelical Church. The slight difference that may exist between ourselves and the members of other reformed churches, does not prevent us from hailing them as brethren. Moreover, as we profess to derive our origin from no one principal founder, and render thanks to God for having through his grace enabled us to reform ourselves, we are willing to extend our sympathy towards all our Christian brethren, whatever may be their denomination. We even hope that our Church will be distinguished by a greater spirit of conciliation, than is perhaps to be found in others. Each of us will be enrolled in the Evangelical Alliance, and will preach the doctrines of union, and concord; faith, charity, and good works.

Whether we shall adopt the Episcopalian or the Presbyterian form of government, I cannot as yet say. To tell the truth, I am not at present much interested in the question, since I consider it altogether a secondary one. It will greatly depend on the Bishops of the Latin Church in Italy. If they receive and promote our views, it is probable that they may, like the Bishops of England, be received by the general body of the Reformers; otherwise, they will be done away with; as is the case in Scotland, Switzerland, and other countries: we shall have pastors in their stead, and among them some will be appointed, as presidents, to offices of greater authority. I am inclined to believe that the change of name will be sufficient to induce the reform. The word bishop is of Greek origin, and would be better rendered by the word moderator, inspector, or superintendent; which would at once get rid of the idle notion of the reformed bishops, respecting the Apostolic Succession, and all its presumed rights and privileges. I maintain the absolute necessity of a complete and thorough reform of what is degraded and abused. As to anything further, I am, for my own part, indifferent about it.

The Italian Church must be built on the ruins of the Latin Church, which is already an anachronism. The Church of Christ must arise from the destruction of the Church of the Popes, which has become a blasphemy and an impiety. I do not believe it possible for the Church of the Priests to be reformed; it must be destroyed, as it is written in the 18th chapter of the Revelations. It is the people of this Church that will be reformed; and it is precisely the object that I myself and a few others are endeavouring to effect.

The religious reformation of Italy, at the time I am now writing, in the month of December, 1850, has already made considerable progress; and, except for the interference of an Inquisition, similar to that which existed in the time of Pius IV. and Pius V., it is impossible, humanly speaking, for it to be checked.

Undoubtedly, in some parts of Italy, it is yet concealed, inasmuch as it is denounced by the present government; and may be said to exist, as was the case with the Church herself, in early times, among the catacombs.

We have seen with our own eyes, the Bible itself persecuted not only in Rome, but in Tuscany also. A scandalous process was instituted against a printer, for having published the New Testament, according to the faithful version of Diodati; at a period, too, when the liberty of the press was pretended to be unrestrained. In Piedmont and Genoa, the people are more fortunate, as the Bible is allowed to circulate among them; and our brethren the Waldenses, since they have obtained their civil freedom, have also had their religious liberty granted them. But in all other parts of Italy even the Jews are better off than we are. They are allowed to assemble together and to open their temples to the public; they can educate their children in their own faith, and they are not subject to the pains and penalties of the Romish Church. The Jews are, at least, tolerated in Rome; but we are not. Still we have our secret meetings, even in the papal city; with a prison staring us in the face, we read our Bibles, and meditate on their contents, and we converse with each other on the essentials of salvation, through our Lord Jesus Christ, and of the true faith, as revealed in his Holy Word: and to these vital points we adjoin all that is necessary for Christian doctrine, at the same time confuting the errors of the Church of the middle ages. And what our brethren are personally engaged upon in Italy, we, who are banished on that very same account, are carrying on in other countries. The day will assuredly come when we shall be re-united, and publicly return thanks to God, for having associated us in the same faith, and saved us through the same hopes. And this day we trust is not far distant.

Eight years have now passed away since I first put my hand to this great work, and it has never, during all that time, ceased to go forward. As a minister of the Gospel, a servant of the Church, I called on my brethren to arise from their slumbers, and witness the brilliant light that was brightening the horizon. I called upon them to break the bonds with which they had hitherto been fettered; and, with the Bible in my hand, I endeavoured to enlighten their eyes, and convert their souls.

Could I know that the day would arrive when I might myself behold the salvation of my country, I would ask of the Lord that I might then depart in peace from this life, singing the song of Simeon,[95] and hoping for the benediction of the Almighty.

I have been accused as a man of extravagant desires, of overweening ambition. I do not deny it. My desire is that the people of Italy should be no longer the slaves of the priesthood, at once the prey and the laughing-stock of the Jesuits; that they should worship God, and not bow down before a wafer, a painted canvas, sculptured brass, or wood, or stone, or dry bones: that this beloved people should be taught to believe in the revelation of God, and not in the false inventions of the priests. These and similar desires have possessed my mind, and led me to implore their fulfilment from the Lord. And as to my ambition, it is to be foremost in this good work, and to teach others to labour effectively, through the grace of God, in the same holy cause.

My preaching in the Italian Church, as I have already stated, began about eight years ago, and I have been continually occupied in carrying it forward. From Corfu to Zante, and from thence to Malta, where, in the midst of opposition, not only from my enemies, but also from my weaker brethren, I established my church.

It was contrary to the opinion and advice of many that I went to this latter place.

"Reflect," they wrote to me, "on the ignorance and barbarity of the people; consider that they are much more subject to their priests and their monks, than they are to their English rulers, and that they will wage an incessant warfare against you. You will endanger your own safety, and run the risk of injuring your cause; you will also endanger us, who are powerless to afford you assistance."

I received this letter in Cephalonia, at the moment I was setting out for Malta, and it came from one whom above all others, I had expected to labour with me, in the vineyard of the Lord. It was displeasing to me; and in the panic fear with which the writer appeared to be possessed, I clearly saw the suggestions and instigations of that evil one, that adversary the devil, who, as St. Peter says, "as a roaring lion, walketh about, seeking whom he may devour,"[96] and who now sought to devour my works.

At this time, too, in order to impede my progress, a Maltese journal, notorious for its bad and abusive character, thought fit to publish several articles against me. In one of them, written by a Portuguese, probably connected with some foreign policy, after stating that I was come among the Maltese to convert them to Protestantism, it was proposed to the people to welcome me with a *chiarivari* of cudgels, stones, and other offensive missiles. This man had previously met me at Zante, when he told me he was himself a Protestant, and wished me all manner of success.

Another writer, who I believe had been an English clergyman, but who, on account of his misdeeds, had lost his situation, asserted that I was well paid for what I was doing by the Bishop of Gibraltar, and that I was nothing more than an agent, for my own private interest. I had met him a short time before in Cephalonia, where he inhabited the same house with myself, and he also, with many friendly protestations, encouraged me in my views.

In a third article I was roundly accused of political intentions; of having led on the two brothers, Bandiera, to their destruction, and of being an impostor and a hypocrite; and the public was accordingly called upon to treat me as I deserved. The writer of this tirade was a miserable Italian, of whose character the less that is said, the better; I congratulate myself on never having exchanged a word with him.

These three articles appeared either the day before or the very same day that I arrived at Malta; but instead of being discouraged or alarmed at their threats, I boldly advanced before my enemies, defied their malice, and provoked their indignation still further, by publishing my writings, and opening the Italian church. These proceedings silenced the reports against me; the fears that were entertained of me gradually faded away; there was no longer any occasion to dread a public disturbance on account of the Italian church; on the contrary, it began to meet with encouragement, when it was seen that it was frequented by some of the most respectable inhabitants of the place. Our congregation began to assume an air of stability. Others were associated with myself in the ministry, and it was my intention to consult them on all matters of importance. In this way I proceeded to compose the liturgy,[97] prepare a collection of hymns,[98] and make other arrangements, so that in the event of my absence, the work of God might still go on.

The Rev. M. A. Camilleri, a Maltese and a Roman-catholic priest, a worthy and excellent person, was the first to associate himself with me. He invited me to his own house, and set about making preparation for the establishment of our chapel. He conducted a religious journal, entitled "The Indicator," which subsequently became the organ of the Italian Church. It was not long before we were joined by a young bare-foot Carmelite friar, called Father Antonio, but whose real name was Pietro Leonini Pignotti, a Roman. He had been for some years at Malta, among the friars of his order, and used frequently to engage in conversation with us on spiritual matters. I admired him for the sincerity and openness of his character, and expected much from the zeal and affection he displayed for the religious reformation of our country.[99] Leonini was followed by Saccares, who was sent to me from the Bishop of Gibraltar. He also was a young friar, of the Capuchin order, from the Roman States, and renounced his obedience to the Church of Rome in order to join us.

In this manner our small family increased in number, and I foresaw that it would continue to do so. My letters from Italy spoke of many persons who were desirous to associate themselves with us; among others, my old pupil in theology, whom I had always esteemed, and augured well of his future destiny, Father Luigi de Santis, a Roman by birth, and curate at the Maddalena in Rome. He wrote to me in the most affectionate style, and it was with great pleasure I communicated the contents of his letter to my friends, who, together with myself, could not but admire how the Lord chose out of Rome herself, the men that were to combat against her.

All this confirmed me more and more in the opinion that the very "set time" was come, when a religious reaction was about to take place in Italy, against the Church of the priests, and that it was conformable to the will of God. Another idea now entered my mind, to connect a college of missionaries with our Italian Church in Malta, from which we might send forth our new preachers throughout Italy. This, however, did not take effect, for it is written, "My ways are not your ways, neither are your ways my ways."

I had already communicated my project to several of my friends; I now spoke of it to Dr. Gobat, the Bishop of Jerusalem, who was passing through Malta, and several meetings were held on the occasion. It was settled that my plan should be proposed to the Malta College Committee in London. Accordingly, in the month of May, 1847, I set out for this capital, in order to arrange as to the best mode of carrying the plan into execution.

The Committee appeared to be pleased with my idea, and to be willing to follow it out. It was proposed to unite my college to their own, and to call it the Theological Branch of the College of St. Julian, at Malta; which was to be placed under my direction, with the understanding that in all important matters I should communicate with the Principal.

I have no doubt that the Committee of the Malta College were sincere in their offer to grant me this support. The readiness with which they entered into my views, their approbation, and the promises they made me, were sufficient to make me believe that the hand of Providence was in the affair. I was not, indeed, acquainted with all the members of the Committee—some of them were not present—but the few objections that were raised, were overruled by a majority of votes in my favour.

Everything was well arranged; one thing alone was wanted, and that was money, which some people deem the most essential of all things; for my own part, I have never given it the first place in my consideration, having always hitherto found it supplied by the good providence of God, when it was most needed.

In the present instance, however, this very necessary article was required, not only for my theological branch, but also for the college itself, or rather for the school for the youths. The mode of procuring it was to be by calling meetings; and for this purpose I made a tour, accompanied by a Secretary belonging to the Committee, through the principal towns in England; holding these meetings at various places, which afforded a large amount in donations and subscriptions.

It is almost incredible, the sympathy which many persons evinced for this Missionary College. My name, the story of my conversion, my protest in my letters to the Pope, the Italian Church, all afforded abundant interest to those who saw that a reformation had already commenced in Italy, through a religious movement at Rome.

My brethren in the cause were immediately summoned to the spot destined for the Theological College. To Leonini and Saccares were added De Santis, and also Cerioni, of Jesi, in the Roman States, who had lately come from Alexandria, where he had been Secretary to the Bishop of Cairo. A fifth came from Smyrna, an Armenian priest named Giovanni Keosse, who stated that he had escaped through the assistance of a bishop, and under the protection of the Austrian Ambassador, from the clutches of the Roman Inquisition, which had laid hold of him at Constantinople. I cannot tell how it happened that this Keosse, on his arrival at Malta, was placed by the Principal of the College among my people. I should have been willing enough to have received him, if he had brought any recommendations with him. But he came in a furtive sort of a manner, and the reports I heard concerning him were by no means to his advantage; so that I began to suspect some evil design on his part; and in fact he soon showed himself in his proper colours.

A bundle of papers arrived one day at the Committee of the Malta College in London; they were anonymous, and contained vile, and at the same time ridiculous charges against Leonini and Saccares. I was informed that Keosse was the author of these slanders; the Armenian, received from motives of kindness, was already a traitor, who stabbed in the dark. I needed no further proofs of his baseness to give him to understand that he must forthwith take his departure: he then thought fit to throw off the mask; he was an agent for the opposite party.

"I think," said one of my friends to him, "you need not wait the coming of Dr. Achilli; he has declared that if you cannot prove the truth of your accusations, he will without ceremony turn you out of the house."

In fact, finding himself discovered, the Armenian did not think proper to wait my return; he departed, saying, he could live no longer where such disorder was going on.

I arrived at Malta in the December of the same year. The accusations against the two priests were proved to be false, and Keosse was declared to be a calumniator; I therefore caused a sitting to be held before the two authorities of the College, the Principal and the Vice-Principal, Keosse being present; and at this sitting he was prohibited from all interference with my theological branch. I imagined that he would also be expelled from the other departments, but he had more favour and protection than I anticipated; he received money to sustain his charges, and to endeavour to substantiate them; and at the same time, through the interest of some of the officials, he obtained the situation of Professor of the Turkish language. So that, although I dismissed him, another brought him back; I closed one door against him, the Principal opened another, for his re-admittance.

Five months of vexation, opposition, and annoyance succeeded. It was in vain that I complained and protested. This Keosse was employed as a tool, to separate me from the Malta College, to make me close the missionary department, and to lose all the ground I had previously gained. Nay, what was the worst of all, he had the art to induce some English clergymen, and others who called themselves Protestants, to oppose themselves to my proceedings.

I have been rather diffuse on this head, as it relates to the history of the Italian Church. Keosse himself, after having accomplished his mission,—the college being destroyed, and myself compromised in the estimation of those who were not acquainted with the business,—after having awakened discord, inseminated scandal, turned Protestantism into derision, and elated the Jesuits with their victory, now turned his back on the Malta Protestant College, and repaired to Rome, to receive the reward of his labours: doubtless he will be made a bishop.

We see, then, that the Italian Church can already boast of persecution, in the treatment of her promoters, who have been oppressed and calumniated, and betrayed by false brethren. And this very circumstance may be adduced as evidence of its divine origin, since the early Christian Church was equally afflicted and unfortunate. Indeed, such trials are promised to all the followers of Christ. Let us thank God that we have been accounted worthy to suffer for the truth.

And yet the Italian Church of Malta was beautiful in promise! The College was her seminary; but she herself was free and independent. My first agreement with the Committee was couched in the following terms:—

"If the College and the Theological Branch are under the patronage of the Bishop of Gibraltar, do not on that account imagine that my Church will also be subject to him. I shall consider it my duty to be equally courteous to him as to yourselves; but neither in one nor the other do I recognise the head or ruler of our church. Furthermore I declare, that neither my companions, nor myself, not being members of the Anglican Church, we purpose to be in communion with all Christian reformed churches whatever, beginning with your own."

These were my very words on accepting my office, and uniting myself to their body. And in accordance with these sentiments I may add, that we occasionally enjoyed communion with the Episcopal Anglican Church, and also with the Scotch Presbyterians; and at our own church, on the Thursday before Easter in 1848, we had the satisfaction of partaking of the holy communion with Christian ministers and members of many denominations.

The Italian Church disclaims the spirit of sectarianism, and fraternizes with every other church that lives in the purity of the Christian Faith; she abhors the spirit of intolerance and exclusiveness. She desires to be Catholic, in the true and original sense of the word.

The Italian Church I had established at Malta augured well, not only for the place itself, but for the whole continent of Italy, and for the island of Sicily also. I do not think it possible for the Anglican Church to prosper in Malta. All the efforts that have been made to that effect, for the last forty-eight years, have proved to the contrary. The English language is not adapted for a people who have received the language of Italy, through tradition, from the Knights of Malta, and from its commercial relation with Sicily and the Levant, whose merchants carry on their traffic in Italian. Besides it is to be noted that the people have no sympathy with the religion of their rulers, when they are on bad terms with their governors. Ireland is a speaking example of the truth of this remark. If reform be at all possible in Malta, it must be of Italian origin, and the Italian language must be employed, both for teaching and for worship.

My esteemed friend, Camilleri, who exclusively devotes himself to the service of his native place, is at length convinced of this fact, and joins me in the work I am undertaking.

It may be urged that the Maltese have a language of their own; but it is neither studied nor cultivated, and is little esteemed; it is entirely confined to the lower orders, and is a spoken not a written language: the Italian, on the other hand, is the language of the educated classes. I have always advanced these arguments to those who sought to ameliorate the religious condition of this people. I have discountenanced the translating into the Maltese language either the New Testament or the English liturgy; as has been done by the Bishop of Gibraltar: since whoever in that country desires to read, chooses the Italian language, which is preferred to all others. And it is on this account that none but an Italian Church can hope to supersede the Latin one; and that only after a long laborious effort. Provided the Italian Church were established in Malta, it would greatly tend to its extension in Sicily, since the place is much resorted to by the Sicilians, both for business and pleasure; and lately indeed by unfortunate refugees. During the whole time that our Church was open, many worthy Sicilians frequented it in preference to any other; and each of these, on returning home, carried with him at least his Bible, with the Christian Catechism, which we gave away on the occasion.

All is now over, through a jealousy the most foolish, the most incoherent I ever heard of. Weak men suffered themselves to be deceived and overcome, and after having made their first false step, had the folly to persist in and vindicate their error. I witnessed the fall of a Church, which yet was "built on the foundation of the Apostles and the Prophets, Jesus Christ himself being the chief corner-stone."[100] I had to lament over the destruction of the work we had effected in the Lord's vineyard, and the dispersion of the labourers. Oh, how many tears have I shed over the destruction of our infant Church! God alone knows all that I have done to raise and preserve it. Those who, to their eternal disgrace, have occasioned this evil will doubtless meet with due punishment. At any rate, I have the consolation of being free from remorse.

These reverses, nevertheless, served to instruct us with respect to the future. I, in particular, had occasion to acquaint myself with many things that I had not known before, and to undeceive myself with respect to many others. I had it in contemplation to commence my work with an appeal to the priests of the Romish Church. Their conversion would naturally have led to that of the laity. I argued with myself that if I could gain over to the Gospel of Christ the present ministers of the Romish Church, and separate them from the Pope's bulls, the people would assuredly follow their example; that the conversion of the ministers could not be a very difficult matter, since as they are all more or less read in the Holy Scriptures I could call their attention to them, and make it evident how widely Papistry is separated from early Christianity. "The Bible will be the touchstone," I said, "to which I can refer the two doctrines, Christian and Papist. The Bible itself will decide the question."

My reasoning was just, and I have found by experience that whenever a priest has consented to undergo the trial, he has finally been obliged to yield, and has acknowledged me to be the victor. The same success has attended my writings; Cerioni has frequently assured me that some articles of mine in the "Indicator" led him to examine the question, and that the consequence was his abandoning the Romish Church; and the same was asserted by two other members of the Theological College, besides many others. Similar success occurred in Rome. Many declared themselves willing to abide by the testimony of the Bible, but as sure as they came to argue the matter, so sure was I to gain the victory. I shall not relate here how many of the priests, seeing that from the authority of the Scriptures the falsity of the Romish doctrines was made manifest, ended by concluding that the Bible was no better authority than the bulls of the Popes, or the decrees of the Councils. I wish to confine myself more particularly to the mention of those who, impressed with the authenticity of the Holy Word, and convinced that the principles of Christianity cannot disagree with its teaching, drew the natural consequence that Popery is not Christianity.

It may be asked, What advantage do I gain in converting a priest from the Church of Rome? I answer, I gain a friend, an associate, in a holy cause; one who, if I desired it, would be ready, for his own part, to nominate me his bishop. If I was an ambitious man, I could assume an authority over most of these whom I have thus won over to the truth,—I could become their head, and establish a Church which should be called after my name; and so add another to the numerous sects which already divide the Christian world. But there is no danger that this will take place; I have invariably rejected the idea, whenever it has been suggested to me, as unworthy of a minister of the Gospel. Priests, above all people, are naturally inclined to sectarianism; they are accustomed to regard the Church as of higher importance than the Bible; according to them, Religion is not the work of God alone, but of God and man together. Hence it is that the Priesthood, in every Christian sect, is that which divides, opposes, denounces, and excommunicates. It is through the Priesthood that we have schisms, and we shall continue to have them so long as in the Church of Christ the believer is not placed before the minister, the spirit before the form, grace and faith before outward rites and observances.

The Roman priests, more than any others, naturally fall into this error; being desirous, even in their reform, to preserve their old customs. But there is another obstacle of no less importance—the priest has been accustomed to live, as they term it, by the Altar. We know it is written, "The labourer is worthy of his hire;" and Jesus Christ himself quotes the old saying, "Thou shalt not muzzle the ox that treadeth out the corn." It therefore is clear, that every minister, of whatever sect he may be, who duly works, has a right to be decently provided for. But this doctrine, though sound in itself, becomes nevertheless objectionable, when it is made a dominant principle, the axle on which the wheel must turn. The minister who serves the Gospel is maintained by those to whom he dispenses its truths; but he is not equally to be so maintained, on the sole ground of his priestly office, when he is unemployed.

It is a difficult matter to drive this idea from the heads of the priests and monks of the Romish Church, the major part of whom are accustomed to an idle life, setting aside the *laborious* duty of saying Mass; so that even when they leave their ancient creed, from motives of conscience and clear conviction, their first inquiry is, how they are to live. Hence it follows that many of them are kept in their allegiance to Rome, because they fear they shall die of hunger if they desert her. Others, on the contrary, deceived by false statements, forsake the Church of Rome, and throw themselves boldly into any reform whatever, under the vain hope of finding the means of becoming rich in so doing. The first err through too great timidity, and the second through too great rashness. Both the one and the other are very little serviceable to the cause. I have had experience with both kinds—with those who before joining me looked for an agreement on my part that I should always be at the expense of their maintenance, and with others who unreservedly associated themselves with me, under the idea that I should, with a liberal hand, supply them with all the money they wanted.

On the contrary, I have been poor ever since I left the Church of Rome; still I never solicited aid from any other than God alone. I admit, however, that His goodness never failed me. I have laboured hard to gain my living, but have never eaten the bread of idleness; and I have sometimes, through my own exertions, been able to minister to the necessities of my brethren. I have never regretted the privations I have had to undergo; I have even frequently concealed them, in order not to be burthensome to others. My companions have seen all this, and can bear witness how I have confided my wants to the care of the Divine Providence, and how often it has happened that some one has spontaneously come forward to our relief, at the moment we most required it; through the agency of man we have been fed by the hand of God.

But the priest who leaves the Church of Rome, persuaded of the truth, yet not converted by it, is always in search of "what he shall eat, what he shall drink, and wherewithal he shall be clothed," and becomes unhappy and desponding if he be not regularly supplied according to what he thinks necessary.

The idea of providing for these priests, and the great difficulty of finding the means of doing so, has, in fact, hitherto prevented me from calling them to me. I had had a sad experience on the subject, when I associated myself with those at Malta. As long as they were well fed, peace and harmony prevailed; but the very day our means failed, they rebelled against me, with the exception of one or two, and turned out ungrateful, unthankful, and altogether unworthy.

This lesson, amongst others, has taught me that in my work of reform I must not seek the aid of priests. They would be nothing but a burthen and a trouble to me. It is not they who constitute a reform, but the believers; and among them it does not appear to me that the priests, as a body, hold the first place; if by the word believer is to be understood a man endued with faith and religious zeal. I hope our Italian Church will institute good laws with respect to its ministers; in the meantime, I shall get my operations forward, without again associating myself too closely with any of the priests who may be converted. I shall exhort them to work as I do, and gain their own bread.

St. Paul "laboured with his own hands;" and why should not a priest, who has not much to do in his ministry, employ his leisure time in some civil or literary employment? I even indulge the hope that we may at last return to the old practice in this matter, when the priests did not form a *caste*, but were merely the heads of the families that were the most respected; and were chosen by the people, on account of their wisdom or piety, to the office of minister or elder.

The inconveniences to which we are now subject in Italy, through the priests, warn us in time, as to what arrangements we ought to make respecting them. It is certain that as to exalt Christ we must abase the Pope, so to raise the spirit of Christianity we must combat the idolatry of mere forms; and that to purify Religion, which has become corrupted by priests, we must in every possible way make war against everything that comes under the head of priestcraft.

## FOOTNOTES:

[93] 1 Sam. iii. 9.

[94] *Vide* M'Crie's "History of the Reformation in Italy;" Baird's "Sketch," &c.

[95] Luke ii. 29.

[96] 1 Peter v. 8.

[97] "Form of Divine Service in the Italian Church in Malta." Malta: 1847. Printed by Vassalli.

[98] "Psalms and Hymns for the Italian Church in Malta." 1848. Printed by Vassalli.

[99] He made profession of his faith in a letter to the General of his Order, published in the *Indicatore,* and circulated at Rome as extensively as possible. Vide Appendix, Indicator I. March 1847.

[100] Eph. ii. 20.

# CHAPTER XV
# MY MISSION

Meditating on the events that had taken place at Malta, I was compelled to acknowledge that the method which I had deemed the best to evangelize Italy, viz. a Missionary College, was not the way that Providence had appointed. In fact, instead of proving an advantage, it turned out to be a complete obstacle to my success, and gave occasion to so much injurious discussion that at length I began thoroughly to be disgusted with it.

I moreover felt a conviction that the mission which I had confided to others would be carried out better by one person alone; at least, that I ought at all events to begin it by myself. Having entertained this idea, and becoming more and more satisfied of its propriety, the next consideration was, where and in what manner my operations should take place.

It was about the end of the year 1848, whilst I was still in London, doubtful whether or not I should return to Italy, when another thought came into my mind, as to the expediency of my first making a voyage to the United States. In the midst of this uncertainty the news arrived that Pope Pius IX. had fled from Rome. This intelligence, which to some occasioned grief and consternation, and to others equal joy and satisfaction, particularly struck me, not so much as a matter of surprise and wonder, but as involving in it the most important consequences.

"So," I exclaimed within myself, "the Pope has fled from Rome—has abandoned the government of his States! The Constitutional Pope has lost his kingdom, he has fallen from his assumed eminence. He is no longer popular, the Romans have ceased to love or to esteem him! he has given them frequent cause of offence, and, on the sixteenth of November, he completed his work of provocation. The Romans are not to be despised—their anger is terrible: in the same degree that they formerly loved, they now abhor the Pontiff! I see him dethroned! He has fled, only to work greater evil; his flight is to betray his people! But he will never return! Woe to him if he should attempt it!"

These ideas continued to haunt my mind; I carefully examined and weighed them over, and discerned a connexion between a political event which was known to everybody, and a religious one which was apparent to myself alone. The times were serious; they occasioned me to fall into a profound meditation, and led me to offer up more fervent prayers to the Lord.

I went about consulting my friends, and amongst others, one whom I hold in the highest esteem and regard, Sir Culling Eardley Eardley. I passed a day with him at his seat, Belvedere, near Erith. We were both silent some minutes, considering whether it would be prudent for me to go to Rome.

"Oh! yes," I exclaimed at last, "the present is the very moment when it would be best for me to go among my brethren, in my native land, to speak of Him who is 'the first-born among many brethren.'[101] The hour is propitious, and I hope I may not lose it; the utmost of my desire is that the door should be opened for me to enter."

"But do you not think," suggested Sir Culling, "that your life might be endangered? You know how incensed those priests are against you! If they lay hold of you!— —"

"Oh! fear them not; I do not believe that they have any longer the means to injure me. The Pope has already lost all moral power in Rome, and he will soon lose his physical power also. Whatever happens, I believe I shall be protected by the Almighty; He has protected me hitherto, and will doubtless continue to do so, more especially when I am exposed to danger in His service."

"Are you of opinion that your presence in Rome will be useful to the cause of the Gospel? and that the Romans, in the midst of their present political struggle, will find time to turn their attention to matters of Religion? Do you suppose that now, when every one is vociferating for civil liberty, they would listen with complacency to a person who should talk to them of religious liberty, of spiritual liberty, of the liberty of the children of God?"

"Without a doubt I do; I understand the Roman character better than any one, and I feel confident that even in the midst of their political agitation, they would be interested in religious concerns; and the more so when they were made to understand that the religion which their priests had taught them was a false one. Among the numerous doctrines that their Church professes, several are not believed by many persons; but it is through instinct and natural good sense that they refuse to accept them, and not from having proved them to be false. No one has hitherto been allowed to instruct the people, or to give them any books that treat of religious subjects in their proper point of view; and more especially is it forbidden to put the Bible into their hands. Now, what would happen if the Romans heard one of their fellow-citizens speaking to them the language of truth, in opposition to the teaching of the priests?—speaking it with the Bible in his hand; and that Bible, moreover, in their mother tongue; and handed over to them, that they might read it themselves, and teach their children to do so, and by it to reform both their faith and morals? Yes! my Romans would be delighted, at the present juncture, to listen to what they have so often desired to hear, and what no one has hitherto been allowed to explain to them. I am perfectly aware that zeal ought to be guided by prudence; I shall therefore not go and declaim abroad, in the piazzas, but shall rather endeavour to find my way into the houses; and before I hold forth in public, I shall commune with individuals in private. I shall, in fact, make to every one I can a personal appeal. It was so that the primitive Church was formed by its Divine Head. The Lord, then, shall be my guide in all that I do."

"Well, then," observed my friend after a pause, "in order to obtain that guidance, it must be the subject of prayer." Upon which we both knelt down, and as the Spirit dictated I besought the Lord to guide us in our proposed work, according as seemed best to His gracious pleasure. My friend also preferred his supplication that the desire which influenced our minds, and the love which inspired our hearts to convey the truths of the Gospel to our brethren, might be graciously strengthened by His Divine assistance; that the doors might be opened, and the paths prepared to facilitate our undertaking.

We both derived comfort from our prayers; and we felt it to be the will of Heaven that I should go to Rome. I made some further remarks on the subject; and particularly that I considered it to be a providential circumstance that I was not impeded by any engagement with the Malta College, but was free in every respect. I remarked too that my mission was not from men, but from God alone; and consequently, that I depended solely on Him, to whom all obedience and glory is due.

These were not, however, the only supplications that were at that time offered up in behalf of my success. I requested of my brethren of the Evangelical Alliance the benefit of their prayers also, that I might be directed by the Lord in my difficult task; and I was sure they would be fervently made, so that I felt myself sufficiently encouraged, and was full of ardour to commence my work.

In the meanwhile the news from Rome became every day more and more important; since after the flight of the Pope, and after he had refused to receive the embassy from the Senate and the People, who solicited his return, the public feeling against the Papal Court every day continued to increase, as well as their dislike to whatever savoured of the priesthood.

Every one delivered his free opinion on passing events; the Roman journals were loud in their denunciations: everything prognosticated the destruction of the Papal government, and with it that the Church,—that hypocritical and tyrannical Church,—would cease to torment the people, and thus the greatest obstacle to their liberty would be removed.

I set out from London on the 8th of January, 1849. I passed through France, recommending the true welfare of Italy to the prayers of our brethren. I took the road through Genoa and Tuscany. The defeat of Charles Albert had thrown a gloom over men's minds; they deplored the sacrifice of so many noble youths in the plains of Lombardy, without any advantage to their country. Nevertheless, the grief they experienced in nowise diminished their courage, or lessened their ardour to engage afresh in their glorious attempt to drive the Austrian out of the land, and liberate the country from a foreign yoke.

I, as a good citizen, felt a lively interest in everything that was going on, and participated in the hopes and fears of these brave people. I often entered into political discussions with them, but it was always with the purpose of introducing religious remarks, which gradually gave a tone to our whole conversation without their being themselves aware of it. I had some pocket Bibles and Testaments with me, and occasionally produced one, to give a text in the original words; it generally happened that others also were desirous of looking into the book, and it usually ended in my presenting them with a copy.

At Leghorn I supplied myself with a large quantity of Italian Bibles, which I carried with me to Rome. As at the time of my landing at Civita Vecchia the Pontifical Government still nominally existed, the officers of the Custom-House, before they allowed me to set off for the capital, were desirous to inspect my books.

"Two cases of books!" exclaimed they.

"Well," said I to them, "I will tell you what the cases contain. They are all copies of one single book, and which book I maintain it is not necessary to subject to inspection. To whom, pray, would you submit it for that purpose? To the head of the Inquisition? Understand then that the book which I take to Rome is the Bible, the true Bible. Do you suppose that the Bible would be objected to by the Inquisition?"

"If it be actually the true Bible," returned one of the officers, "I should say it would not."

"But if it be not the true one?" suggested another.

"I can assure you it is," I rejoined, "you may, indeed, yourselves readily imagine, that an ardent lover of his country, as I am, would never introduce a false one into Rome."

"Can we see it?" asked a third.

"Without doubt," I replied; and opening one of the cases, I handed four Bibles to them, which was one apiece; "will you allow me, gentlemen, to present each of you with a copy? it will serve as a remembrance."

Great was the satisfaction of the whole party on the unexpected acquisition. They could not sufficiently admire the gift, and thank me for it. I had myself already inwardly returned thanks to God, who had granted me to enter into my native country under such favourable auspices.

I arrived at Rome on the evening of the 2d of February. The coach stopped as usual at the Porta Cavalleggeri, under the lofty walls of the Inquisition.[102] I raised my eyes to survey the massive boundary that was erected to shut out the Holy Office from the profane gaze of the passer-by. Alas, what horrors have been enacted within its circuit! What direful prisons exist around the grand hall of the tribunal! Some immediately under the roof of the building, exposed to the suffocating heat of summer, which renders them almost as close and unendurable as a furnace; others, which are excessively cold in the winter, on the basement, and into them the water filters from the adjacent grounds, and occasions a perpetual humidity. The dungeons are deep underground, like burial vaults, and in the middle of them is a cemetery, for the bodies of such as have been put to death within the walls. These wretched places have only been discovered recently, and were laid open to the inspection of the people during the time of the Republic.

In the midst of the court-yard rises the vast edifice where the cardinals meet at stated periods, (besides their weekly sittings at the Minerva,) and the councillors every Monday prepare the decisions. In the same building are the grand Archive Chamber, over the door of which is written "*Scommunicato è chi entra,*" the Chancery the Secretary's Office, and the secret Printing Office: the various apartments for the different offices attached to the establishment, as well as for the servants, the officials, and the gaolers: the places of punishment also, where in former times the unfortunates under accusation were tortured in various ways, by the cord, by fire, by boiling water, and other atrocious inventions, which it would be too painful to describe.

These places now present a different aspect, and appear to be appropriated to other purposes; so that it might hardly be discovered that they had originally served for chambers of torture, were it not that here and there an iron ring affixed to the wall, and other indications of that sort, afford too sure evidence as to their former uses.

This little description has arisen in my mind on having occasion to speak of the locality: as I have before said, all was concealed at that time behind lofty walls, but I was well acquainted with the precincts. I remembered my own imprisonment, when, more than for myself, I grieved for so many other victims sacrificed in that abode by superstition, by fanaticism, and not unfrequently by private vengeance.

In the midst of these melancholy recollections, I felt grateful that I was permitted to revisit my beloved country, to which I was returning, not from any motives of earthly interest, but from a sincere love for higher and heavenly considerations. I was not the bearer of gold, or of other worldly treasure, but of a treasure infinitely more valuable. I felt a pride in entering into Rome laden with Bibles; and it appeared to me as a dream, that I was permitted to do so, without any one presuming to interfere with me. I subsequently ordered another package to be forwarded, not only to myself, but also to other brethren, who were associated with me in the same good work. In the meanwhile, an extensive edition of Diodati's New Testament was published at Rome. The Bible, therefore, it might now be said, had entered and taken peaceable possession of the city, and was distributed among the citizens.

I had always admired the Roman people, so ready to receive the truth when it was pointed out to them. Whoever asserts that they are a prejudiced race, does not sufficiently reflect on their shackled condition; it is to their teachers we must look.

The Romans are papists through necessity, since they are never permitted to listen to any others than their popish priests, or to open a book which is not of papistic tendency. To be judged candidly, they should first receive, as other nations do, a liberal education. I am convinced that their natural good sense is such, that if the truths of Christianity were once fairly laid before them, they would accept them readily. Still it is not the work of a moment, and a fit time is required to unfold them.

It is not to be questioned that the first half of the year 1849 was for Rome a time of liberty, but it was also a time of agitation. A new order of things engaged the attention of all classes; and the minds of all ranks of persons were in a state of commotion, divided between hope and fear. The subject of all their conversation, the primary object of all their thoughts, were public affairs, political measures, and the existence of civil rights. Threatened on all sides from the earliest period, they knew that without a special Providence their Republic could not continue to exist; in such a precarious state of affairs, the majority dared not compromise themselves with the priests; certain of a reaction from the papal government, on the first opportunity. They were aware that of all the dangers they had to dread, the most fatal one was to be suspected of heretical tendencies.

In Rome, the Bible itself is heresy, as the priests assert it is from it that all heresy proceeds. Therefore, a man who studies it, is suspected of doing so, in order to find a pretext to separate himself from the Romish Church; so general is the idea that the sacred Scriptures and the papal Church are not in agreement. The suspicion is increased, if the version consulted be one of those that are prohibited in Rome. Among all the Italian translations, the most odious, and most proscribed by the priests, is the famous one of Diodati, which that learned and holy man brought out in Geneva, about the end of the sixteenth century. Admirable as it is, and the most correct according to the Hebrew and the Greek, its text might serve as a standard for others. A few years ago this Bible was scarcely known in Italy, even by name; in order to obtain a copy, it was necessary to apply to some Englishman, who could himself only introduce it secretly; and woe to him in whose possession it might afterwards be found!

What then were the grand fears respecting this book? That whoever read it was certain to have his mind alienated from the Church of Rome. A higher eulogium could scarcely be bestowed upon it. Its extraordinary fidelity and extreme perspicuity, notwithstanding the difficulty of rendering perfectly one language into another, will always render it a work of the greatest use.

In distributing this Bible I was accustomed to dwell on its value, to those who were not already acquainted with it, and also to explain the mode of reading so as to understand it. The chief rule is that the Bible can never contradict itself: obscure passages should be explained by others more clear. "The Bible explains the Bible," is the canon of St. Augustine. It is not true that the Fathers are necessary to interpret it; they may sometimes be useful, but more frequently they do harm, since each of them has a different system.

The Church of Rome orders the study of the Fathers in preference to that of the Scriptures; and this she does because in the diversity of their opinions the reader becomes bewildered, and is obliged to have recourse to her for explanation. The grand maxim of the Church, that no private man can be a judge of the Holy Scriptures, is true in one sense; no private individual can impose his own understanding of the Holy Word upon another person; it being revealed to every one for his own especial good. He may, for the edification of others, reveal the fruits of his own experience; but no man can be the spiritual master over another. We have one only spiritual

Master, and that is our Lord Jesus Christ. This observation applies to all persons, even to the Pope himself; who, if he be a sincere believer, and an intellectual man, may comprehend the Word of God, as any other sincere believer and intellectual man, whether priest or layman, may comprehend it: if, on the contrary, he be ignorant and stupid, he is not more capable of comprehending it than any other person of the same description. The privileges of the Popes are as unfounded as their pretensions.

Among intelligent people—and there are such in the Church of Rome—one of the chief objections against studying the Scriptures is an idea of their wanting perspicuity. I was asked by one person how it was possible for him to understand so obscure a work. "Why not?" I replied; "are not you as good a judge as the Pope? Nay, if you are a believer, and he is not, you are in that case a better judge than he can be."

"But to understand the Scriptures in a proper manner, it is necessary to read the Fathers!"

"And who has told you so? Doubtless persons who wish to discourage you; since it requires no little resolution to undertake the reading of the Fathers,—a series of more than forty volumes in folio!! No, no, read your Bible, and never trouble your head about the Fathers."

Every day I was thus occupied in conversing about the Scriptures. At first I sought out for persons to introduce the subject to: in a little time I was myself sought out by them. My house became a general rendezvous, and it frequently happened that from morning till night I had not a moment to myself; so many persons were calling on me, either to ask for Bibles, or to discourse with me on what they had already been reading. Many whom I had never seen before came and introduced themselves to me, requesting a Bible, and several repeated to me the very topics I had argued with others; which showed me how widely the truth might be spread through mutual communication. I had at that time but few of the female sex among my converts; I have however been informed that many have since received the truth from their husbands, their fathers, or their brothers.

Besides the Bible, I circulated a few tracts which I had written expressly for the purpose; and I also availed myself of those I had published at Malta, and in Tuscany, through the medium of friends. The most acceptable of all these was that "On the benefit resulting from the death of Christ," by Aonio Paleario; published at Siena, in 1543. This valuable little book, which treats expressly on our justification by faith, and is, in my opinion, the best explanation of the two Epistles of Paul to the Romans and the Galatians that I have yet seen, was so vigorously sought out, and destroyed by the Romish Church, that of fifty thousand copies that were printed during the Author's lifetime, it would scarcely be possible at the present moment to find even a single one in existence; and I myself owe the restoration of it to accidentally discovering an old translation of it in English, in my first visit to London in 1847, which I retranslated into the original Italian. The Author was burnt by the Inquisition, on account of this work, along with the renowned Pietro Carnesecchi, a most learned and pious prelate; and Cardinal Moroni, after a wearisome imprisonment, narrowly escaped a similar fate. His offence, as well as Carnesecchi's, was having put this little treatise of Paleario's into circulation.

Two extensive editions of my translation were published in Florence, and of these I distributed many copies among my friends in Rome.[103]

The experience I had gained in these matters taught me that the present moment was a favourable one to sow, to plant, and to graft; and that we might hope our labours would be visited and nourished by the sun and the rain from heaven. We are indeed assured that when the seed is thrown into good ground, in the vineyard of Christ, it not only takes root and flourishes, but also bears fruit. It is true that the wild boar of the forest has since entered in, and with his savage tusks rooted up, wasted, and destroyed; but a portion of the seed yet remains in the ground, and in due time, with the blessing of heaven, will not fail to bring forth good fruit.

It was my constant endeavour to avail myself of every opportunity to lead the conversation to religious subjects: not a day passed without making some progress, and in all places I kept my object in view. Sometimes a discussion took place in a friend's house, and frequently in shops and other places of business; and as it is customary in Italy, as in France, for the most respectable people to frequent *Cafés*, both morning and evening, I did not neglect to visit them likewise, in the hope of meeting some to whom my discourse might be acceptable. The few good and faithful friends who laboured in the same cause acted as I did, and gave a tone to the conversation in these places, as well as in the clubs and other places of public resort.

Sometimes when we had got a few persons together, we repaired to one of the halls of the Campidoglio, or to the ruins of the Coliseum. In the latter place we had on one occasion a very interesting meeting. It was on a fine afternoon in May, and the French army, outside the walls, were carrying on their barbarous and most unjust siege. I had many friends in Rome at the time, who had come up from the provinces, and were desirous to hear about our Reform; I therefore appointed them to meet me at the Coliseum; several Romans also were of the party, and altogether we formed a numerous body. I opened the Bible, and began to read to them the first verse of the fifth chapter of the Epistle to the Romans, explaining to them the signification of the expression, of being justified through faith. I then proceeded to read the first verse of the eighth chapter of the same Epistle, and commented on the meaning of the words, "to be in Christ Jesus." I next inquired of a boy who was present, if he could repeat to me the Ten Commandments, which when he did as he had learned them from his priest, I took occasion to show, that according to the Church of Rome, instead of ten commandments there were only nine, since the second, as it is given in the twentieth chapter of Exodus, and the fifth of Deuteronomy, was wanting. It is impossible to describe the amazement of my hearers on discovering this deceit on the part of their Church, against which they did not fail to exclaim, in no very measured terms. It was towards evening, and we were seated among these celebrated ruins; the moon was rising and began to shed her yellow rays upon the broken arches around; the scene was picturesque and impressive, and while our breasts were saddened by the contemplation of these remains of Roman grandeur, our souls were still more oppressed by the thought of the desolation that had fallen on Christianity itself.

One of my favourite resorts was the *Circolo Popolare*. Those persons who take it into their heads to calumniate the Romans on every occasion, designate this assembly as a democratic club, expressly organized, not merely to uphold the Roman Revolution, but to sow discord and disorder in society, anarchy in the government, and to effect the complete demoralization of the people; and in support of their assertion they cite the evil that was effected by the popular clubs in France. I, who was in Rome all this time, and took no part in the Government, nor held any office under it; I, who am also a Roman, and one who holds in the highest esteem principles of order, moderation, and justice,—I can declare what the *Circolo Popolare* really was. It was a club where citizens of every rank and condition met together, to promote, by their united counsel and operation, the liberty and national independence of their country. It was founded in the time when moderation prevailed, and Pio Nono favoured the cause of liberalism, and put himself at the head of the people; and he was supported by intelligent and just men, actuated by sincere patriotism, and free from self-interested motives. I was myself a member, as was the Count Mamiani, the Abbé Gioberti, the Marquess Savorelli and many more, whose characters were sufficient to stamp respectability upon any place they frequented. The rooms were open every evening, and there were always a number of persons present, to read the journals, to talk over the news, and not unfrequently to discuss political affairs, either legislative or financial.

In war time, the conversation turned on the position of the enemy, on our own fortifications and means of defence. In the midst of these discussions there arose the cheering thought of the protection of the Almighty, the acknowledgment of His good providence in our prosperity, and a sense of His justice in times of adversity. The consideration of these points was more particularly assigned to myself. I was the messenger of "good tidings from Zion;" always good to such as are willing to receive them. My ministry took a new form, a new character: I was a Christian citizen, and under that title I was acceptable to all classes, and the more so, as I was not suspected of looking out for proselytes; my style of conversation having nothing dogmatical in it. Indeed, I entered the more readily into political matters, since I rendered them subservient to the cause of religion. Pio Nono was my type of popery; the betrayer of his people, the bombarder of Rome, of Bologna, and of Ancona, as he was, he yet was not, in my estimation, the worst of Popes: from every one of them, I asserted, the same treatment must have been expected in similar circumstances. It was not so much the Pope, as the papal system that was to be abhorred, accursed, and sent back to the infernal world, from which it originally came.

The city of Rome owes its present state of desolation to the popes: it is they who have made it what it is. The desert between the Coliseum and the church of St. John Lateran is a record of Gregory VII., the paramour of the Countess Matilda: the ruins of the Borgo, sometimes called the city Leonina, recall the treachery of Clement VII., the bastard of Medici; who, from recent investigations, has been suspected of himself bringing in the army of Bourbon, and authorizing the sacking of Rome, with all the horrors related in the history of that period. The popes, to raise palaces for their, so-called, nephews, and to erect their churches, have destroyed the finest and most interesting monuments. And to what cause is to be attributed the scarcity of inhabitants in this city, which at one time in itself alone contained double the number of the present inhabitants of the whole of the Papal States? To the policy of the popes, who to shine the more conspicuously in insulated darkness, like a will-o'-the-wisp in a fog, have always desired a city of the dead, surrounded by a desert *campagna*. The system itself, therefore, is to be attacked, and not so much those who are at the head of it. They die, but the system is always living: and consequently men fitting for its service are never wanting. If I had been Pope, I might not have been any better one than Gregory VII., or Clement VII., or Pio Nono. I know that if some of the Italians had Pio Nono in their power, they would handle him very roughly; I, on the contrary, would not harm a hair of his head. I would, however, take care to place him where he should no more have it in his power to injure society. But what others would do to him personally, I would do to his Office; to his pretended spiritual authority, and to his ostentatious, nay, blasphemous, dignity. I would have the Papacy itself judged by the rational and religious in civilized society, and by them condemned to the ignominious death which it deserves.

In this manner I was accustomed to deliver my sentiments on such topics as were presented by the occurrences of the day. Generally our political discussions terminated in religious reflections, as it was natural they should do. At that time all classes of the people felt what an insult, what an outrage it was on humanity, to have their city besieged in the manner it was, by an enemy equally base, hypocritical, and inconsistent.

One day as I was walking along the Corso, a bombshell fell in the Piazza Colonna: "Ha!" exclaimed a Roman, "here is a gift from Pio Nono." "Yes," I observed, "it is a Bull that he sends us from Gaeta." This remark was mightily approved of, and the idea was so generally taken up, that the bombshell, for a whole fortnight, was kicked about the streets of Rome, under the title of the Pope's Bull. Afterwards, drawings and engravings were handed about, representing the bombshells that were showered upon Rome, with the following words inscribed upon them: *Pio Nono to his beloved children, health and apostolic benediction. Pope Pius the Ninth, in lasting memorial of the event. Pius the bishop, the servant of the servants of God.*

Unquestionably, the Pope could not have succeeded better than he has done, had he studied the means ever so deeply, in removing from the minds of the people all respect for the Papacy, and in exposing more completely its imposture, than by besieging and bombarding Rome, and the other two principal cities of his dominions. He never reflected that the altered state of the times would occasion a result exactly opposite to that which he anticipated. In fact, he has absolutely lost all that he intended to regain. The mere deprivation of his temporal dignity would have been a far less misfortune to him; he would then have preserved his spiritual power. Now, however, he has forfeited both. How much longer, we may ask, will he, or any one in his place, retain possession of the government of the Roman States, now that all trust and all veneration for the Papal dignity is for ever done away with?[104]

These reflections often came into my mind, the short time that Rome was a Republic; and they were strengthened when I afterwards saw the city taken possession of by French soldiers, and the old abhorred government once more imposed upon the citizens. It would be a difficult matter to render any people so subservient, and most of all the Romans, as to submit long to a government merely effected by force; it can only be upheld by France and Austria, so long as their bayonets are at hand to support it: and these bayonets are wielded by Papists! Is not this the last proof that was wanting to show that the Church of Rome is opposed to Christianity, which never has recourse to weapons of destruction? Is it possible to love a religion that is obliged to seek the aid of arms?—that to return to the place from which it has been driven, calls in foreign troops, selects deadly artillery, lays siege, batters down the walls, and showers into the town shells, grenades, rockets, and other projectiles?—that slaughters, destroys, and commits every ravage in order to replant a standard which at once displays and disgraces the sign of the cross?

At our *Circolo*, religion and politics were brought side by side; the throne of the Popes by the Cross of Christ. One evening a member arose and addressed the assembly as follows:—

"I think we are wrong in continuing any outward show of respect for the religion our priests lay down to us, which is, in fact, no religion at all; though they seem to think that, like Midas in the fable, who had the power of turning everything he touched into gold, so whatever they lay their hands upon must, of necessity, become holy, sacred, and divine. Until just now we had the *Apostolic* custom-house, and the *Apostolic* coat-of-arms! Did the Apostles then collect customs in their kingdom? or had they their coats-of-arms, their sumptuous carriages, and their richly-caparisoned horses?"

"St. Peter," observed another, "made it his boast that 'silver or gold had he none.'"

"But what," said I, "has the Pope to do with St. Peter? I maintain that he never was in Rome at all. Even if he had been, there is no reason why the Pope should call himself his successor."

"What!" inquired another, "have you good argument to show that St. Peter never was in Rome?"

Hereupon I brought forward the strong reasons that exist against the supposition, and the still greater absurdity of the assertion that he occupied the Pontifical throne for twenty-five years.

"At any rate," I added, "even granting that he had been here, that circumstance could not possibly have invested the Romish bishops with any right or privilege, since they themselves have never ventured any attempt to prove that he bequeathed to them the right of succession at his death."

Another evening we had a long conversation on the subject of the Saviour and His Gospel; when one of our party, who had been listening with much attention, demanding a hearing, said:

"Let it not surprise you, brother citizens, that I, who am as deeply interested in public matters as yourselves, now make a proposition which may seem to be altogether a private matter, an affair between God and man.

Is not this hall sacred to the rights of the citizens? and have we not these rights from God? Every time that we meet here in the service of our country, this hall becomes a Temple in which the Deity presides. In destroying the government of the priests, and in depriving the Pope of his authority, we have most certainly no intention to offer any offence, either to religion or to God; we assert unequivocally that the religion we are desirous to profess is not one of human councils, or of vain traditions, and we are not disposed to admit that the Pope is God. Nay, so far are we from imagining that we have outraged the Deity in deposing the Pope, that, to undeceive all those who may have entertained such a notion, I propose that our *Circolo Popolare*, instead of remaining under the auspices of Pio Nono, should be placed under the immediate protection of God Himself. To which end, I move that Jesus Christ, the Son of God, who died for our salvation, should be declared the only Head and Lord of the *Circolo Popolare*, and that his statue should be placed here accordingly."

"Let it be so," exclaimed several voices at once, "we agree to it."

It was necessary, before the proposition could be carried, that it should have a certain number of signatures, and I gladly affixed my name to it. Oh! who can express the satisfaction I experienced at so signal a manifestation of a sincere religious feeling. I saw in it the operation and fruit of the Bible. It is needless to add that it was carried amid general acclamations, and these excellent young men thronged round me afterwards, rejoicing, and exclaiming:—"We have done right; we have exalted Christ and abased the Pope. Glory and honour to the Lord Jesus Christ: to the Pope confusion and disgrace. He has dared to excommunicate us; we, in our turn, will excommunicate him. It is the Church which has the right to excommunicate, and the people constitute the Church."

Yet this noble outburst of pure religious feeling has been basely misrepresented, by the enemies of civil and spiritual reform, as the language of profanity. France—traitorous and degraded France—joined in the senseless outcry, with the hypocrisy that has marked all her proceedings under her present most unworthy president; though she must well know how universal, in Catholic countries, it is to put all places of public resort under some saintly protection or other. If in this instance the Romans wisely chose to range themselves under the banner of their Saviour, rather than under that of any one who might be impiously exalted by the priests to share in the honour and worship due to Him alone, they had, at any rate, the example before them of the Florentines, who did the same thing in the time of Savonarola; that unhappy monk, who yielded up, amidst the flames lighted by the Inquisition, the life that he had devoted to unmasking the enormities of the Papal Church, and her instruments the priests.

With equal disingenuousness was it pretended to be understood by the same enemies of truth, whether moral or religious, that the motto of the Roman Republic, *Dio e il Popolo*, God and the People, signified The People is God, *Dio è il Popolo*. Thus wickedly did they bear false witness against their neighbour, and seek to confound right and wrong in the minds of those who would otherwise willingly have been led to form their opinions according to the rules of candour and justice.

At this juncture, when the Pope was struggling with the people for the possession of power, the Romans displayed great courage and enthusiasm. It was not imagined that a people sold to the Church would have possessed such a spirit of independence. The priests had declared that the Romans would not know how to go on without the Pope and the Cardinals: whereas, any one who was present in Rome in the year 1849, can bear testimony that they never were so full of contentment as when they had shaken their intolerable priestly yoke from their necks. Of all the misfortunes, of all the evils that befell them on their defeat, the most insupportable was the sight of the Cardinals and the Pope once more parading in the streets of their city. In the provinces the feeling against the purple dignity was even stronger still. The Legations were ready to call for the usurpation of the Austrian, rather than be again subjected to the Priests.

The short time that it was allowed me to enjoy my liberty in Rome, I had no time to occupy myself with looking after the neighbouring towns, except so far as writing letters to them, sending them Bibles, and deputing some of my friends in those quarters, to speak to the people the words of truth. It was my intention if the Republic had lasted, to take a circuit in the country, in order to extend my mission. But everybody knows how soon we were surrounded by hostile troops, so that it was impossible for me to go beyond the walls of the city.

I was frequently advised to betake myself to some other place; but I doubted the sincerity of these councils, and suspected some treachery; for the bigoted priests, and the Jesuit party, as they were termed, regarded my being in Rome with an evil eye; I have reason indeed to believe that they hated to see me among the living, and were most anxious to number me with the dead. My friends continually cautioned me to beware of them, and above all, not to eat or drink in the company of priests, friars, or their partisans; and I was so far influenced by their apprehensions, that I have not unfrequently refused invitations from persons of whom I had cause to be distrustful.

Before I received these cautions, however, soon after my arrival in Rome, I paid a visit to the Dominicans belonging to the Minerva, to see after my friends there. The general of the Order, Father Ajello, was my principal inducement; he was a worthy old man, whom I had known in Naples, and highly esteemed. I was received by him with every possible kindness; he brought old times to my remembrance, and spoke gratefully of the attentions I had shown him in my office of Prior; with him I willingly took a cup of chocolate, which is the usual compliment the friars offer their guests.

And here I may observe of these friars, that some of them are at present exactly in a similar state of mind to what I was myself, while among them; that is to say, greatly desirous to be acquainted with the truth; as was the case with the blind man in the Gospel, when he exclaimed: "Lord, that I might receive my sight."[105] The opportunity only is wanted, or some impulse to occasion them to open then eyes to the light. Should any one ask them why they remain as they are, they might probably reply as the cripple at the pool of Bethesda, "Sir, I have no man to put me into the pool."[106] I have myself, on various occasions, seen so many persons who have evinced their desire for the truth which leads to the putting on of the new man, that I feel confident if the Lord would grant us to breathe the air of liberty once more, in our much-loved country, we should see, even from the very monasteries, men come forth as preachers of the Gospel, Apostles of the Truth.

A very small number as yet have had the courage actually to issue from their dens of corruption and death; and in those who have attempted it the step has not been altogether complete. Either from the want of sufficient means, or that the period which Providence has assigned for these great changes has not yet arrived, these brethren, who might make themselves so useful, are for the present content to remove themselves a short distance from Rome, and to take no further measures.

I have had the same experience, with others. Three years since a dear friend of mine in Rome, struggling between light and darkness, life and death, called upon by the Spirit to come forth, and retained by the flesh in bonds, wrote to me at Malta such moving letters, as almost brought tears into my eyes. "Pray for me," he exclaimed, "pray that the Lord may enable me to overcome in this conflict; pray that the Spirit may triumph over the flesh."

I showed his letter to my friends, and besought them to add their prayers to mine for the relief of our brother, who was undergoing the same struggle that I had myself endured, and the severity of which I knew full well. Soon after, I left Malta to visit England, which I then did for the first time. My route lay through Switzerland and France, and wherever I met any of our brethren in these countries, I did not fail to ask their prayers also, that our friend in Rome might have the strength to break asunder the bonds in which he was held, and to vanquish his spiritual adversaries. It appeared that our united petitions in his behalf to the Fount of mercy, were not without success, since before I returned from London to Malta, our convert was already there, expecting my arrival. He is now a diligent labourer in the Lord's vineyard, and it is to be hoped that our earnest supplications may be beneficial also to many others, who are now undecided and wavering. We are indeed often disappointed in our most sanguine expectations, and deceived in our most flattering prospects; but all we have to do is to commit ourselves to the care of the Divine providence, after having ourselves done our utmost, as faithful ministers in Christ.

In my last visit to Rome, I entertained the idea that among the various monasteries with which the city abounds, many would be found who would listen to the word of God with enthusiasm, and that a considerable portion of the monks would unite with me in the good cause. Accordingly, on my arrival I made a circuit among the monasteries, declaring the necessity of separating Christianity from Popery, as utterly incompatible with each other. I entered into the discussion of various particulars, and although I met with considerable opposition, the major part of my hearers listened to me with docility, and evidently derived advantage from my arguments. But when on the very point of conviction, of declaring their disbelief of the Romish faith, and of professing their adherence to the true principles of Christianity—when they were just prepared to abandon the Mass—it was then, even at the decisive moment, that I saw them doubtful, apprehensive, and vacillating in their resolution; and it ended with some of them avoiding me from that time, as if the very sight of me reproached them with their weakness.

I had an interesting meeting, in the church of Santa Maria Maggiore, with my old friend and companion, Father Borg, a Dominican, and one of the Penitentiaries belonging to that *Basilica*; a good man and a sincere one; a papist from conviction, and thoroughly conscientious. He had been a Professor at the same time with myself, in the monastery Di Gradi at Viterbo. He was acquainted with every particular of my life; but I had not at that time let him into the secret of what was going on in my mind, with respect to my religious belief, as I deemed him unfit to give the matter impartial consideration. He had seen with the utmost surprise and consternation the events that had befallen me, and ignorant of what was passing within me, he could not in any way satisfy himself as to the great change I had experienced. From the time I had left Viterbo we had never met, but I felt assured of his regard. I could not, therefore, now remain in Rome without paying him a visit, and as nothing at the present moment forbade my doing so, revealing my sentiments.

Accordingly, I set off one morning for the church of Santa Maria Maggiore. The canons were chanting their regular service in the choir, and my friend was seated in his confessional, waiting for sinners to come before him to receive their pardon, and holding in his hand his long rod,[107] with which to touch the heads of those who should kneel before him. He did not expect to see me; I passed before him smiling, and saluted him; then turned back again, and did the same: at last he recognised me, and stretched out his hand to me, scarcely crediting the evidence of his senses.

"What, Achilli?"

"Yes, at your service. How do you find yourself?"

"You here?"

"Yes, I am come on purpose to pay you a visit."

"But tell me, are you not a Protestant?"

"My dear Borg, what does your question imply? I have nothing to protest against yourself."

"But against the pope?"

"I assure you I have nothing whatever to do with him."

"You are, then, a heretic!"

"Oh, no, my friend, I am a Christian; I believe in the Lord Jesus Christ, and in His Gospel."

"And in nothing else?"

"Is it necessary to my salvation to do so? Is it not written, 'Believe on the Lord Jesus Christ, and thou shalt be saved, and thy house?'"[108]

"Everybody here has declared that you have become a Protestant."

"I repeat to you that I am a Christian—hear the profession of my faith—a Christian according to the Bible; all that is written in that holy book I believe, and nothing that is not to be found therein."

"Then you do not believe in tradition?"

"Certainly not in that of the Decretals and of the Canons, which are exclusively of the Church of Rome, and in support of which she can produce neither authority nor reason; I believe in the traditions of the Church Universal; which includes not merely the Romish Church, but the Greek also, and all the reformed Churches in Christendom. For example, it is a true tradition that certain books are the true writings which compose the canon of the Holy Scriptures."

"Well, but do you not believe that there are seven Sacraments; that the Church has the power to absolve sins; that in the sacrament of the Holy Supper there is present the real body and blood of Christ?"

"My dear friend, what a world of questions all in a breath! Had we not better discuss them separately? Every one of them requires a long dissertation. But I can tell you I do not believe that you have ever had power to pardon the sins of any one, notwithstanding your office of Penitentiary, unless they were offences committed against yourself."

My friend, upon this observation, hastily quitted his confessional, in his eagerness to cope with the argument, and invited me to follow him to his own room, in the College of the Penitentiaries adjoining the church. I found there two other old Penitentiaries, whom I had formerly esteemed as my masters, Father Galleani and Father Chiappa. They were both glad to see me, and hearing that Father Borg had engaged me in discussion, they lent an attentive ear to it, in order to aid their colleague, if it should prove necessary. Thus I found myself alone against three stout adversaries.

"You do not believe, then," rejoined my friend, "that our confessors, approved by the Church, have the power of absolution?"

"I believe they may have, if the Church alone is sinned against."

"And if it be against God?"

"In that case God alone can pardon, or one who has received power from Him to do so. We read that Jesus Christ alone has that power, and this furnishes a convincing proof of His divinity. His enemies were wiser than they were aware of, when they said, 'Who can forgive sins, but God only?'"

"But the Church has received the power through St. Peter, along with the keys."

"Keys signify, in the spiritual sense, no other power than that of intelligence. We say, the key of the mystery, the key of the business, the key to an enigma, or to a cipher, or to characters. Therefore Christ, when he speaks of the keys of the kingdom of heaven, means us to understand, knowledge and intelligence in heavenly things, or in the essentials of the Church. By the words, 'Whatsoever thou shalt bind on earth shall be bound in heaven: and whatsoever thou shalt loose on earth shall be loosed in heaven,'[109] you understand binding and loosing, pardoning and the reverse. Well then, if such be the sense of the passage, the sins that are to be pardoned are those which we commit against each other; and it was with reference to our duty on such occasions that Peter asked of Christ, 'Lord, how oft shall my brother sin against me, and I forgive him? till seven times?'[110] If therefore I offend you, Father Borg, (which I would not willingly do, if conscious of it,) and confess the evil I have committed, it is your duty to forgive me."

"Your interpretation respecting 'the kingdom of heaven' is altogether new to me. Why should it be called the kingdom of heaven?"

"My good friend, it is the kingdom of heaven for which we supplicate the Lord, in the prayer which He has Himself given us, 'Thy kingdom come;' were it otherwise, we ought to say,—May *we come* into thy kingdom. And it is the same kingdom of which Christ speaks to His disciples, when He says to them: 'Because it is given unto you to know the mysteries of the kingdom of heaven, but to them it is not given.'[111] Now here are the keys of the kingdom of heaven given to *all* the disciples; that is, to *all* believers. In fact, the privilege granted to Peter, was also granted to all the faithful alike. Christ says, 'Verily I say unto you, Whatsoever ye shall bind on earth shall be bound in heaven: and whatsoever ye shall loose on earth shall be loosed in heaven.'[112] But to put the matter beyond doubt, the very same power of pardoning sins is given to *all* the disciples; 'Receive *ye* the Holy Ghost: whosoever sins *ye* remit, they are remitted unto them; and whosoever sins *ye* retain, they are retained.'[113] Do you imagine now that Jesus Christ at that time made so many penitentiaries of His disciples, or that He granted them the reserved cases in Bulla Cœnæ?"

"But St. Thomas Aquinas does not understand it in that way," observed Chiappa; "read his work."

"My dear master, it is better to read the Holy Scriptures," replied I; "in them only should we believe. I know quite enough of Thomas Aquinas; you yourself may remember how much time I wasted over his works! I am sorry I did. I feel myself now called upon to make up for it by giving my whole attention to the Holy Word; not only to counteract the impressions I formerly received, but what I have also taught to others, when I myself was blind and leading the blind. You refer me to Thomas Aquinas, and I refer you to the Bible."

"How! you reject the authority of the Angelic Doctor, he to whom the celebrated Crucifix spoke, saying, '*Thou hast written well of me, Thomas.*' You dare to contradict him! and make your appeal to the Bible! None studied it more than he did, none understood it so fully. Do you pretend to say that you know it better?"

"But," said I to him, "you are now going upon another question. I think it would be as well to settle the original one first."

"I cannot argue," replied he, "with one who doubts such authority. You know what Pope John XX. said of Thomas Aquinas: that whoever departed from his doctrine, *semper fuit de veritate suspectus.*" So saying, up rose Father Chiappa, and abruptly left the room.

Father Galleani was a more quiet disputant. From the subject of Confession, we passed to that of Transubstantiation, and to the propitiatory Sacrifice of the Mass. When I found myself engaged in this argument, I confess, that losing sight of moderation, I assailed the Popish system with great warmth, and inveighed against the impiety of its doctrines, so injurious to the sacred mystery of the passion and love of Christ.

"I cannot conceive, my dear master," I observed, "of an idea more degrading to Christianity—a bread god! I say bread, since what the Church of Rome calls the Body of Christ is actually neither more nor less than bread. It was bread in the hands of Christ Himself, when He said, 'This is my body,' and it is as bread that it forms the mystery of the Eucharist. Christ brake no other substance than the bread, nor ate any other Himself, nor gave any other to the Apostles. Unquestionably it is a figurative sign, a representation of the Body of Christ, which having suffered upon the cross has become spiritual food, a vital nutriment, for all true believers. Bread itself can only be eaten in a natural way; Christ living in the body, could not be eaten without occasioning His death. But you will tell me that it is a miracle. I answer that God can unquestionably work miracles, but he cannot act against Himself—Christ living and conversing as a human being, could not be eaten without ceasing to converse and to live. Tell me, moreover, how could Christ substantially eat Himself? This monstrous belief was never that of our fathers, who always considered, when they met together to eat this bread, that it was a symbol of the natural body of Christ, and of His mystical body, the Church. And this is the true signification of the Sacrament. Neither in one view nor in the other can the words be taken in their literal sense."

"But you are aware that the Angelic Doctor, St. Thomas, asserts that the whole of Christ is in the Sacrament in actual substance, under the form of bread and wine; and that it is not *circumscribed*, as water in a basin nor *definitive*, as the soul within the body; but *sacramentally*, spiritually, and substantially present at the same time."

"But if it be one, it cannot be the other: the substance of the body of Christ is physical and not spiritual; if it be substantial it cannot be spiritual, and *vice versa.*"

Here we were interrupted by Father Borg, who, finding I gave up no one point, and that the argument was pushed on to contradiction—I with the Bible in my hand, and my opponent with his Thomas Aquinas—thought best to put an end to it by changing the discourse. God grant that what I then advanced may be like seed thrown into good ground, which in due time produces its fruit of life eternal!

After my first few visits to the monasteries, I began to perceive that I was looked upon with suspicion, and had to encounter many sour glances. I thought it better, therefore, to give up my mission among these people for a while, unless they themselves should come in search of me. In fact several, of various orders, did come, more especially towards evening, wearing a secular dress, and requesting me to keep their visit secret.

At no time did I feel more impressed with the importance of the mission which the Lord had confided to me than in the latter days of the Republic. It was then that I witnessed prodigies of conversion, not among the priests or friars, for they, seeing the probable restoration of the papal government at hand, quickly relapsed into their accustomed notions, and were ready once more to submit their necks quietly to the bonds that held them captive alike in mind and body;—it was among the laity, the professional men, and men of science, the tradespeople and artists, that the greatest progress was made. Some few were of mature age, but most of them were young men, who were enabled, through the blessing of the Almighty, to open their eyes to the light, and to rejoice their hearts with the love of truth. Many whom I had never before seen came to tell me that they had heard of my ministry, and had become acquainted with the doctrines I taught; and desired to open their minds to me, and to co-operate with me in the establishment of a Church, in which Christ should be supreme, and His Holy Word recognised.

Some of the best informed among them could give me very sufficient reasons for their belief; others were anxious to correct their ideas, and to get rid of their errors: I assisted as many as I could with my own instructions, and supplied others with useful books for their perusal. But as much as possible I showed them from the Bible itself the arguments connected with our subject: I endeavoured to avoid all appearance of undue authority, and to unfold my views in a familiar and friendly tone, as one brother with another, and occasionally we engaged together in prayer. In this, however, I took care to avoid any approach to a set form or ritual, leaving that to be adopted upon mature deliberation, when our Church could openly assemble without danger.

During the first month or two I had prayer meetings at my own house, every Sunday and Friday; at which, as Christians before God, we all assembled. But these it was soon found necessary to discontinue, as they were looked upon with a jealous eye by the priests, evidently with the intention of revenging themselves, at some future time, when the old order of things should be restored, against such of us as might then remain in Rome.

I thought it best therefore not to compromise any of my converts, and gave them to understand that I could no longer receive them, at that time, as a congregation. Nevertheless, on Sundays I admitted a few to private worship; and sometimes we met at each other's houses, or in some artist's studio, where it was our custom to read a portion of the Bible, and offer up our prayers: and I am assured that many still continue to do so, in such a manner as to evade the search that is made for them without ceasing by the government, the despotic and uncharitable government of the Priests. May the Lord continue in all those who have thus far received the truth, that fervent spirit which shall enable them to hold fast together, until it shall please Him to reunite us, free citizens, under liberal laws, such as His gracious providence has bestowed on other nations!

On the 2d of July the French troops entered Rome. An army of forty thousand men, with all the resources of military art, had laid siege to the city, and for three months remained under its walls; one-third of which time was passed in hard fighting, with heavy loss on both sides, but chiefly on theirs. After a continual thundering of artillery, a bombardment in fact of fifteen days, a breach was effected and mounted: but nevertheless the city was not entered until the enemy learned that no further resistance could be maintained; when the wearied, half-famished troops, covered with dust and scorched by the sun, made their inglorious entry into Rome, with a tremendous park of artillery, and every hostile demonstration, to receive from the entire populace unequivocal marks of scorn and derision, even from the women and children.

In those unhappy days I did not leave the house. Grieved to see the overthrow of a government which the majority of the people had ardently longed for, the only one fitting for our country, in the estimation of every one who is no longer content to endure the deadening influence of the Papal yoke,—indignant at beholding a foreign power so disgracefully violate its own honour, its own laws, in order to invade and oppress a people that had no way offended it, I preferred, as many others did, to remain at home, that I might neither see nor hear what was going on. I was sufficiently rewarded for doing so, in a series of agreeable visits; from morning till night I had persons with me conversing on religious matters, and I had frequent opportunities of distributing the Bible among them, and through them to others.

On the 24th of June I had entered into the married state. During the seven years that I had been emancipated from Rome, I might at any time have done so. And at first I had seriously thought of it, seeing that I was at the head of a small establishment, and imagining that a wife would greatly lighten the burthen of it; besides the advantage she would have afforded me in a more free and confidential intercourse with the sex. But I objected to it for two reasons: first, because, having engaged in so difficult an undertaking as that of a religious reform in Italy, I foresaw it would be incumbent on me to journey about to different places, and that therefore I must be alone, in order to do so without hindrance or impediment; and, secondly, that my enemies might not, with their accustomed calumny, assert that my desertion of the Romish Church had been solely prompted by my desire to renounce my celibacy. For although that in itself might have been accounted a sufficient reason to abandon the faithless Church, so prophetically described by St. Paul as "forbidding to marry, and commanding to abstain from meats,"[114] yet I should not have wished it to be said that I had been actuated by that motive only, and not by higher and more spiritual ones. But I afterwards saw the necessity and even the duty of such a step, since by taking it I should place myself in a state of equality with other men. The words of St. Paul to Timothy, "A bishop must be the husband of one wife," I consider to be something more than mere advice that Christian pastors should marry. For my own part I have always inveighed against the law of celibacy, and invariably have advised my friends to enter, as early as they prudently might, into the conjugal state. Why should not I then do so, whilst yet in the prime of life?

"What a scandal to the Church," I observed one day to some Romish priests, "is this vow of celibacy among the clergy. And after all, if considered synonymous with that of chastity, where is it kept sacred? Rarely indeed! by either bishop, cardinal, or pope. As to the lower order of priests, what with temptation from within and example from without, the vow is continually violated; and if the observance of it be alike injurious to nature and to society, as it unquestionably is, can it be good in itself, or proper to be enforced?"

"Well, then," said they, "show us how we can release ourselves from our vow."

"The Republican Government," I answered, "have made a law which declares that these vows shall be no longer binding, and that every citizen shall enjoy equal rights. This law, which was issued in the month of May last, authorized all of us to marry, since the sole legal impediment was the pretext of a binding vow of celibacy."

"It is very true," observed one of the priests, "we are now at liberty to get married in Rome; but no one as yet has had the courage to set the example."

"Then I will," I exclaimed; "I promise you that before this Government is at an end, I shall be married, and so set the example of a holy action in Rome."

Shortly after this conversation I offered my hand to Miss Josephine Hely, the youngest daughter of Captain Hely; an amiable young lady, carefully and virtuously brought up, and happily for herself, as for me, imbued with Protestant principles, by a dear friend of hers, Mrs. Tennant, the wife of the Rev. Mr. Tennant, the minister of the English Church at Florence. This lady had always manifested a mother's tenderness for her, and it is in grateful acknowledgment of it, on the part of my wife, and equally on my own, that I pay this testimony to her worth. We were publicly and solemnly joined in holy matrimony on the 24th of June, 1849, according to the rites of our Italian Church; but as the government which authorized that act has since fallen, or rather has become suspended, we took care, on arriving in England, to have our marriage duly registered, at the Parish Church of St. Martin in the Fields.

I was convinced, in the very commencement of my conjugal life, that I had not been too sanguine in my hopes of finding a congenial companion and valuable helpmate, in my destined and beloved partner. The similarity of our religious views, the facility with which she expressed herself in my native language, which was indeed hers also, and her ardent desire to co-operate with me in my designs, all made me look upon my union with her as another of the precious favours for which I had to be grateful to the Lord; equally likely to increase my own happiness, and to extend the sphere of my usefulness to others.

My dear wife loved me as the wife of a minister of the Gospel ought to love her husband. She was aware what the followers of Christ had to expect. I had myself forewarned her that if she anticipated comfort in my affection, and delight in my society, she would also have to experience much trouble. On our very wedding day I told her that the lot she would have to share with me would in all probability be more marked by tribulation than by joy, and that in this world we might be called on to suffer in the flesh—for the spirit cannot be injured—to endure persecution even unto death: she bowed her head in resignation to the will of Heaven, and assured me that she also was desirous to become a handmaid of the Lord, and was ready to do His will.

It was ordained that we should soon be put to the proof. Scarcely a month had passed over our heads, when a sudden stroke divided us. Was this misfortune foreseen by me? Had I no indication of its approach? It would be folly in me to say that I did not expect it. But so it was, I had no help for it. The hand of Him who is mighty to save kept me in Rome in the midst of danger and alarm. Even my wife, who is naturally timid, seemed at that time endued with a courage that rendered her insensible to the imminent peril that awaited me. We talked much together, concerning the difficulties of my position, without being able to come to any positive decision. In short, we saw the storm approaching, but knew not how to avoid it. Some advised me to be circumspect; others spoke out plainly of the probability of my being put into prison. But I laughed at them.

"Why do you not get away?" asked one of my best friends. "Do you not know that already arrests are being made on every side? Do you think it likely that they will spare you, who have rendered yourself so obnoxious to the priests?"

"My dear friend," I replied, "the present government have but one fault to charge me with, that of having abandoned the Church and reformed my creed, and, as a natural consequence, if you will, entered into matrimony. Now for this pretended crime I am only responsible to the Inquisition. The civil tribunals have nothing against me; I am no political offender. It is well known that ever since I have returned to Rome I have lived as a private citizen, and never held any office under the Republic; so that I am easy on that score. As to the criminal courts, thank Heaven, I have no cause to fear them; nor in that of the Vicar-General can any charge be laid against me for immorality. But do you think that the Tribunal of the Inquisition can ever be re-established? under the protection of France too? It is not to be thought of. At any rate, without the Pope and the Cardinals there can be no Inquisition in Rome, and they are not likely to return just yet. Indeed, I shall not wait for them; I shall be far away before they come back."

"Your reasoning is very good; but do you imagine justice will be done to you? have you never heard the logic of priests? *Stat pro ratione voluntas*: they have only to desire, and your ruin is certain."

"My dear friend, prudence is very desirable; but not so that restless apprehension which takes possession of the mind, to the exclusion of all other feelings, and leads us to imagine danger where none exists. Our Lord authorized His disciples, when they should be persecuted in one city, to flee unto another; but who, as yet, has persecuted me? If I fly without such persecution, what answer shall I give to the Lord, when he shall say to me: 'Shepherd, I had entrusted a flock to your care, I had even given you my lambs to feed, and to guide into the paths of salvation; you were their guardian; and behold, you saw the wolf approach, and you fled. You are not their true shepherd, but a hireling who careth not for the sheep. Leave it to Pio Nono, who is no true shepherd, to desert his flock; but you—' Ah! my friend, above all I should dread so terrible and so just a reproof. I will only fly when the Lord, who has placed me here, enjoins me to do so. Until He declares His will, I shall remain where I am."

At this my friend shook his head, and said, "Since you are resolved, may the Lord keep and protect you. He will either remove the danger from you, or——but whatever be His pleasure, may His gracious will be done."

"Amen," I answered.

Towards the end of July, I was informed that another case of Bibles had arrived, directed to me, and was lying at the Custom-house.

"Alas!" I exclaimed, "my poor Bibles have come too late!" The Custom-house had returned to its old system; the inspector of books was again upon the alert, on the part of the master of the Sacred Palace; it would be impossible to get them out of his hands; still I resolved to make the attempt; not indeed personally, but through the mediation of others; and the attempt was fatal to me. My Bibles were confiscated, and were turned into an evidence sufficient to condemn me. The endeavour to introduce the Bible into Rome is a crime not to be pardoned, "neither in this world nor in the next;"—it is reckoned as the real sin against the Holy Roman Church; a more direful one, in her estimation, than that against the Holy Ghost.

"Now, indeed," my friends observed, "there is cause for fear. This case of Bibles is a body of crime: hasten out of Rome; delay not a day."

I confess I did indeed feel a cold shudder, even to my very bones, as I thought of it. I saw that my fate would be the same as that of the books. If they were shut up, could I hope to remain at liberty? This occurred on the 26th of July; I might have got away, but I had always accustomed myself, especially in times of trouble, not to rely on my own judgment, or act from my own will. As a believer in the Divine providence, I desired in all things to be governed by the will of God; and accordingly I sought in prayer His guidance, determined to act as His influence should direct me. He appeared to require a sacrifice of me; my testimony to Himself, and to our Blessed Saviour. My flight would have characterised me as an apostate, a deserter from my duty. Could I terminate my mission so unworthily? Should I, by a single act, lose all that I had obtained with so much exertion? I remembered the prayer I had offered up on entering Rome, "Lord, as in this same city Thou didst send thine Apostle Paul to overthrow idolatry, and to announce the glad tidings of salvation; and didst ordain that he should remain for the space of two years within these walls, so grant to me, thy servant, that being also sent here in thy service, I may remain here at least for the term of one year, in the continual exercise of my mission, through Jesus Christ our Lord." This prayer, which I then offered up in faith, could not but be granted; and divine favour is not given by halves. I therefore considered that as I had yet only been six months in Rome, there were six more that I had to remain, to do the Lord's will—it mattered not under what circumstances I should be placed, I had still my work to do. The Apostles even in prison continued their labours. Whatever it pleases God to appoint for the future, it is my duty at present to remain in Rome.

These reflections imparted so much comfort and satisfaction to my mind, that I look back upon these days as the happiest of my life. I regarded my dear companion with confidence and holy joy, and more than once asked her if she too were not willing to do the will of the Lord, and whether He sent us joy or tribulation, to bless His holy name.

"Ah! yes," she replied, "have we not frequently promised it to each other? Was it not our prayer when we were first betrothed, and was it not renewed on the day of our marriage? I am ready to submit to the will of the Lord."

This also was an inexpressible satisfaction to me. To see a beloved wife, whom only one short month before I had received as a precious gift from heaven, so well disposed to make the greatest sacrifices for the love of God! Everything tended to confirm me in the thought that it was my duty to wait with resignation the fate that should be allotted to me.

From the 26th to the 29th I remained at home, distributing the Bible and speaking of the Gospel of Christ, to all who came to me. From an early hour in the morning until late in the evening I had a perpetual throng of visitors. On the evening of the 29th I felt more than usually tired, having been engaged in speaking the whole of the day. My wife was not very well, and at about eleven o'clock we retired to rest. At twelve, I heard a violent knocking at the front door. It was the Inspector of the Police, with three officials from the Inquisition, escorted by six of the *chasseurs de Vincennes*. Yes, the soldiers of the French Republic, after having destroyed a government as legitimate as their own, now lent their assistance to the tools of the Pope, to execute the orders of the Inquisition!

These nocturnal visitants evidently came for the purpose of arresting me. I asked by whose authority they acted. The Inspector, Signor Volponi, replied, "By authority of the Prefect of Police," (at that time an officer of the French Republic.) We exchanged but few words. I commended my wife to the care of the Lord, leaving her with her brother Henry and her sister Elizabeth, who at that time were living with us, and allowed myself to be taken away to the palace of the Governor.

The next morning the chief bailiff came to reconnoitre me; and after some deceitful words and lying promises, on the part of the Prefect of Police, sent me off, under an escort, to the Inquisition; where I was placed in a cell wherein two priests were already confined, on the charge of having taken part in the affairs of the Republic. They knew me by sight, it appeared; though I did not myself recollect having ever seen them before.

There were altogether in the prisons of the Holy Office, at that time, about fifteen priests; not one of them was accused of any pretended heresy, but all of having written, as well as spoken, against the temporal power of the Pope.

My two fellow-prisoners soon became on friendly terms with me. Their desire to hear me deliver my sentiments on religious matters made them forget everything else; they were famishing after the doctrines of the Truth, of the Word of God. I had not a Bible with me; I had not been allowed to bring one; but I cited passages from memory, and as I was well acquainted with the Vulgate edition, I quoted the Latin text; and I frequently heard such remarks as, "Oh, I was not aware of it!" — "Indeed! I never reflected on that before!" — "You are quite right; your argument is undeniable."

The authority of the Church was the grand topic; we continually returned to it; the Primacy of the Pope, as derived from the Apostle Peter. What a surprise it was for them to hear themselves contradicted in this belief, which they had regarded as an absolute axiom; to be told that among the Apostles no one was head or chief; that Jesus Christ never gave any distinct diploma to St. Peter; and that on the contrary, He expressly declared that no one should be lord or master over the others, since they were all brethren.

"But Peter," said they, "was always foremost in speaking; he answered for the rest, without being called upon to do so, as one having authority."

"St. Peter," I replied, "was characterised by his great boldness, which indeed often amounted to presumption: his words to our Lord were: 'Though all men should be offended because of thee, yet will I never be offended;'[115] and, again, 'Though I should die with thee, yet will I not deny thee!'[116] You know how this proud boasting ended. He was also bold when he requested Jesus to enable him to walk upon the water; but this daring soon gave place to fear, and he began to sink. His presumption even went so far as to 'rebuke' his Lord and Master, when He told His disciples 'that he must go unto Jerusalem, and suffer many things ... and be killed.'[117] And did not Peter well deserve the reproof he then received: 'Get thee behind me, Satan, thou art an offence unto me: for thou savourest not the things that be of God, but those that be of man'?[118] So much for the authority of this Prince of Apostles, as he is called, and his claim to supremacy, dignity, and infallibility in the Church! St. Paul, at any rate, does not seem to admit it, when he says, 'But when Peter was come to Antioch, I withstood him to the face, because he was to be blamed.'[119] It is to be noted that this took place at Antioch, where, according to the Church, of Rome, St. Peter established the first pontifical chair, and, consequently, where he may be supposed to have spoken *ex cathedra*."

My poor friends had no more to say. One of them was extremely docile, and from the first was disposed to admit the authority of the Bible. The other was equally desirous to understand the truth, but he could not divest his mind of its old prejudices: he was pained to see the idols of his temple destroyed. We discussed these subjects every hour of the day, and during part of the night. An oppressive, suffocating heat prevented our sleeping; what little breath we had we employed in these discourses, and in occasional prayers. The second day after my arrival, the least docile of my new friends yielded to my arguments; both were now converted to my opinions. Towards evening we were engaged on the important question, as to the sole mediation of Jesus Christ, to the exclusion of that of the Virgin Mary and of the saints, when suddenly the door of my prison opened, and I was laid hold of by two of the officials of the Inquisition, and by them taken out and delivered over to a party of carbineers, to be conducted to the Castle of St. Angelo.

My two friends were in despair at seeing me removed; one of them could scarcely refrain from tears. I shared in their emotion, and invoked the blessing of Heaven in their behalf.

Arrived at the castle, I was confided to the guidance of a single carbineer, who took me within side, and led the way to the upper part of the fortress, where the secret prisons are situated.[120]

"Can you tell me, my friend," I inquired of the carbineer, who seemed a good sort of a man, "why I am removed from the Inquisition to this castle? Is it better or worse, with respect to accommodation?"

"Pretty much the same," he replied. "As far as I can learn, it appears that you have been removed from the Inquisition, because the great wall that lately surrounded it is now destroyed, and the prison is not considered sufficiently secure. I believe too, that it has been deemed expedient to place you out of the way of the priests who are confined there. You are looked upon with great mistrust in consequence of your dealings about the Bible. You know it is prohibited in Rome."

I was now locked up in the remotest part of the fortress, *la Gemella Seconda*.

### FOOTNOTES:

[101] Romans viii. 29.

[102] These walls were thrown down during the Republic, so that at present the Inquisition can be seen on every side.

[103] A third Edition of this work has been recently published in London, by the Religious Tract Society, for the benefit of the Italians in England.

[104] *Vide* Appendix. Reply to the Allocution of Pius IX., in the Consistory of Gaeta, 20th April, 1849, published at Rome during the last days of the Republic, and circulated there after the entry of the French troops.

[105] Mark x. 51.

[106] John v. 7.

[107] The Penitentiaries of the four principal Basilicas of Rome hold a long rod or wand, in sign of their extended power to absolve even the most enormous crimes.

[108] Acts xvi. 31.

[109] Matt. xvi. 19.

[110] Matt. xviii. 21.

[111] Matt. xiii. 11.

[112] Matt. xviii. 18.
[113] John xx. 22, 23.
[114] 1 Tim. iv. 3.
[115] Matt. xxvi. 33.
[116] Matt. xxvi. 35.
[117] Matt. xvi. 21.
[118] Matt. xvi. 23.
[119] Galat. ii. 11.
[120] There are also dungeons underground, so horrible that no one has been known to survive in them more than a few days; they are like wells, completely dark, and wet. But these are no longer made use of.

# CHAPTER XVI
# THE CASTLE OF ST. ANGELO

Conducted into this cell, in which from some unseen cause there was a most offensive odour, I was shown in one corner a mattress that seemed to have served as a bed for dogs.

"There," said my gaoler, "you can take your rest when you like. We cannot leave you any light, for it is altogether prohibited in your case. It is a new regulation, which is not in force with respect to prisoners for political offences. We do not know, at present, on what charge you are brought here."

So saying the gaoler retired, closing the first and second doors; and I remained in darkness in the middle of my dirty cell, oppressed by the heated unwholesome air which I could scarcely breathe. I was abandoned by man, but my God was with me. Hence, though deprived of everything, I felt I was not utterly forsaken. Fatigued and exhausted, I needed repose; but without food, which for three days I had scarcely tasted, I could not sleep. I passed the night in prayer to my God, and found comfort in the remembrance of the sufferings my Saviour endured for our sakes.

Sometimes my thoughts reverted to my Christian brethren, and particularly to those who, as I well knew, continued to love me.

"Oh!" said I to myself, "if they could know of my imprisonment, I am certain they would put up their most fervent prayers to the Almighty: my dear friends in England—brethren of the Evangelical Alliance—friends in France and in Geneva! God, thou wilt listen to the supplications of thy children, and grant their prayers!"

The following day, by the little light which glimmered through a high narrow window, I could better examine my habitation; and found the bad smell proceeded from the pavement, the bed, and still more from a wooden box, placed at the outside of the window, as if to obstruct both the air and the light, and that contained a quantity of filth and rubbish, which there were no means of removing; as it was fastened down at the outside, and had on the inner side an iron grating, which, together with the bars of my window prevented any access to it. My inviting mattress was to serve the double purpose of bed and chair. The walls, on which my eyes must necessarily rest as soon as I opened them, were scrawled over with monstrous figures and dolorous inscriptions in charcoal, by those who had been confined there. I thus learnt that this cell had contained thieves, assassins, and amongst others the notorious Abate Abbo, of whose horrible crimes and cruelties I have already made mention.

At a certain hour of the day I was visited by the gaoler, who said to me courteously:

"I am sorry you should be treated in this manner. I know who you are, and I know what you are accused of; you have cause to rejoice in your alleged offence, but at present it is expedient that you should resign yourself to this hard treatment; perhaps I may be able in some measure to soften the rigour of it. Suffer patiently, and put in practice what you teach others."

"My kind friend," I replied, "you have a heart formed for compassion. The exhortations and professions that I hear from your lips show me you intend to do all you can to cheer my imprisonment; and even though you should not be permitted to offer me any other charity, I shall always be grateful for this—that I receive your sympathy. Oh! believe me it will be requited to you by Him who has said through Jesus Christ, 'Whosoever shall give to drink a cup of cold water only, in the name of a disciple, verily I say unto you, he shall in no wise lose his reward.'"[121]

"And where is it that Jesus Christ says these words?"

"In the Gospel written by St. Matthew."

"I would willingly read it, if I understood Latin."

"It is to be had in Italian—good Italian; I will tell you where you can procure it, by asking for it in my name."

This man in a very short time became my friend. I can now speak of him without fear of doing him any injury by my disclosures, because I have heard that he has given up his employment, and is no longer in the Roman States.

He was not the only gaoler, but he was one of the chief amongst them: he was nevertheless always in fear of his subalterns, who watched him very closely, and informed against him whenever they had any excuse for so doing; insomuch that however cautious he might be, he was frequently reproved by the superior, for being too indulgent.

These prisons were all filled with people thrown in for various imputations, and consequently subject to various courts.

Eighteen different tribunals, some lay and some ecclesiastical, were re-established in Rome, on the return of the priests; besides these there were the Inquisition and the French court martial. The greater part of the prisoners did not know under what judges they would come, or what crime was to be imputed to them. Thus passed away six months, and none of them yet knew by whom, or for what offence, they were going to be tried. As to myself I was very soon told on whose accusation I was placed there, without, however, being informed upon what charge.

Captain Gennari, who had the custody of those detained in the fort, came after a few days to tell me that I was under the tribunal of the Inquisition;—that the Commissary of the Holy Office, Father Cipolletti, had sent for him, to tell him I was to be watched with the utmost vigilance, and treated with the greatest rigour; without seeing any one, or communicating with a single individual, either verbally or in writing: in short, without light in the evening, or anything whatever beyond what was absolutely necessary to prolong my existence. This official communication was sufficient to prevent my flattering myself that I should meet with gentle treatment, or even with common humanity, unless I obtained some indulgence from the good nature of the gaoler.

Captain Gennari, when he spoke to any one of his mode of acquitting himself in his office, used to say—"I do my duty as a soldier, and if my own father were imprisoned here, from whatever cause it might be, I should not treat him any better than the rest." Nevertheless, this impartial man knew how to relax his severity towards those who could afford to be generous.

My imprisonment continued with unabated rigour, and all the consolation I found was in the comfort of the Holy Spirit, and the kindness of the good gaoler. He redoubled his visits, and often came twice during the day to condole with me.

"Tell me," said he, one day, "what I can do for you, to render your confinement less irksome."

"You can do me one favour, which would be the greatest of all under this heavy tribulation. You know my residence, where my wife now is; go, and inquire for a book for me, the book that I constantly read, and the not having it with me now is my greatest trouble—that is, my Bible. In this way you may render me a double service. Tell that dear creature, also, that I am in good health and perfect tranquillity of mind."

"Yes," said he, "I can serve you so far, and I promise you I will."

On the morrow, he came back in high glee.

"Your wife and all the rest salute you, and she sends you the book."

"God be thanked!"

My good gaoler offered to take care of my Bible for me, and asked me to make him acquainted with its contents. No one can imagine how I enjoyed the first time I read it to him; and he continually contrived opportunities for availing himself of my instructions. I spoke to him one day of the gaoler at Philippi, and how he was called by God, and taught by the holy apostles. Another time I read to him the parable of the Prodigal Son which touched him so much, that he would read it again himself.

"Oh, what a noble book is this Bible!" he exclaimed; "but do the priests believe that it contains the word of God?"

"They say they believe it," I replied, "but their actions contradict their assertion; in fact, they neither read it themselves nor let others read it."

"I understand why—this book does not approve all that they say. If we were to read it attentively, could we afterwards believe in their childish stories?"

Whenever I expounded the Scriptures to him, he seemed as if he could not look at the pure doctrines of Christianity, without confronting them with the corrupt practices of popery.

One time he did not visit me as usual, but another came in his place.

"Is it true," said my new gaoler to me, "what they say of you, that you are put into prison for reading the Bible? But how is that?—is it prohibited? Is it not the book of God?"

"Yes, certainly it is the book of God; this the pope confesses; nevertheless he does not wish it to be read, because he says that no man but himself can understand what God says."

"Would God, then, have spoken not to be understood? Is it likely that God would speak only to the pope, and a few others, like the kings of the earth? I believe that God has spoken for all, and that what is written, is written for all."

"My good friend, you show more intellect than the pope, and more good sense than all his priests. Do not let them impose upon you. Read the Bible, you will obtain one ... ask for it in my name, and it will be given to you."

Three or four other gaolers came to me; all spoke, more or less, the same language; these were all soldiers. Were they not more worthy than cardinals? But of all these men the first was the one to whom I was the most attached, and he, by the mercy of God, was the most attached to me. I was his counsellor in his difficulties, his consolation in his afflictions. I was, he said, a friend and a father to him: and he was of great benefit to me, for he frequently was able to temper the severity of my imprisonment.

"I know," said he one day, "why they do not wish you to hold any communication with others. It is that you may not speak to them of the Bible, of the Gospel, of Jesus Christ. I will not be the means, however, of depriving those who would derive profit from it of this opportunity. I will open the door that communicates with some other cells, where several have already begged me to allow them to speak to you; M. Gazola has often made the request. I know that you will always do good, and never harm to any one; now I will willingly give you an opportunity to do this good, and I trust that God will protect us both from the power of our enemies."

"Oh! my dear friend," said I to him, "it is surely the Lord who has inspired you; do not doubt that He will be with us, if we faithfully serve Him."

After this time, the door of my prison was occasionally left unfastened, so that I might communicate with those who were confined in the same part with myself. Several that could not visit me in the day-time came at night. I am sorry that I cannot at present enter into more particular details, since, at the time I am writing, the major part of my fellow-prisoners are still in confinement, and the remainder are either in Rome or in the Papal states, and consequently under the jurisdiction of the Inquisition. I could otherwise relate many things which our good brethren would be delighted to hear; I may however make the general remark, that whenever I communicated with my fellow-prisoners, our conversation invariably turned on religious matters; it was a subject of rejoicing for us when our prison doors were opened, which each day the gaoler was requested to do at as early an hour as possible. I continued my lectures for the space of a month, and during that time my Bible was in frequent circulation among them.

The treatment experienced in this prison is certainly not so bad, in most cases, as it is in every other within the walls of Rome. The Castle of St. Angelo is chiefly set apart for prisoners of distinction. Cardinals and prelates who fall into disgrace with the pope are confined in it. For this purpose there are a variety of apartments; in one of them are shown the iron rings that had the honour of securing the cord with which the celebrated Cardinals Caraffa, Coscia, and others were hung. Pope Clement VII. was likewise a prisoner in this fortress, at the time of its occupation by the Imperial forces, which he himself had called into Rome. The records of this edifice, which, as everybody knows, was originally the mausoleum of the Emperor Adrian, would throw considerable light on the history of the papacy, and unfold many of the evil deeds of the popes. It has been the scene of the most unheard-of cruelties, as well as of the most shameless and revolting obscenities. The well-known orgies of Pope Alexander VI., which were celebrated partly in the gardens of the Vatican, and partly in the Castle of St. Angelo, have left a stain upon its walls that can never be effaced. Like the Pope's bulls, it serves *"ad perpetuam rei memoriam."*[122] In one of the halls are the notorious pictures by Julio Romano, of which it would be difficult to decide whether the artistical skill they display be more admirable, or the subjects they represent more grossly indecent and detestable. Colonel Calandrelli, one of the most valiant defenders of the republic, and a triumvirate, after Mazzini—a gentleman equally learned in the history of his country as he has shown himself brave in her service, has assured me that he has a work ready for publication, in which the whole history of this celebrated castle is unfolded from authentic documents.

My imprisonment was a source of much trouble and uneasiness to the three cardinals whom the pope had commissioned to take the reins of government. They frequently sent for Captain Gennari to inquire concerning me, and to give fresh orders respecting my safe incarceration. I remember on one occasion the good gaoler having kindly opened for me the door of communication, hastily returned, and with his hand made signs to me to re-enter my cell with all speed, that he might again close the door. Another time, very early in the morning, while I was yet lying on my before-described mattress, the outer door was opened in a very unusual manner, and I heard the voice of Captain Gennari, who loudly called out: "Here he is; come in, Sir, and certify for yourself that Signor Achilli is here;" then opening the door of my cell, he called to me by name, and on my replying to him, observed to his companion, "You hear the voice of Signor Achilli, do you not? Be assured the Cardinal's orders will be duly attended to." Then putting his head into my cell, he whispered to me, "He comes from the Cardinal-Vicar, with fresh orders as to your more close confinement."

After this my poor gaoler began to take fright, and durst no longer allow me to have my door opened as usual: he assured me that he was alarmed for me, as well as for himself; as the first thing that would be done, in case his indulgence was discovered, would be his own removal, and the appointment of another in his place, who would have orders to treat me with greater severity. I afterwards learned that a new prisoner, who had been placed in a cell near my own for some misconduct two or three days before, had informed his father confessor that he had seen me go out and converse with other prisoners; and from what he heard, it appeared to him that I had preached Protestant doctrines to them, and that they had become my followers. The confessor told all this to the cardinals, but, fortunately for me, he had the reputation of being so great a liar, that he obtained no credit with them for his statement, however true it might be; so I heard no more of it.

In the midst of these apprehensions, and with the possibility of finding myself put into irons, my courage never gave way, neither did my zeal diminish in the cause of my friends. I continued, as often as I could, my accustomed discourses, as if I were at liberty, and in a land of freedom. I took no precaution as to whom I addressed myself; my sole care was to render my subject intelligible, and to impress on the mind of my hearers a lasting idea of its importance: with the learned my arguments were more scientific; with the uninstructed, more simple and familiar.

In this way my mission continued to progress even within the walls of a prison. The cardinals, in ordering my incarceration, imagined they had put a stop to my operations, whereas they only accelerated them. We laughed, inside the castle, at the wise precaution of sending me where many of the bravest and the best of the Roman citizens were at that time confined. The city itself was a desert in comparison with the prisons, which were full to overflowing. Had I been allowed to remain unmolested in my own house, I could not have obtained half the success I met with among my fellow-prisoners. Unquestionably I suffered very much in my confinement, separated from my dearest friends, and tormented by the thought of the grief they must feel; but in the midst of these sorrows, I derived consolation from the idea, that the grand work on which I was engaged was, through the grace of God, and the blessing of his Divine providence, steadily advancing. I rejoiced, too, that it was carrying on in Rome, and at the very time, too, when, through foreign compulsion, everything was returning to papacy, and to Pio Nono; who had not only destroyed his own work of liberty, but even the small remains of it that had existed under his predecessors.

At a period when the most horrible slavery was imposed on us through the *generosity* and *consistency* of the French nation, I alone remained free; I, the most hated of all, the most detested by the pope and the cardinals, even more so than Mazzini himself, I had the privilege granted me by the representatives of the two governments, to make war against the pope and the papacy, with undiminished advantage and success. And this was all they gained in shutting me up in the fortress of St. Angelo.

Every time they renewed their persecution of me, I think my power increased. I am not a man to be easily put down. In considering myself as a servant of the Lord, I feel as a rock, on which the tempestuous ocean spends its utmost fury in vain.

The severity of my imprisonment denied me the gratification of seeing any of my friends who were at liberty, neither was it in the power of my kind-hearted gaoler to be of service to me in the matter. There were too many doors to pass through; each of them had its own separate turnkey, and it was hopeless to think of conciliating them all. The only person who had hitherto been allowed to visit me was the English consul, Mr. Freeborn, who had, when I was first taken, obtained permission to do so from the French general; but the cardinals interfered afterwards, and gave orders that no permission should be valid except what came from the Inquisition or the pope, so that an end was soon put to his visits.

A deputation from the Evangelical Alliance, composed of my two good friends, Mr. Tonna and M. Meyrueis, the one an English and the other a French gentleman, who were sent to intercede in my behalf, were also, on application to the cardinals, refused admittance. On referring their petition to the pope they were again denied, and I found that I was more rigorously treated after it; more closely confined to my cell, and threatened with even greater severities.

Nevertheless, through the blessing of God, I never before enjoyed such perfect tranquillity of mind; never in society had I been conscious of more cheerfulness, and when I was drawn into conversation I inspired others with the same feeling. I bade them trust in the providence of God, who would restore to his people their rightful liberty. Hence arose a long discussion on this divine attribute. I let every one propose his objections, which it was a pleasure to me to answer. Another time I was consoling one of my companions for the injustice of the tribunal that judged him. "Oh, my friend," said I, "you look for justice from men. Can you expect it from those who do not fear God? Is not justice an attribute of the Deity? No man can be just who departs from God. How then can justice be restored amongst us? Only by regaining the knowledge and faith, the fear and love of God. And what we say of justice may equally be said of truth. There can be no truth among a people, where the pope is exalted into the place of God. From the earliest times he has been a liar, and his lies obtain credence even in other countries, because they emanate from Rome. If we, then, no longer admit them, let us be the first to denounce that popery by which Rome is oppressed and dishonoured."

These discussions could not fail to produce their effect; which was gradually to withdraw those who listened to them from popery, and to lead them unto God, through Christ. The blessing of God is with those who honour Him, and I hope myself to reap the fruits of what I have sown. I relate these things, not to take pride in them as my own work, but as proceeding from the bounty of the Lord. I should not have come to prison by my own choice, but for wise ends it was so decreed by Divine providence.

Whoever views my imprisonment merely as the work of man, sees in it only injustice and cruelty; but those who regard it as the permission of God, discern in it abundant proofs of his wisdom and love. Many a time have I blessed God for the favour He showed me in choosing me to commence the great work which will be redemption to the Romans, and regeneration to all nations. It has commenced, and is now in progress. To carry it on, God has chosen persons who would not have been thought of by us, any more than we should have thought of Galilean fishermen becoming the apostles and promulgators of a doctrine which was to influence the whole world.

The reformation of Rome is entrusted to Romans. On the reformation of Rome depends that of Roman Catholicism. Those who would concur and co-operate in this work must do it by succouring the Romans.

"Do you think," said one of my companions in prison, one day, "our reform will go on? Will Rome ever be reformed? Will Italy ever become protestant?"

"I believe," replied I, "that Rome will be reformed one day, like London, Berlin, Edinburgh and Geneva."

The question whether Italy will ever become protestant was discussed by me one evening, with the Abate Gioberti, at Paris, in December 1847. He referred me to some pages of his 'Modern Jesuit,' in which it is maintained that Italy never will be protestant: I, on the other hand, referred him to history, to the true history of our country, which shows how great has been the tendency towards protestantism in Italy, and what efforts have been made to promote it. I agreed with the learned Abate that the title of Protestant, as expressive of a division, or religious sect, should be avoided. The Italians, and amongst them the Romans, profiting as they ought to do by three centuries' experience of other nations who have abandoned popery, could not properly denominate themselves anything but Christians. Were they once to renounce the pope, none else could impose upon them either doctrine, form, or name. The questions which to this time have agitated protestantism, and which now divide England into various parties— episcopalian and presbyterian—baptist, methodist, &c. &c., would never disturb the peace of Italy. On right principles the Italian church would be organized with great simplicity, and every one left at full liberty to worship God in the manner best suited to his own spiritual views. What I now call the Italian church does not assume to be a national church, with exclusively privileged forms of government; no, it presents itself to Italy as its ancient church, in the unity of faith and spirit; but in diversity of form, government, and modes of worship. Being thus associated with all the Christian churches throughout the world, it would have nothing exclusively Italian but the language.

In these conversations with my friends, I had the satisfaction to think that what was said to few would be repeated to many. What I uttered within the walls of the castle, in a secret cell, was quickly circulated throughout Rome, and spread abroad, making an impression that could not be effaced. In this manner five months of my imprisonment had already passed away, and I was yet left in ignorance of the crime by which it had been incurred.

I had forwarded my protest to the French government, and the strongest remonstrances had been sent to Paris by my dear brethren of the Evangelical Alliance, yet there appeared to be no prospect of my release; but I may say, with sincerity, that since I have consecrated my life to the Christian ministry, so long as I am engaged in its service I am satisfied. I was now in the full exercise of this ministry during my imprisonment, and no one who has heard my narrative can doubt the satisfaction it gave me. Thus far, therefore, I was contented with my situation; and if I could have supposed that the Roman government would not alter it, but that I might continue to pursue the same course, I should in truth have besought both God and men to leave me in it; because I might perhaps have been more useful, imprisoned in Rome, than at full liberty elsewhere.

But the priests were tired of enduring my boldness and audacity. They took it as an insult to them, that I continued in prison to repeat the very same offences for which I had been incarcerated. All my friends declared to me, that I must either be released and sent out of Rome, by the contrivance of foreigners, or that I should be put out of the way altogether, by the priests themselves.

Reflecting on this idea, I began to think whether it was the will of God my life should be sacrificed; but a voice within seemed to tell me—no. I had done too little, as yet, to see my work so soon crowned with success.

It was the 24th of December—a solemn day in Rome, full of kindly feelings as well as of superstitious observances. On this day good wishes are exchanged and presents made amongst friends; favours are granted, and the boon that should then be asked it would be deemed a sin to deny. We prisoners wished happiness to those who opened our doors, and they cheerfully returned our salutations. My good gaoler, full of benevolence, came to me before I had risen.

"Good morning," said he, "and better luck; I bring you good news."

"What news?" said I.

"An order is come from the French general Baraguai d'Hilliers, to let two gentlemen speak with you—undoubtedly two of your friends; and what is still more satisfactory, it is with the consent of the cardinals."

"Do you know the names of these friends of mine?"

"Only one of them, 'Doctor Bambozzi and companion,' so it is written."

"My dear fellow, do you really believe these can be my friends? If they were so, do you think the cardinals would let them speak to me? They did not give this permission to those two who posted all the way from England and France to obtain it. I do not know who Doctor Bambozzi is, and I cannot imagine what he can want with me."

"But if they be not friends, what can they be?"

"Enemies, assuredly. No person sent by the cardinals can have any occasion for an order from a French general."

"It may be a trick—one of those tricks so frequently played off in priestly Rome. Baraguai d'Hilliers does not know the priests; they may be plotting together something to compromise him."

This visit, announced with so much ceremony on Christmas eve, did not take place till the last day of the year. The supposed friends were the Fiscal Judge of the Inquisition, Monsignor Bambozzi, and his Secretary, Avvocato de Dominicis.

Monsignor Bambozzi is one of the most courteous of men. Those who, hearing of the Fiscal Judge of the Inquisition, might picture to themselves an austere man, with a crafty sinister air, would find they were quite mistaken in their idea. No, he is a very polite little man, a sacristan priest, paying compliments to everybody, always smiling, with his snuff-box in his hand ever ready to offer a pinch. The other was a poor needy-looking personage, with nothing unfavourable in his aspect, and evidently following his occupation to earn his bread.

I was first desired to give an exact description of myself. The prelate then made a sign to the other to write, and began to dictate to him in Latin.

"A certain man (homo quidam) appeared before me declaring himself to be—What is your name?"

I told him my name, my age, &c. He went on:—

"Giacinto Achilli, son of —— born at —— aged —— &c., dressed," (here followed the description of my dress from head to foot)—"confined in this prison, &c.; being asked if he knows why he is detained in prison, answers ——Answer this question.

"'It is what I wish to know. I have been six months confined here, and have never yet been told, nor do I know the cause of my imprisonment.'

"Interrogated whether he knows under what tribunal he is now examined, answers—

"'It is what I wish to know.'

"And being told that he is examined by the magistrates of the Holy Roman Universal Apostolical Inquisition, answers—

"'I am glad of it. Speak frankly.'

"Admonished to tell the truth, and to recognise in this fact the justice of God and not the vengeance of man, he replied to the first part—

"'I promise to tell the truth:' on the second he was silent."

At this juncture, Monsignor Bambozzi drew out a quire of paper, covered with writing, and began to read the first page; from which I perceived it was the minute taken down the second day of my imprisonment, by a judge of the cardinal-vicar's: consisting of a general interrogatory on the whole of my life—that is to say, my education, my studies, my public functions, my occupations, my journeys, and especially that to the Ionian Islands, Malta, England, &c., till my return to Rome; what I had done during the Roman Republic, and finishing with my imprisonment. All this confronted anew with numerous questions, formed the subject of my first interview with Monsignor Bambozzi and his companion.

In a moment the news resounded through St. Angelo, that the judges of the Inquisition were come, with the special permission of the French authorities, to take possession of me. The indignation this intelligence excited was great; and was expressed in no very measured terms, against both the priests and the French. I smiled amidst the universal excitement; but I may safely say I was the only one who did so.

Four days afterwards the judge and his companion were again announced; and I had to submit to a fresh and very long interrogatory, carried on like the former one in Latin.

First, as to why I had abandoned the Order of the Dominicans, from which I had received, even up to the latest moment that I was connected with it, the greatest proofs of esteem and good-will; insomuch, that I had been promoted, whilst yet in my youth, to posts so high and important that they were difficult to be obtained even by the aged.

Secondly, why I had afterwards abandoned the ministry of the Roman Church, my theological functions, the mass, and other religious duties; thus showing myself thankless and ungrateful for the education I had received, and for the interest taken in me at Rome?

Thirdly, what complaint I had to make, if any, of the lenient correction I received on my being summoned before the Inquisition in 1842, the sole object of which was to recall me to the right path?

Fourthly, and lastly, why I had left Rome, and quitted Italy altogether, to take refuge in Protestant countries; thus making myself a public subject of conversation, to the scandal of my best friends, and the fearful injury of my own soul?

To these questions I calmly and briefly replied—

First, that with regard to leaving the Dominicans I had been induced to do so from motives of conscience, though I still retained a grateful remembrance of all the kindnesses I had received from them; and that what I had done was with the full permission and licence of Pope Gregory XVI.

Secondly, that it was equally from motives of conscience I had left the ministry of the Roman Church.

Thirdly, that far from bringing any complaint against the Inquisition, I had quietly resigned to it all the charges of the ministry, testifying thereby to every one who might be willing to understand me, that from that time I intended no longer to be connected with the Church of Rome in any way whatsoever, regarding myself as subject to no one, in matters of faith, save God alone.

Fourthly, that my leaving Rome, and Italy altogether, was the natural result of the steps I had previously taken; that whether I went to the English or Spanish dominions, or any other, could be a matter of consequence to no one, provided I lived an upright life, wherever I might be; and as I felt conscious that this had been the case hitherto, I did not consider myself called upon to render an account of my actions to any man.

I had reserved to myself a more lengthened and argumentative conversation, when Monsignor Bambozzi should enter upon the question of matters of faith; he not only, however, left that subject untouched upon, but even turned it aside when I endeavoured to lead his attention towards it: nay, he went so far as to order the gaoler to let me take the air every day, for about a quarter of an hour, on the terrace of the castle, saying that he was quite satisfied with me, and that we were perfectly agreed. Yet how he could imagine we were so, when my opinions had been diametrically opposed to his, and all my answers a direct rebuff to his questions, I cannot understand. The fact is, that the Inquisition has always been about as anxious after truth, for its own sake, as Pontius Pilate was, in the presence of the Lord.

Both my judge and his companion, however, upon taking leave of me this second time, shook hands with me, saying, that I should see them again shortly.

Eight days elapsed, when I was once more asked for. "It is Bambozzi," cried my fellow-prisoners; and I went down stairs laughing, in the expectation of seeing him again; but in his place I beheld a priest of the Oratory, alone. He was full of compliments and civilities, on our meeting; and I asked him at once his name, and the cause of his visit; for as soon as he opened his mouth, I perceived by his accent that he was not an Italian. He replied that he had come to see me purely out of good-will; and showed me his name in the title-page of a book: "Dr. Augustine Theiner, of Prussian Silesia, Professor of Ecclesiastical History in the College of the Propaganda in Rome." He went on to say that he was grieved to find me in such a situation, but that still all might turn out for the best, if I would only be teachable towards God, and the Holy Mother of the Roman Catholic church. This at once brought us to the question, whether the Roman church alone had a right to be called Catholic? I maintained that it was *a church*, but not *the church*, and by logical consequence could not be called universal, for the simple reason that Rome was not the whole world:—that the Pope was Bishop of the Roman church alone, and not of the Catholic church; the proof being that many hundreds of bishops exist in the church, some dependent upon, and others independent of Rome; without reckoning all those Christian churches which pride themselves on having no other bishop than Him mentioned by Peter: "For ye were as sheep going astray, but are now returned unto the Shepherd and Bishop of your souls."[123]

He asked me, smiling, what my church was? I told him it was that of which St. Paul speaks:[124] "The general assembly and church of the First-born which are written in heaven." To a few other questions I replied to the same purport. He exhorted me to read his book, printed by the Propaganda, in which he had shown me his name; and then took his leave.

This book is a "History of the Reformation in Sweden," written, it would appear, on purpose to blacken the fame of those staunch Reformers, the good King Gustavus and the excellent Oloff Peterson; and to have the opportunity of using every description of epithets, the most offensive he could find, against Luther. It has had the honour, as the author told me, of being translated into French by M. de Montalembert, and into English by Dr. Newman, who is also become a priest of the Oratory. A second and third visit from Dr. Theiner, who came to me with other books of his own writing, which he earnestly requested me to read, were occupied with continual questions on the Roman church; he resting upon certain passages of the holy Fathers, to prove that it is the Catholic church, and I upon passages from the Fathers also, to show that what they called Catholic, was the Roman church together with all others, those only excepted which deviated from the teaching of the Holy Scriptures, and from the faith of Christ,—the Roman Church being so different in our days, and especially since the Council of Trent, from what it was in those of the holy Fathers, that if they were now living they would be the first to protest against it, and to separate from it; that before the present Roman church could be called Christian, a reformation in it was indispensable; the Jewish and the Pagan elements being so mixed up with both its doctrines and worship, that there hardly remains in it a shade of primitive Christianity: that let but the pope undertake this reformation, we would be with him, otherwise we must remain separated; nor should his threats terrify us, nor his Inquisition rob the Christians of Italy of their faith or their union; that I had shown an example to the brethren how to propagate in this country the pure and simple doctrine of Christ; that the Bible, and the Bible alone, was sufficient to destroy the whole edifice of the pope; and that on the day when I saw reprinted in Rome the New Testament in Italian, and moreover beheld the avidity with which the Romans received it, I exclaimed, "The death-knell of the Papacy is sounded."

My heart almost leaped out of my breast with joy, at having been able, in the prisons of the Roman Inquisition, to render this testimony to the truth and to the religion of Jesus Christ.

"I am as happy as possible now," I said to several of those good friends who were with me in prison, and who asked me every time they saw me how I got on with the papal theologian. "I am only afraid that, feeling how firm I am, Padre Theiner may discontinue his visits, and tell the cardinals and the pope that every attempt to bring me back to the Roman church is useless."

He had in fact, at his second visit, shown me a letter of the Cardinal-Vicar, in which he appointed him, by the pope's desire, to come to me under the guise of a visitor, to hold conferences with me, and to discover some way of recovering me to the faith.

At the end of each visit, however, I had always requested him to report faithfully everything I had said to him; adding that every day I felt more and more firm and fixed in my purpose; and that if it should please God that I should be released from prison, I should, with the aid of His Holy Spirit, continue my mission with all the more vigour, from perceiving by His having conferred on me the grace of being allowed to suffer six months' incarceration for His name's sake, that it could not be otherwise than acceptable in His sight.

At the same time, I bade him, and the pope and cardinals likewise, to remember, that the persecution to which I had been subjected could not be approved or justified even by Roman Catholics themselves; and that if it had no other effect, it would at least have the most desirable one of ultimately working the abolition of the Roman Inquisition, never more to be restored.

Padre Theiner and I were, on this third visit, in the full fervour of our controversial arguments, when the captain of the castle came to inform me that two *chasseurs de Vincennes* were arrived to take me to the French Council of War, to give evidence in the trial of Signor Cernuschi, Deputy of the people, under the Republic.

How I, separated as I was, and had been for six months, from the rest of the world, by a decree emanating from the Inquisition, could be summoned by a foreign authority to appear before a military tribunal, was what I could not comprehend; and my theologian was still more astonished at it than I was. The captain added that he had the permission of the Cardinal-Vicar. "Let us go, in the name of the Lord," was my thought.

Padre Theiner accompanied me to the carriage, I got in, and two soldiers, armed with carbines, took their places by me, one on each side. The tribunal was held at the Ecclesiastical Academy in the Piazza Minerva, the great institution of the Dominicans, who were, as I have already stated, the founders of the Inquisition; and I have often reflected since upon the retributive justice of Providence, in appointing that very place for the sitting of the tribunal which was to break down the power of that villanous establishment, by setting one of its victims free, to disclose its iniquities to the world.

The *Capitaine Rapporteur* was alone; he put a few questions to me concerning Cernuschi; and said certain things to me, which I forbear to mention; as well as some other things of little import to any one but myself; for fear of causing trouble to parties still remaining in Rome, and consequently subjected to the treacheries and basenesses of a government at this present moment one of the most tyrannical, and at the same time the most degraded, in Europe. I was then remanded to the castle.

The next day, the 19th of January, Dr. Theiner again called upon me, and we recommenced our discussions with more animation than ever. Our subject was the bishopric of St. Peter at Rome, and the privilege of succession bequeathed by him to the pope; he intent on demonstrating, I on confuting it. Our arguments lasted till nearly dark, and no doubt would have lasted longer still, as we were neither of us inclined to cut the matter short, had they not been suddenly interrupted by the entrance of the gaoler, with the information that the two *chasseurs* were come again to take me to the Military Commission.

I held out my hand to my disputant. "Farewell!" said I to him, "farewell, Padre Theiner; offer my respects to the Cardinal-Vicar, and thank him from me for your visits; I assure you they have given me real pleasure. I hope we may both of us derive profit from them, and be confirmed by them, more and more, in the word of God."

I again pressed his hand, and then got into the carriage, and seated myself between the two soldiers.

This time my vehicle was an open one, and as it traversed the long way from the Castle of St. Angelo to the Piazza della Minerva, I saw and was seen by many persons. I was regarded with curiosity. It was, indeed a singular spectacle to behold a prisoner of the Inquisition under the guard of the French Republic.

I found the *Capitaine Rapporteur* even more conciliatory in his deportment towards me than he was before, and I felt persuaded that he entertained a personal sympathy towards me. I will not, however, repeat our conversation. I will only say that it cheered me greatly, and made me feel so thoroughly as if I were my own master, that I determined to try if it could really be the case.

I walked into an ante-chamber, where I saw several sets of military garbs and accoutrements. In a moment I found myself in the uniform of a French soldier. I proceeded towards the doors on the landing; they were open; not a single individual anywhere to be seen, to oppose my egress. It was half after five in the evening, consequently dusk. I did what any one else, I suppose, in my situation would have done, and I did it with a smile of confidence and joy. I descended into the Piazza della Minerva, passed through the Strada Pie-di-Marmo, the Piazza del Collegio Romano, and walked down the Corso, in my military garb. Unrecognised, uninterrupted, I arrived at a place where I changed my dress. Here I found money prepared for me; a passport and a carriage with post-horses were soon ready, and at seven in the evening I beheld myself beyond the walls of Rome!

I offered up my thanksgiving to the Lord, and implored his blessing upon my country, my brethren, and the infant church, which will one day shine forth in all the lustre of truth, so that it may again be said of the Romans, that "their faith is spoken of throughout the whole world."

In six hours after leaving Rome I arrived at Civita Vecchia, where I rested till morning. I then delivered several letters, and afterwards went on board a French steamer of war. The whole of that day I passed in port, engaged, the greatest portion of it, in returning my grateful thanks to my Almighty Father, and praying to Him to provide for me in all respects. I likewise, finding I had an opportunity of getting it posted, wrote a farewell letter to my brethren in Rome.

The next day we sailed for Toulon, whence I proceeded to Marseilles, and thence to Lyons; where I stopped a day, to embrace my excellent friend, Mr. Fisch, and other brethren, who felt as if they could not bless and thank the Lord enough, for my unexpected liberation. In Paris I was greeted with the same rejoicings. Oh, what enjoyments has the Christian life, even in this world! In my own case all that I have suffered now seems sweet and delightful to me. It is indeed to my body like a dream; but to my spirit it is a precious and enduring reality. Never, I hope, shall I forget the gratitude, which, under God, I owe to the brethren of the Evangelical Alliance, who have indeed set an example with regard to myself, of the most edifying Christian charity.

At Paris I laid aside my incognito, which in fact was of no use to me after I embarked at Civita Vecchia; but the French government, through whose assistance I had escaped, stipulated that I should not resume my own name before I reached Paris. It was consequently my duty to obey. Several among the old ministry assured me that they would have gladly lent me their services, had they been in power; but as that was not the case, they rejoiced in seeing it done by others: they seemed indeed to be of opinion that the way in which my liberation had been effected, was the only one that could have been adopted to avoid a dispute with the Pontifical government; that, on the other hand, had I been suffered to remain in prison, it would have been a lasting disgrace to France, to have it said that the power of the Inquisition was restored and upheld through her medium; they added that if assistance had not been afforded me at an earlier period, it was only because it had been given out that I was confined on account of moral delinquencies, and not for my religious tenets.

"And I," said the ex-minister, "was one of the first to be misled by these charges; but when they were all proved to be malignant inventions, brought forward only to injure you, there was but one wish on the subject, and that was to see you set at liberty."

Notwithstanding this flattering testimony of the ex-minister, I have no doubt there were many, even among the French, who would much rather I had remained in the power of the Inquisition; the Jesuit party especially, among whom were several members of the National Assembly, were loud in their outcries against me, and renewed in their journals their old calumnies, which had so often been answered before, and to which the act of the government itself, in liberating me, was more than a sufficient reply.

I shall not here relate all the kindness and affection I experienced on the part of my friends, on again seeing me among them. One of the first visits I made was to our dear brother in the Lord, the Pastor Frederic Monod, who retained me under his roof all the time I remained at Paris. I had scarcely sent in my name, when the whole of his numerous family came out to welcome me, and fervent were the praises and thanksgivings that were offered up by them to the Giver of all good, who had delivered me from the hand of my enemies, and from them that sought to destroy my soul.

"Come," said my good friend, "let us go to my brother Adolph's; our friends are met together there on your account; they have not yet heard of your liberation, and are at this very time consulting together on the best means to adopt, in order to influence the government in your behalf."

We accordingly proceeded together to the house. Frederic entered first, while I remained at the door. "Brethren," he exclaimed, "before you proceed any further in your deliberations, you will rejoice to learn what a signal favour it has pleased heaven to grant. Our brother Achilli has, through the mercy of God, without any assistance of ours, been released from his imprisonment. He is now in France; he has arrived in Paris, and is actually at the door of this very house; he is come to salute you, and to offer up conjointly with yourselves his thanksgivings to the Lord."

At this moment I entered, and great was the joy with which I was received by these dear brethren. After we had returned thanks for the great mercies we had experienced, I, following the example of St. Peter, "beckoning unto them with the hand to hold their peace, declared unto them how the Lord had brought *me* out of the prison."

I had now only one thing wanting to complete my contentment, which was the restoration to me of my dear partner, the sweet solace of my troubles, and the sharer of my hopes. And this additional blessing was soon granted to me. At the time of my leaving Rome, my wife was at Florence; but as soon as she heard of my arrival at Paris, she set off to rejoin me, under the protection of some friends.

About the middle of February we returned together, after a most eventful year's absence, to England; where, ever since my arrival, I have received the same, and even increased tokens of regard and interest in my welfare, that I had done before, and of which I shall always retain the most grateful remembrance. Nevertheless I view my mission as inseparably connected with my native country; to resume my labours there, sooner or later, in the establishment of a reformed Italian Church, is the holy ambition of my heart, the unceasing object of my prayers. Meanwhile I endeavour to preserve the germ of it alive, by celebrating Divine worship, "pure and undefiled before God," and imparting religious instruction on the Sabbath, and at fit seasons, to as many of my unfortunate fellow-refugees, and others of my countrymen, as show themselves desirous of it; trusting that "what is sown in tears may be reaped in joy," and that the great "Lord of the harvest" may be pleased to send His labourers therein, and to bless their efforts and their hopes.

### FOOTNOTES:

[121] Matt. x. 42.

[122] Every Papal bull commences with these words.

[123] I Pet. ii. 23.

[124] Heb. xii. 23.

# APPENDIX

Letter

To Cardinal Lambruschini, *Secretary of State.—Vide p. 41.*

Corfù, Nov. 1842.

Most Reverend Eminence,—

I have reason to be grateful for the singular attention your Eminence has manifested towards me, in so repeatedly recommending me to the care of the Governor of the Ionian Isles, in Corfu. I am aware that the Papal Consul, Signor Mosca, has done his utmost that I should be again given up to the authority of the Inquisition; on the contrary, however, I have, in consequence, been the more sedulously protected by this respectable Government, which glories in granting an asylum to all honest persons from the shores of Italy, particularly to such as come from the Papal States. It was in this same country that the Neapolitan emigrants, and among them the Papal Consul himself, were so cordially received in the year 1821. An equally kind welcome was also extended to the exiles from Modena and Romagna, in the year 1831, to many of whom were granted public employment, and the rights of nationality.

I do not myself belong to that honourable body who, for the sake of their country, have been exiled by their monarch. I am a voluntary exile, in consequence of the priestly domination and despotism which prevails to a greater extent than ever; and I have sought refuge among strangers, hoping to pass the remainder of my life secure from the outrageous oppression with which we were continually visited by our wretched rulers, in consequence of their heart-corroding suspicions and alarms. From the first moment that I landed among these noble-minded Greeks, I found hospitality, personal security, liberty of conscience, peace, and tranquillity. I chose this spot as being near to Italy, and where kindred spirits lament over the present disastrous state of affairs, and endeavour to preserve themselves and their children from similar misfortunes. Above all, I came here because I felt a presentiment that I shall be called upon to maintain the cause of the Cross; and I am desirous, moreover, to be ready to defend myself from those who, having before so unworthily attacked me, will doubtless renew their molestations, unless I am present to refute their calumnies.

I need only refer to the late letters written to the Consul and others, to my injury, the falsehood of which your Eminence well knows; not to mention the numberless schemes put in practice to annoy me. But are you not aware that it is in my power to cover my adversaries with confusion, and render them infamous in the eyes of the whole world, simply by narrating things as they really are? Yet, I shall rather check this spirit of reaction, unless I am absolutely constrained to allow it in my own vindication.

My sole desire is to possess and enjoy peace in my own mind; to have my understanding enlightened; to feel the influence of goodness in my own breast, and to be guided in all things by Him who alone is wisdom and light, "the way, the truth, and the life." I declare to you, Signor Cardinal,—I declare to all your brethren of the Sacred College, and to the Pope himself, that from this very moment I intend no longer to be conjoined with the sect of the so-called Roman Catholics, of which the Pope is the head, Rome the seat, and the Canons the law. I renounce all belief in Papistic doctrines, as being opposed to the Gospel, the only light left us by Jesus Christ, the only volume of religious truth, the single code of faith, the sole rule and guidance for our moral conduct; as such, I desire in all things to be obedient to the injunctions of that Holy Gospel, and to follow it in its original purity, divested of all the corruptions introduced by the Church of Rome, which subject the Word to the domination of a *soi-disant* Vicar of Jesus Christ, a high priest intruded upon the Universal Church. Thus I hope to return to the early faith established by Christ, promulgated by His Apostles throughout the whole world, and professed by His true disciples, our forefathers, to whom neither Pope nor Cardinals were necessary, and who lived together in peace, as brethren; arrogating to themselves no superiority over others, nor any right to command their fellow-servants in the cause of religion, their only distinctions being titles of affection and kindness; knowing that God, who contemneth the proud, and severely rebuketh those who are clothed in purple and fine linen, regardeth with favour the meek and lowly of heart, and him who having two cloaks gives one to his neighbour who has none.

My religion, therefore, is no longer that which God has abandoned to the false prophets; but that which He visibly protects upon earth; that which He has himself brought forth out of the corruptions which the followers of pomp and wealth have occasioned, to the destruction of true morality, the profanation of what is holy, the falsifying of the very truth itself. My religion is that which has been purged from the Romish infection by men raised up for that purpose by the Almighty himself; and to whom was also given the power and grace to rescue half Europe from the abyss of papal contamination. And now is the time that the people of every nation are called upon to join in this reform; and I doubt not they will come from every quarter for that purpose, weary of belonging to an abominable sect, which so greatly dishonours the Gospel by the immoderate luxury of its court, and the ignorance and vices of its entire priesthood.

I rejoice that finally, after so many trials and tribulations, the Lord hath effectually called me to Him, through the truths of faith; and as I owe Him thanks for all His dispensations, I am more particularly called upon to bless His holy Name for having enabled me to turn this last persecution of the Romish priesthood to such good account. Behold me then always a true Roman with respect to my country, but no longer so with regard to religion; a Christian, but no Papist. And as such, in the path that opens before me, I trust I shall be enabled to lead others also unto the truth.

I flatter myself that we may now enter into a sort of agreement with each other. I, for my part, solemnly engage to relinquish every privilege I have received at your hands, and expect that you, in return, will give up all right to exercise authority over me. Let there be a complete divorce, a wall of separation between us. I do not indeed imagine that I shall be further molested, at any rate I shall be but little disposed to put up with it. My intentions are nevertheless far from hostile: now that we are divided, let there be that peace betwixt us which, as long as we were united, never could exist.

Communicate the contents of this letter to the whole Congregation of the Holy Office, to whom I am indebted for the first idea, not of my reform itself, but of my declaration of it; as I am now to your Eminence for this full and solemn protest.

P.S. Your Eminence must know, that among the events which took place the day I left the Inquisition, one was the depriving me of a valuable watch, by one of the Inquisitors in the name of the Holy Congregation, for what reason I cannot tell. As the loss of it was very disagreeable to me, I did not fail to make many urgent requests to have it back again, but all in vain. Poor watch! as it had been my constant companion for ten years, I suppose it was imagined it also had imbibed a portion of heresy, and who knows what terrible sentence may not hang over its head! I maintain, however, that my watch has always been *true* and *faithful*, and *regular*, and if it has no claim to *infallibility*, it is solely because it has never belonged to the Pope: it belongs to me, and I have no intention to resign it to others. If, therefore, the Inquisition does not think proper to restore it to me, I shall be under the necessity of making my complaint public; which I shall assuredly do in the Maltese and London Journals.

I have the honour to be, &c. &c.
Giacinto Achilli.

*To* Gregory XVI., *Bishop and Sovereign of Rome,* Giacinto Achilli, *Minister of the Italian Catholic Church.—Vide p. 42.*

Letter I.

However known my sentiments may already be to you, from several letters, which I have recently written to your two Cardinals, Polidori and Lambruschini, I still regard it as desirable to make a more ample declaration to yourself, so as to throw greater light on my faith, and to leave no longer in doubt the form of religion which I follow and profess.

Believe not, Holy Father, that I am urged to this step by any feeling of resentment in consequence of the injuries done me in Rome by certain of your ministers; or that I wish to avenge myself thus, for the hundred days during which I was shut up, last year, in the Inquisition without any just cause. May God pardon you your offences as entirely as I pardon you that act, though it brought upon me heavy sufferings! I have been enabled to derive benefit from it; and that which by you was designed for my injury, the all-wise God has turned to my advantage. So that now, on reckoning up my account, I find that my gain has been far greater than my loss; that my sorrow has been turned into joy; that the plot has turned against the plotters, to whom nothing has remained but remorse for the attempt, and the shame of a miserable defeat.

Holy Father, if you really fear God, you know sufficiently that He is not to be trifled with—we cannot lie to Him, nor purpose one thing and say another. Allow me, then, now to summon you into His presence, to discuss your faith and my own; for we are both equal before Him; the Decalogue and the Gospel are equally imposed upon us both. Excepting these, I know no other law to direct me in my belief and in my actions; and I am convinced that there should be no other for any one who calls himself a Christian.

Tell me, I pray you, whence you derive those of your dogmas which exist not in the Gospel, and those numerous doctrines which are not to be found in any book of the Scriptures? I am entitled to ask you; for, after examining your lauded fountains of tradition, your theologians, and the Fathers, so dishonestly edited,—I have found superabundant fraud, both in interpretation, assertion, supposition, and inference; for all seem to be concentrated in the object of making the Pope universal sovereign; establishing him as head and lord of the entire Church, with full and absolute power of loosing and binding—that is, of destroying and building up,—declaring his Church, as a spiritual kingdom, superior to every state, to every people, to every dynasty; so that, according to this theory, the power of the pope is made to absorb every other power; from that of God Himself, who alone, in other times, judged men to life or to perdition, down to that of the lowest baron, who can only have from the pope the legitimate power over his vassals.

Such fables might be told in the vaunted days of Gregory VII.; when they were coined with the design of extending the papal mantle over the whole world; subjecting to him, as far as possible, the kingdoms of Europe and Asia. Such was the object of the Crusades. Such was the object of the foundation of the numerous Orders,—enrolled, under various devices, for the purposes of the popes, and sent to the most remote countries, to preach, together with the Gospel, the primacy, the sovereignty, the infallible, irresistible, fearful omnipotence of the Most Holy Bishop of Rome; under pain, if they did not, of being severely punished, and with the promise, if they did, of being rewarded, after death, with the honours of the altar.

History, Holy Father, teaches us this, whenever we read it with the necessary discernment. These Orders, however, increased, spread, and were laden by Rome with privileges, exemptions, and even riches; for the monks, yet more than the priests, played the papal game, and related to the nations the holiness of the popes, how they were chosen by the Holy Spirit, and how Christ and the Virgin conversed with them familiarly. Happy, then, did those consider themselves, who could obtain an *Agnus Dei*, or other favour; whilst for an indulgence, silver and gold were spent without restraint. Hence the immense riches which, from every quarter showered upon Rome, and rendered the popes proud, their courts insolent, their city the most beautiful in the world.

But times changed; that is to say, many well-informed persons amongst the faithful, perceived the imposture of these sellers of Christ; and first with words, afterwards by acts, revolted against the disorder which not only blinded them with error, but despoiled and oppressed them.

And now came the epoch of the Reformation—of that religious rising which, excited by God, and guided by the Spirit of the Lord, succeeded in enlightening and persuading half Europe to separate from the theories of popery, without fear of offending religion,—nay, rendering justice, by so doing, to that Gospel which the popes had adulterated, which Rome had profaned, which had been made an instrument of extortion and falsehood, by the aid of priests and monks. But this lesson, honestly given to them by nations, was not enough to correct the popes; even the half of their proselytes who remained to them, were sufficient to maintain their courts in all their luxury; and one hope comforted them, that by the use of skilful artifices, they might destroy the work of Luther and of Henry VIII., as they had done that of many others.

Holy Father, how has this hope for three centuries failed your predecessors! Nay, you yourself have had the grief of losing several districts, in the north and in the south, which called themselves yours, without any hope that they will ever return to you again.

If you wish to know the reason, I can tell it you. It is because our times are no longer in accordance with the impostures that you sell by your monks, who, full of ignorance, superstition, and knavery, still hawk about the fables of Rome. The world will no longer listen to your universal primacy, because every one knows that it does not extend beyond the two millions and a half of people, which, by the deference of the sovereigns of Europe, it is still permitted you to govern by force of arms.

Your indulgences, your relics, are specifics which are gone out of use. The excise upon sins, which you enforce once a-year, to be paid through your privileged exactors, is, be assured, paid by the generality in false money; inasmuch as now nearly every one comprehends that, however great may be the authority you possess, that power assuredly is wanting to you which belongs to God alone. Still it is to be bitterly lamented, that a great part of Europe yet tolerates that trickery of yours—a spectacle revolting to the good sense, not to say to the religion, of mankind—that a priestly juggler should boast of being able to transform, by virtue of certain words, a portion of bread and wine into Deity. Too great, O Holy Father, too great is the abuse attempted to be practised on your adherents; placing them in the very condition of those who were once taught that gods might be born in a garden. Why so far outrage your friends as to make them afterwards ashamed of themselves, when they come to reflect upon the fraud? It makes them hate and curse you when this happens. In these our days, when even children are angry at being deceived, men have sufficient self-respect rather to bear blows than to be treated with fraud and delusion.

And do you know what follows? The gravest of all evils—the total loss of religion. Roman Catholics, if not quick in taking refuge in some reform or other, become Atheists, the first moment that having their eyes open, they perceive they have been drawn into such gross errors. They feel an indignation which makes them discredit everything; believing that there can be nothing good where so many evil things are presented to them to swallow. Just as when in a most exquisite dish we find foreign substances which offend our senses, we do not endeavour to separate them, but rather reject the whole; so it happens to Papists, when they perceive the falsity and fraud which lie hidden under the Roman faith.

What now will you say, Holy Father, if I prove to you that by means of popery men become more wicked, and are so speculatively? The power that you claim of granting absolution of sins,—to whom does it secure pardon? Who is there that, having fulfilled the condition you lay down of confession, does not feel persuaded that he has settled his accounts, to open them again with equal extravagance? Where are the greatest numbers of robbers, traitors, adulterers, if not in the midst of your Roman Catholics? And why? Because it costs them nothing but to cast themselves at the feet of one of your plenipotentiaries, to cancel every iniquity. If you have been at Naples, you know of whom it is that the churches are full; who it is that beat their breasts before the altar, who are those that weep all day at the confessionals! And such as Naples is, such are all the other countries more or less papistical.

But there is still more to observe. Who are generally the most wicked persons in every locality? (I speak only of Italy, indeed only of Southern Italy—a country emphatically Roman Catholic.) Forgive me, Holy Father; but it is a matter of fact,—priests and monks; whatever iniquity, wickedness, and abomination has ever existed upon the earth, you will find among them. Haughtiness, luxury, ambition, pride,—where do they most abound? In your temples. There the excessive love of money, falsehood, fraud, duplicity, cover themselves with a sacred veil, and are almost in security from profane censures. And oh! how great are the horrors of the cloisters (*sepulchra dealbata*), where ignorance and superstition, laziness, indolence, calumny, quarrels, immorality of every description, not only live, but reign. The most abominable vices, long banished from all society, have there taken refuge; and there will they continue miserably to dwell, until God, outraged by them, shall rain down upon them the curse of Sodom and Gomorrah.

Am I exaggerating? or do not you yourself, while reading this paragraph, utter the sigh of sorrowing conviction? But who are to be blamed for such evils? Mankind, you will tell me, evasively. But I reply: Are not the immense mass of Protestants also a part of mankind? and do not they live quite differently? Worshipping the same Deity, followers of the same gospel, their temples are truly the house of prayer; their Sundays the Lord's-day, their ministers patterns of probity and morality. Can this be denied concerning the Protestant clergy in general? But against the Roman Catholic clergy thousands of accusations can be most justly made. Will you venture to deny it? You must first hide the episcopal prisons of your State, and numerous other places of punishment for ecclesiastics;—you must prevent the world from knowing of the Ergastolo of Corneto, full to overflowing with priests and monks, whom you send there yourself, when they become intolerable to you. Find me anything like this in Germany or in England—countries eminently Protestant. Can you deny, then, that your popery renders men more wicked?

It follows, from what has been said, that such a religion is the pest of society; insomuch as it conceals the truth, disfigures the gospel, promotes error, favours ignorance and bigotry. Hence comes the ruin of poor Italy, which, owing to this system of belief, is in many parts desert, the country uncultivated, the commerce in a deplorable condition. Italy, once the queen of the world, is now the servant and slave of other nations. Kings consulting with their confessors how best to oppress their people! Jesuits restored to the ascendant! Monks continually enriching themselves! While all the rest of the world is progressing, Italy alone is going back, on account of her popery, which degrades, debases, and renders her contemptible in the sight of God and man.

Holy Father, are you grieved by what I say? I rejoice not in your grief, but in the hope that it may be for your benefit. It rests with you, if you will, to change the system. Be not ashamed of having erred till now. You will be *the man* of the age; a man glorious in all history: you will be the true apostle of Jesus Christ, if, renouncing the vanity of your primacy, which can last to you but little longer, you lay down the titles and the dignities which do not belong to you. You, better than any other, can bring back to Italy the religion of Christ in its purity; taking away all that has been maliciously invented, to defraud the faithful for the profit of the clergy. The imposture is now thoroughly seen into; there are no longer persons who believe in Confession, in the Mass; in the sufferings of Purgatory, in the patronage of Saints. Your indulgences have lost all their credit; your excommunications are totally valueless: your bulls and canons only raise a smile.

How is the world changed in regard to you! Once all Catholics, even the least earnest, spoke of the pope with respect. Now even your own court speaks ill of you. Accusations against yourself personally, which circulate through the world, and state things in the highest degree disgraceful, originate with Romans. You will call this the work of Satan, but I must, with more suitable language, call it the hand of God; that terrible hand which is preparing your punishment.

It will happen to you as it happened three centuries since, to Pope Clement VII. Germany and England then separated from Rome under his eyes: Poland and Spain are about to do the same under yours. Hasten, Holy Father, to accept the call which Heaven makes to you. Despise not the voice of God, as your ill-advised predecessors despised it. Your measure is now full. In the first days of your pontificate you saw the most violent revolution that ever happened in your States,—the sincere expression of the opinion and wishes of every one. It was echoed and applauded by all Italy. Italy wishes for you no longer; Italy no longer believes, respects, or loves you. It was requisite, at that time, for the Austrians to interfere. Will they do so again? Or, if they do, will they be able to extinguish the flame?

Regard not who it is who gives you these suggestions. I am less hostile to you than you imagine. Nay, I protest to you that I have no hostility in my heart, except towards your doctrine and policy; I have none towards yourself, whom I regard with religious affection, and for whom I desire the holy light of God, to promote your repentance and that of your brethren.

Corfu, January 15, 1843.

*To* Gregory XVI. *Bishop and Sovereign of Rome,* Giacinto Achilli, *Minister of the Italian Catholic Church.*

Letter II.

It is not party spirit—it is not a vain-glorious craving to contend with you,—but the love of truth, the interests of religion, and the charity of the gospel, which induce me to write to you again.

It has ever been the custom in the Church of Jesus Christ for the elders to treat with the bishops, upon the most important matters. Thus Jerome did with Damasus, and Bernard with Eugenius. I do not set myself up as a judge. I only wish to be a truthful witness, in a cause where there are a thousand accusers. The issue lies between you and the Church—that is, between the Christian people and one Bishop of Christendom. No question could be more important, from the subject to which it relates, the parties who compose it, the period at which it is raised. The subject is the faith of the gospel, the only law given to Christians. The parties are a multitude against a few; a people against individuals; the Christian Church against its pretended lords. The period is the nineteenth century. The terms of the question: whether the world at large should continue to believe in you, to obey you, to follow you, wherever you are pleased to lead it. You support the affirmative, which others deny. I will openly deliver my solemn testimony.

The Christian world will no longer believe in you, because you have deceived it, and because you continue in your intention of deceiving it. It believed you as long as you announced the truths of religion, as they are written in the book of the common faith. To you, as more instructed than others, it allowed the faculty of explaining the mysteries of charity, the symbols of the Divine Word. Your speech ought to have been simple and pure; but you adulterated it with false doctrines, with fallacious arguments, with meanings extorted from the philosophy of the pagans,—you explained the gospel by the theories of Plato and the sophistries of Aristotle. The world no longer knows what to believe.

Your doctors exalted themselves above the apostles; they perverted the holy expressions of those Epistles which men of God left for the instruction of the faithful. A new Word prevailed above the old—an earthly and human over the heavenly and Divine. The faith, the patrimony of a free people, was made over to a caste which domineered over them. The property of the simple was usurped by the cunning; the inheritance of the poor of Jesus Christ was extorted from them by the rich; who, clad in purple and gold, disdained the title of brethren and friends—the only appellation of Christians—and chose instead to be called fathers and lords. And the people were deceived by them.

Yes, the people; they who constitute the Church, were deceived by the ministers of a religion which knows nothing but the people, which is given to the people only—by which, whosoever aspires to be the first, is condemned to be the last,—the people who, as St. Peter says:—

"Laying aside all malice, and all guile, and evil speaking; as new-born babes desire the sincere milk of the Word, in order to grow thereby, after having tasted that the Lord is gracious: to whom coming, as to a living stone, disallowed indeed of men, but chosen of God and precious, they are built up as living stones, a spiritual house, an holy priesthood, to offer up spiritual sacrifices acceptable unto God by Jesus Christ ... a chosen generation, a royal priesthood, an holy nation, a peculiar people, which in time past were not a people, but now are the people of God; which had not obtained mercy, but now have obtained mercy."

Yes, the people, deceived by you, have good reason no longer to believe in you. You have deceived them with your doctrines—your own, not those of the gospel; invented for your own profit alone; not for the benefit of men's souls, to which you have even denied consolation, when they could not give you silver and gold in payment for it. You deceive them with your practices, when you, so avaricious, preach disinterestedness; you, so impure, chastity; you, so vindictive, forgiveness; you, so insubordinate, submission; you, so turbulent, peace; you, so self-indulgent, temperance; you, so indolent, industry; you, so immoral, holiness.

Thus to this day you have deceived the people; and they have ceased to believe in you; perceiving that God did not dwell in you, that God no longer spoke through your untruthful lips.

How, indeed, could they longer believe in you, when your words were in open contradiction with the Word of God—your institutions with its principles?

God pardons him that believes and repents—you declare none pardoned but through outward works! God will be worshipped by believers in spirit and in truth; He prohibits sculptures and images, in order that no one may ever give worship and homage to another.

Oh, how many things have you taught, how many divers practices have you adopted! How have you changed the temple of prayer, the mystic table of the Lord's Supper, the simple hymn of the faithful, the pure preaching of the Word!

Who ever saw in the ancient Churches—who could have anticipated in the modern ones, the golden ornaments of your sacerdotal crowns and vestments? so that, on solemn days, your whole person shines in the temple like a sun; to which the dazzled eyes of a deluded multitude of disciples are turned, substituting, alas! the senses for spirit, earth for heaven, man for Deity.

Fatal illusion, which has caused such great evils throughout Christendom! these appearances are supposed to be faith, and in these religion is made to consist. Deny it if you can. What is, in fact, the faith of the people, and what must it be from your practical instruction? That, of course, which they see and hear with you. And what else do they see and hear, but superstitions and errors? To whom are the solemn days dedicated? To the saints. Concerning whom are the most glowing orations made in the Churches? The saints. Who is over the altars? A saint, at full length; with, or perhaps without, a small crucifix, scarcely visible. Which way do the people turn on entering the temple? To the spot where they see an image exciting to their feelings. And what follows? They worship that image. And you priests, spectators of that worship, are silent. You are consistent in being so, for none but yourselves deserve to be blamed for this abuse,—you, who place the image there—you, who relate its miracles, so as to enamour the simple who trust you! You are silent also because it is your interest to keep so. Oblations, gifts, offerings, follow the adoration. But are not the people deluded? What matters it, if only the priesthood be profited!

The people, however, will not believe themselves deluded, in doing what they see you do. Who is there among you that does not adore the saints, does not adore and kiss their relics? It is useless to urge the distinction about sorts of worship, which you make in the schools. The people know it not, because they have never been taught it. It is shut up in your books, from whence it never comes out, except to be learnt by those who have to support and defend it against every attack. In short, it is the doctrine of controversy, not of practice.

If you regulated the practice by the doctrine, you would prohibit kneeling before images and relics; but you are the first to kneel. You would not permit the use of incense to relics and images, practised from antiquity in honour of God alone; but it is you who offer incense to them. You would not tolerate even the candles on the altar, to inspire the people with a high idea of the majesty of God; but you light them yourselves. You come upon us with the distinction of the school, between the worship and the adoration of images.

Who are you who dare to distinguish, where the law precludes all distinction? It is God who says in the Second Commandment, "Thou shalt not make unto thyself any graven image, or any likeness of any thing that is in heaven above, or that is in the earth beneath, or that is in the water under the earth: thou shalt not bow down thyself to them, nor serve them." But you have purposely taken this commandment out of your Decalogue, dividing the last into two, in order to complete the number ten.

Need I remind you of all the other inventions by which you have deceived the people; making them believe that you have found them in the Scriptures; and that they have, moreover, the suffrage of a constant tradition within the Church? The people having now learnt to read, take the Bible in their hands, and look for your doctrines in it. Where, they ask, is the precept for auricular confession, of which the Church of Rome makes an express command, and has declared it a sacrament? Not a word of it can be found in the gospel, nor the slightest allusion to it in the letters of the apostles. But perhaps it was practised by some Christians in the early ages? For the first four centuries of Christianity, it was not known even by name, and when it began to spring up, it found more opponents than followers; no one even venturing to reduce it into a precept. The people search the Bible for the famous doctrine of purgatory; and how great their surprise to find that our Lord Jesus Christ, who brought life and immortality to light, with the double eternity of rewards and punishments, has never mentioned purgatory, nor have His apostles.

You send them to read a sentence of the Book of the Maccabees, and wish Judas Maccabeus to teach the Christian people what Jesus Christ did not teach. But the people, who are not wanting in sense, ask their priests what is the value of that Book of Maccabees? The priest, if he have any conscience, is obliged to reply that it is one of the Apocryphal books; it having never been received by the Hebrews, from whom we are bound to receive faithfully the books of the Old Testament; it not being written originally in their language;

never being quoted, either by Christ, or by His apostles; consequently, not received in the ancient Catholic Church, and only inserted among the sacred books by the Council of Trent; to whom it was an object to authenticate the doctrine of purgatory. So much for the Scripture proof. Now, let us go to the tradition of the ancient Catholic Church.

You will admit that, for two centuries, prayers for the dead, and still more the doctrine of purgatory, never entered men's heads. Tertullian, that imaginative mind, which saw so many other things upside-down, was the first to recommend prayers for the dead; without, however, mentioning purgatory. Towards the end of the fourth century, Augustine, another African mind, spoke more decidedly both of prayers, and of a sort of suffrages for the dead. However others choose to act, shall we rely on the authority of his discoveries? Even the purgatory of Augustine was not an existing fire, but one which is to be lighted up at the final destruction, through which then, and not previously, souls shall pass. This theory is of perhaps equal value with his theory respecting the Antipodes, whose existence that learned man denied!

The case is similar with all the other dogmas which, since the time of Gregory VII., have originated in the Church of Rome. Is the Christian Church bound to receive the wicked inventions of Honorius III., proposed and sanctioned by him in the Lateran Council (1215)? Shall she adhere to his famous dogma of transubstantiation, invented by the heretic Eutychus, unknown in the first ages, and ably contradicted by Pope Gelatius? (*De Duab. Christ. Natur.*) Shall she abide by the impious doctrine that the sacrifice of Christ, offered once for all, as a full satisfaction, even to the end of the world, should be renewed every day, by hundreds, by thousands, by hundreds of thousands of priests, who say that they are authorized to offer it, both for the living and the dead? Most enormous sacrilege, to which the whole Bible is opposed, and which the Apostle Paul loudly condemns in his Epistles! What elder, or bishop, in the first centuries, ever allowed himself to celebrate your mass, or the sacrifice which you call unbloody; or to make use of anything but the simple commemoration of the supper of the Lord; very far removed from that idea with which you have clothed it in the ages of error and ignorance? Is the sacrament which you now celebrate the original august mystery of the Divine food, instituted indeed in substances of bread and wine, but containing spiritually the body and blood of Christ, which are communicated to His Church, that is, to the multitude of believers, not materially and physically, as you say, but in virtue of faith? Yes! if you will but celebrate it with that simplicity with which it was celebrated by the first bishops and elders of the Catholic Church, we will come willingly to receive it at your hands. Celebrate it in all its extent, and the people will approach the eucharistic table, to eat of the Divine bread, and to drink of the Divine cup. But the people desire both the one and the other, and cannot yet understand the reason for which you have taken the cup from them.

Is it not the precept of Christ that every believer should drink of that cup, as well as eat of that bread? Was not this the practice of the primitive times of Christianity? The Greek Church has always retained that practice, and the Reformation immediately resumed it. The people have as good a right to the cup as have you priests;—even better than you, since you cannot avail yourselves of it without the Church properly so called. In taking it alone, you perform an act contrary to His institution, which is to "communicate,"—that is, to take it together, as the word itself teaches you. Yes! Only on this condition will the people remain united to you, that you be faithful in the exercise of the ministry, not altering the faith, not changing the practice, not deceiving them in anything.

They are willing to confide in you as the appointed servants of the Church, in the offices of religion. But instead of this you think of nothing but to command. The yoke of Christ, which He made easy, and His burden, which He made light, you have rendered so heavy and insupportable that the people refuse to bear them. Something very different from indulgences and benedictions is now needed to satisfy the people. In the present day fables please none but children, and lies are no longer tolerated by any. The Christian people desire from us, the ministers of its Church, the Word of Life as announced by Jesus Christ, as preached by the apostles, as written in the sacred books of our faith.

If, instead of chaplets and *Agni Dei*, which are deceptions, you, the bishop of Rome, were to give the Bible to the people, you would see how readily they would follow you! But it must be the Bible translated into their own language, so that they may comprehend it. Give them the Bible! Bestow on them those sacred books which Moses and the Prophets, the Evangelists and the Apostles wrote for the people, and not for the priests only! Give the people that which is their own; they have a right to it of which you cannot deprive them. It is the testament of our God, who left His people the heirs of His holy Word; in reading which, faith will be granted, and to the belief of which are attached salvation and life.

Who gave you the power to deprive the people of their privilege and highest benefit? Fear lest God end by avenging His oppressed ones, and causing a curse to fall upon you.

You venture to excommunicate the people, if they read the Bibles which a beneficent Christian society has taken pains to print in all languages, on purpose that all nations may enjoy the benefit of reading them. You condemn the charity and the religion of those good men, who, in their zeal for souls, undertake this work with much expense to themselves! O Pope Gregory, what manner of spirit are you of? As one of the bishops of Christendom, you should have a care to feed your flock; on what will you feed them if not on the pure and holy Word of God? You ought, therefore, to be well disposed towards all who take this Word from the holy originals in Hebrew, and Greek, and faithfully translate it into the vulgar tongue, so as to enable you and other bishops to administer it to your flocks. You ought yourself to accept these sacred volumes from their hands, and, accompanying them with the warmest expressions of paternal solicitude, recommend them to the reading and the study of your children. What do I say? You ought, on your own account, to print them, and not wait for others to supply you with them. You would then see the faithful in your Church apply themselves eagerly to that Divine book, and draw from it food and nourishment. But, alas! you do just the opposite. You do not print it, and you do not choose that others should print it. You never give it to the people, and you do not wish that others should give it. I will add what I hear is said,—you do not read it, and you do not wish that others should read it. And for this you allege, as your sole reason, the pretext that the people are not capable of understanding it. Sure enough, they do not understand it in Latin; but they would understand it in their own language. The Germans and the English, to whom their own Churches impart it, understand it; why should it not be understood by the French, the Italians, and the Spaniards?

You say, in your Encyclical of last March, that the Council of Trent, in order to explain the Bible to the people, provides that in each cathedral church a canon should be charged to deliver, every year, certain lectures on the Scriptures. And think you this is enough? I know of this provision, and I know, too, how it is practised. Would that this were done in all the cathedrals, and that the number of lectures amounted to twenty in a year! But, let me ask you, has every village its cathedral and its theologians authorized to lecture on the Scripture? Away with such excuses! why abuse the inexperienced with illusive words, which only mock the people? The fact is, you do not wish the Scriptures to be read at all, still less to be read aloud, by any one who, having no interest in flattering you, would consult them in order to investigate your doctrines. Those humble souls to whom the Lord would reveal the knowledge which he denies to your theologians, would find in them the falsity of your system; instead of believing in you, they would begin to believe in Jesus Christ, who announces to His people salvation by faith, and not by works; remission of sins to sinners by grace, and not by penance; satisfaction by the merits of the Redeemer, and not by those of good men; Jesus Christ the sole Mediator with God, not the Virgin and the saints; Christ the Head and Chief of the Church, not Peter nor you; Christ alone perfectly holy, Christ alone infallible.

These, and other such things, the people would find in the Bible, if they read it. And the consequence would be, that they, being the many, finding themselves deceived by you, who are the few, would summon you to judgment, for having too long kept them in error; to the serious injury of religion, as well as to the danger of their own souls. Think you that the antiquity of dates, the traditions of canons, or the authority of the Fathers would then serve to defend your cause? The people, with the Bible in their hands, after having confuted your errors and those of your Councils and of your Fathers, all of whom were uninspired men, were but too liable to err, as in fact they did err—the people would pronounce such a sentence as would oblige you and your theologians to return to the Bible, that is, to the true Catholic Church of the first three centuries; reforming, by this means, what has been added since, whether by the desire of novelty, or by the spirit of ambition and interest.

Do you know what the people are? They are the Church of Jesus Christ. We are the ministers, or servants, of this Church; and we therefore depend upon the people. This truth, announced by Jesus Christ, and openly taught by His Apostles, but which men have wilfully denied, begins now to revive. The people, whom it has been attempted to deprive of their privileges, now begin to reclaim them. The man who now reads in his own language the Epistles of St. Peter and St. Paul, discovers in them his own privileges; he reflects on the usurpation practised upon him, and claims the rights to which he is entitled. The people, as constituting the Church, to which the ministers are servants in the dispensation of mysteries and in the office of preaching, will then have the help of Christ, even to the end of the world. On this People-Church the promises of the Redeemer descended, and we only participate in them as part and ministers of the people.

Bishop of Rome! continue, if you will, as long as men will allow you, to sit on the throne of the Cæsars, who are dead; but invade not that of Jesus Christ, who lives and reigns. He is the only Sovereign of the People-Church, nor does He allow himself to be represented by others. He governs it at all times by His own laws, nor does He suffer others to usurp His rights, by substituting their laws for His.

And does it follow that He must be longer silent, because He has borne with you in silence until now? It is now nearly the middle of the nineteenth century. Do you not see the providence of God in operation over all material and earthly things? When was there ever such progress in enlightenment, such knowledge of the arts of industry? Remote nations approach each other by the easiest means, connect themselves in the most rapid manner, and form plans for a degree of union, of peace, and of prosperity, such as has never before existed. Nations which slept for ages, have woke up full of vigour and energy; their steps are those of a giant; their look is that of the eagle; they measure the earth, in its vastness, and overrun it in all its extent. The people of our day differ widely from those of by-gone times; their wants are more strongly felt, their language is more decided.

In former times, no Roman could have been found to speak to his pope with frankness. You have now found one who spares you not; who dares to present himself before you: not on his knees, to adore you, but erect, to speak to you with freedom, and to tell you what he thinks. And with him are thousands, nay millions, who partake his views. And who is this man? An Italian, a minister of an Italian Church;—a Church which assembles to pray to God in the Italian language, and to listen to the reading of His holy Word. And in whose name does he minister? In that of God. By whom chosen and received? By the people, who are the Church; and previously by yourself, and by the Church of the priests; if, indeed, that Church of yours be really a Church, consisting, as it does, of priests only, without people. You are called the Latin Church, but where is the Latin people? From the time that the language of the priests has ceased to be the language of the people, priests and people no longer form one Church; unless by the word Church you mean a theatre, with a stage for the actors and a space for the spectators. The country from the Alps to the sea is Italy; its inhabitants are called by all the world, Italians; its language is Italian, and has been so for four centuries. Where is there room for a Latin Church? Such did exist before God extinguished it; but God has extinguished it, and man cannot maintain it in existence.

Yes, Pope Gregory, Italians we are, and Christians we are resolved to be. What shall be the name of our Church? Answer, or the people will answer for you, "The Italian." The Italian Church we are, by the will of God and in the name of Jesus Christ who presides over us. Will you join us? You, too, are an Italian. You, too, are a Christian. Nay, you are a minister and an elder, as St. Peter designated himself; and among the elders we will recognise you as a bishop, whenever you will return with us to the Christianity of primitive times; otherwise we must part.

Understand that in religion there is no compromise, and we are persuaded that the religion of the first three centuries is alone the pure and true Christianity. Can you deny this? You are a conscientious man; do justice, then, to your country, since the providence of God has made you pope, that is to say, Bishop of Rome, in the nineteenth century. Blame us not, that in wishing to be Christians, we refuse to be *Romanists*. Within the present century, heaven and earth will contradict you; posterity will condemn you; and an Omnipotent God will pass your sentence, dooming you to be the last of a series which has existed long enough, by coming down to our own days.

July, 1844.

*Letter to* Pius IX. *Bishop and Sovereign of Rome,* Giacinto Achilli, *a Minister of the Italian Catholic Church.*

It is not unknown to you that I addressed two letters to your exalted predecessor, Gregory XVI., making a full retractation of the Romish doctrines which I had professed, more or less, up to 1841, and declaring to him my entire belief in Divine Scripture alone, to the exclusion of everything else. In this faith I intend to live and die, so help me God and His holy Word!

Being appointed, however, by the will of the Lord, a minister and elder in His Church, I cannot abstain from the exercise of that employment without entailing upon myself God's anger, and committing a culpable desertion of duty. My ministry is consecrated to the Church of Jesus Christ, and I am deeply impressed with the obligation of fulfilling my vocation. "The Pastor and Bishop of souls" gives me both the command and the strength to discharge my duties. The Church, which is the people, calls me to serve it. I must be faithful to my ministry, rendering a good account of the charge entrusted to me.

I have been bidden to keep in remembrance "that true faith which is in me," and "to keep alive that gift of God which is in me by the imposition of hands," seeing that God "has not given us a spirit of fear," but of strength, and of love, and of a sound mind. Therefore, "I must not be ashamed of the testimony of our Lord." "I know in whom I have believed, and I am persuaded that He is able to keep that which I have committed unto Him against that day." I therefore "keep the form of sound words which I have heard, in faith and love which is in Christ Jesus." "I keep that good thing, which was committed unto me by the Holy Ghost, which dwelleth in me." I profess before God and the Lord Jesus Christ "to preach the Word, to be instant in season and out of season, to reprove, rebuke, exhort with all long-suffering and doctrine." I purpose to be vigilant in everything, "to endure afflictions, to do the work of an evangelist, to make full proof of my ministry."

Such being my office, such my obligations, here I stand before you, Holy Father, "studying to show myself approved of God, a workman not needing to be ashamed, rightly dividing the Word of Truth." I know that the elders who have performed well the duty of ruling should be "reputed worthy of double honour; especially those who labour in the Word and in doctrine." You are the elder to whom was recently committed the charge of ruling over the Church of our country; and this charge was committed to you by other elders, who divide amongst them the various offices of that Church, or who are called to preside over other Churches. You the overseer, or bishop, of the Church of Rome, took upon you the heavy responsibility of feeding that portion of the flock of Christ, and of strengthening your brethren with good example and holy doctrine; your brethren, who look to you for counsel and direction, and depend in a certain degree on you, regarding you as an elder brother, whose judgment and prudence may aid their timidity and weakness. On you, therefore, it devolves to propose to them that which is of God and of the Lord Jesus Christ, and which tends to the welfare of His Church. You it behoves to restore the truths of religion to their primitive purity; to take away every extraneous admixture; to separate the good wheat from the tares, in order to give to the Christian people the nourishment of faith and of salvation. Your brethren look up to you in this matter, which ought to be conducted with harmony, in order to preserve the union of the Christian Churches: and although each possesses over his own Church an equal authority, they nevertheless hesitate to act without you; they expect you to set this work in motion, and to be their model in the reformation of doctrine.

Yes, Holy Father, the reformation of doctrine is the serious business to which you and your brethren are called by the people to turn your earnest attention; for it is well known to all Christians, that upon the purity and holiness of the doctrines of the Church depend the purity and holiness of the actions of believers. Now, the doctrines which proceed from man are neither pure nor holy; seeing that "God hath concluded them all in unbelief, that He might have mercy upon all." Therefore, none but the doctrines of God are the truth in religion; all others are lies.

Think you, then, that those are doctrines of God, which are not contained in His Book, but are opposed to the sacred precepts of His holy Word? Have you ever compared the doctrines taught in primitive times with those of later ages? Have you ever compared the dogmas of the Decretals with the doctrines of the Bible? I have compared them, and have shuddered in amazement, that so many strange novelties, amounting to an actual renunciation of the ancient faith, the pure creed of our fathers, should ever have been introduced into Christianity.

Strip yourself, then, of that fatal prepossession that your predecessors were holy and infallible. Examine carefully the sources of the existing belief.

Observe what is from God, and what proceeds from man. Man has erred in presuming to legislate in the things of God. Not only singly, but in the aggregate, men have erred. The Divine assistance was no doubt promised, but it was for preserving the ancient doctrines, not for framing new ones; the Holy Spirit is with those who believe in the ancient Scriptures, but not with those who tamper with the Divine Word. In the middle ages the ministers of the Catholic Church revelled in innovation, and from that time the desire for change has grown upon them to such a degree, that primitive Christianity can no longer be recognised.

Think you that it was ever permitted to men to add their ideas and thoughts to the ideas and thoughts of God, or to take anything away from the Divine Book? Are you not rather persuaded with me that whosoever does this, on him are denounced the chastisements of God, as it is written in the last verse of the Divine Revelation—"God shall take away his part out of the book of life, and out of the holy city, and from the things which are written in this book?" To add to the meaning, or to change it! to overturn, on certain points, the entire system and spirit of the Divine Legislator! I ask you, who were an elder before me, and a ruler among the elders, are such things to be endured? However ancient these errors may be, however concealed by some or acquiesced in by others, shall prescription prevail to this extent? No! not any antiquity can establish the abuses of religion; and even if the whole world were combined to maintain error (supposing such a thing were possible), even that would not hinder its destruction by any single person who had with him the Word of Truth.

This, then, is the point at issue;—the abuses of Rome have existed long, and obtained for a long time the support of the multitude; do they for that reason cease to be abuses? Her errors have been adopted, applauded, followed; do they on that account cease to be errors? And must not abuses and errors be reformed wheresoever they may be found, or however long they may have existed?

But with whom does it rest to effect a reform in matters of religion? Who is to promote it, and by what means? I reply: first, the bishops; then, the elders; afterwards, all who have a zeal for religion. The instrument of reformation is simple; viz. the Word of God as it stands written in the Sacred Scriptures, pure as our forefathers received it, powerful in itself to change the face of the whole universe. The truths of that inspired volume constitute the whole of Christianity; out of it there exists no truth for the Church. Be it yours, then, with the Holy Bible in your hand, to reform the doctrine corrupted by your predecessors! No one can do this work so well as you; no one so much as you is bound to do it by conscience and by special obligation.

Let this consideration sink deep into your mind, how sad is the present state of religion in Italy, that country with which you are most closely connected! Where, now, can be found among us that holiness of faith, whence alone proceeds holiness of works? When we look for Christianity, what do we see around us? Infidelity or superstition. Infidelity in all those classes who call themselves enlightened; superstition in all those who follow the teaching of your priests. On the one hand, are men who have cast off all belief, and have rejected Christianity with popery. Seeing that both Gospel and Canons have come to them through the same hands, they have concluded that both must be lies; that both being preached to them with the same fervour, nay, the Canons sometimes exalted above the Gospel, both have been contrived only to shackle consciences, to degrade the spirit of man, to subjugate the people to the rule of an individual, who has had, in all ages, an insatiable appetite for power! Thus, not distinguishing the work of man from pure Christianity, which is the work of God, they have rejected everything alike, and live the life of infidels. On the other hand, we behold men who receive implicitly all that is taught them—to whom all is gold which is sold by the priests—to whom all is sacred which has any show of religion or piety—men who, not caring for faith, seek only for good works; and, thinking little or nothing about God and Jesus Christ, run after saints and the Virgin,—relics, images, and indulgences!

These two classes, generally speaking, comprise all the Christianity of Italy; and to this unsoundness is to be referred the reigning immorality, the want of energy of mind, the absence of virtue and of union among our citizens. "The Church which divides the races within our country" was the great subject of lamentation to that immortal genius, who, three centuries ago, on the banks of the Arno, revealed to the world the wickedness of princes. "The Church which demoralizes the people" with its doctrines even more than with its practices, is the lamentation which I, a son of Italy, a minister of the Italian people, raise aloud to heaven; and which, with all the strength that is in me, I would echo in the ears of all good men who love our country. Yes! from the Church, or rather from those who call themselves the Church, proceeds all that series of evils which degrades our beautiful land, and lowers our finely gifted people in the eyes of the stranger. Nor will I ever cease to lift up my voice, until, in this respect more than any other, our beloved Italy shall be seen reforming herself, and returning gloriously to holiness of faith, purity of morals, and mutual love among our citizens.

And you, Holy Father; are not you, like me, an Italian? do not you, like me, feel burning within you the sacred love of country—"*la dolce carità del natio loco?*" Oh! I will not so wrong you as to suppose you now destitute of a sentiment which has hitherto distinguished you; a sentiment which ought rather to grow stronger in your mind, now that, as bishop of the most ancient of cities, you occupy the most glorious of thrones. To you the applauding people ascribe a generous liberality; from you are expected good laws, and ameliorations in the difficult details of government. From you they hope to receive that in which they would receive everything—which by a single act you have the power to give them—a religious reformation. Whoever thinks correctly knows that on this point depend social improvement, public prosperity,—in a word, every good thing which, by the favour of Divine Providence, citizens are capable of enjoying. Without this, we shall always remain in wretchedness, unhappiness, disunion. Without this, there will never be contentment, nor any tranquillity among the people. The spirit of restless change will continue to agitate them—to their own injury, it is true, but also to the destruction of yourself, and of others who are their princes.

Let us then have reform in the Church; but what reform, and in what particulars? Must I repeat it? Remove everything invented by popes, decreed by popes, designed for the interest of popes. All this is popery, not Christianity; and we are resolved to be henceforth Christians, not papists. The reformation will be complete, when once the sentence is uttered, "The Bible, and nothing but the Bible."

For instance, that you, Pius, should be Bishop of Rome, is not contrary to the Bible. But *this* is contrary to it, that you should assume a bishopric over those sees which have already another bishop; for all bishops are equal; each one the pastor of his own flock, and each independent of the other. For my part, you should have my vote to be bishop of *all* Italy, were *all* the other bishops removed; but you cannot rightfully co-exist. That elders, too, should exist, is in accordance with the Bible—and you may call them priests, if you will; but as for friars, they are contrary to the Bible; their vows are repugnant to the Gospel and to nature, whatever your theologians may say of them; and their ministry useless, at least, if not hurtful, to the Church.

What, again, do we mean by the Church? You know well that in the Word of God it means the Christian people. It is contrary then to the Bible for the Church to mean the priests only. Let it please you, Holy Father, to consider well, for a moment, this point, which is at present of the highest importance. Do you believe that what has been usurped should be restored? Let it, then, be by your means that the people resume their ancient rights, and repossess the Church according to their right. But what Church will you restore to the people of Italy? The Latin? But where is now the Latin people, or the Latin language? Do you not perceive what a scourge God sent you, when the priests of Rome wished to appropriate the Church to themselves, and to make it their private property; declaring themselves princes and governors, and the people subjects and slaves to the Church of the priests? It was a chastisement not unlike that which God sent in the valley of Shinar, when daring men set themselves to build the famous tower which was to reach to heaven. Audacious priests, in the thirteenth century, also attempted to raise themselves into a spiritual power, intending to hold the people for ever in subjection. But God sent among them by degrees the spirit of confusion, rendering their language unintelligible to the people, so that people and priests were compelled to separate. With the priests remained the ancient language, in which they had dictated laws at variance with the Gospel; and, sometimes in Christ's name, sometimes in the name of Moses, had oppressed, burned, tortured the people; a language associated with crimes which daily mounted up to the throne of the Omnipotent, provoking the infliction of condign punishment,—such crimes as prayers addressed in the temple to saints instead of to God; the Word of Truth exchanged for fables; and Christian teaching founded no longer on the ancient doctrine of the Bible, but on the new doctrine of the Canons. The whole language of Catholicism, having become exclusively Romish, had adulterated the things of God, the doctrines and maxims of the religion of Jesus Christ.

So grievous a scandal drew down upon Rome the anger of the Eternal, who seemed, as it were, to repeat the ancient words, "Let us go down, and there confound their language." That beautiful idiom, which originating in Latium among the descendants of Romulus, grew with the greatness of ancient Rome, the language of Virgil and of Tully, became confused and lifeless; and Rome, the new Babel, beheld issuing from her bosom and growing up at once, a generation of sons who understood not the language of their fathers. The Church of the priests felt the heavy blow which came upon it from heaven; but, instead of weeping and humbling herself before God—instead of repenting, and correcting her faults, she persisted in her error, and launched her anathemas against the people; declaring, like the haughty synagogue of old, that it was enough for her to comprehend herself,—as for the people, if they did not understand her language, so much the worse for them!

What followed? People and priests were divided. The Church and the nation became separated for ever; the Church and the priests called themselves Latin, while the nation and the people called themselves Italians. This is a great fact which has not hitherto been sufficiently regarded. The people, ever under subjection to the tyranny of the priesthood, had not the spirit to resist oppression, scarcely even to open their eyes to look upon the chains it had imposed upon them. In the meantime, the priests laboured to impress them with a belief that such was their natural condition. Slaves by the will of the strong, they were taught to believe themselves so by the fatality of nature, and the will of God.

But enough! The eyes of the people are shut no longer. They have opened them; they have beheld their chains. Like a lion they have burst through them. They threaten their former oppressors with a look that may well make them tremble. Their roaring was like the waking up of nature, indicating a grand change in the face of the world. The people have declared that the times are gone by when they would submit to be badly governed by their pretended masters; and that they are now the arbiters in their own affairs. We priests are specially bound to do justice to the people; for to us, more than to others, has their cause been confided. Be it ours, then, to enlighten them; which is the first thing they need. Be it ours to assist and protect them, with that holy ægis which they themselves have confided to us. Let us unite with them in the true religion of our forefathers. When God extinguished our Latin language, he meant thereby to punish us priests, and not the people. Let us submit to that punishment. The Latin language has corrupted the truths of the Catholic Church, and, therefore, God has extinguished it. Let our Church rise again in the Italian language, and let this be the ancient Church of apostolic times. Anathema to the Church of the middle ages! Thus, alone, can we priests become again united to the people; thus, alone, can we recover the Church. For—once more let it be said—the Church means the people; bishops and priests being only the ministers of the people. It is not in the nature of things that the language of the Church should be other than the language of the people. Italian is our language, and Italian must necessarily be that of our Church.

This Church it is which I desire to serve as a minister. Will not you, Holy Father, serve it as bishop? Gladly would I then return to you; and with me many who are now alienated from you would gladly return. Thenceforth they will have no cause to separate from the Church, for Jesus Christ will truly reign in it, and with Him will reign union, peace, concord, charity. Oh, what a sight were this! "How good and how pleasant it is for brethren to dwell together in unity!" Thus united in the Italian Church, we should remove everything which separates us from other Christian Churches. Germany, England, Switzerland—all other countries at present divided from the communion of Rome, would be again united with us in one faith. Nations would be drawn together in the bonds of brotherhood. And you, Holy Father, would be the blessed instrument by which would be realized the Divine prophecy, "There shall be one fold and one Shepherd."

"The grace of our Lord Jesus Christ, and the love of God, and the fellowship of the Holy Ghost, be with us all. Amen."

Malta, 1846.

## EDICT.

*We,* Fr. Vincenzo Salva, *of the Order of Dominicans, Master in Theology, Inquisitor General of the Holy Office of Ancona, Sinigaglia, Jesi, Osimo, &c.*

It having been determined fully to re-establish the disciplinary laws relative to the Jews living in our jurisdiction, and which we have hitherto in vain endeavoured both by entreaty and exhortation to carry out in the several ghettos of Ancona and Sinigaglia; we, authorized by the venerated despatch from the Holy Inquisition of Rome, dated 10th June, 1843, in which we are expressly enjoined and commanded to enforce the observance of the Pontifical Decrees and Ordinances, especially with respect to Christian nurses and servants, and the sale of possessions, either in the city or in the country, whether bought and held before the year 1827, or after that period,—we ordain as follows:—

1.—That at the expiration of two months from the present period, all Christians, male or female, employed as servants in the Ghetto, either by day or night, are to be discharged, and the Jews are expressly prohibited to employ in future any Christian whatsoever in domestic affairs, under pain of such fine as the Pontifical Decrees have appointed.

2.—That every Jew possessing real property of any kind whatsoever, or any annuity or mortgage, shall, within three months from the present date, dispose of the same by an actual *bonâ fide* sale; at the expiration of which term, if the order be not complied with, the Inquisition shall cause the property to be peremptorily disposed of by public auction.

3.—That no Jew, much less any Jewish family, shall inhabit or carry on business in any town or village where there is no Ghetto; and such as are at present acting in contradiction to this law, are hereby commanded to enter into their respective Ghettos, within the period of three months, or they will be prosecuted accordingly.

4.—That no Jew shall be permitted, more especially in towns where there is a Ghetto, to *sit at table and eat with Christians,* in any eating-house or tavern.

5.—That no Jew shall sleep out of his Ghetto, nor enter any Christian's house for familiar conversation.

6.—That no Jew be allowed, under any pretence whatever, to induce Christians to pass a night in the Ghetto, more especially women.

7.—That no Jew shall employ as day-workers, any Christian men or women, in their houses in the Ghetto.

8.—That no Jew, male or female, shall be allowed to frequent the houses of Christians, or *enter into friendship* with them.

9.—That the law which prohibits the Jews to travel about the State without a licence, shall remain in full force.

10.—That the Jews are expressly forbidden to traffic in church ornaments, or in books of any description, or to buy, read, or keep any prohibited book whatsoever, under penalty of a fine of one hundred crowns, or *seven years* of imprisonment. And in case any Jew, already possessing such, neglects to bring them to the Tribunal of the Holy Office, he will be liable to the same penalties.

11.—That the Jews in the removal of their dead bodies shall not be allowed to use any *ceremonial rite*, or public display; more especially are they enjoined to *abstain from all singing of psalms,* and carrying of lights through the streets, or out of the Ghetto, under penalty of a fine of one hundred crowns, the forfeiture of their lights, and corporal punishment to be inflicted on the *nearest relatives of the defunct.*

Any person infringing these laws and regulations will be subject to the penalties and fines imposed by the Holy Office. And that no one may plead ignorance of their existence, it is hereby ordered that a copy of the present Edict be published, and fixed up in the synagogue, which shall be deemed equivalent to serving it personally on every separate Jewish individual, as well on those in Ancona, as on such as may reside in other places belonging to the same Ghetto.

Given at Ancona, from the Holy Office,
this 24th day of June, 1843.

F°. Fr. Vin. Salva, Inquisitor General.

The above Edict, published in the year 1843, and authorized by Rome, is a sufficient answer to those who pretend that the Inquisition is no longer what it was three centuries ago. We have here the decree of the very essence of the Roman Court, composing the Holy Office—fifteen Cardinals, thirty Councillors, &c. &c., with the Pope at their head.

We are returned to those delightful times in which the Neapolitan, Caraffa, better known as Paul IV., and Michael Ghisler, called Pius V., lighted their funeral piles, and inflicted their tortures; and when, not to be behindhand with his predecessors, the monk Felice Peretti, called Sixtus V., proclaimed a crusade against the poor Israelites. O glorious days, when the holy indignation of Rome was responded to by the ferocious bigotry of Spain, the religious fury of France, and the papal fanatics throughout Italy!

Who is there that would not delight to see those good old times restored, when Christian men enjoyed the pleasing spectacle of the public burning of fifty thousand Moors, by Ferdinand and Isabella of pious memory, and as many Jews consigned to the flames alive, through the various countries of Europe? Who would not wish to act over again the famous day of St. Bartholomew, and a hundred other deeds more or less celebrated, but all testifying the zeal of the holy Roman Inquisition?

And what is the reason why these spectacles, so *creditable* to the human race, are no longer to be witnessed in these days? Is it that the people are no longer instigated by that species of devotion which rendered the burning of their fellow-creatures alive, on account of their difference in religious opinions, a matter of such consolation and enjoyment? The zeal of the Romish Church remains the same, and our popes have not lost their holy desire for the conversion of the whole world by fire and sword to their sacred doctrines. How is it then that these glorious days do not return?

Let us, however, confine our remarks to the present Edict, in which the Inquisitor equally shows his profound knowledge of jurisprudence and of morality. The Jews are spoken of as being under his jurisdiction; but I cannot understand whether this jurisdiction be political or religious. The first he has nothing to do with, as his authority is purely ecclesiastical; and as to the second, I would ask, what right has he to exercise it upon persons of a different religion? It is idle to say that the Pope has conferred it upon him, since he himself has no right over such as are not baptized. To usurp any authority whatsoever, is a crime, in the eye of the law of every nation. The Inquisitor is consequently either extremely ignorant, or most daringly presumptuous thus to defy a principle acknowledged and submitted to by all civilized people.

He says that he has hitherto in vain implored that the laws of discipline relative to the Jews should be maintained in full force, and therefore takes occasion to issue anew a mandatory Edict. Surely those who call themselves Masters in Theology, ought at least to understand common honesty. Could laws be considered as conscientiously binding which were the result of sheer hatred towards an unoffending community? And were not the subjects of it justified in evading them as much as possible?

As to the 1st article, that all Christians are to be dismissed from the service of Jews, what can be more arbitrary and unjust? The Inquisitor would have done better to have laid his interdict upon the Christians, in forbidding them to go to the Jews, rather than to compel the latter to shut their doors in their faces. And, concerning these very Jews in your own jurisdiction, Mr. Inquisitor General, you know how charitable they have always been;

you know what service they rendered us in the time of the cholera; how, in this very city, they assisted the poor, and condoled with them under their sufferings; and how charitable they showed themselves on every occasion.

Before, then, you forbid the Jews to employ Christian servants, tell those who are in want of bread to seek it at your convents, at the doors of the Inquisition.

As to the 2d article, touching the disposal of the property of these people, what can be said in its justification? Whether they retain it or not, I suppose they are equally liable to be called upon for the government taxes. There is one of this race, however, who must be a sad trouble to you; one who has lately possessed himself of an enormous extent of property, and has claims upon the very estates of the Church, even to the palaces of the Pope, the prebendaries of the Cardinals, the revenue of the bishops, and the whole body of the clergy, friars, nuns and all, which are absolutely mortgaged to him, to the extent of many millions. Now, is it an agreeable thing, O Father Inquisitor, that this great Jew, this powerful Baron Rothschild, should be invested with such awful authority, as to be legally justified in driving the Pope from the Vatican, should Cardinals Tosti and Lambruschini be behindhand in their accounts? This wealthy baron is, in fact, master of half the Pontifical State; and if things go on at the same rate, *super Cathedram Petri sedebunt Israelitæ*. What remedy will you propose, my dear Inquisitor, if, on the Pope's neglecting to pay, this Jew, Rothschild, seizes on the church-property? You threaten the poor Jews of Ancona with forced sales, but the Baron may put the whole of you up to auction at once.

If this article was designed to evade such a catastrophe, I doubt if it would be of any avail. Rothschild is too well supported to have his rights invaded even by the Holy Roman Inquisition. This unjust attack is indeed altogether as unwarrantable as it is impolitic. What would you say if the Grand Sultan were to issue a decree that all the Catholics in his dominions should be constrained to sell, within three months, whatever property they might possess, merely because they were Catholics? Yet you set him and others an example of this crying injustice, for no more defensible reason.

The 3d article savours strongly of the monk. To oblige all the descendants of Israel to live cooped up in their Ghetto, as in a monastery. Perhaps you feared that the Christians might turn Jews, if free intercourse were permitted between them; or do you rather apprehend that the Jews might become Christians? Rarely does the former take place. It is the latter, then, that you dread, for you know very well that the Jews profit the Inquisition far more than the Christians. The real object of this law, therefore, must be to estrange the two parties, and to sow enmity and dislike between them, so as to cause them to live in perpetual vexation, and discord, and distrust.

The 4th is a singular article,—that no Jew shall be allowed to eat at the same table with a Christian, or in any public eating-house or tavern out of the Ghetto. It would be well if every one could make it convenient to take his meals at home; but when, from the nature of a person's occupation, or any other cause, this cannot be the case, what is he to do? To the *trattoria*, or eating-house, every one is admitted; there is no distinction made there between the Jew or the Turk, the Christian or the Heathen. The noble sits by the side of the plebeian. He is the most respected who spends the most; he is the best served who pays the highest. Every one is admitted, even the thief and the assassin. The Jew alone is to be forbidden! But what a disgrace it is to prohibit the Jew from eating in company with the Christian, when Christ himself, the Divine Head of our Church, sat at meat with the children of Israel, even with the Samaritan and the Sadducee, and imparted to them the benefit of His instruction.

How shall we in future have the courage to persuade these people that we are partakers of that most holy religion which began with Adam, and had the Jews for its early fathers? How, in proof of our assertion, present to them the code which is contained in the books of Moses and the Prophets, by us, as well as by them, believed and reverenced? With what face can we boast to them of our Gospel as abounding in precepts full of peace and love? Will they not reply to us by pointing to the laws of the Roman Inquisition, the famous Edict of Ancona, where all is division and hatred? Are you a preacher, brother Salva, and is such your doctrine? To be consistent, you ought to begin your sermon with the duty of religious intolerance, evangelical persecution, and Christian cruelty. Speak the same language in your pulpit as you do in your Edict, and observe the good effect it will produce upon your audience.

Your 5th article prohibits the Jew from sleeping out of his quarters, and from any friendly intercourse with Christians. Well done! So the Jew is for ever to remain a Jew, and avoid all opportunities of being converted; he is to forego any advantage he might derive from conversing with us. But perhaps you imagine the race to be so bad that good Christians might be injured in communicating with them; indeed your Edict treats them as such throughout. But whoever consults the calendars of our tribunals will find that in all our towns there are very few Jews who figure in the list of criminals; a sufficient proof of their regularity of conduct, their obedience to the laws, and their respect for the authorities.

In the 6th, it is stated that no Jew shall allow any Christian man, much less any Christian woman, to sleep in the Ghetto. The inuendo here conveyed might not inappropriately be retorted upon the friars, notwithstanding the closed gates of their monasteries. They may thank the Jews for not publishing the story of a certain Vicar of the Holy Office, who frequently, under cover of the darkness of night, was accustomed to find his way into the Ghetto, certainly not for the purpose of preaching morality to its inmates. I should advise you, then, Father Inquisitor, not to be over curious in your researches, when there is need of so much indulgence in your own proceedings.

The 7th is a very extraordinary prohibition, forbidding any Jew to employ a Christian as a day-labourer in his house in the Ghetto. So that they are not allowed to have the services of bricklayer, carpenter, or builder, all of whom work by the day, and it is well known that the Jews themselves do not exercise these employments. This law, in fact, was made to oblige the Jew every time his house required repairing, to go to the Inquisition, with all due reverence and respect, and *not empty handed*, to get leave to have his work done, without which he is liable to a heavy fine.

In the 8th, the Jews are forbidden to contract any friendship with Christians. For charity's sake, poor children of Israel, pay no attention to such nonsense. Be as good friends with us as you can.

We esteem you as our fellow-citizens, notwithstanding our difference of religion; we regard you as brothers, since we both call God our Father, and both of us ascribe honour and glory to Him.

The 9th article relates to a licence with which every Jew must provide himself, before he can be allowed to travel about the State—a licence which the Inquisitor alone can grant—which must be referred to the decision of the bishops and vicars; and the infringement of any of the rules it contains, subjects the offender to arbitrary punishment, besides imprisonment and a fine of three hundred crowns. In this licence it is forbidden to dwell with, or to enter into familiar conversation with Christians. Now it is only in a very few of the towns in the Roman States, that a Ghetto is to be found. It follows then, that as their business leads the Jews to visit places where there is not any, they are obliged, in that case, according to the conditions of their licence, to live with their beasts, in their stables.

The 10th prohibits the Jews from dealing in church ornaments, and in books of every description. This is of no great consequence as respects the future; but in the meanwhile what is to be done with such of these forbidden articles as they may already have in their shops? they must make a present of them to the Inquisitor, for it appears that unless they do so, there is a fine of three hundred crowns to pay, and imprisonment to undergo.

As an appendix to this new decalogue which is directed against the living, the Inquisitor has thought proper to add an order or two respecting the dead; forbidding the Jews, in burying them, to make use of any ceremony or rite, or to carry any lights with their funeral processions, or *to sing psalms*. What, does your anger then extend even to the dead? are they too to be punished? Would your canon laws prohibit the decent performance of those last sad offices which are held sacred by all nations, respected by all classes of people? Every religion has its form of worship, every form of worship its peculiar rites, every rite a proper ceremonial form. These things, although extrinsic, and not strictly essential, are nevertheless established by custom, and observed with befitting reverence. Can you deny that the Jews have a right to practise their own religious observances? He that is born a Jew and remains one, must die and be buried as a Jew. How can you, then, prohibit the necessary ceremony at their funerals? You keep them among you, and allow them the exercise of their religion. Their dead have a claim to sepulchral rites, which can only be performed in the manner their own religion prescribes. The Catholics, the Protestants, the Greeks, and the Armenians, the Arabs, and the Chinese, have each of them, according to their peculiar views, established their funeral ceremonies, which, however imposing they may be to those of their own creed, may appear trivial and insignificant in the eyes of others. Nevertheless they are not to be despised, any more than their religion itself, although neither understood nor approved by others. But to forbid these children of Israel to sing the Psalms of David! their own prophet-king! Good heavens! And you yourselves recite these very prayers in your own sepulchral ceremonies! What greater right have you to them, composed as they are by a Jewish monarch, than the Jews themselves have? They, moreover, recite them in the language of King David himself, in their original Hebrew, a language full of harmony and pathos and lofty meanings; whereas you declaim them in a barbarous dialect, which you call Latin, but which in reality has nothing of the graces of Latium: the version is badly translated, too, incorrect, and every way imperfect.

According to your ideas, then, not only the Jews are forbidden to honour their dead, but the Greeks also, although Christians; since, in this country, their rites and ceremonies are prohibited, and all, in short, who dissent from the canons of the Vatican, and attribute no authority to the Inquisition. You alone are at liberty in this respect, you alone are entitled to the benefit of prayers and spiritual song, since in you alone are to be found faith, holiness, and salvation!

In the meanwhile look at the tolerance that prevails throughout the rest of Europe. But could you with any justice complain if you were yourselves treated as you treat others? Is it fair, that in Greece, in Russia, in the Ionian Islands there should be Romish churches, Romish worship, Romish processions, and other public ceremonies, whilst, in the Roman States, the Greek Church, its rites and ceremonies, are not permitted? Equally might the Romish Church be banished from England, because in the Pontifical States the Anglican Church is prohibited.

But the forbearance of others increases your insolence; their kindness only augments your pride, and their religious feeling your impiety. O wicked race, how long will you deceive mankind!

Behold, O Italy, what manner of men are your priests, your ministers of religion! They who ought to alleviate your woes and render your chains less galling, whose duty it is to shed the balm of consolation on your wounds, they, on the contrary, engender strife and disgust among you; every hour they recall to your mind your past shame, your excessive credulity, your blind adherence, your too great submission. They pretend to lament over your illiberality, your religious incredulity, only that they may the better devour your substance. They, rapacious vultures, greedy wolves, they are the bad shepherds of whom the Prophet speaks. God of Israel, God of our fathers, remember the promise thou hast made through the mouth of thy servant, Jeremiah: "Woe be unto the pastors that destroy and scatter the sheep of my pasture! saith the Lord.... Behold, I will visit upon you the evil of your doings.... I will gather the remnant of my flock out of all countries whither I have driven them, and will bring them again to their folds: ... And I will set up shepherds over them who shall feed them: and they shall fear no more, nor be dismayed.... Mine heart within me is broken because of the prophets; ... because of swearing the land mourneth; ... their course is evil, and their force is not right. For both prophet and priest are profane; yea, in my house have I found their wickedness.... I will bring evil upon them, the year of their visitation. I have seen folly in the prophets of Samaria; ... also in the prophets of Jerusalem: ... they are all unto me as Sodom, and the inhabitants thereof as Gomorrah. Therefore thus saith the Lord of hosts concerning the prophets; Behold, I will feed them with wormwood, and make them chink the water of gall: for from the prophets of Jerusalem is profaneness gone forth into all the land. Thus saith the Lord of hosts, Hearken not unto the words of the prophets that prophesy unto you: they make you vain: they speak a vision of their own heart, and not out of the mouth of the Lord.... In the latter days ye shall consider it perfectly. I have not sent these prophets, yet they ran: I have not spoken to them, yet they prophesied.... I have heard what the prophets said, that prophesy lies in my name, saying, I have dreamed, I have dreamed.... Which think to cause my people to forget my name by their dreams which they tell every one to their neighbour, ... The prophet that hath a dream, let him tell a dream; and he that hath my word, let him speak my word faithfully. What is the chaff to the wheat? saith the Lord.... Therefore, behold, I am against the prophets, saith the Lord, that steal my words.... Behold, I am against them that prophesy false dreams, ... and do tell them, and cause my people to err by their lies, and by their lightness; yet I sent them not, nor commanded them: ... Therefore, behold I, even I, will utterly forget you, and I will forsake you, and the city that I gave you and your fathers, and cast you out of my presence: and I will bring an everlasting reproach upon you, and a perpetual shame, which shall not he forgotten."[125]

*Letter to* Cardinal Caracciolo, *Archbishop of Naples.*

Capua, August 27, 1835.

Eminentissimo e Reverendissimo Padrone,

This, my most respectful letter, will be presented by Father Giacinto Achilli, a Doctor of the Dominican Order, who was lately proposed to me as a preacher in the Metropolitan Church of Capua, by Father Jabalot, the Master-General of the Order; to whom I applied for a serviceable and talented person to occupy the pulpit during the period of Lent.

It would be difficult for me to express to your Eminence the satisfaction that this same Dr. Achilli has given to the Clergy and to the people. He has now fixed his residence in Naples, in the Monastery of St. Peter the Martyr, which may be greatly benefited by his superior talents in Philosophy, Mathematics, and Theology; all which sciences he taught in Viterbo, his native place. He is desirous to place himself under the protection of your Eminence, to whose exceeding kindness I therefore venture to recommend him; more especially, as I know the favour with which your Eminence regarded Doctor Salsano, also a Dominican, on account of his singular talent and virtues; and it is to be hoped, that Dr. Achilli, who is certainly in no wise inferior to him, will prove himself equally agreeable to your Eminence. The Master of the Sacred Palace, Buttaoni, whose learning is well known in Rome, frequently consulted him in the revision of new publications, when he was residing at the Minerva; from which circumstance, it is evident in how high a degree of esteem he was held; and how worthy he is of the favour of your Eminence.

I avail myself of the present opportunity to offer my humble duty and respects, and most respectfully kissing your hands,

I remain,<br>
Most Reverend Eminence,<br>
Your most humble and devoted Servant,

F. Card. Serra, Archbishop of Capua.

The above letter, which is written with all the attention to etiquette and ceremony that the Cardinals observe towards each other, may serve as a model to those who wish to study the code of politeness received in the Court of Rome.

Letter.

*Fr.* Antonio di Gesu, *formerly Pietro Leonini Pignotti of Rome, to the General of the Order of Carmelite Friars at Rome, Health.*

Some time ago you summoned me to Rome to give an account of my belief. Nothing was ever more agreeable to me than your invitation, since I have always desired to bear testimony to the truth. I should not have hesitated in the least to obey you, if I had imagined that I could as freely have confessed my opinions at Rome as I do at Malta. But at Rome, as you well know, there are certain theologians, who for any dissent expressed against their views, immediately raise the cry of *heresy*, and conclude with Thomas Aquinas, *"that heretics should be burned."* Willing, therefore, to spare myself any such proceedings as you would, doubtless, have thought it necessary to put in force against me, had I presented myself before you, I judge it best to give you no other trouble than will accrue to you in examining my present belief, such as I now hold it, and, with the help of God, hope to keep it to the hour of my death.

I believe then all that God has revealed to us in his holy word, in which he has clearly pointed out to us the way, the truth, and the life we ought to follow, in order, through the assistance of Christ, to enter into his kingdom. I consequently believe, with the true Catholic Church, all that is taught in the Apostolic and the Nicene creeds.

I do not believe in the traditions of the Church of Rome, which are altogether false, and fabricated for interested purposes, partly from errors in the writings of the early fathers, and false interpretations of Scripture, and partly from foolish superstitions, which are by the Church called *pious*, although contrary to the spirit of the word of God.

I believe that Jesus Christ instituted two Sacraments—Baptism, and the Holy Supper: the first, when he said to the Apostles, "Go ye therefore, and teach all nations, baptizing them in the name of the Father, and of the Son, and of the Holy Ghost;" and the latter, when he said, "This do in remembrance of me."

I do not believe that Jesus Christ ever instituted the sacrament of confirmation, since he gave no commands respecting it. The imposition of hands is a simple rite in imitation of what was done by the apostles. Acts viii. 17. The anointing is entirely of Romish invention. Neither is there any mention of auricular confession in the New Testament. St. James exhorts the faithful to confess their sins to one another, that is, to ask forgiveness of each other for mutual wrongs. Of extreme unction not a word is said in the whole of the Bible. Ordination is nothing more than a simple rite, a ceremony consisting in the imposition of hands, praying God to give to his people good and faithful ministers. And matrimony is merely a contract between the parties, and the priest is enjoined to implore the Lord to bless the union. These five last have by no means the same claim to be regarded as sacraments as the two first. And even these two are altered and injured by the Romish Church, since in baptism water alone should be used, and not salt and oil; and in the Holy Supper common bread should be used, as it was originally, and as it has always been in the true Catholic Church.

I believe that original sin consists in the corruption of human nature descending from Adam. I believe that justification is solely the work of grace, without regard to works, as the Apostle teaches in his Epistle to the Romans.

I do not believe that original sin consists in following Adam, as the Pelagians say, and as the Church of Rome teaches; neither that it is washed away by the water of baptism. Born as we all are to natural life, we are re-born unto spiritual life "by water and the Holy Spirit." Neither do I believe that our own works in any way contribute to our justification, the works themselves being the effect of justifying grace. Jesus Christ has not said that those who work will be saved, but those who "believe and are baptized." And speaking of works, he has declared that when we have done all that is commanded us, we are to acknowledge that we are only "unprofitable servants."

I believe that Jesus Christ has once for all made propitiation for our sins, in that one sacrifice, which was ordained for our eternal redemption, he being a high priest for ever after the order of Melchisedec.

I believe that any other sacrifice is false and deceitful; any other propitiation is sacrilegious. Consequently, I deny the pretended propitiatory sacrifice of the Romish Church, as impious and heretical, contrary to the teaching of the Gospel, to the Epistles, and to the doctrine and practice of the ancient Catholic Church.

I believe that in the Sacrament of the Holy Supper, Jesus Christ communicates himself, through faith, to the believer, in the substance of the bread and wine, in a real and spiritual manner, so that eating that holy bread, and drinking of that sacred cup, with true faith, we receive through the word of Christ, the resurrection and the life.

I do not believe that in this sacrament the substance of the bread and wine disappears, and that of the actual body and blood of Christ is substituted in its stead, as the Church of Rome teaches, in which she follows the notion of the heretic Eutychus—"This *is* my body," is to be understood as "John *is* Elias," and that passage in Exodus, "It *is* the Lord's passover." *Esti* in the Greek signifies *represents*. St. Luke explains the meaning in the following words, "This cup *is* the New Testament in my blood." And in this sense alone the ancient Church understood it.

I believe that the Sacrament of the body and blood of Christ are received, when the bread and wine are eaten and drank according to the order and the warning of Christ, "Except ye eat the flesh of the son of man, and drink his blood, ye have no life in you."

I do not believe that in receiving one half alone, the whole sacrament is received, it being indivisible according to the will of the Divine institution, and was so understood in the Church for twelve centuries, and continues still to be so in the most ancient Christian Church, that of the Greeks.

I believe that, according to the Holy Scriptures, the souls of the dead are forthwith consigned to their eternal destiny; the elect and the justified to the joys of heaven; the wicked and the reprobate to the abyss of perdition.

I do not believe in an intermediate or third place or state, between heaven and hell. If purgatory exists at all, there is no reason why it should not always have existed, and have been mentioned in the Scriptures as well as heaven and hell. I do not believe that the Almighty created it only in the fifth century of the Church, and revealed it to St. Augustin alone, to become after the lapse of ten centuries a dogma of faith.

I believe that the saints, who are known as such to God only, stand in his presence, and together with the angels adore Christ and the majesty of God.

I do not believe that the saints know anything about us, nor that they can in any manner interfere in our concerns: certainly, we owe them no worship, since like ourselves they are created beings; neither should we invoke their aid, which they are unable to bestow. Jesus Christ, says St. Paul, is our sole mediator; He continually intercedes on our behalf with his divine Father, and exhorts us to come unto Him. His mother, who in one solitary instance attempted to intercede at the marriage feast of Cana, had for her sole answer, "Woman, what have I to do with thee?" I do not believe that the reliques of saints are to be worshipped, since God in his second commandment prohibits all worship but to himself alone. Why has Rome hidden this commandment?

I believe it is right to hold the memory of the saints in due estimation, and to place their portraits among those of our friends and relatives.

I do not believe that any images, whether of Christ, of the Virgin, or of any saint, ought ever to be worshipped, as an act especially forbidden by God.

I believe that Jesus Christ has left to the Church the power which the ministers exercise in public, to absolve,—that is, to declare that all those are pardoned who believe in the satisfaction He has made, and who humbly implore forgiveness.

I do not believe that Jesus Christ pardons in virtue of our works, neither on account of the merits of his mother, or of the saints, none of whom have a superabundance; and much less for the mere asking of the Romish Church, in its notable discovery of indulgences.

I believe that the Church of Jesus Christ is the congregation of all the faithful who are baptized, and who believe in neither more nor less than what is taught in the Holy Scriptures, which Church is one, holy, catholic, and apostolic, having Christ for its head. And I believe that this Church exists separately, among the different languages and nations, as in the time of the Apostles.

I do not believe that there is a mother Church superior to the rest, having dominion and power over all others. And I am of opinion that Rome, who arrogates to herself such dominion, has in reality no Church at all; since God, who has destroyed the Latin language among the people, has also, at the same time, destroyed the Church which existed in that language, the people and the priests having become totally separated through this difference of language; nor can the Church be restored until it is regenerated.

I believe that the faith and the confession of the Apostle Peter is the faith and confession of the true Church of Christ, the foundation and the pillar of truth. I believe that this faith should be preserved pure and intact among believers, who are bound to reject all innovations which, through error or ignorance, are introduced into Christianity; and that obedience is due to God and not to man.

I do not believe that the blessed Apostle Peter ever left any successor either at Jerusalem or at Rome,—which latter city he probably never visited. All true believers are his successors; and I believe it to be a blasphemy that a miserable sinner like myself should dare to call himself the Vicar of Jesus Christ,—his representative upon earth. I do not believe that He has any need to be represented, since He, much better than any man, or than the whole race of men, sees and provides for the necessities of his Church. No obedience whatever should therefore be paid to a man who impiously calls himself the successor of St. Peter and the Vicar of Jesus Christ.

I believe that all the canon and other laws of Rome are contrary to the spirit of the Gospel; that all the Councils and Synods, including that of Trent, held in support of Rome, and favouring her interests, are false and erroneous, and that their memory will always be a disgrace to Christianity. I believe that of all the errors that have infested the Church, the worst and the most detestable is that of Popery, as all the articles I have thus far enumerated sufficiently demonstrate, and against which, I, therefore, as a servant of God, and a minister of Jesus Christ, loudly protest, and condemn.

I do not believe that any Christian can ever live tranquilly under a system which is contrary to the Bible, whose doctrines are so many heresies, and whose practice is impiety throughout. I do not believe that any one who has heard and received the truth, can conscientiously remain conjoined to those who are opposed to it. The least pardonable sin is that of unfaithfulness.

I will conclude then in the same words by which you, professing the most unworthy belief of Pius IV., deceive yourselves; in opposition to which I have expressly modelled this my present profession of faith. This true Catholic faith, out of which no man can be saved, and which I now freely profess and truly hold, and which, by the blessing of God, I hope to retain pure and undefiled to my last breath, I, Pietro Leonini Pignotti, minister of the Italian Catholic Church, promise, swear, and make oath, to uphold, declare, and preach, to the extent of my ability, that it may also be received by those who are committed to my charge. So help me God and his holy Evangelists. Amen.

Reply

To the Allocution of Pius IX.

*At the Consistory of Gaeta, held on the 20th April, 1849.*

Since you oblige us to reply to your address, we intend to make it clearly evident to whom are to be attributed *"the disastrous storms," which,* you tell us, *"overwhelm your State, and plunge the whole of Italy into confusion and disorder."* Not to insist upon the fact, that the State properly belongs to us the people, and not to you, a repudiated monarch, we shall offer our remarks, not to your colleagues of the Consistory, whose opinions we value not, but to our own brethren, our fellow-countrymen, who share with us in the affection and interest for the public weal; so that no one may be ignorant how much and to what end we have laboured. *"And may the Almighty,"* (we use your own words,) *"grant that men, made wiser by these most unhappy events, understand that they cannot occasion a greater injury to themselves than by deviating from the paths of truth, of justice, of honour, and of religion."* If you suffered yourself *"to be led away by the wicked counsel of evil men; and to learn of them to deceive and to ensnare, we, on the contrary, shall make evident to the whole world with what care and solicitude and brotherly love we have endeavoured to promote the real good, the tranquillity, and the prosperity of the people,"* our brethren, no longer your subjects, in our Republic, which you obstinately persist in calling *"your Pontifical State;"* and which is most truly *"the fruit of our great care and affection. In these words we condemn not only yourself, but all those most deceitful workers of such great evils, attributing to every one his proper share."*

And here, above all, it delights our minds that *"many of our people, aware of having been miserably deceived by you, have now closed their ears to your words and to your counsels, and opened them,"* instead, to the righteous doctrines of the friends of the people, of the holy evangelists, who, pointing out *"the right path of virtue, and treading in the ways of honour and justice,"* aim alone at encouraging the mind, *and directing the understanding in the pursuit of truth."*

All are at present aware of your utter deceitfulness, and constant disregard to truth; and they cite, as the first proof of it, your famous amnesty, on account of which, with unparalleled effrontery, you so often reproach us, and which you pretended was to restore peace to so many families, including, be it remembered, your own, and those of your relations. And we, at first, gave credit to your assertions, wondering that a pope could do so much. But to our extreme surprise we discovered that our names were secretly handed over to the Austrian police of Italy, that our persons might be under surveillance. And among the exiles who received the amnesty, there were many to whom your consuls refused passports to return to their homes; while others had to undergo such humiliating treatment, that many chose rather to remain in exile than purchase a degraded freedom at such a price.

It naturally followed that those who returned did not consider themselves under great obligation to you, individually, but felt themselves more and more confirmed in the necessity of getting rid of your race altogether, as a race that never forgives.

*"It grieved you"* to see the people meet in assemblies, from which issued the sparks of a fire you had attempted to cover over with ashes; but which the more you endeavoured to extinguish it, the more it fed itself and

flamed forth; neither did the Edict of the Secretary of State, in April, 1847, produce any other effect than to make evident your own apprehension and that of your government, concerning matters which had no other aim than to protect a people against the artifices and the control of him, who, from the first, intended, after having granted them a moment's relief, to oppress them afresh. It was very natural that your endeavour should be resisted, and that the people who had roused themselves from their lethargy, should not suffer themselves to be cast into it again. A vigilant people will not remain inert. To you, who feign to be ignorant of its most heavy grievances, it has spoken and it has written. Why then did you not listen to it? You complain of its language and its threats! It is the genius of a southern race to be resentful; towards those who turn a deaf ear to our complaints we feel anger, and to the restive beast we are accustomed to use the whip. You have a peculiar faculty in playing the deaf and the restive, and we very naturally apply to it the treatment it deserves.

According to your account the conspiracy of July, 1847, was not a real one, "*but contrived for the express purpose, by public agitators.*" And pray did you make this notable discovery at Gaeta? Is it not true that when you showed some intention towards useful reform, the adherents of the government of your predecessor, those men of vengeance and of blood, who had filled the prisons and crowded the scaffold with their innocent victims,—those men with whom to love their country and to praise the sacred name of Italy, was a crime;—is it not true that they conspired to our injury and against yourself? And was it not the object of this conspiracy "*to plunge the City of Rome into civil war, with slaughter and destruction; until the new institutes being entirely abolished and done away with, the ancient form of government should be restored*?" Whence arises then your present madness, to deny a fact which you had full proof of, and which you yourself admitted at the time? Is it true then no longer? And have these conspirators, because they have paid court to you at Gaeta, suddenly become "*patterns of goodness, eminent for their religion, and distinguished for ecclesiastical dignity*?" Since you have remained out of Rome, how dear they have become to you. It was well for them that you quitted it, and it is through them that you will never more return.[126]

"*It was,*" as you say, "in this time of agitation *that it was proposed to form a Civic Guard.*" We know full well with what jealous eyes you look upon this institution—what a dagger it is in your heart. "*Hastily assembled by your own act,*" it was after your departure only that "*it was completely organized and disciplined.*" If you could now behold this Guard which has received the title of National, you would be compelled to acknowledge it the finest spectacle that Rome affords. It is to this body we owe the tranquillity and good order which never existed before. It defends our country against the aggression of your satellites. It is composed of the flower of our citizens, and has exulted in the cry, *Vivà la Repubblica, à basso il Papato."*

Do you not blush at the remembrance of that solemn piece of deceit which you termed a Council of State? Was it not natural for us to imagine that in this Council the will of the majority should prevail over that of the minority? that the influence of the people was to be equal to that of the priests? that yourself, a single individual, and by no means infallible, might have the courtesy to submit your individual opinion to that of the many? Otherwise, for what purpose is the Council assembled?—to cause us to undergo the usual humiliation of finding laws imposed upon us in opposition to our own wishes?

As to your glorious Allocution in the Consistory of Oct. 1847, of which you still make boast, we shall leave those to judge who have read the production. For us it was as an apple of discord, thrown among the people of Italy, in order that they might mutually distrust each other, and that all might withdraw themselves from the holy cause of emancipating their common country. And that was no dream of an armed foreign intervention secretly invited and even implored for, by a conspiracy of cardinals and the monarch, to root out, as they said, every germ of what they were pleased to call sedition. And were not you, who, in February, 1843, spoke deceitful words of comfort in order to tranquillize men's minds,—were not you foremost in this demand?

Still we continued to deceive ourselves: many persevered in their opinion that you were good and liberal, and every day expected to see civil and progressive institutions emanating from your decrees; the Romans, still devoted to you, were willing to ascribe every delay, every retrograde movement, every deceitful promise, to the intrigues of evil-minded persons, and to believe that the Jesuits, who were most assiduous about your court, prevented the expansion of your bounty. It was through affection for yourself that we called out for their suppression. Already expelled from other Italian States, why should they continue to hold sway in Rome, where you yourself contributed to render them the more odious? It was not, therefore, so much personal hatred towards them, as love towards our country and yourself, that induced the Romans to rise against the abhorred sons of Loyola. A proof of this is, that not one of them was ill-treated, or even prevented from remaining in the city, provided he kept himself quiet and unobtrusive.

The removal of the Jesuits was so far beneficial, that on the 14th March, a Statute was issued which appeared to us to regard our necessities, and to give evidence of your surpassing liberality. It was read with avidity, and we asked ourselves if the government had really become constitutional. Many reports were spread. The more credulous were transported with extravagant enthusiastic delight; the more sagacious, before they gave way to hope, required time, to see the fulfilment of the promise; long, and sad experience had taught them to distrust the specious professions of a pope. With sincerity and right feeling you might have conducted us to a Republic, but such was not accordant to your character nor to the innate genius of your caste. A republic to be proclaimed by a pope in his own States, would be as impossible as for the devil to turn Christian. You were right, therefore, to exclaim against those who, to tell you what they had fondly dreamed, broke in upon your slumbers, with so little ceremony. You too have had your dream, conjured up through an association of ideas very different from theirs, which you have confided not to their ears alone, but to the hearing of the public at large, when you state that the Republic they wished for "had no other *object in view than perpetual agitation, the removal of every principle of justice, virtue, honour, and religion; and to introduce and spread abroad on every side, with loss and ruin to all human society, the fatal and horrible system of Socialism, contrary to all natural right and reason.*"

This was an ugly dream, and, doubtless, arose from a diseased imagination. But that was no dream which you have since related to us with such satisfaction, how you had, to our injury, opposed the Italian cause, secretly at first, and afterwards more openly. Our youth who flew to arms in the righteous cause, assured you of their intention to seek the sanguinary Croat, where the battle raged the fiercest. And you feigned to approve of their holy design, blessing their banners, and auguring from heaven itself auspicious omens for their victory. Was it not you who expressed to Charles Albert your grief that you could not assist him as you wished? And when was it that Rome discovered your real intentions, and your secret orders not to pass the confines, if not when they heard from your own lips your celebrated Allocution of the 29th April, 1848? Bitter remembrance of an act that destroyed all the hopes of a people, at that time, devoted to you! It is evident, then, that your love for the Italian cause, and all your speeches and professions, were priestly and royal deception. And you dare bring to our recollection those times in the past and the present year; when, in the former, you abhorred to shed the blood of the Croat, and in the latter you thirsted for that of the Romans!

On the 29th of April last, the army of Louis Buonaparte displayed itself beneath the walls of Rome, with a direful train of artillery, of cannon and of bombs, to slaughter in your name all those Romans who should maintain that you, a Christian prelate, ought not to govern them as king. A fatal day was that for Rome; the most disastrous in our annals; the most disgraceful to the Papacy!

Since matters are in this state, strike out from your Allocution words that you have no right to utter: *"that you, elevated, although most unworthily,"* (most true,) *"through the inscrutable decree of Divine Providence, to the summit of apostolic dignity, to exercise upon earth the office of Vicar to Jesus Christ,"* (a false and blasphemous assertion,) *"you receive from God, the fountain of Charity and Love, your mission to regard with paternal affection, all mankind, of whatever country or race, to watch over and to promote their safety, and not to impel them to slaughter and to death."* That these words are false is evident from your own confession that you have yourself brought and impelled against us, in fratricidal war, Austria, France, Spain, and a portion of Italy.

To whom are to be attributed the slaughters at Bologna, at Ancona, and beneath the walls at Rome? You were averse to a just war, for the safety of Italy; not so to that most unjust one which had for its object the replacing of yourself, the most abhorred of sovereigns, upon a throne which you had yourself deserted, and from which, *"through the inscrutable decree of Divine Providence,"* rather than through any effort of ours, you had been removed.

Who will pardon your mis-statement of facts, your outrage upon individuals? Language has no words more abusive or scornful than those you have employed against us, who, you assert, are guilty of the heavy offence of despoiling you of your territory, and that, too, after having constrained you in so many ways to grant a reform which was true, stable, and conformable to our wants. But it is not the empty name of a republic that satisfies us; it is a wise, a provident, and a just government, that we require. Call our present one what you will; it is that which we have always wished for, and to which we have a just right. It is one which we endeavoured to urge upon you, because the Papal Government removed you too far from us. Some who fancied you a wise and considerate prince, believed your influence might be beneficial, and without delay proposed that you should rule the destinies of Italy. You, however, it appears, considered this proposition *as extremely insulting.* In fact, it was not from a pope that Italy could hope for her redemption. The popes, at the head even of a republic, would have finished by subjecting the whole of the country, as they did at Rome, where the Church became the incubus of the State, although at one time denominated a republic,—*Sancta Dei Ecclesia et Respublica Romanorum.*

This attempt, then, having been made as a last proof of devotion towards your person, it was inevitably forced upon our conviction that no other hope remained for us than what might arise from the separation of the priestly and royal functions. The Church was to be the sole empire for the priests; Rome and Italy would together arrange a form of government for themselves. But this simple act, full of justice and moderation, you stigmatise as the fruit of *"the most unbridled licentiousness, audacity, and depravity,"* and they who are actuated by love for their country and mankind are stigmatised by you as *"enemies both of God and man."* ...

How entirely has the spirit of falsehood possessed you! When have *"the streets"* as you say, *"been sprinkled with human blood?"* when have *"the most deplorable sacrileges taken place, and the most outrageous violence been offered to your person in your own house?"* What infamy for the Head of our Church to be guilty of such scandalous untruths! You declare also that *"traitors, infuriated, and threatening, indulged in all sorts of deceit and violence to terrify the good, already sufficiently intimidated."* We ask you, Who were these traitors, and when were these intimidations employed? All the world knows that you were not yourself more legally chosen pope, than the Constituent Government was authorized by the whole of the Roman people, in fair and unbiassed freedom of election....

The love of empire, that sways the base and ignoble mind, is more present with you than the love of the people or a regard for humanity. It is in vain you endeavour to hide it; nevertheless, it is ridiculous in our days to talk of a temporal throne in the apostolic seat, in the Holy Roman Church. The Apostles possessed none, and could consequently give no right to inherit any. The words of our Divine Master are moreover in direct opposition to such possession, enjoining them to arrogate to themselves no titles of authority. "After these things do the Gentiles seek;" "but be ye not like them;" and many more passages might be adduced to the same effect....

If, however, it be alleged that our progenitors gave to the High-Priest of Rome the office of governor, we, by the same right, have power to take it away. In like manner, the sister Churches of France, Austria, and Spain, may, if they choose, make either a king, an emperor, or a president, of their chief-priest. We have no right to object to their doing so, and all we ask in return is that they should not trouble their heads about us.

Your dethronement was occasioned by your ill-government and oppression, in which you followed the example of other despots; and moreover, you did so in the name of St. Peter, and even of Christ. And all the temporal power and trust you placed in the hands of the clergy, a measure injurious alike to the interests of the Church and of the people. The most talented were employed in the service of the State, the most ignorant in that of the Church; the former were active and rapacious in acquiring wealth, and the latter supine and superstitious in the duties of their calling; the one party rolling in luxury, and the other poor and needy, so that by degrees they began mutually to hate each other.

This monstrous union of Church and State has thus gone on until the present period. Profane and sacred things have been so jumbled together that good sense and right feeling with respect to them have altogether been lost. The progress of civilization on every side except among ourselves, rendered our situation still less endurable, so that among all classes the two powers were held in slight and derision. In proportion as they ceased to love the prince they began to despise the priest. By the one the laws were transgressed, by the other the offices of religion neglected. The sovereign laid his snares, and the priest through his negligence brought the Church into discredit. Meanwhile, the obstinacy of the popes, to keep the two powers united in their own person, threatened them not only with the loss of the State, but of the Church also. It was, therefore, a kindliness towards yourself, and a love for religion, that induced us to decree, that in order to guarantee the Roman pontiff in the free exercise of his spiritual power he should no longer wield the temporal sceptre. It is necessary when the whole body is threatened with gangrene to cut off the morbid portion....

We ardently desire to see established the religion of Christ, as holy and saving, and this, we conceive, may exist without bishops or priests;—the invisible and universal Church, which includes believers in all parts of the world; of which Christ alone is high-priest and Head. And this invisible Church does not do away with a visible and material one, which is divided among all people and nations, and of which every one has a right to choose that form which appears to him the best. Many of these Churches have no bishops, as the German, the Scotch, the Helvetic, and the evangelical Churches of France and Italy. Who is the bishop of the Church of the Waldenses? No one. And yet it is full of zeal, has existed from the eleventh century, and after so many fierce persecutions and massacres still presents a body of twenty-four thousand believers.

It is possible, then, to be good Christians, and to form a visible national Church on such a model without the aid of bishops. At any rate, you cannot deny that a Church can change its bishop for a sufficient cause. Do you think it then absurd or contrary to the precepts of the gospel that the people of Rome, who may be termed the whole Romish Church, should repudiate you as an apostate-bishop, a traitor, a bombarder, and that they should elect another, faithful, true, and beneficent?

Those who were asleep have now awakened, and they no longer trust your words. When you went out from Rome, the Bible entered in; the Bible, persecuted by the popes! and the gospel of Christ and the holy writings of the Apostles, faithfully translated into the Italian language, are now in the hands of the people, who read them, and find there neither popery nor the pope.

Take care that it does not happen to yourself in Italy, as it happened to your predecessors out of it, who, desirous to obtain more, lost all. They who last February took from you the temporal power, intended by so doing to guarantee and ameliorate your spiritual authority. From the 30th April to the present period, you have rejected every friendly advance, and violated every law in presenting yourself before the walls of Rome, surrounded by bayonets and cannon; and you announced to this city your return and your solemn entry with bomb-shells and incendiary acts among the wounded and the dying. Is this the entry of a bishop? Is it in such a manner that the pretended Vicar of Jesus Christ returns to his people?...

Let us suppose, by way of argument, that you, environed by thousands of bayonets, should effect your return to a city overpowered by foreign violence, what would you find at Rome?—a people capable of loving you and serving you as formerly? No, indeed; you would find a desert. The city which has abhorred you as a prince, and through you has learned to despise the whole race from which the popes have descended, is no longer disposed to receive your laws, to pay you tribute. Over whom do you expect to reign? Over the few who followed you to Gaëta? or those who here and there have remained favourable to the old system? Even of these there are none that really love you; it is to the system, and not to yourself personally, that they are attached....

It is in vain you exaggerate the disorders of our government, and in disgraceful language descend to the lowest scurrilities, calling Rome "*a den of furious beasts*" and those who dwell there "*apostates, heretics, communists, and socialists—bent on disseminating their pestiferous doctrines, and corrupting every heart, and possessed with a daring and sacrilegious desire of seizing upon the property and revenues of the Church.*" If this property and these revenues belong, as you say, to the Church, then we have done no other than restore them to their rightful owner, rescuing them from the hands of lawless spoilers. The people constitute the Church; the property of the Church then is the property of the people. And the priests and bishops, considered as servants to the Church, are to be maintained by the people. By divine command the tribe of Levi was supported by the other tribes. Christ also directs that the ministers of his Gospel are to be maintained by the faithful, when he says, "for the labourer is worthy of his hire." This was the practice in the early times of Christianity, and to them we must return.

If our former ministers are content to return to the Church under this new arrangement, we are willing once more to receive them; otherwise, we must look out for servants who will be more zealous for heavenly riches, and less greedy after the wealth of this world.

Is it because these doctrines have been established for more than eighteen centuries, and are based on the Gospel and the writings of the Apostles, that you call those who profess them *apostates and heretics*?

We have *"despoiled the temples of their ornaments!"* That is, we have taken their superfluous silver to coin into money, to supply the place of that which you and yours have concealed or carried away. We have *"turned religious houses to profane uses!"* Yes; some of the haunts of the lazy and the worthless we have given as habitations for the industrious poor, who live as God has commanded them to do, by the sweat of their brow. In the eyes of those to whom idleness is sacred and labour profane, we have certainly committed a crime, but for us *heretics and apostates,* we imagine we have done a holy work.

We have ill treated *"the sacred virgins!"* The chronicle does not say so. They have never been more safe and more respected than by ourselves and our government. Who it was that ill treated the sacred virgins under your own government, is well known to you, without our taking the trouble to repeat it. Pay a little more regard to truth, and be silent on these matters, unless you wish us to reveal what for the sake of charity we do not mention.

We have *"most cruelly persecuted, imprisoned, and put to death the most worthy and excellent ecclesiastics and holy monks; venerable and esteemed bishops, even such as were elevated to the degree of Cardinal, we have barbarously driven from their flocks, and thrust into prison!"* You accuse us of what, for reasons of state, we ought to have done, but which, through too great consideration, we abstained from doing. All wicked and insidious traitors, spies and conspirators, whether priests, monks, bishops, or cardinals, who sought to bring ruin upon the people, we ought undoubtedly to have hanged, in reward for their infamy. That we did not do so was, perhaps, through an overweening regard for their persons. Pope Gregory, and his cardinal, Lambruschini, on the slightest suspicion of liberalism, tore from the bosom of their families citizens far more useful and respectable than these priests and monks, consigned them to horrible dungeons, or after a mock trial, handed them over to the public executioner. All the vengeance we took, was, on the commencement of our revolution, to pardon all those accursed wretches who did not die with Pope Gregory; and our government calmed the fury of the populace, who, on account of their crimes, were eager for their destruction. It was a grief to us when some of those who had received pardon at our hands again sought to irritate the people, who then knew themselves to be masters. Certain death would have been their fate had not our government shut them up in confinement.

Certainly, when any one was taken with arms in his hands, and firing upon our people, as the curate of Monte Mario, the priest Racchetti, and another or two were, the people conceived they had a perfect right to take the law into their own hands, and get rid of their enemies, without writing to you to ask leave to do so. You may thank Providence that our people are so mild and so obedient to their governors as they are, or you would have had some of your monasteries visited, and the ribald monks turned out to pay you a visit at Gäeta. In the provinces likewise, every here and there, a band of factious insurgents roamed about, headed by a priest or a monk, and protected by a bishop or a cardinal. Was it not an unheard-of act of mercy to spare the lives of such wretches? And is it on account of such acts that you complain of the Republican government?

We felt an extreme repugnance, which the government of the priests never felt, to shed the blood of the citizens, considering them not in the light of subjects, but as brethren. And we grieve that all do not share with us in these fraternal feelings.

As to the *exhausted treasury*, to whom was it owing, if not to yourselves? We, on the contrary, in a short space of time, restored the finances, and put the administration of them into the best possible order. Who paralysed the exertions of commerce, and with unjust laws and enormous duties forced all the capital of the provinces to the seat of government? Who, on the other hand, reformed the laws, reduced the duties, and gave encouragement to commerce, if not the Republic? Certainly, commerce greatly suffered, and still continues to do so, in consequence of the siege and bombardment, by your favourites, of Bologna, Ancona, and Rome.

What falsehoods you state with respect to "*heavy contributions imposed upon the nobility, property plundered from individuals!*" Many of the nobility never contributed a single farthing, whilst many, not noble, paid large sums into the treasury. Is it not yourselves who teach that the superfluity of the rich is the patrimony of the poor? But who was ever plundered by us? Can you bring a single example to justify your assertion? If not, we have a right to stigmatize you as a calumniator. Neither can you bring any proof of your other most injurious assertion, that we "*interfered with the personal liberty of all good people, destroying their peace, and even threatening their very lives with the dagger of the assassin.*" The audacious nature of this falsehood is apparent. Have we not abundant testimony of the good character and conduct of our government, from persons of every nation, from the representatives of foreign powers, who are ready to certify that none of these excesses were ever perpetrated under the Roman Republic? How frequently they took place under the government of the popes, I need not relate; how many innocent individuals were torn from the bosom of their families, how many lives sacrificed, it were painful to disclose. The reign of the late Gregory furnished numberless examples, and your own reign, too, is not without its share in these enormities.

Let us now advert to that glorious confession of yours, of having sought from foreign powers an armed intervention to replace you on that throne from which you were removed more through your own weakness and folly than through any act of ours: and which you have had the simplicity to publish, in order, as it seems, that history may hand down to posterity this last ignominy of the papacy. Four foreign armies were invited to Rome to place the last of the popes upon a throne which is renowned for having the early pages in its history marked by fraud and usurpation; the succeeding ones by extortions, deceits, civil wars, the barbarities of the Croats, and the horrors of the Inquisition; and the last with the destruction of liberty, with parricide, and the bombardment of Rome, the great act on which you pride yourself. Do you, then, imagine it possible that you can return to fill a throne, so abhorred by Rome, and by all Italy? It is only possible through the support of foreign armies, bayonets, cannon, and all warlike means! It is only to be effected by the shedding of blood, and slaughter of thousands sacrificed to sacerdotal fury and ambition! Can you return to Rome to hear the cries of mothers, deprived by you of their dearest hopes, of widows whose husbands have been slain through your agency? And in the midst of such universal grief will you return smiling and joyful? How long, John Mastai, will you continue to insult our country, and how long is she to endure your presence? The presence of one who has allied himself with kings to betray the people, who united in friendship with the Bourbon of Naples, in order to devise the best means of oppressing every generous mind, of eradicating from the sons of Italy every noble sentiment! O insensate men that we were, to believe you, to trust in your deceitful promises, to the disappointment of your hopes, to the ruin of our happiness! Do you not believe that the Almighty is the judge of our cause; that he is powerful to abase the rich and the proud, and to exalt the poor and the oppressed? If you make an appeal to the canonical laws, we refer to those of the Gospel.

Christ has taught us to bless those who curse us, to do good to those who hate us, and to pray for those who despitefully use us and persecute us. But you begin to curse those who have always blessed you, to hate those who have done good to you, and to persecute those who have prayed for you. You who alone could have preserved the country, and have restored what was lost, joined yourself to our enemies to ruin and destroy us. And you dare to call yourself the Vicar of Christ! Is Christ then divided? is there a Christ opposed to the gospel? If so, you doubtless are his Vicar, and we have nothing more in common with you; neither the country which you have betrayed, nor the faith which you have denied. Keep possession of your Church; it is no longer ours: and enjoy your kingdom, since we are no longer your subjects. Go where your wishes lead you, but dare not again to place foot in a city which accuses, judges, and condemns you. Who could endure to raise their eyes to encounter those of a traitor? Who could receive a benediction from a hand yet stained with blood? No one, indeed, could consent to enter the temple with a hypocrite, who at the very time he was planning by the basest means to wreak upon us his cruel vengeance with fire and slaughter, had the assurance to give breath to the following words, which, to undeceive the present and to warn the future generation, not without a sensation of extreme horror and disgust, we venture to repeat:—

"*Lastly, venerable brethren, resigning ourselves entirely to the inscrutable decrees of the wisdom of God, with which he operates his glory, while in the humility of our heart we render Him infinite thanks for having made us worthy of so great suffering for the name of Jesus, and for having rendered us, in a degree, similar to Himself in His passion, we are ready in faith, hope, patience, and in gentleness, to suffer the most severe pains and trials, and, for the sake of the Church, to give even our very life, if by the shedding of our blood her calamities could be remedied.*"

Such impudence of declamation amid such atrocious deeds, for ever closes the page whereon, in characters of blood, is registered the perpetual downfall of the Roman Pontificate.

FOOTNOTES:

[125] Jer. xxiii.

[126] Unhappily, this prediction has not been verified.